Science and the Dao

From the Big Bang to Lived Perfection

Livia Kohn

Three Pines Press

Three Pines Press
P. O. Box 530416
St. Petersburg, FL 33747
www.threepinespress.com

9 8 7 6 5 4 3 2 1

Printed in the United States of America
This edition is printed on acid-free paper that meets the American National Standard Institute Z39.48 Standard.
Distributed in the United States by Three Pines Press.

Cover Art: Earth in Dao, by Brent Cochran.

Library of Congress Cataoging-in-Publication Data

Names: Kohn, Livia, 1956- author.
Title: Science and the Dao : from the Big bang to lived perfection / Livia Kohn.
Description: First [edition]. | St. Petersburg, FL : Three Pines Press, 2016.
| Includes bibliographical references and index.
Identifiers: LCCN 2015044751 | ISBN 9781931483322 (alk. paper)
Subjects: LCSH: Taoism and science
Classification: LCC BL1942.85.S35 K65 2016 | DDC 299.5/14165—dc23
LC record available at http://lccn.loc.gov/2015044751

Contents

Preface

"But that goes against everything we know and understand in Western science. It defies the biophysical laws . . . You don't emit energy! That's not the nature of things." Thus Bill Moyers exclaims in *The Mystery of Chi* video when confronted with Master Shir, a martial arts and qigong practitioner who uses his thoughts to direct *qi* 氣 or "life energy" toward people, either warding them off or pushing them over. Moyers's position is symptomatic for the traditional Western approach to Daoist claims—be they cosmological, philosophical, physiological, or practical in nature. It not only reflects a general disdain of science-based thinking for anything odd, strange, or unexpected, but also continues the age-old contempt of the Confucian establishment for Daoist religious visions and techniques, which was duly transmitted to early sinological pioneers, such as James Legge (1815-1897; see Girardot 2002), and from there entered the mainstream of Chinese studies.

However, since the video's production in 1993, we have come a long way, and the interface between Daoism and science has unfolded in numerous, often unexpected ways. Rather than developing a "Taoistic" science as described by Abraham Maslow, characterized by harmony, receptivity, patience, and non-interference, free from all "presupposing, classifying, improving, controverting, evaluating, approving, or disapproving" (1966a, 13, 96, 100), scholars are using discoveries and evidence of the sciences to show a strong confluence of traditional Daoist visions with modern understanding.

The sciences in this context are the hard natural sciences, such as physics, biology, astronomy, chemistry, medicine, and the like, that work with three strands of valid knowing, based on empiricism and experimentation: hypothesis, experience of data, and falsifiability (Wilber 1998, 190). That is to say, the scientific method sets out with a hypothesis or idea it wants to test, an initial "instrumental injunction," a practice, an exemplar, a paradigm, an experiment; this always lays out a particular way toward verifiable knowledge. Second, it works with "direct apprehension," the immediate experience of data assembled based on the practice or experiment. Third, it strives for "communal confirmation (or rejection)," a double-checking of results by replicating the experiment (Wilber 1998, 155-56). Typically, the three strands give rise to a new paradigm—a theory combined with "a particular technique taken as an exemplar for generating data" (1998, 158)—which leads to a yet higher, different level of knowing.

For example, in the 19th century, it was official dogma that, as Thomas Jefferson stated in 1807, "it is easier to believe that two Yankee professors would lie than that stones should fall from heaven" (Kwok 2013, 15; Beauregard 2012, 138). Chemical analysis and microscopic examination of meteorites gradually convinced the scientific community in the 20th century that rocks did in fact fall out of the sky. By 1969, only 2100 meteorites were known; by 2012, that number had increased to over 45,000 (Kwok 2013, 15). Today every child knows that stars are made of condensed gases or solids that are in constant motion and, yes, fall on us at regular intervals; watching meteor showers is a prime pastime that keeps numerous people up well into the wee hours. By the same token, "there is today almost no scientific theory which was held when, say, the Industrial Revolution began about 1760. Most often today's theories flatly contradict those of 1760; many contradict those of 1900" (Bronowski 1965, cited in Beauregard and O'Leary 2007, 202).

The emergence of new theories and paradigms has speeded up in the last few decades, due mainly to advanced technologies that allow insights into farther and farther realms of the universe (e.g., the Hubble telescope) and explorations of smaller and smaller units of the bodymind (e.g., fMRI brain imaging; DNA analysis). It is also due to the increasing acceptance of quantum physics and string theory, as they move far beyond the Cartesian and Newtonian paradigms and present a powerful understanding of what reality is like, a reality that—as pioneering visionaries already noted in the 1970s (Capra 1975; Zukav 1979)—looks more and more like what Daoists (and other Asian thinkers) have described all along.

However, even within this overall atmosphere of rapid change, there are still dominant paradigms that only shift under great duress and with much resistance (see Kuhn 1970). An example is the belief that human health and disease are largely determined by genes, still dominant in the medical profession, which stands in stark contrast to increasing evidence for epigenetic impact and the biological adaptability of cells (Chopra and Tanzi 2015; Lipton 2008; Francis 2011). It is often difficult, even for the brightest and most learned, to "sever emotional attachments to old ideas, discard familiar tools, argue with superiors and people of authority, or risk one's position and security, in order to fight for the elusive truth. As a scientist today, it is much easier to go with the flow and ride the bandwagon, especially when research grants and tenure are at stake" (Kwok 2013, 207).

This means that breakthroughs, especially those relevant to Daoism, tend to come from the work of iconoclastic, visionary, and often disdained—and even persecuted—scientists. They are outsiders or mavericks, people who overcome the limitations of dominant models, do not shy away from unexplored territory, or let themselves be scared off by apparent absurdity (see McTaggart 2003). Forced into organized institutions for reasons of funding, many end up following the dominant mode during the day but, driven by curiosity and the search for truth, work on issues of personal concern or unexplained oddities in their free time. "Some live long enough to see their ideas vindicated" (Kwok 2013, 208), others remain in the shadows of the dominant doctrine and even lose their positions and standing.

Science being continuous exploration, more and more far-out ideas and practices, however unorthodox, are coming under its scrutinyleading to a new and more open understanding. As scholars and scientists take Daoist claims seriously, moving toward an increased integration of science and religion, they begin to explain why its cosmological visions make sense in scientific terms and why specific practices have certain concrete, measurable, physical effects. For example, biochemical and hormonal studies have shown that the particular food choices, herbal supplements, self-massages, and visualization techniques used by followers of women's alchemy (*nüdan* 女丹) do in fact lead to the "decapitation of the red dragon," i.e., the ceasing of menstruation, which in turn creates stronger health and vitality (see Réquéna 2012).

Far from demystifying the religious claims of the Daoist tradition, exploring the scientific correlates of its cosmology, physiology, psychology, and practices enhances its credibility and makes it more accessible to modern people. At the same time, it offers additional perspectives to scientific understanding as well as new dimensions of practical application. In other words, the project represented in this book is a new and enhanced level of translation—of Daoism into Western science as well as of theory into practice—with beneficent effects for both.

I myself have been involved in the academic study of Daoism as much as in its self-cultivation practices for most of my career, beginning with taiji quan at Berkeley in 1976. For the most part, the urge to practice came from books, thinking and theory leading the way toward concrete experience. This work, however, came about the other way round: practice stimulating questions and leading to academic inquiry.

After suffering a shoulder bursitis in 1999, I joined a gym and began taking yoga classes. I was so enamored with the practice that I signed up for teacher training at the Kripalu Institute in the summer of 2002. Besides ample practice, the course taught the history and philosophy of yoga and offered classes in anatomy and physiology, linking ancient techniques with modern medical understanding. Not only opening my eyes to the possibility of integrating science and religion through practice, the training inspired the question: Where, then, is yoga in China?

This resulted in several years of research on Chinese body cultivation, focusing specifically on the tradition of healing exercises (*daoyin* 導引), the precursor of modern qigong, in its medical and Daoist dimensions. Over time, this led to the publication of an edited volume (Kohn 2006), an analytical study (Kohn 2008a), and an anthology of translations (Kohn 2012). In a next step, I moved on to apply the methodology to forms of meditation—looking at various practices in terms of history, worldview, current status, and matching science, and developing a model of six distinct types (Kohn 2008b).

From here, I proceeded to revise and expand my earlier work on medieval Daoist meditation, centering on "sitting in oblivion" (*zuowang* 坐忘) (Kohn 2010a). While researching the comparative dimensions of the practice, I came across the work on behavioral kinesiology by John Diamond (1979) and David R. Hawkins (2002), highly creative and radically inspiring mavericks in the field of psychiatry. I was stunned not only by the closeness of their body and energy vision to the Daoist model, but also by the practicality of their approach, the measuring of *qi*-flow via muscle testing. This was the starting point of the current book. It also resulted in a first related talk on "Daoist Body Cultivation and Behavioral Kinesiology" at the First International Summit on Laozi and Daoist Culture in Beijing in 2009.

Two opportunities arose in 2011 that set me more firmly on the path toward this work. I agreed to translate a study relating qigong to quantum physics from the German, which gave me a good grounding in the basic concepts and terminology of modern physics (Bock-Möbius 2012). And I encountered Core Health, a quantum- and kinesiology-based way of releasing, expanding, and directing the flow of life energy that not only closely echoes Daoist cosmology but also applies visualizations quite similar to the Inner Smile. Deeply impressed with the practice, I took all the classes offered, underwent facilitator training, and co-authored the book *Core Health* with the founder, Dr. Ed Carlson (Carlson and Kohn 2012). In the process, I learned about more and different dimensions of science as relevant to self-cultivation, including most importantly Bruce H. Lipton's work on the immediate impact of beliefs and emotions on the functioning of human cells (Lipton 2008).

While presenting talks along the lines of "Daoist Cultivation in the Light of Modern Science" in various formats and venues, I responded to a request from the Daoist College Singapore and wrote a lengthy analysis of the *Zhuangzi*, discussing the text in terms of both historical development and philosophical content (Kohn 2014). Gaining a deeper insight into Zhuangzi's worldview and his understanding of how the mind works and how we can work with it, several questions arose: How does all this play out in the brain? What does mind-fasting mean in terms of neuropsychology? It is possible to be free from emotions? If so, how does it work neurophysiologically?

At that point, I envisioned a project on "Zhuangzi and the Brain." Reading up on neuroscience, I started by examining the practice of sitting in oblivion in relation to the functioning of memory and the process of forgetting, presenting my findings at the 9th International Conference on Daoist Studies in Boston, June 2014 (published in Kohn 2015). Receiving a great deal of interest and an overall positive response, plus some insightful comments, I continued the work, but soon realized that the brain alone would not do the trick. There are, after all, so many different aspects to Daoist cultivation and so many different dimensions of science! Expanding ever further, the inquiry mushroomed into the multifaceted volume before you.

My heartfelt thanks go to all the scientists and scholars cited in the bibliography, without whose work I would have no ground to stand on. I am much indebted particularly to my academic colleagues for their helpful comments on papers and presentations as well as to the Core Health crowd—teachers, fellow facilitators, and participants—for their ongoing inspiration. I would also like to thank the members of Florida Qigong for their participation in various seminars that allowed me to test out connections between Daoist practice and scientific understanding, as well as my husband Tom for his continued patience and loving support.

Chapter One

Stars Are Us

The Astrophysics of Cosmic Unfolding

Traditional Daoist cosmology centers on Dao 道, literally "the way." The term indicates the way things develop naturally, the way the universe moves and living beings grow and decline. The concept of Dao is not limited to Daoism, although the latter takes its name from it. Rather, it is part of the general Chinese understanding of the world, which appears in all different philosophical schools—albeit in slightly varying interpretations. This is why A.C. Graham calls his book on early Chinese philosophy *Disputers of the Dao* (1989). Dao in this general sense is the one power underlying all. It makes things what they are and causes the world to come into being and decay. It is the fundamental ground of all: the motivation of evolution and the source of universal being (Jahnke 2002, 53).

The *Daode jing* 道德經 (Book of Dao and Inner Power) says, "The Dao that can be told is not the eternal Dao" (ch. 1). Still, it is possible to create a working definition. Benjamin Schwartz, in his *The World of Thought in Ancient China* (1985), describes Dao as "organic order" organic in the sense that it is not willful, not a conscious, active creator or personal entity but an organic process that just moves along. However, beyond this, Dao is also order—clearly manifest in the rhythmic changes and patterned processes of the universe, the stars and the natural world. As such, it is predictable in its developments and can be discerned and described. Its patterns are what the Chinese call "self-so" or "nature" (*ziran* 自然), the spontaneous and observable way things are naturally. Yet, while Dao is nature, it is also more than nature—its deepest essence, the inner quality that makes things what they are. Governed by laws of nature, it is also the inherent power that makes these laws.

In other words, it is possible to explain the nature of Dao in terms of a twofold structure: "Dao that can be told" and "eternal Dao." One is mysterious and ineffable, a force at the center of the cosmos; the other works at the periphery, visible and tangible in the natural cycles of the known world. About eternal Dao, the *Daode jing* says:

> Look at it and do not see it: we call it minute.
> Listen to it and do not hear it: we call it faint.
> Touch it and do not feel it: we call it subtle. . . .
>
> Infinite and boundless, it cannot be named;
> It belongs to where there are no beings.
> It may be called the shape of no-shape,
> It may be called the form of no-form.
> Call it vague and obscure.
> Meet it, yet never see its head,
> Follow it, yet never see its back. (ch. 14)

Dao as the ground and inherent power of all existence is entirely beyond ordinary human perception; vague and obscure, it cannot be known or analyzed. The only way a person can ever get in touch with it is by letting go of common modes of perception, by transcending ordinary human faculties, by becoming subtler and finer and more potent, more energetically subtle, i.e., more like Dao itself (Johnson 2014a, 58).

Dao at the periphery, on the other hand, manifests in the give and take of various pairs of complementary opposites, in the natural ebb and flow of things as they rise and fall, come and go, grow and decline, emerge and die. As the *Daode jing* says:

> To contract, first expand; to weaken, first strengthen.
> To destroy, first promote; to grasp, first let go.
> This is the subtle pattern [of life]. (ch. 36)

All things flow in alternating patterns; life is in constant motion. In a continuous flow of becoming, everything always moves in one direction or the other: up or down, toward lightness or heaviness, brightness or darkness, growth or decline, life or death—yin or yang 陰陽. All that grows must decline; all that declines and dies must transform into new levels of being.

Stages of Unfolding

The universe as a whole being a manifestation of Dao, in its innermost essence it *is* Dao. Dao gave rise to all creation and to everything that exists. It did so in stages of gradual cosmogonic unfolding, described with several key variants in the literature. The classical passage is in the *Daode jing*.

> Dao brought forth one.
> One brought forth two.
> Two brought forth three;
> Three brought forth the myriad beings. (ch. 42)

The notion of "one" (*yi* 一), originally a simple numeral, includes the idea of oneness. The "ultimate ancestor of everything" (Puett 2002, 318), it represents the formless, omnipresent integration of the cosmos (Capra 1975, 131). The state of Dao at the brink of creation, it is not a material or visible entity, a potent creator, a metaphysical reality, a number that initiates all numbers, or a single entity opposite to the many. Rather, oneness as wholeness, integration, overall unity, uniformity, and non-duality is a fundamental quality of Dao (Gu 2009, 162, 243), the unity and coherence it gives to the world (Wang 2012, 48; Kohn 2014, 83).

One divides and brings forth two, but this division is not like the biological division of cells, which results in two separate entities that yet contain the complete information of the original one. Rather, it is an internal division, a creation *within*, a splitting into two different parts, named in the *Daode jing* as yin and yang. These two parts or forces then energetically combine and unfold a third actor on the cosmogonic stage, identified in the *Huainanzi* 淮南子 (Book of the Master of Huainan; trl. Major et al. 2010) of about 150 BCE as yin-yang combined or in harmony (see Major 1993). On this basis, then, all beings come forth, all material existence develops.

In other words, rather than looking like this:

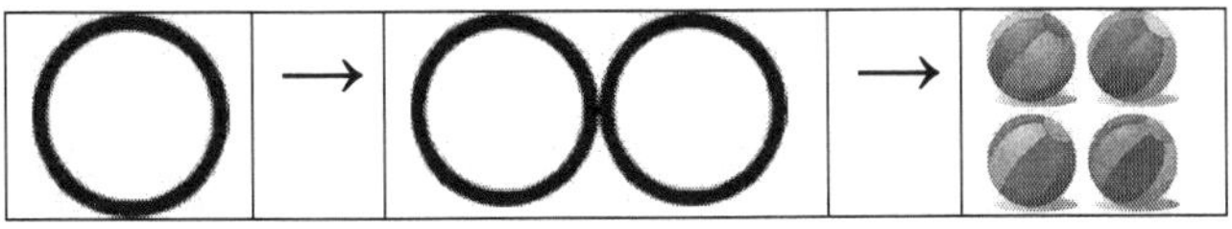

Daoist cosmogony looks like this:

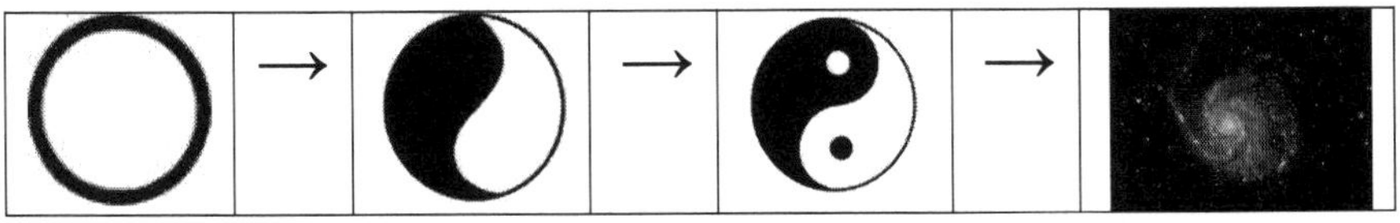

Beings and life appear in the dots: the white in the black and the black in the white, where yin and yang intermingle in endlessly new mutation and transformation, giving rise to everything that exists including living beings. Rather than splitting or separating, the action of cosmic unfolding in this system is thus a diversification, an "opening" (*kai* 開), not accidentally the term later Daoists use to describe creation.

Other early sources describe the opening of the world from primordial nothingness as taking place over similar stages including original chaos (*hundun* 混沌), time and space (*yuzhou* 宇宙), yin and yang, heaven and earth (*tiandi* 天地). The latter intermingled to bring forth the more concrete aspects of the world: water and fire, air and soil, temperature and density, eventually leading to the emergence of living creatures.[1]

A yet different way of looking at the emergence of the world is by systematizing pre-creation into a series of stages, a model that first appears in connection with the *Yijing* 易經 (Book of Changes) and from there makes its way into Daoism, described notably in the *Liezi* 列子 (Writings of Master Lie) (ch. 1; Graham 1960, 18). Named "grand" or "primal," they delineate the gradual unfolding of life energy in the cosmos, from the original state of chaos to the existence of all beings.

These stages were duly adopted in religious Daoism, as it arose in the second century CE with the emergence of the first organized movements, such as Great Peace (Taiping 太平) and the Celestial Masters (Tianshi 天師) (see Hendrischke 2000). Daoists generally tend to present cosmological and spiritual concepts in more mythological terms, so that, for example, they represent the notion of spirit (*shen* 神), the fundamental cosmic force of all life and key factor within humans, in spirits or gods, describing them in vivid detail and with various manlike characteristics (Kohn 2005, 37). They accordingly see Dao both as an inherent power of order in the universe and as a divine figure, divinizing the ancient philosopher Laozi now known as Lord Lao (see Seidel 1969; Kohn 1998a). Laozi as Dao, symbolizing the inherent tendency toward order within all movements and patterns in the universe, thus guides the world actively from chaos to creation.

An immortal with magical powers, he not only makes sure the world grows into existence but also shows a clear purpose of salvation, which he fulfills by appearing in visions and issuing revelations, providing guidance to local spiritual leaders and thus also bringing about the Daoist religion (Seidel 1969, 60-73; Kohn 1998a, 12). The understanding is that Dao at the root of creation is more than unconscious, organic order; it has a distinct purpose, a divine thrust, a spiritual direction and continues to guide the world even (or maybe especially) after the emergence of humanity and culture.

---

[1] *Huainanzi* 3; Major 1993; Major et al. 2010. Recently excavated manuscripts have added further variety to traditional cosmogony. For a study, see Wang 2015.

The longest and most detailed description of Laozi as Dao creating the world appears in the 6th-century *Kaitian jing* 開天經 (Scripture of Opening the Cosmos, DZ 1437;[2] trl. Kohn 1993, 35-43; Schafer 1997), a text of the Northern Celestial Masters whose main focus was on Laozi as central deity of Dao (see Kohn 2000). It begins with a graphic description of the utter nothingness of primordial chaos, where Lord Lao arises as the first seed of Dao. Descending in regular intervals and issuing forth sacred scriptures, he teaches the world to evolve in just the right way, advising rulers and guiding civilization on its course. The early stages of this development, which the text pursues down to the historical rulers of the Zhou dynasty, adopt the periodization scheme of the *Yijing* and the *Liezi*, but here each stage lasts for millions years and ends in destruction before a new phase begins. For example,

> In the time of Grand Antecedence, Lord Lao descended from barren emptiness to be its teacher. His mouth issued the "Scripture of Opening the Cosmos" in one section and forty-eight times ten thousand scrolls. Each scroll had forty-eight times ten thousand characters. Each character was one hundred square miles in size. In this way he taught Grand Antecedence.
>
> In Grand Antecedence, for the first time he separated heaven and earth, the clear and the turbid. He divided boundless galaxies and vast nebulae, set up shapes and signs. He secured north and south, and ordered east and west. He opened the darkness and made light, and positioned the four universal mainstays. (1b)

Cosmic Spheres

Another major difference to pre-Qin cosmology is that religious Daoists add a new dimension to the creative process by expanding the pure, formless Dao at the universal root into a primordial manifestation at the nub of creation—a manifestation that is still pure but no longer quite so formless. Before giving rise to the world as we know it, Dao (or rather Lord Lao) brings form a series of cosmic spheres, called *tian* 天, lit. "sky" or "heaven." Consisting of oscillating and glittering materials, inhabited by gods that change shape continuously, and housing divine scriptures that blend in and out of existence, they represent a realm where oneness is intact—both a primordial stage of creation and a continuously present high-energy level of the universe. Here gods, heavens, and scriptures participate fully and are vividly present (Johnson 2014b, 11). They

---

[2] Texts in the *Daozang* (Daoist Canon), abbreviated DZ, are cited according to Schipper and Verellen 2004.

have the ability to merge back into ultimate formlessness, but can just as easily move forward and become solidified in worldly appearances.

This vision is first documented in the *Santian neijie jing* 三天內解經 (Inner Explanations of the Three Heavens, DZ 1205; trl. Bokenkamp 1997, 204-29), a text of the Celestial Masters dated to about 420. Like ancient cosmogony, it begins with life energy, but here it does not simply unfold naturally but relies on the guidance of Lord Lao. Also, it no longer moves from one to two to three, but from one to three to nine, producing celestials (gods, heavens, scriptures) in the process. "Three" here is no longer yin and yang in harmony but three primordial energies, called beginning, primordial, and mysterious (1.2b). They appear in different colors (green, yellow, white) and are immediately identical with the three highest heavens of Daoism (Highest, Jade, and Great Clarity), which in turn are also the central gods (Three Pure Ones) and most sacred scriptures (Three Caverns) of the religion (Kohn 2002, 121). Ultimately one and part of the primordiality of the universe, they represent an entirely separate Dao-level of existence.

From the tripartite division of the as-yet uncreated universe, a set of the nine cosmic spheres emerges, recalling ancient Chinese cosmology that divided the sky into nine layers, the earth into nine continents, and cities into nine squares (see Major 1978; 1984). From here, the Daoist universe further expands to encompass enormous numbers of layers—sometimes as many as five hundred million (Kohn 1995, 139)—most commonly described as the thirty-six heavens.

Their pinnacle is the Heaven of Grand Network (Daluo tian 大羅天) with its capital of Mystery Metropolis (Xuandu 玄都), also known as the (Mountain of) Jade Capital (Yujing shan 玉京山). Here the great celestial scriptures are stored, managed and guarded by the highest of deities, powerful representatives of Dao and elevated immortals (Kohn 1995, 56). The thirty-five heavens beneath it divide into five groups. There are first the Three Clarities—Highest, Jade, Great—the heavens that represent the three major schools of Daoism with their respective gods, scriptures, talismans, incantations, and a host of divine administrators.

Below them are the four Brahma Heavens, named after the central deity of the Hindu pantheon who represents the purity of the universe and the four ideal mental states (*brahmaviharas*): equanimity, love, compassion, and sympathetic joy. These four are the home of true believers, human beings of superior purity transposed into these divine realms of pure bliss. They can advance to become immortals in the Three Clarities or, like bodhisattvas, decide to return to the lower realms if they decide to assist humanity in its quest for peace and perfection.

The lower twenty-eight cosmic levels are called the Three Worlds and adapted from Buddhism. The lowest six form the World of Desire; the following eighteen are the World of Form; and the four heavens above them constitute the World of Formlessness. They are open to humanity, each person gaining residence according to his dominant way of life: determined by passions and desires, guided by ethical rules and virtues, or spiritually advanced with a strong sense of intuition and rightness. The highest participate in the World of Formlessness and are poised for ascension into the Brahma Heavens or even the Three Clarities as they increasingly transcend physicality and come to live more and more in pure energy and spirit (Kohn 2002, 122).

The Stars

The concrete location of these various cosmic layers is in the stars. The most important among them is the heavenly pivot or celestial pole, the ultimate geographical core of the universe, known as North Culmen (Beiji 北極) or Palace of Purple Tenuity (Ziwei gong 紫微宮). It is the residence of the Great One (Taiyi 太一), the divinized form of great oneness (Johnson 2014b, 64-66). The power that controls everything, this central location is not represented by any particular star or constellation. Having no "obvious physical presence," it is rather "the marvel of an efficacious 'nothing' at the center of the rotating dome of the sky" (Pankenier 2013, 92), a giant hole at the galactic center (Rees 2000, 36).

Next in importance is the Northern Dipper (Beidou 北斗), ruler of fates and central ordering power of the universe. Already the *Shiji* 史記 (Historical Records, dat. 104 BCE) notes,

> The Dipper is the carriage of the emperor; it is placed in the center, . . . governs the four cardinal points, separates yin and yang, and determines the four seasons. It balances the five phases, arranges the divisions [of time] and the levels [of space], and sets the various measures. (Robinet 1989, 178; 1993, 212)

The Dipper consists of nine stars, two of which are visible only to highly advanced adepts. Represented by specific deities, each called various by technical (astronomical), traditional, and spiritual (Daoist) names, they the Seven Primes (*qiyuan* 七元) or the Nine Perfected (*jiuzhen* 九真) (see Kohn 2000; Johnson 2014b, 67-74). Another major constellation is Cassiopeia, called the Flowery Canopy (Huagai 華蓋), located opposite the Dipper and covering two major celestial quadrants, to the west and north. In addition, the sun, moon, and planets play a central role in Daoist cosmology, ordering time and space and radiating pure celestial energy throughout.

The starry realms are the home of various celestial beings: pure gods of Dao, emanating from original cosmic energy; immortals, successful practitioners of spiritual cultivation; demon kings, converted spirits of high rank and power; and ancestors, departed humans. The reside in glittering palaces of indestructible materials, notably gold and jade, live on pure cosmic energy, persist over millions of years, and have unlimited powers of transformation. As the *Fafu kejie wen* 法服科戒文 (Rules and Precepts Regarding Ritual Garb, DZ 788; trl. Kohn 1993, 336-43) describes it,

> [They wear] garments made from flying clouds and floating mists, pure spontaneity and wondrous energy, made from the precious radiance of the nine colors. . . Some are thickly embroidered with dragons and phoenixes, with the flowing shapes of mountains and rivers. Changing a thousand times and transforming ten thousand times, they cannot be described. . . . None possess any material solidity whatsoever: they appear and disappear without constancy. (3a; Kohn 1993, 340)

The celestial realm of the stars is organized hierarchically and houses the celestial administration, strictly ranked divine figures who supervise human life and fate. But their connection to humanity is closer than that. As the *Chisongzi zhongjie jing* 赤松子中戒經 (Essential Precepts of Master Redpine, DZ 185; trl. Kohn 2004a, 155-68) points out, each human being receives a personal star at birth, which shines or dims in accordance with his or her celestial standing. Everyone who comes to life is connected "to one particular star, which may be big or small, but in each case governs the person's longevity and shortness [of life], decline and prosperity, poverty and wealth, death and life" (1a). This star is used by the celestial administrators, notably by the Director of Fates (Siming 司命) and the Director of Emoluments (Silu 司綠), to gauge people's moral mettle by "placing a talisman of the Great One on people's heads to examine whether they are full of sins. In accordance with their finding, they then make a subtraction from the life expectancy" (2a). Although most people begin life with a standard longevity "of 43,800 days, i.e., 120 years of life" (1b), this may change rapidly as their behavior does not measure up (Kohn 2004a, 17).

To enhance the starry presence in their lives, Daoist visualize celestial denizens in the body, generally viewing it as a microcosmic replica of the entire cosmos. A variant creation myth, adapted from the ancient Vedic tale of Purusha (see Lincoln 1975), accordingly describes Lord Lao's body as transforming into the world.

> Laozi changed his body: His left eye became the sun and his right eye the moon. His head was Mount Kunlun, his hair the stars. His bones turned into dragons, his flesh into wild beasts, and his intestines into snakes. His breast was the ocean, his fingers, the five sacred mountains. The hair on his body was transformed into grass and trees, his heart into the constellation Cassiopeia. Finally, his testicles joined in embrace as the true parents of the universe. (Kohn 1995, 54; 2002, 112; see also Schipper 1994)

The original pure body is in fact the universe; it is the stars and the residence of the gods in its physical form on earth (Kohn 2002, 116). Daoists activate this divine, cosmic dimension of themselves by expanding themselves into the universe, engaging in ecstatic excursions to the stars, and visualizing the interior of their bodies as the palaces and halls of the gods, seeing them reside within in precise detail.

The practice typically begins with a period of purification and ritual preparation, the placement of talismans and recitation of incantations. Ecstatic visits to the otherworld usually begin with a tour around the far reaches of the earth, then move on to an imitation of the planets' movements, especially of the sun and the moon, gradually making the body into a replica of the universe and gaining control over its rhythm.

Once perfectly aligned, adepts reach out to visit the higher spheres of the planets and superior heavens, eventually approaching the central ruling power of the world in the Dipper in a practice known as "pacing the void" (*buxu* 步虛) (Schafer 1977; Andersen 1990). From here, they transcend to the empty pivot, the quiet center of Dao, thus becoming one with the root of creation. On their way, moreover, they encounter numerous gods and immortals, from whom they learn cosmic secrets and receive instructions for further attainment. By ecstatically traveling through far-off, cosmic reaches, Daoists increasingly become denizens of the otherworld, often finding their heavenly life more rewarding and more real than their existence on earth (see Robinet 1989; 1993).

Within the body, they see divine entities, often described as infants to symbolize their raw power and original purity, in their five inner organs (*wuzang* 五臟) and three major energy centers, the so-called elixir fields (*dantian* 丹田). They activate starry constellations in different parts, so that, for example, the lungs become Cassiopeia. Most importantly, they visualize the Three Ones (*sanyi* 三一), gods representing the three life energies at the root of creation (see Andersen 1980) that govern the twenty-four fundamental powers of the human body, corresponding to the twenty-four periods of the year and the twenty-four essential constellations in the sky (Kohn 2002, 110).

They also activate the Eight Luminants (*bajing* 八景), starry constellations and energy centers first described in the *Huangting jing* 黃庭經 (Yellow Court Scripture, DZ 331, 332), a 4th-century text on visualization of body gods and interior cultivation that today appears in an Outer (*wai* 外) and Inner (*nei* 內) work. Closely associated with the school of Highest Clarity (Shangqing 上清), in its older (outer) form, it precedes the revelations (see Kroll 1996; Robinet 1993, 55-96). Adepts further enhance the so-called Ninefold Empyrean (*jiuxiao* 九宵), deities representing the nine heavens as outlined in the *Jiutian shengshen zhangjing* 九天生神章經 (Stanzas of the Vital Spirit of the Nine Heavens, DZ 318). Doing so, they merge with Mystery Metropolis, the seat of the central heavenly administration, housing thousands of gods and immortals. Moving even further inward, they eventually activate the Palace of Purple Tenuity, the residence of the Highest Lord in the North Culmen and core of all power in the universe (Schafer 1987, 56). The overall goal of the practice is a cosmicization of the self through the body, a change in personal awareness from the limited human to the overarching universal, a shift in identity from bounded I to cosmic vastness.

The New Cosmology

The very same goal is also at the center of a new cosmology emerging from the scientific community in cooperation with the comparative study of religions. Called "scientific cosmology," it understands the universe less as a "container for everything else" than as a "dynamic evolving being" that is defined according to an overarching social consensus, a "mask fitted on the face of the unknown universe" (Harrison 1985, 1; Primack and Abrams 2006, 19; see also Tucker 2011). Based on new physics discoveries about nature and the stars in the light of the growing environmental crisis, it presents the first scientific story of nature and the origins of the universe (Abrams and Primack 2011, 6), striving to open up "patterns that connect humanity to a vaster destiny—a vital participation in earth's unfolding" (Swimme and Tucker 2011, 111). Its goal is to make us "know who we are and see from a cosmic perspective . . . , see ourselves as part of universal evolution, . . . and think cosmically and act globally" (Abrams and Primack 2011, 37, 77, 239; www.earthweareone.com).

Human beings, scientific cosmologists argue, are in a unique position, in size and conscious awareness right in the middle of a vast circle of dimensions, between a total of sixty orders of magnitude in the entirety of creation, from the galactic, humongous and vast, to the subatomic, tiny and minute.[3] Humanity at the present time is also at a crucial moment in the unfolding of the universe, close to the midpoint of our solar system, at about the halfway point of the life-span of the sun, i.e., 4.6 billion years from both its origin and its projected end.[4] We are at the midpoint of complex life on earth, about half a billion years after the arising of the first animals and half a billion years away from the extinction of all life when the sun begins to die and its heat evaporates the oceans and destroys almost all life forms on earth (Abrams and Primack 2011, 85; Kwok 2013, 63).

Now, moreover, is a peak moment of astronomical observation. "There will never again be so many galaxies visible," since they are speeding away from us with the ever increasing expansion of the universe (Abrams and Primack 2011, 81-82). Before too long our own Milky Way will merge with the neigh-

---

[3] Abrams and Primack 2011, 30-31; Primack and Abrams 2006, 160; Rees 2000, 8.

[4] Abrams and Primack 2011, 84; Kwok 2013, 63; Rees 2001, 7; Swinne and Tucker 2011, 119-20.

boring galaxy of Andromeda—2.7 million light years away—to form Milky Andromeda.[5] All this means that right now is an extraordinary moment for humanity, a "worldwide turning point that can only happen once in the evolution of our planet" (2011, 261). The turning point is further characterized by exponential growth, both in human population and use of natural resources, creating a great urgency to develop in new and more evolved ways (2011, 86-88).

The key to taking best advantage of this unique point in time and unfold planetary and human evolution toward a "future vaster than ever imagined" (2011, 79) is the development of universal awareness within the individual and a cosmic society on the planet. Rather than seeing ourselves as limited entities with a relatively short life expectancy and a narrow (and often obscure) purpose, we need to realize that we are "the sum total of our history," and this history is the history of universe, which goes back close to 14 billion years. We need to see ourselves as part of universal evolution and connect to the vastness of space and the enormity of cosmic time consciously and personally, directly and experientially. "We are connected to the universe in our bones, our history, our atoms, and our minds" (2011, 78). We have to make the active choice to see and experience ourselves in this way.

This choice of attitude is not a casual one. If we take this seriously, integrate science and meaning, claim our centrality in the universe, and begin to see and live from a cosmic perspective, we have "the power to overturn the fundamental institutions of society" (Primack and Abrams 2006, 275). No longer seeing ourselves as irrelevant, we can step up to cosmic responsibility and stop wasting the resources of the planet, prevent the extinction of further species, and reverse the effects of global warming.

We can begin to think in terms of having enough instead of always needing more (see Twist 2003). We can start acting as one big integrated organism rather than as unrelated individuals and interest groups, becoming planetary citizens, appreciating the ecological interconnectedness of all, and seeing ourselves as an integral part of the system in which we live (Sounds True 2009). Following the new understanding of evolution, we can find success by being powerfully cooperative, creating potent networks, garnering deep-rooted support from the community, and furnishing optimal living conditions for everyone (Wright 1994). And we can come to see life as win-win or non-zero sum game, where all participants benefit in one way or another, there is more to go around, and cooperation produces greater profits (Wright 2000).

To sum up, by developing a cosmic consciousness along the lines described by medieval Daoists we can reach a state then called Great Peace. Today this matches the ideal of "phase lock," a state where individual oscillating rhythms fall into a deep pattern of energetic resonance, a state nature always

---

[5] Primack and Abrams 2006, 239; Primack in Tucker 2011, 1.2; Tipler 1994, 55; Tyson and Goldsmith 2004, 117.

favors and tries to make happen. As we build deep connections and genuine community among our own circles and the people of the world, we participate in this moment of global transformation, joining all in cosmic awareness, and creating the collective harmony that is the next step in our evolutionary journey (Williamson 2002).

Star Organics

The first step toward this cosmic consciousness is to explore and experience our connection to the stars—again in close similarity to the Daoist project. For one, as residents of the earth, we move constantly along with them. We may sit quietly in an armchair, peaceful and relaxed, apparently unmoving. Yet in fact, we are hurling through space at unimaginable speed. We move with the earth as it rotates on its axis at 1,000 miles per hour (mph) and revolves around the sun at 66,000 mph. More than that, we speed along with the sun on its way toward Lambda Herculis at 45,000 mph. With our solar system, we spin around the Milky Way at 483,000 mph; and with the entire Milky Way galaxy, we hurl through space in the ever expanding universe at 1.3 million mph. Far from being solid and stable, we are in constant motion at speeds far too fast for our limited imagination (www.astrosociety.org/uitc).

By the same token, our bodies consist of fifty trillion cells; each cell contains a hundred trillion atoms; and each atom is made up of billions and billions of subtly vibrating energy strings (Greene 2003, 14). These strings, moreover, began with the Big Bang 13.7 billion years ago. At first highly condensed into a tiny but immensely powerful point, the universe exploded, and within one second, protons and neurons began to bind as nuclei of hydrogen, helium, lithium, and deuterium, thereby reducing the overall processing speed.[6] Within three minutes, matter and radiation coupled together, and the first stable nuclei formed. Undergoing various stages over the next 300,000 years, matter and energy began to decouple, and the optically dense universe became transparent to cosmic background radiation (Hawking 2001, 78).[7]

At this point, it gave rise to the first hydrogen atoms—the core material of all existence and the beginning of our nervous system (DeSalle and Tattersall 2012, 30-31; Rees 2000, 40). Over the next thousand million years, clusters of hydrogen and helium formed the first stars that, under the impact of millions of degrees of heat, underwent nuclear fusion and began to synthesize heavier

---

[6] Primack and Abrams 2006, 143; Rees 2001, 43. A hydrogen atom can encode four million bits of information; a proton, on the other hand, being much smaller, encodes about forty (Vedral 2010, 187).

[7] For more on the Big Bang, see also Gleiser 2010; Hawking and Penrose 1996; Penrose 2004, ch. 27; Tucker 2011, 1.1; Weinberg 1979.

nuclei.[8] Over the following 15,000 million years, new galaxies formed—initially small and irregular—with solar systems condensing around stars, while atoms began to link and form complex molecules of initial life-forms (Hawking 2001, 78; Potter 2009, 160-70).

Stars, moreover, do not live forever. Although they last several hundred million years, they too get old and die, and in the process become redder, brighter, and larger, reaching a stage known as asymptotic giant branch. Only then—in what amounts to about three days of an eighty-year lifespan—do they produce carbon, the basic element of all organic life (Kwok 2013, 64; Ferreira 2006, 151). As they develop strong stellar wind, this carbon together with other essential building blocks of organic life, such as nitrogen, phosphorus, and sulfur (Tyson and Goldsmith 2004, 176), ejects from the star's outer atmosphere and moves into space. Eventually the wind removes the atmosphere of the star completely and exposes its core, at which point it becomes a planetary nebula, "a death cloud of middle-sized stars" (Abrams and Primack 2011, 43). In this form, it expands and gradually disperses into the interstellar medium. Visible for only 30,000 years, it eventually becomes a white dwarf and is no longer luminous (Kwok 2013, 74; Potter 2009, 180). While on average a star dies every year, only few of them go supernova, which means they explode in a widely visible blast—the best recorded historically occurred in 1604, the most recent was observed in 1987 (Ferreira 2006, 152; Kwok 2013, 77; Rees 2000, 40-43).

Whatever form the star's death takes, the various molecules it produces fly widely through space and rain on other celestial bodies, including about 40,000 tons of stardust that fall on the earth every year (Potter 2009, 206; Schrijver and Schrijver 2015). Since all organic life, moreover, originated with the stars, we too are in essence "all star stuff" and "literally made of stardust" (Abrams and Primack 2011, 39; Primack in Tucker 2011, 1.3).

> Human bodies consist of molecules: water, protein, DNA, sugar, and fat. Each molecule, in turn, is made up of hydrogen (61%), oxygen (26%), carbon (10%), nitrogen (2%), calcium (0.2%), phosphorus (0.1%), and sulfur (0.1%), and more. We take in atoms in the form of molecules by eating, drinking, and breathing—our body is a *giant chemical factory*, all parts of which have once been part of a star. (Kwok 2013, 37)

Not only is the carbon in the carbon dioxide we exhale with every breath originally part of planetary nebulae (Abrams and Primack 2011, 43), but the history of the universe is in every one of us. "Every particle in our bodies has a multibillion-year past, every cell and every bodily organ has a multimillion-year past, and many of our ways of thinking have a multi-thousand-year past. Each of us is a kind of nerve center where these various cosmic histories intersect" (Primack and Abrams 2006, 151). In other words,

---

[8] Cox and Forshaw 2011, 216-17; Primack and Abrams 2006, 147; Rees 2000, 40.

> The iron flowing in your blood was made in a supernova explosion some 4.6 billion years ago. Floating through the vastness of space, it became part of the earth as the solar system came into being, and now, through food, it has become part of your body. To carry this idea further, the hydrogen and other elements found throughout your body were created at the birth of the universe. They have existed for 13.7 billion years, along with the universe, and are now part of you. (Takano 2014, 50)

Everything we are, every atom in our being has at one time or another been part of a star (Kwok 2013, 40; Primack in Tucker 2011, 1.1). Consisting essentially of galactic nuclear waste, we *are* the stars (Rees 2000, 52).

We do, moreover, continue to communicate with them—not only intentionally through visualization or ecstatic excursions as undertaken by medieval Daoists and modern energy practitioners (Primack and Abrams 2006, 152-54), but also unconsciously on a cellular basis. "Each individual being (including humans) not only communicates within its own species but also across large evolutionary and planetary distances, using molecules rather than the senses. Bacteria, for example, communicate through quorum sensing, i.e., by sensing the presence of other cells or organisms, then responding to them as appropriate" (DeSalle and Tattersall 2012, 63). "Every electron, every proton, and every neutron in your body is constantly exploring the universe at large, and only when the sum total of all these explorations is computed do we arrive at a world in which the actions in your body tend to stay in a reasonably stable arrangement" (Cox and Forshaw 2011, 174).

All organic matter constantly emits energy, radiation at extremely low frequencies, most commonly measured in geomagnetic and geoelectric fields, but also clearly present in the human brain and the greater universe. Through patterned string vibrations, we actively entrain with all sorts of external fields that reach through the planet into the galaxies and to the far reaches of the cosmos (Oschman 2000, 97-99). The resulting connection is instantaneous, part of universal nonlocality and quantum entanglement (Beauregard 2012, 211; Tiller et al. 2005, 197). "On the most basic level, the universe appears to be a web of particles that remain in contact even if there is no transfer of energy or information" (Nadau and Kafatos 1999, 185), forming what Max Planck called the Divine Matrix (Dames 2011, 14). Becoming conscious of this fact and enhancing our sense of this intrinsic, overarching interrelatedness is an important step in creating the cosmic consciousness and universal identity essential to future evolution as much as to medieval Daoist practice.

The Multiverse

Our solar system resides in the Milky Way galaxy, which has over 100 billion stars, 2.5 million among them similar to our own sun. The universe as a whole has more than 100 billion galaxies similar to the Milky Way (Kwok 2013, 1; Rees 2000, 53). Galaxies form clusters, attracted to each other by high levels of gravity. The cluster, to which the Milky Way belongs, our so-called local group (Abrams and Primack 2011, 17), includes one other major galaxy, Andromeda, plus thirty-four minor ones, making a total of thirty-six (Rees 2000, 53; 2001, 49)—coincidentally the number of medieval Daoist heavens. The nearest cluster beyond that is Virgo, containing several hundred galaxies; further out, there are even larger aggregates, known summarily as the Great Wall, plus further galaxies in different shapes: irregular, elliptic, disk, and spiral (2000, 54; Duncan in Tucker 2011, 1.2).

Given the vast expanse of the universe and the immensely huge number of galaxies, combined with the fact that organic matter is present throughout due to the ongoing death and explosion of stars, it is entirely plausible that, "in a suitable environment and with sufficient time," intelligent life can develop in other areas (Murdin 2009, 310). Since we ourselves are essentially stardust and come from out there—are in fact "alien life" ourselves, there might well be "other alien life to be discovered" (Potter 2009, 206). Even if only one percent of one percent of all stars in the universe had some form of life, that would still be an enormously large number (Sagan 2006, 114; Davies 2007, 177).

Life beyond the earth, as a possibility already indicated by Giordano Bruno in 1584, has been a hotly debated topic throughout the 20th century (Dick 2001). Scientists today pursue it with ever advancing signal-processing technology in an exploratory field known as Search for Extraterrestrial Intelligence (SETI; www.seti.org; Tyson and Goldsmith 2004, 286), despite the fact that any communication across the vastness of space would take a very long time to arrive. Plus, even if it got here, it might well be in a code too advanced for us and thus entirely unintelligible (Sagan 2006, 115, 118; Rees 2001, 27-28).

Still, the vision that arises is fascinating. As Marcelo Gleiser describes it,

> Imagine a vista with valleys and peaks stretching in the distance. Different valleys in the landscape correspond to different universes, each with its own properties, possibly even with distinct values for the constants of Nature. In some, the speed of light may be greater than ours; in others, lesser. In one, light does not exist; and in another, electrons have different electric charges and masses. There is no time in the landscape; it represents only a mapping of potential universes. (2010, 70; see also Davies 2007, 169; Susskind 2006)

Besides potential realms of intelligent existence in similar solar systems within our own and neighboring galaxies and the possibility of organic life in areas far beyond, string theory proposes the concept of parallel universes that are right next to ours but work in a different dimension (see Tegmark 2004; for a fictional account, see North 2014). Striving to unify relativity theory with quantum physics, string theory proposes that particles are not points but subtle strings of energy that vibrate in different energy patterns (Alexander 2009, 64; Greene 2003, 142-45; 2004, 348-60; Hammond 2008, ch. 8). These strings come in two major forms—loops and snippets. Loops are free agents that can move around and fly off into space; snippets, on the other hand are half-loops with something like suction cups at the end (Greene 2011, 134). They are attached to a two-dimensional string, an energetic constellation formed like a flag or a tablecloth that can wrap around space and is called a "brane," an abbreviation of "membrane." A three-dimensional string, moreover, could be infinitely big and envelope space in a bubble, not unlike a fish-tank (Greene 2011, 130).

This, then, would constitute a universe. Since light cannot travel across the brane, another braneworld or parallel universe could be just millimeters away—like the next slice in a loaf of bread—and we could not sense it, although we might be able to connect to it on an intuitive level (Greene 2004, 391-94; 2011, 135). In other words, in this understanding, our cosmos is not a universe but a multiverse, where we occupy only a tiny pocket (Alexander 2009, 65; Greene 2003, 366; see also Carr 2007; Penrose 1997). While some braneworlds might be extremely small, such as Planck size of 10^{-33} centimeters, some might be much larger, e.g., 10^{-4} centimeters. This being the case, one could test for its existence by measuring gaps in gravity (Greene 2011, 135). Universes in this model come in various forms and shapes: quilted, bubble, and more, opening the possibility of life forms vibrating in different energetic frequencies and with constituents and intelligences, potentially even self-aware beings quite different from us, literally next door (2011, 132, 136; Rees 2001, 169-70).

Either model—extraterrestrial life in other galaxies or intelligent existence in parallel braneworlds—outlines a vision quite compatible with the Daoist understanding of gods, spirits, and immortals residing beyond our realm yet communicating with us (see Kaku 2006).

In addition, string theory also opens the possibility of a cyclical rather than linear history of the universe, again coming closer to the ancient Daoist vision. If universes are wrapped in branes, two branes could conceivably collide, creating a cataclysmic explosion that would annihilate both and lead to the emergence of a new one. In other words, the Big Bang would not be a one-time starting point, from where the universe expands until its ultimate extinction, but a recurring event that occurs every so often in billions or trillions of years, creating cyclic multiverses in "cycles that have always happened and always will" (Greene 2011, 139; Rees 2000, 150; see also Penrose 2010; Mersini-Houghton and Vaas 2012).

The Inevitability Factor

Rather than a thing, the universe or multiverse, therefore, is an ongoing activity, a process that continuously creates and transforms existence (Duncan in Tucker 2011, 1.2). It does so in one particular way and none other, providing the optimal conditions for the arising and decaying of stars and the creation of life. "In a multiverse model, . . . most of the universes would be barren, unable to sustain any kind of life" (Greene 2011, 202). Our universe happens to be the one where things work just right for conscious beings to emerge out of the laws of physics and the constraints of biology" (Gleiser 2010, 219; Rees 2001, 21; see also Ward and Brownlee 2000). If the universe after the Big Bang had expanded just a tiny bit slower, it would have re-collapsed into a giant black hole; had it expanded just a tiny bit faster, it would have exploded into nothing but dust. It moved exactly at the rate necessary for life to come forth (Primack in Tucker 2011, 1.1).

This holds true even after the generation of planet earth. Life could only develop in the so-called goldilocks zone of a planetary system: neither so cold that water freezes nor so hot that it evaporates, and the earth had just the right distance from the sun for that to happen (Murdin 2009, 312; see also Davies 2006; 2007). "We exist because the sun burns at the right rate and because the masses of the electron and proton are as they are. Were any of these slightly different, or the forces not so finely tuned, neither we ourselves nor anything that we know would be here" (Close 2011, 353). "We owe our existence to the fact that the sun has been pretty much stable for four and half billion years, allowing a steady environment for life to have developed and flourished on earth. Had the sun's brightness or temperature been changing, even on million-year time scales, the development and sustaining of life would have been much more difficult" (Kwok 2013, 63). "If Jupiter had not been there to protect the earth from bombardment, it is hard to imagine how life on earth could be possible" (Potter 2009, 202).

All manner of things have to come together just so to make life possible, forming part of a universal pattern, an inherent organic order. Stars and elements cannot but do what they do—"their behavior is built into the order of the universe" (Abrams and Primack 2011, 62). By the same token, the earth's magnetic field is just right to ward off cosmic rays: were it weaker, there would be no atmosphere and the planet would be barren like Mars; were it stronger, there could not be any life. Similarly the amount of uranium is just right. Were there less, the earth would have cooled too fast and become inert; were there more, the planet would have been too radioactive for life to develop (Potter 2009, 204).

Even timing is uncannily accurate. "If man and his technology had appeared on the scene several billion years earlier, the separation of uranium-235 [crucial for making atom bombs] would have been easier. If man had appeared later—say ten billion years later—the concentration of uranium-235 would have been so low as to make it practically unusable" (John von Neumann in Potter 2009, 204n6). That is to say, both animate life and human technology as we know it required the galactic environment to be just so and none other. Or, as Carl Sagan puts it, "It is no more likely that the origin of life could occur spontaneously by molecular interaction in the primitive ocean than that a Boeing 747 would be spontaneously assembled when a whirlwind passed over a junkyard" (2006, 101-02).

"Everything in the universe has to be about the size it is" (Abrams and Primack 2011, 31; Potter 2009, 202). Even human beings cannot be any other way. "If we were much smaller, we would not have enough atoms to be complex; if we were much larger, our speed of thought and internal awareness would be too slow. Only in this size and setting could [reflective] consciousness evolve" (Abrams and Primack 2011, 33). Does this, then, mean that, as Joel Primack says, "the universe must have known that life was coming" (Tucker 2011, 1.1)? Does it mean that cosmic evolution is teleological, "a purposeful cosmic strategy with life as its goal" (Davies 2007; Gleiser 2010, 220)? Does it justify the assumption that humanity is central, as described in the so-called anthropic principle?[9]

Not necessarily, but it means that there is a certain inevitability to the cosmic enterprise, a sense of underlying structure (Davies 2007, 17; see also Stenger 2011). Although working through evolutionary selection (see Dawkins 1986), the universe presents a quality of cosmic unity, reveals some force or pattern pervading all existence, which chaos theory describes as the "fractal geometry of form and process" that appears in "intricate, repetitive patterns" throughout the world (Jones and Culliney 1999, 644-45). It also appears as a claim of oneness in Greek thought (Gleiser 2010, 22-24) and the vision of a purposeful divine creator in Western religions. [10]

Cosmic Numbers

Further evidence emerges from certain so-called cosmic numbers: always stable, they form the mathematical underpinning of the universe (Tipler 1994, 91). For example, gravity is inevitably 10^{36} times feebler than electric forces, expressed as the number *N*. Were it even a little bit stronger, it would stunt the evolutionary potential of stars; were it just a small amount feebler, matter would not hold together (Rees 2000, 30). Similarly, the number 0.007, known as Σ, defines nuclear efficiency, i.e., how firmly atomic nuclei bind together, how the atoms on

---

[9] Barrow and Tipler 1986; see also Primack and Abrams 2011, 98; Harth 1993, 12; Linde 2004; Penrose 2004, 756; Tipler 1994.

[10] Primack and Abrams 2006, 277; Ostriker and Mitton 2013, 261; see also Wolf 1996.

earth were made, and how long a star will live (2000, 47). The ratio is essential to enable "the crucial first link in the chain—the build-up of helium from hydrogen" (2000, 49). Were it any different, stars could still form but they would have no nuclear fuel and deflate quickly: life would not be possible.

In addition, there is omega Ω, a number that measures the amount of material in our universe, defining the relative importance of gravity and expansion energy. It must never be greater than one, lest the universe collapse upon itself. As it turns out, all the 10^{78} atoms in the observable universe are fine tuned to remain in the permitted range, hovering around 0.25 to 0.3 (Rees 2000, 73, 84). Next, lambda λ, Einstein's cosmological constant, defines the degree of cosmic repulsion that balances gravity, i.e., a cosmic "antigravity." It cannot be zero, since gravity would cause the universe to collapse, but it cannot be very much either. It has a tiny but constant value that keeps the universe expanding steadily but not too fast (2000, 96).

The number described as *Q*, moreover, is 1/100,000 or 10^{-5}. It represents the ratio of any two fundamental energies as they are bound together, i.e., it describes how much energy would be needed to break them apart or the force of gravity that holds them together. Being very small means that the universe is fundamentally homogeneous, presenting a matching texture throughout (Rees 2000, 106; 2001, 80-81). Finally, there is *D*, the number of dimensions, centering on three. Zero dimension means points; one dimension means lines; two dimensions are surfaces; and all solid objects come in three dimensions: forward and back, up and down, right and left (2000, 134). The various forces of nature, such as electricity and magnetism, moreover, all give off fields in particular shapes, described as flux (Greene 2011, 143), forming the foundation of a three-dimensional world. A fourth physical dimension would require a much larger size of objects, showing that the inherent stability of planets and other objects depends on their three-dimensional nature (Rees 2000, 135; Penrose 1997, 21).

All these numbers and other constancy factors show that the universe evolved under the auspices of an inherently balancing force or power, that it moves toward homeostasis and always in a direction that favors perpetuity and the emergence of life. As chaos theory has it, "all 'bodies' self-order through random repetition out of chaotic atomic flows and decay back again into these flows"(Stevenson 2006, 303). David Bohm, moreover, describes it in terms of two levels of order—quite akin to the two aspects of Dao in ancient Daoist thought. One is the external, visible order of things in this world; the other is the underlying structure, orderly in its own way but much more subtle: explicate and implicate or unfolded and enfolded.

> In the [*implicate* or] *enfolded* order, space and time are no longer the dominant factors determining the relationships of dependence or independence of different elements. Rather, an entirely different sort of basic connection of elements is possible, from which our ordinary notions of

> space and time, along with those of separately existent material particles, are abstracted as forms derived from the deeper order. These ordinary notions in fact appear in what is called the *explicate* or *unfolded* order, which is a special and distinguished form contained within the general totality of all the implicate orders. (1980, xv; see also Targ 2012, 206-07)

This essentially means that not only is there an underlying order in the greater universe and all its parts, but also that "each event and each appearance in the world is a manifestation of a much larger process" (Peat 1997, 106; Bohm and Hiley 1993, 357; Talbot 1991, 46). The larger process is ubiquitous and pervasive, linking everything together in closely integrated wholeness, i.e., ultimate oneness.

> The quantum world is fundamentally holistic . . . and indivisible. In every observation, the observer and the observed are linked by a quantum. Since the quantum cannot be broken apart in any way, during an observation, the observer and the observed must be considered an indivisible whole. (Peat 1997, 106)

> Quantum concepts imply that the world acts more like a single individual unit, in which even the "intrinsic" nature of each part (wave or particle) depends to some degree on its relationship to its surroundings. (Bohm 1951; Peat 1997, 106)

This also means that our traditional boundaries of local and nonlocal, mind and matter, body and consciousness are overcome, giving instead rise to the notion of an overarching subtle energy field whose strings vibrate in different frequencies yet are always one.

Chapter Two

Piping with Heaven

Particle Physics and Subtle Energy

The subtle energy that forms the field of all existence in the Daoist tradition is *qi* 氣. *Qi* is the concrete aspect of Dao, the basic material building block of the universe, the fundamental stuff of nature. Ancient sources associate it with mist, fog, and moving clouds. The character for *qi* as it first appears in the oracle bones of the Shang dynasty (1760-1122 BCE), consists of two parts: an image of someone eating and grain in a pot. Combined, these parts signal *qi*, the quality that nourishes, warms, transforms, and rises. *Qi*, therefore, is the foods we eat and the air we breathe. More subtly, it is the life force in all matter including the human body and as such is the ground of all vitality, the ongoing process of aliveness (Zhang and Rose 2001).

By extension, *qi* also denotes anything perceptible but intangible: atmosphere, smoke, aroma, vapor, a sense of intuition, foreboding, or even ghosts. There is only one *qi*, just as there is only one Dao. Yet it, too, appears on different levels of subtlety and in different modes. At the center, there is primordial, prenatal, true, or perfect *qi*—intangible, invisible, inaudible, dark, and mysterious. At the periphery, there is postnatal or earthly *qi*—like the measurable Dao, it is in constant motion and perceptible in form, sound, and light—matching the three major ways of human perception and the fundamental quality of energy (Vedral 2010, 183). Thus, it can be classified according to categories such as temperature, density, speed and direction of flow, as well as its overall impact on human and natural life.

Yin and Yang

The most fundamental classification of *qi* flow is in terms of "phase energetics," the movement of energy either up or down, forward or back, rising or falling, and so on. The dominant model here is that of the interchange of the two dynamic forces yin and yang. Originally indicating the sunny and shady sides of a hill, they soon acquired a series of associations: bright and dark, light and heavy, strong and weak, above and below, heaven and earth, ruler and minister, male and female, and so on. Commonly presented in the well-known circle with two black and white curved halves, they represent the interlocking of energy patterns in an ongoing process of balancing and ordering, of continuous enfolding and unfolding (see Graham 1986; Wang 2012).

Yin and yang describe the energetic dynamics and reality patterning of everything in the universe. In concrete application, they indicate different kinds of action:

yang	active	birth	impulse	move	change	expansion
yin	structive	completion	response	rest	nurture	contraction

These characteristics are in turn associated with items in daily life:

yang	heaven	spring	summer	day	big states	ruler	man
yin	earth	fall	winter	night	small stats	minister	woman

father	life	noble	marriage	soldiers	speech	give
mother	death	common	funeral	laborers	silence	receive

While Westerners commonly assume that yang is "better" than yin, the Chinese view demands that neither is better, stronger, brighter, or more preferable, and the two forces do not represent good and evil. On the contrary, the yin aspect of things is just as important as the yang, because you cannot have one without other. They are not opposites but complementary phases of *qi*-flow, one bringing forth the other in close mutual interdependence, one inevitably necessitating the other (Kohn 2005, 21).

Smooth *qi*-flow, then, is the entrainment or vibrational harmony among different phenomena, objects, or aspects. Various modes are possible. Superimpose two waves of identical pattern: hill matches hill, valley matches valley, and the amplitude of the original wave pattern is doubled. This is called constructive interference or the "productive" (*sheng* 生) pattern of *qi*-interaction. Superimpose two waves of opposing pattern, and the exact opposite happens: they cancel each other out and the wave vanishes into a straight line. This is disruptive interference, the creation of disharmony and the "obstructive" or "overcoming" (*ke* 克) form of *qi*- interaction (Johnson 2000; 2014a, 4-5).

In the case of varying wavelengths, moreover, some phases match each other while others do not. This results in a curve that goes up and down, is far apart at one point, then meets again and parts again. The overall tendency of yin-yang dynamics is, like the universe as a whole, to fine-tune toward balance and seek the optimal level of functioning. Sooner or later a rhythmic pattern of interaction emerges, present in both the natural and human world.

Another aspect of *qi* is that it is ubiquitous and not limited by constraints of space or time. This means that any vibration anywhere resonates fully with all others—from the most minute realm within a human cell to the most expansive order of galactic vastness. The way in which we are made of stardust and continue to communicate and connect to the stars, then, happens via *qi*, through an all-pervasive energetic unity combined with the variable oscillations of subtle energy.

In other words, the ideal of harmonious *qi*-flow and entrained vibrations represents a completely resonant system. The waves of one entity impinge on another so that it moves in the same frequency. This, in essence, is the definition of health and harmony in Chinese culture. The *qi*-vibrations of each part in body, society, or nature resonate smoothly with all others. We as people resonate harmoniously with the people and things around us; society and nature resonate perfectly with each other in a state of optimum energy transfer.

Sound

Not only tangible in the vibrational frequencies of all matter, *qi* is also strongly present as sound (Johnson 2014b, 251). As a result, the entire universe is humming along in the joining of many different *qi*-sounds. The *Zhuangzi* 莊子 (Book of Master Zhuang; d. ca. 290 BCE), accordingly talks about three different types. They are the "piping of humanity," the sounds people make when they speak and interact; the "piping of earth," the sounds of nature in all the different places on the planet; and the "piping of heaven" the creation of the universe in its diversity through Dao (Kohn 2014, 44). The description of the "piping of earth" is most vivid and also applies to the other forms. The text says:

> They roar like waves, whistle like arrows, screech, gasp, cry, wail, moan, howl. Those in the lead cry out *yeee*; those behind cry out *yuuu*. In a gentle breeze, they answer faintly; but in a full gale, the chorus is gigantic. And when the fierce wind has passed on, then all the hollows are empty again. Have you never seen the tossing and trembling that goes on? (ch. 2; Watson 1968, 36-37)

The notion that *qi* can be perceived as sound also plays an important part in ancient musical theory (DeWoskin 1982), military strategy, and divination, where the manifestation of certain earth energies is observed with the help of pitch-pipes in a method known the "watching of the ethers" (*wangqi* 望氣; Bodde 1959; Loewe 1988; Sawyer 1993). Moreover, the relation of *qi* to breath and sound had an important influence on ancient Chinese diagnostics in that numerous illnesses were believed to be cause by the "winds" (Kohn 2005, 16).

Medieval Daoists expand this understanding to see Dao as a tone of a certain wavelength that pervades and encompasses all, i.e., a certain quality of *qi* that underlies and furnishes all existence. Individual things and beings, then, on the basis of this *qi*-quality or Dao-tone begin to "pipe" in their own way. In addition to Zhuangzi's piping of heaven, earth, and humanity, Daoists also acknowledge the sounds produced by various material entities and all sorts of individual living beings. These noises may or may not harmonize. The perfect pitch of Dao as implicate order and the tendency toward optimization, deeply embedded in every being though it is, may or may not be joined by the music of the myriad beings (Kohn 2007, 44).

This means that the more out of tune any individual (including plants, animals, and ghosts) is, the more "evil" he is from the point of Dao, the more unhappy he feels, the less fortunate he appears. Such "evil" is not fundamental; it is not rooted in the cosmos. It is merely a deviation, a change in pattern; it is a different wavelength, an unmatched pitch. Conversely, the more sagely one becomes, the more one is in tune with Dao. As Robert Neville points out in his discussion of the sage, "The more of God and the world which one possesses, the less one is a separate possessor. To follow up the musical metaphor: one becomes yet another chord in the harmony of the whole" (1978, 48).

Beings have the potential to be either in tune or out of tune with the true pitch of Dao. The universe equipped them with the individual power of producing their own tones. The power and beauty of the Daoist universe lies exactly in this freedom that is yet a form of bondage. The bond of Dao is an inner tendency, a feeling of belonging, a natural affinity for the right sound, the most harmonious vibration, a deep longing for peace and harmony. As soon as beings are out of tune with the overall symphony of life, they feel the need to return to the perfect harmony they had before they were born. Like fish out of water, they feel at odds in their *qi* and estranged from Dao (Kohn 2007, 45).

Cosmologically the overarching purpose of existence, therefore, the goal of all the various aspects of fine-tuning, is to create a perfect match in all tones, to lead the world from cacophony to spherical harmony. Getting involved in life on earth is how Dao (as Lord Lao) realizes itself through *qi*, creates greater harmony in an ever-growing cosmic orchestra. The sage, then, is one who has found perfect pitch in all his thoughts and actions. He happily goes along with the piping of Dao and never adds even a trace of disharmony to the cosmic symphony.

Light

Another dimension of *qi*-presence in the universe is in the form of light. Daoists commonly refer to it as "spirit light" or "spirit brightness" (*shenming* 神明), indicating a particular manifestation of "spirit." The subtlest form of *qi*, spirit is a cosmic force of extremely fast oscillation that pervades the entire universe; concentrated in the heavens in the form of spirits, gods, and immortals, it is a holy force to be held in awe (Roth 1990, 18). The *Zhuangzi* says, "Pure spirit reaches in the four directions, flows now this way, now that: there is no place it does not extend to. Above, it brushes the sky; below, it coils on the earth. It transforms and nurses the myriad things, but no one can make out its form. It is one with heaven" (ch. 15; W 169; Kohn 2014, 62).

Within human beings, spirit is an active, organizing configurative force that connects people to the finer and subtler levels of life and exerts a powerful transformative influence (Porkert 1974; Johnson 2014b, 226). It is without limit or judgment and comes before all sensory affects and emotional reactions (Lewis 2006, 22). An integrated whole that is not subject to increase or decrease, it works mainly with precognition and intuition (Roth 1990, 23, 16), opening us to heaven and cosmic oneness (Puett 2003, 257). It remains in its lodging place, the body as form (Kuriyama 1999, 167), as long as it stays clear of vexations, predisposed desires, and intentional harnessing (Roth 1990, 17). "Be unseeing and unhearing, guard spirit in stillness," Guangchengzi says in the *Zhuangzi* (ch. 11). Manifest in individual awareness yet impossible to be perceived directly—as when concentrated in gods, ancestors, and other divine forces—its vitalizing force pervades all aspects of the human being (Kohn 2005, 34; Zhang 2002, 171).

The notion of spirit light originally related to the ancestral cult and first appeared in the ancient expression for ancestral spirits in the sense of "blossom of brightness." Philosophers, next, defined inherent potency as the "light of inner vision" that direct outer behavior toward goodness. Thus, spirit as the agent active in human potency is the force of light, which in turn is the visible pure *qi* of yang. The personal light of inner vision, moreover, is the same as the light of the cosmos. As both participate in one another, they become the stronger the more harmoniously they shine forth. This is the power that renders ritual objects potent (Vandermeersch 1985). It is also a key feature in early shamanic works, such as the "Yuanyou" 遠遊 (Far-off Journey) poem in the *Chuci* 楚辭 (Songs of Chu; trl. Hawkes 1959), where the protagonist flies through Great Brightness and absorbs cosmic power in various colors (Nicholson 2004, 4).

The Daoist concept of spirit brightness is a direct continuation of these ancient notions. Many Daoist practices thus aim at strengthening the inner light of the adept (Robinet 1993, 60; Johnson 2014b, 45), inner observation being foremost among them in the Tang (Kohn 2010a, 91; see also Kohn 1989a; Johnson 2014c, 23). The notion of the personal star each human being receives at birth described in the *Chisongzi zhongjie jing* closely relates to this: it shines or dims in accordance with people's health, goodness, and spirituality, reflecting the power of spirit within.

Daoist practice involves enhancing and increasing the spirit brightness within. To this end, they undertake various forms of meditation, including also the active visualization of "luminants" (*jing* 景) within, starry entities that radiate throughout the person. The most important scripture in this context is the *Huangting neijing jing* 黃庭內景經 (Scripture of Inner Luminants of the Yellow Court, DZ 401, 402; trl. Saso 1995; Zhou and Archangelis 2010), which details the visualization of radiant deities in different parts of the body, thus cosmicizing the individual (see Kroll 1996; Robinet 1993, ch. 2). As adepts get closer to realizing Dao, they get lighter and brighter: the higher they ascend and the purer the spirit becomes, the more light they radiate, shining forth along with the sun, moon, and stars (Kohn 2010a, 100).

Body and Mind

Qi is the basic material of all that exists. It animates life and furnishes functional power of events. As such, *qi* is also the root of the human body and mind; its quality and movement determine human health. *Qi* in human beings can be discussed in terms of quantity, since having more *qi* means stronger metabolic function. This, however, does not mean that health or harmony is a byproduct of storing large quantities of *qi*. Rather, there is a normal or healthy amount of *qi* in every person, every animal, every plant, and every society, and health manifests in its balance and harmony, its moderation and smoothness of flow. This flow is envisioned in the texts as a complex system of waterways with the Ocean of *Qi* (*qihai* 氣海) in the abdomen; rivers of *qi* flowing through the upper torso, arms, and legs; springs of *qi* reaching to the wrists and ankles; and wells of *qi* found in the fingers and toes. Even a small spot in this complex system can thus influence the whole, so that overall balance and smoothness are the general goal.

Human life is the accumulation of *qi*; death is its dispersal (*Zhuangzi* 22). After receiving a core potential of primordial *qi* at birth, people throughout life need to sustain it. They do so by drawing postnatal *qi* into the body from air and food, as well as from other people through sexual, emotional, mental, and social interaction. But they also lose *qi* through breathing bad air, overburdening their bodies with food and drink, and getting involved in negative emotions, frustrating thoughts, and excessive sexual or social interactions.

It is thus best to keep mentally calm, breathe deeply, and eat moderately in accordance with the seasons. One should relax in the spirit, move smoothly, exercise without exertion, and match activities to current needs. This is how one keeps balance and creates health. As the *Lüshi chunqiu* 呂氏春秋 (Spring and Autumn Annals of Master Lü), a text from about 260 BCE, has it:

> One wants the skin to be tight, the blood vessels to allow unimpeded motion; the sinews to be firm and the bones hard; the heart, mind, and will to be concordant; and the life energies to flow. When this is happening, agents of disorder [sickness] have nowhere to abide and pathology has nowhere to be produced. The abiding of agents of sickness is the origin of pathology, which is blocking the flow of qi. (ch. 4; Knoblock and Riegel 2000)

Health is not just the absence of symptoms and ailments. It is the presence of a strong life energy and of a smooth, harmonious, and active flow of *qi*. This is known as the state of *zhengqi* 正氣 or "proper *qi*," also translated as "upright *qi*." The ideal is to have *qi* flow freely, thereby creating harmony in body and mind, a balanced state of being in the person. Radiating outward and constantly interacting with life on all levels, this personal health matches health in nature, defined as regular weather patterns and the absence of disasters. It also connects to social health in the peaceful coexistence and strong community among families, clans, villages, and states; and it manifests on the cosmic, galactic level in the regular course of planetary trajectories and the regular firing of the sun. This harmony on all levels, the cosmic presence of a steady and pleasant flow of *qi* everywhere—from the farthest reaches of the universe to the minutest cells in the body and mind—is what the Chinese call the state of Great Peace (*taiping* 太平), an ideal venerated by Confucians and Daoists alike (Eichhorn 1957).

The opposite of health is *xieqi* 邪氣 or "wayward *qi*," also called "deviant *qi*," "pathogenic *qi*," "heteropathic *qi*," or "evil *qi*" (see Kaptchuk 1983; Porkert 1974; Seem 1989). It describes *qi* that has lost the harmonious pattern of flow and no longer supports the dynamic forces of change. Whereas *zhengqi* moves in a steady, harmonious rhythm and effects daily renewal, helping health and long life, *xieqi*, disorderly and dysfunctional, creates change that violates the normal order. It looks like this:

When wayward *qi* becomes dominant, the *qi*-flow can turn upon itself and deplete resources. The person, organization, or community no longer operates as part of a universal system and is not in tune with Dao as the life force around them. *Xieqi* appears when *qi* moves too fast or too slow, is excessive or depleted, or creates rushes or obstructions.

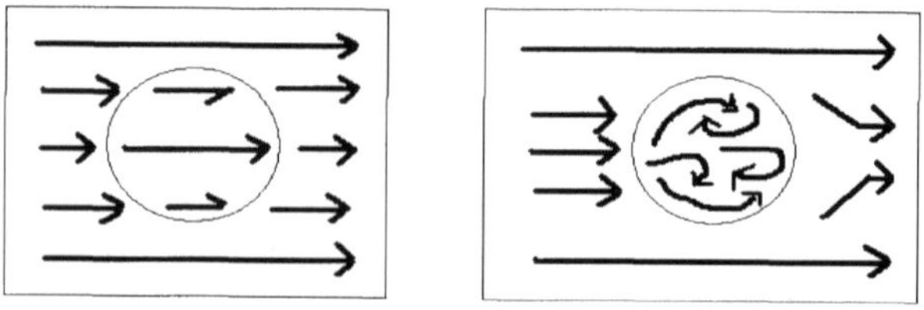

Qi can become excessive through outside influences such as too much heat or cold or through inside patterns such as too much emotion or stimulation, physical or mental. Excessive *qi* can be moving too fast or be very sluggish, as in the case of excessive dampness. Whatever the case, from a universal perspective there is no extra or new *qi* created, but localized disharmonies have arisen because the ongoing *qi* process has become excessive and thus harmful, distorting our being *qi* in the way subtle energetic vibrations move and change.

Similarly, *qi* can be in depletion. This may mean that there is a tense flow of *qi* due to nervousness or anxiety, or that the volume and density of *qi* have decreased, which is the case in serious prolonged illness. However, more commonly it means that the *qi* activity level is lower, that its flow is not quite up to standard, that there is a thinner than normal concentration of *qi* in one or the other body part. In the same vein, perfection of *qi* means the optimal functioning of energy in the body, while control of *qi* means the power to guide the energetic process to one or the other part (Kohn 2005, 13).

Body and mind in this system are thus different aspects of the same vibrating *qi* that is constantly oscillating, arising, and moving on, just as reality overall consists of an interlocking web of fields that each pulsate at their own rate, either in harmony or interference with each other. Nonlocal in nature, *qi* can be anywhere and exchange information with anything else instantaneously. This means that even a small disturbance in any field carries into all the others; even a tiny repositioning toward harmony affects the whole, with no separation between the physical, mental, and spiritual.

The body being a conglomeration of various vibratory fields, there can never be just one single cause for any given symptom, but the interconnection of the whole needs to be examined. Nor can the body be viewed in isolation, but should be seen in relation to the many fields outside: family, society, nature, stars, and so on. Corrections come accordingly in many different forms and should have an effect on the entirety of the system, applying a strong harmonizing rhythm to any given part of the vibrational pattern. Eventually the flow moves back into its harmonious rhythm and health is recovered. Through systematic *qi*-enhancement practices, moreover, people can achieve a fully tuned system that is not only perfectly healthy but may also attain long life and even immortality.

To express this with a metaphor taken from physics literature, the human body, society, nature, and the planetary fields can be imagined as a huge bowl of fairly rigid jelly with raisins in it (Bentov 1977, 29). Vibrate one part of it, and the rest also vibrates. One section cannot move without the other, and even the slightest touch to one single raisin will immediately transmit movements to all the others and the body of the jelly. The same also holds true for human beings. We all have electrical charges in and around us, which are measurable and can be felt (Johnson 2014a, 235). These charges are the body's energy field: it interacts not only with its own organs and parts but also with the field of things around it and the greater universe—from the planet all the way into the Milky Way and beyond.

Electromagnetism

The subtle energy at the root of the universe that Daoists call *qi* has been identified variously in the course of modern physics (Oschman 2000, 5-23; Rosch 2009, 297-99). One candidate is electromagnetic energy, based on Stephen Weinberg's "groundbreaking revelation of modern cosmology: that the universe as a whole is bathed in electromagnetic waves of the microwave kind, with a dominant contribution from wavelength around two millimeters" (Gleiser 2010, 55; see Weinberg 1993).

According to this understanding, all living organisms give forth an electromagnetic field that consists of electrical currents of different kinds and frequencies, including the human body with its bioelectric fields (Rosch 2009, 299-300).[1] Matching the fundamental "law of physics that all material comes in two forms: particles and antiparticles" (Tipler 1994, 53), everything is charged either negatively or positively. At the negative pole, the electrons spin counterclockwise; they have a calming effect on the nervous system and connect to the geographical direction of the north. On actual magnets, this pole is color-coded green, blue, or black. At the positive pole, electrons spin clockwise; this motion has an activating, stimulating effect on the energetic environment and is linked with the south. On magnets, it is color-coded red. Not only does this match the Daoist classification of energy movements into yin and yang, but all magnetic fields have the basic properties of attraction and repulsion, another yin-yang pair (Philpott et al. 2000).

[1] For more on the body's electrical circuitry, see Becker 1982; Becker and Sheldon 1985; Nordenstrøm 1983; Oschman 2000; 2003; 2004; Tiller 2004a; 2004b.

In nature, the strongest magnets are the metals iron, boron, and neodymium; they commonly exhibit a steady or permanent state of magnetization. The strength of a magnet depends on its composition, size, and amount of flux. It is commonly measured in gauss, a low degree being under 1000, while a high level of magnetization is over 6000, rising up to one or more tesla, i.e., units of 10,000 gauss. Typically, magnets are stronger on the inside and weaker on the outside, their strength dispersing further with increasing distance (www.bio magnetic.org).

All living beings produce low-frequency electric currents or biomagnetism, since they too consist of electrons and ions, and their functioning depends on circuits and fields of energy (Oschman 2000, 38, 86; Johnson 2014a, 223). Exposure to a negatively charged field is biologically normalizing: alcalizing and oxygenating, it steadies the pH value of the blood (7.35-7.45). It resolves cellular edema, reduces symptoms, and enhances relaxation and sleep. It also inhibits the replication of microorganisms, cancels out free radicals, and strengthens melatonin and growth hormones. Overall, magnets can be very helpful in processing toxins, relieving pain, and enhancing health (Becker and Sheldon 1985; Oschman 2000, 74-79).

On the other hand, exposure to a positively charged field—much yang in Daoist parlance—is stimulating and growth-enhancing. An experiment with several loaves of bread clearly shows that mold develops much faster when placed near a positively charged magnet (Philpott et al. 2000). While it may enhance plant growth, it disrupts the natural functioning of the body. It is thus best to be prudent and avoid too close contact with highly charged objects, such as power lines, electric outlets, and appliances (Philpott et al. 2000; Becker 1990).

The most powerful magnetic field in our lives is the earth, in itself a vibrantly alive organism (Johnson 2014b, 117). Called Gaia after the Greek name of the earth goddess and first described by Alexander von Humboldt (1769-1859), the living earth—as much as the universe as a whole—has a tendency toward optimization and expansion, balance and harmony (Capra 1996, 23). In a history of 1,000 million years, it should statistically have developed climatic changes toward extreme temperatures. However, this never happened. The earth has always returned to a temperate level, which shows that it tends to optimize varying conditions by developing new agents that produce gases or chemicals that counteract problematic situations. Thus, the earth can be understood as the sum total of all individual modifications in planetary development, the total living interconnected network of all species (Capra 1996, 100-01; Lovelock 1979, 1-4; Tipler 1994, 18-19).

Gaia, like other living organisms, has vital organs at its core and redundant organs on its periphery. It is much easier for it to alter things on the outside, but it resists changes in things deep inside. For example, during the many ice ages, all beyond 45 degrees latitude, both north and south, froze over, covering about 30 percent of the earth's surface. Even with this amount of freezing, the planet still functioned, since its core in the center remained untouched. It is, therefore, less dangerous to alter climates and physical conditions in the far north or south of the planet and more hazardous to modify things around the equator. The cutting down of the rain forests thus has a greater impact on global conditions than any changes affected around the poles, but any activity that interferes with the earth impacts the health and fortune of all living beings (Lovelock 1979, 15).

On the other hand, direct physical contact with the earth opens people to its powerful electromagnetic impact and has a positive affect on health. Like a TV cable, consisting of a copper conductor shielded by wire mesh to prevent data from leaking and disturbances from entering, has a shield grounded in the earth (Ober et al. 2010, 27-28), so earth balances electrons, protecting and stabilizing flow of data, we can absorb the beneficent flux of earth energy. Any immediate skin contact—walking barefoot, lying down, or touching the ground (Ober et al. 2010, 101)—re-establishes the energetic connection and restores life energies. It equalizes the body to the earth's energy levels, synchronizes the biological clock, and calms nervous system, creating an abundance of negatively charged electrons and thus producing an overall healing effect (2010, 94-95; www.earthing-institute.net; McTaggart 2007, 102, 211).

The Quantum World

Another candidate for the subtle energy field of *qi* that underlies electromagnetic patterns is the subatomic world of quantum physics. Discovered in a series of breakthroughs in the early 20th century—from Albert Einstein through Niels Bohr, Werner Heisenberg, Erwin Schrödinger, David Bohm, John Bell, and others[2]—it is in no way like the world we have known and makes electromagnetism look tame and simple. The quantum world is not solid, stable, or continuous, but instead comes as what David Bohm called plasma, a fourth state of matter akin to ether that is neither solid nor liquid or gaseous, but composed of infinitely small particles in constant agitation (Peat 1997, 25, 65). The tiny particles consist of quanta, the energy that electrons absorb or emit when changing energy levels, as well as gluons, the forces that hold atoms together. The most basic subatomic particles behave like both particles and waves, and many of

---

[2] For a short, comprehensive survey of the development of quantum physics, see Bock-Möbius 2012. Other informative works include Barad 2007; Close 2011; Fayer 2010; Ford 2004; Hawking and Mlodinow 2010; McTaggart 2003; Pagels 1982; Penrose 2004, chs. 21-26; Radin 2006; Rosenblum and Kuttner 2011; Talbot 1991; Vedral 2010; Zohar 1990.

these particles take part in universal supersymmetry and form pairs like yin and yang, where one cannot exist without the other (Peat 1997, 48). [3]

These particles, moreover, are not entities but process, continuous motion of inward collapse and outward expansion. "An electron is not one thing but a totality or ensemble enfolded throughout the whole of space. Sustained by constant influx from the implicate order, a particle may appear to be destroyed but is not lost. It has merely enfolded back into the deeper order from which it sprang" (Talbot 1991, 47). In itself a manifestation of the whole universe, the particle/wave seems inherently random. It is impossible to know both its exact momentum and location at the same time—in fact, there is an inverse relationship in that the more information one has about the former, the less is known about the latter, and vice versa (Bohm 1951). The whole of the universe being present in each of its parts at all times (Nadeau and Kafatos 1999, 197), quanta can be at more than one place at a time. Not manifest until observed as particles, they cease to exist in one place and appear in another without any obvious way of getting from here to there, and any observation affecting one also affects its twin, no matter how far apart they are (Denney 2002).

In other words, the subtlest units of reality are in one state of being at a time, but can exist on multiple levels and in multiple states, like Schrödinger's cat:[4] latent or manifest, dead or alive, or anything in between—representing a plethora of possibilities. Imke Bock-Möbius illustrates it vividly.

> We are taking a leisurely walk in the mall and would like to have an ice cream. Soon, we see a stand with an ice cream machine that has two levers: chocolate and vanilla. We order a cone but do not specify the flavor. Leaving the selection to the salesperson, we do not know which one we will receive. As long as the ice cream has not yet come out of the machine, both flavors are still possible. This means, the ice cream exists in a state of overlap between two states, which may lead to either chocolate or vanilla ice cream. The extrusion of the ice cream matches the so-called measurement process [in quantum physics], in which one of the two possibilities becomes reality. (2012, 66-67)

This means that everything in the universe is in a state of constant flux and ongoing change and transformation. The cosmos consists of unlimited possibilities in a vast quantum field that consists of vibrating energies, waves and particles, which change their state trillions of times in one second. Still,

---

[3] Supersymmetry is a fundamental characteristic of the universe. "The particles of nature must come in *pairs* . . . every known particle must have an as-yet-undiscovered superpartner particle" (Greene 2003, 173). See also Close 2011, 346-50; Ferreira 2006, 190-91; Gleiser 2010, 101; Greene 2011, 107-10; Hammond 2008, 154; Penrose 1994; 2004, ch. 31.

[4] On the thought experiment known as Schrödinger's cat, originally published in 1935, see Bock-Möbius 2012, 66-68; Haroche 2004; Penrose 1997, 71; 2004, 804.

they tend to cluster and pattern in certain ways, centering at magnetic field lines and creating harmoniously oscillating structures (Gleiser 2004, 649; Penrose 1994, 351). Ideally, in David Bohm's vision, not just the natural world and the human body, but also society should function like plasma—with each part being integrally connected to all others and the whole being greater than the sum of the parts (Bohm 1980; Peat 1997, 67; Talbot 1991, 35).

Human beings as part of this quantum world, too, consist of vibrating atoms, constantly oscillating, arising, and dissolving: ultimately, we are all fluid, without solidity or firmness. All existence rests on quantum potential, an underlying energy soup that pervades all space and, unlike gravity or magnetism, does not diminish with distance or strength (Talbot 1991, 39). Our reality, then, much as described in ancient presentations on *qi*, is an interlocking web of fields that each pulsate at their own rate and can transform in an instant. These fields can come into harmony with each other and mutually support and increase their amplitude. But they can also interfere with each other and create disturbance. "Electrons are not scattered because, through the action of the quantum potential, the whole system is undergoing a coordinated movement more like a ballet dance than like a crowd of unorganized people" (Bohm 1987, 38; Cox and Forshaw 2011, 175; Talbot 1991, 41).

Since all fields ultimately interlock, even a small disturbance in any one of them carries into all the others—like raisins in jelly. We are connected closely to everything around us and to the greater universe. This holds true for everything, including the mind. Just as bodily transformations are of unlimited possibilities, so the mind is ultimately nonlocal, sharing a fundamental property of the entire universe: it can be anywhere and exchange information with anything else instantaneously.[5]

A good way of describing this interconnectedness is in terms of the hologram, a light phenomenon discovered by Denis Gabor in the 1960s, where "a coherent light from a laser is passed through a half-silvered mirror. Part of the beam goes on directly to a photographic plate, while another part is reflected so that it illuminates the whole structure." [6] Both rays eventually meet at the plate, creating a three-dimensional image that reflects the original structure. The interference pattern creates wholeness in every single part of the process (Bentov 1977, 16-17; Talbot 1991, 40; Vedral 2010, 182).

As a result, "the tangible reality of our everyday lives is really a kind of illusion, like a holographic image. Underlying it is a deeper order of existence, a vast and more primary level of reality that gives birth to all the objects and appearances of our physical world in much the same way that a piece of holographic film gives birth to a hologram" (Talbot 1991, 46; Penrose 1994, 348; see also Grof and Bennett 1992, 7-9). This closely matches the Daoist under-

---

[5] Talbot 1991, 43; Nadeau and Kafatos 1999, 4-5; Targ 2012, 202; Targ and Katra 1998.

[6] Bohm 1980, 145; see also McTaggart 2003, 83-84; Talbot 1991, 15.

standing as well as the vision of the Buddhist *Huayan jing* 華嚴經 (*Avatamsaka sūtra*, Flower Garland Sutra; trl. Cleary 1984). Here the universe is a complex network, depicted as 84,000 mirrors within mirrors, the so-called Jewel Net of Indra, where every single part interconnects with every other part and where all is mirrored endlessly in all else (see Cook 1977; Gimello and Gregory 1983).

This notion is also borne out in recent explorations in the science of networks, which have shown that everything is utterly interconnected with everything else in different levels of complexity (see Ellis 2004). Even as many as seven billion human beings connect by no more that six steps through the workings of "small worlds," weak ties linking clusters of strongly tied communities into complex webbings (Buchanan 2002, 37). Shown to be true on many different levels of life, this pattern is ubiquitous. "It is not a coincidence that the wiring of the human brain turns out to have the very same small-world structure as our social networks, nor that these patterns turn up again in the Internet and the World Wide Web, in the way words link together in human language, or in the food webs that underlie the world's exosystems" (2002, 197). The structuring of *qi*, in other words, is what makes the world go round.

Double Dark

Quantum electrodynamics, i.e., the marriage between quantum physics, electromagnetism, and relativity requires the existence of a specific form of energy, something like the plasma state that underlies the visible and tangible universe (Ostriker and Mitton 2013, 239). Physicists identify this as dark or invisible energy, stuff that acts both on subatomic scales and across the largest distances in the cosmos. Ubiquitous and elusive, the yin to the outwardly visible yang, it is a form of vacuum energy, a wavelike property in the very fabric of space.[7]

According to basic relativity theory, space and time are not fixed but set in an empty stage, bending in reaction to matter. The equivalence principle says that any accelerated motion in a non-gravitational field creates the presence of a gravitational field and thus the same feeling. That is to say, gravity defines the background space (Alexander 2009, 56-57). Matter in the visible universe is gradually expanding, like someone blowing air into a balloon. So as to avoid either its collapse due to gravity or its dispersion due to expansion, the universe needs a counterbalancing factor, something Einstein proposed first as the cosmological constant (Ferreira 2006, 200), today known as dark energy. An invisible and strangely repellent fluid, it evenly fills all space and makes up about 68 percent of the entire universe (Alexander 2009, 58). Dark energy acts on gravity to make the fabric of space accelerate; it has both negative pressure and posi-

[7] Alexander 2009, 54-55. For more on dark energy, see Ferreira 2006, 219; Greene 2011, 160-62; Ostriker and Mitton 2013, ch. 7; Primack in Tucker 2011, 1.1.

tive energy, is in fact an infinite amount of the cosmic constant in a state of continuous expansion, pervading the entirety of space (Alexander 2009, 59-60, 62).

Another factor that combines with dark energy to form the so-called Double Dark is dark matter, which makes up close to 27 percent of the universe. This leaves about five percent, including the mere half of one percent that is visible matter as we know it plus invisible atoms, hydrogen, and helium (Peat 1997, 65; Primack and Abrams 2006, 115; Abrams and Primack 2011, 49). Unable to see it with telescopes, physicists infer the existence and properties of dark matter from its gravitational effects on visible matter, radiation, and the large-scale structure of the universe. Primeval and part already of the Big Bang, it probably is made up from weakly interacting massive particles: it emits or absorbs no light, infrared heat, radio waves, or radiation of any sort (Rees 2000, 73; 2001, 72-75).[8] In other words, it is an underlying level of Dao-existence, a field of subtle energy close to primordial *qi*, a storehouse of cosmic potency.

Strings and Photons

Integrating quantum field theory with electromagnetism and general relativity, and also accounting for the workings of gravity, is the focus of the currently most prominent theoretical framework of modern physics: string theory. Taking the understanding of *qi* to a yet subtler level, its core concept is the idea that within each atom—a hundred trillion of which make up a single human cell—there are multiple billions of tiny energy strings that come in different formats and vibrate at various frequencies.

This means that, instead of thinking of the most fundamental building block of the universe as a single-point particle, physicists are now visualizing it as a rubber-band-like length. Instead of seeing particles moving about and turning into waves every so often, they understand strings to be omnipresent, in constant vibrational connection with everything else, appearing in various clusters and combinations and thereby forming all the different dimensions of matter and energy, whether dark or visible, cosmic or concrete (Greene 2011, 91; www.superstringtheory.com). "Each of the preferred patterns of vibration of a string in string theory appears as a particle whose mass and force charges are determined by the string's oscillatory pattern. . . . Far from being a collection of chaotic experimental facts, particle properties in string theory are the manifestation of one and the same physical feature: the resonant patterns of vibration—the music, so to speak, of fundamental loops of string" (Greene 2003, 15-16).

[8] Dark matter is also discussed in Ferreira 2006, 192-97; Hammond 2008, ch. 2; Murdin 2009, 298-99; Ostriker and Mitton 2013, ch. 6; Primack in Tucker 2011, 1.8; Tyson and Goldsmith 2004, 72-73.

The universe, then, works like sound waves that naturally come into resonance: if we pluck the string of one violin, the matching string on a violin sitting next to it begins to vibrate in the same frequency (Greene 2003, 143). This can also be made visual: if we apply the violin bow to sheet metal with sand on it, distinctive sand patterns appear of standing waves or nodal points that form both active and quiescent areas, moving in a harmonious alternation between up and down, activity and rest (Bentov 1977, 9-11; Greene 2003, 100). However, it is not limited to things that are physically close, but in accordance with the holographic nature of the universe, reaches throughout all existence. It is, moreover, possible to work out the "notes" of the "music of string theory" and thereby "explain the observed properties of the elementary particles" (Greene 2003, 146-47).

The sound produced by subtle energy, in its specific nature determined by the exact manner of vibration and particular string tension (Greene 2003, 149), can appear as random acoustic disturbance (voices, traffic, random notes, body movements) or in rhythmic patterns (notes, tunes, acoustic frequencies). When several sounds come together, they can be either in harmony or disjointed. Superimpose two sounds of identical wave pattern so that hill matches hill, valley matches valley, and the amplitude of the original wave pattern is doubled. This is constructive interference, what Daoists call the "productive" pattern of *qi* flow. Superimpose two sounds of opposite wave pattern, and they cancel each other out so that the wave vanishes into a straight line. This is disruptive interference, the creation of disharmony, described in Daoism as "obstructive" movement (Bentov 1977, 12-13).

Nature favoring balance and harmony, the overall tendency is that rhythmic patterns of interaction emerge. Like numerous instruments coming together in a musical orchestra to create a symphony (Gleiser 2010, 69; Greene 2003, ch. 6), subtle energy moves toward harmonious flow and full entrainment, i.e., a completely resonant system, a creative union on all levels and in all dimensions—the fundamental wholeness of the universe (Bohm 1951). The perfection of self and world, that is to say, is reached when all beings and things, perfect in themselves and fully realizing their special uniqueness, hum on matching wavelengths and frequency in a state of optimum transfer and total resonance.

The concept of resonance and harmony also applies to light, consisting of waves of photons moving together, their color, i.e., their wavelength, determined by the energy they carry (Greene 2011, 155). Light, radiated from the sun, is present in plants and forms the source of energy during photosynthesis, the process of converting light to chemical energy and storing it in the bonds of sugar. As other living beings and also humans eat plant foods, they too absorb photons while metabolizing the plant matter into carbon dioxide and water. We exhale the carbon dioxide and eliminate the water, but what happens to the photons? As discovered by Fritz-Albert Popp, "when taken in by the body, the energy of these photons dissipates so that it is eventually distributed over the entire spectrum of the electromagnetic frequencies, from the lowest to the highest; this energy then becomes the driving force for all the molecules in our body" (McTaggart 2003, 43; Popp 2002).

Photons switch on the body's processes like a conductor launching each individual instrument into the collective sound: flowing at different frequencies, they perform different functions (McTaggart 2003, 43). Overall, biophoton emissions create a perfect communication system, transferring information to the various cells in the organism. While DNA is capable of sending out large ranges of frequencies, working like the ultimate tuning fork in the body, its fundamental functioning relies on photonic emissions (2003, 44). "These emissions have to be of low intensity, because the communications occur on the quantum level" (2003, 47). Still, they determine the body's functioning. "Changes in the electrical charges correlate with growth, sleep, regeneration, light, water, storms, the developments of cancer—even the waxing and waning of the moon" (2003, 48; see also Becker and Sheldon 1985). What's more, health is a function of the coherence and harmony of the light waves, "a state of perfect subatomic communication" (McTaggart 2003, 52). Healthier cells as much as healthier foods carry lower and more coherent intensity of light, a brighter and more potent radiance of spirit in Daoist parlance.

Moving beyond the body, light radiance and wave resonance also connect individual beings with other living things and material entities—life ultimately being "information processing by natural selection," even machines are in some way alive (Tipler 1994, 125), although nowhere near as powerful. As we interact with others, with nature, and with the material world, we engage in a constant exchange of information via photons, what Popp calls "photon sucking" (McTaggart 2003, 53). This may explain how schools of fish, flocks of birds, or swarms of fireflies act in perfect and instantaneous coordination (Buchanan 2002, 48), why people are so susceptible to trends and political machinations, and why certain medications and remedies work—they all create a high level of coherence (McTaggart2003, 53). On the other hand, energy dispersing methods such as acupuncture or homeopathy can heal because they absorb resonance, pulling out rogue energetic frequencies in the body (2003, 54; Becker and Sheldon 1985, 235; Oschman 2000, 69-71). As Daoist and Chinese physicians have claimed for millennia, health comes down to the alignment and harmonization of energetic functions, which manifest as light, described in modern physics in terms of biophotonics.

Nonlocality

Quanta and other subatomic particles vibrating throughout all existence means that everything interacts with everything else and is essentially alive—including not only humans and animals (see Schul 1990), but also plants and minerals. Like all other organisms, plants are aware of their surroundings, react to stimuli, and contain a basic nervous system (DeSalle and Tattersall 2012, 70). Their vibrant aliveness is the subject of international meetings on the neurobiology of plants that began in 2005 (www.plantbehavior.org); its most powerful demonstration appears in experiments by Cleve Backster that go back to the 1960s (Tompkins and Bird 1973; McTaggart 2007, 147; Panati 1974, 112-16). A lie-detection specialist who ran a school for polygraph examiners, Backster impulsively attached the electrodes of one machine to the leaf of his tropical palm-like houseplant, then gave it some water and watched an astoundingly powerful reaction.

Lie detectors work with a weak electrical current that runs through wires attached to a subject on one end and to a machine on the other. In response to mental images or surges of emotion, the electric current will cause a needle to move or a pen to write, thus measuring the subject's degree of energy involvement. The most powerful way to stimulate such involvement is by threatening a subject's well-being. As Backster found out, plants react just as strongly to threats as people do—even more so, since they pick up the mental intent of the person before physical action and are able to do so even over great distances. Since plants do not have the same kinds of senses as animals or people, their method of communication and reception is different. They connect on the level of cellular functioning, communicating purely with life energy, functioning in the nonlocal mind or entanglement of the quantum world (Attenborough 1995). Subtle energy here emerges as the universal language of communication (Penrose 2004, 582).

Plants have a variety of responses at their disposal: they can be alternatively enthusiastic and anxious or go into a deep faint like animals playing dead. Part of the transformation of all life, they appreciate being of service to others and may even "wish to be eaten, but only in a sort of loving ritual, with a real communication between the eater and the eaten" (Tompkins and Bird 1973, 8). In addition, since they connect energetically to all life, they can affirm or deny the truth of certain statements. In one experiment, for example, Backster hooked a lie detector to a philodendron while asking a visitor about his date of birth, listing a series of years. While the visitor answered "no" to each year, the plant indicated the actual year of his birth "with an extra high flourish."

Another feature he demonstrated was that plants had memory and could point to the perpetrator of a crime they had witnessed. They would also bond to their caretakers, being aware of what happened to them even while many miles apart. During a 700-mile flight across the country, the plants at home reacted to their caretaker's emotional stress every time the plane touched down for landing. By the same token, they would be aware when other living creatures suffered, such as the death of bacteria due to hot water being poured down the drain in a kitchen sink (1973, 15).

All this suggests that aliveness and sentience are not limited to more complex sensory beings such as humans and animals and do not even stop at the cellular level: "It may well go down to the molecular, the atomic, and even the subatomic" (1973, 12). It also shows from a yet different angle that—as formulated in quantum physics, string theory, and Daoist cosmology—the entire universe is a closely interconnected, holographic organism, where each part is in immediate close connection to all others and where each actively contributes to the whole at all times.

This close interconnection further extends to the mineral and planetary realms, including also physical structures and the earth as a living organism. It accounts for the efficacy of magnet and earthing therapies as well as the effect the placement of buildings and furniture has on people's minds, energy, and good fortune as formulated in Chinese *fengshui* and Indian *vastu*. Both work with the macrocosm-microcosm correspondence and seek to utilize or alter natural processes for purposes of curing sickness and securing general well-being (Rossbach 1983; Kingston 1997). Energy not only flows through the spaces we live in, but it *is* our environment, both natural and manmade. All objects exert their own draw and pull, and we are in constant close interaction with them—we are part of them and flow in the same realm.

Chapter Three

From Chaos to Consciousness

The Evolution of Humanity

While we consist of and flow in one and the same cosmic energy, as human beings we have also developed reflective, discriminating, ego-based consciousness—as opposed to perceptual consciousness, the faculty of awareness and perception common to all living organisms and shared widely in the animal world (Griffin 1992, 10-11; Shettleworth 2010, 146). Reflective consciousness means the ability to think about a thought and be self-aware in a discriminating, analytical manner, characterized by selectivity, exclusivity, chaining, and unitarity (Harth 1993, 139).

Rather than "a biological given," it is "a specifically human ability built upon the basis of the power of language" (Jaynes 2006a, 91). It came about as the result of an ongoing process of evolution, differentiation, and culture—"the ensemble of customs and technologies that played and continue to play an essential role in the evolution of our behavior" (Cavalli-Sforza 2000, 173). Daoists as well as Western thinkers and psychologists tend to describe this process in terms of four stages of increasing awareness, separation, and complexity, ultimately leading to discriminating consciousness.

On the one hand, discriminating consciousness is a necessity in life as we now know it, since it allows us to gain control over, and enhance engagement with, our environment and grow into new and ever more potent dimensions. On the other hand, it also constitutes a major problem, because it alienates us from our immediate connection to body, nature, and the greater universe. How, then, did discriminating consciousness come about? And what exactly is it?

Differentiation of *Qi*

Both ancient Daoists and contemporary scientists posit that the universe has a beginning or primordial state, from where it emerged into plurality, starting with the division into two complementary forces, called yin and yang in Daoism and matter and antimatter in science. From here, cosmic energy differentiated further, described variously in ancient sources.

Thus, the *Daode jing* has the well-known sequence from Dao to oneness and on to two (yin-yang), three (harmony), and all beings (ch. 42). The *Wenzi* 文子 (Book of Master Wen), an early philosophical work that was lost and later reconstituted, sees life arising from oneness, then move on to heaven and earth, the four seasons, yin and yang, humanity alone, and hard and soft, to eventually result in the myriad beings (ch. 3). The *Heguanzi* 鶡冠子 (Pheasant Cap Master), a political expansion of the *Daode jing* from the late Warring States starts it with the one energy and moves through intention, planning, naming, form, affairs, connections, and seasons to beings (ch. 5; Wells 2013, 107-11).

Recently excavated manuscripts, as discussed in detail by Wang Zhongjiang (2015), add to this variety by offering four further models of cosmic unfolding. First, the *Fanwu liuxing* 凡物流形 (All Things Flow in Form) describes it in terms of beginning with oneness, then—like the *Daode jing*—moving to the two, the three. From there, however, it continues to the mother to result eventually in "combination" (*jie* 结) (see Chan 2014). The *Hengxian* 恒先 (Constancy Before) speaks of Constancy Before, a state of complete chaos and nondifferentiation, from which things evolved through space (*huo* 或), energy (*qi*), material existence (*you* 有), and beginning (*shi* 始) to culminate in the passage of time (*wang* 往) (see Brindley et al. 2013; Brindley 2016).

The *Taiyi shengshui* 太一生水 (The Great One Brings Forth Water), excavated at Guodian, begins with Great Oneness, which gives birth to water, from which arise heaven and earth. They connect back to Great Oneness and water, then bring forth spirit brightness (*shenming*), followed by yin and yang, the four seasons, cold and heat, dampness and dryness, to result in the ongoing cycle of the years (*sui* 岁) (Henricks 2000, 123-29). The *Huangdi sijing* 黄帝四經 (Four Classics of the Yellow Emperor), a group of texts uncovered at Mawangdui and thus dating from the early Han, finally, has the universe begin with oneness, from which spring heaven and earth, yin and yang, the four seasons, and hard and soft, to result eventually in the myriad beings (see Chang and Feng 1998; Yates 1997).

They all have in common that they outline an unfolding from singularity to plurality, from the one to the many, from yin and yang into more subtle and practical complexities, including features of time, space, solidity, and temperature. In the Han dynasty, Chinese cosmologists came to see the key modalities of yin and yang, and thus cosmic energy, in terms of the five phases (*wuxing* 五

行). They describe an ongoing movement and modulation of all life, a recurring rise and fall of *qi* from yin to yang and back to yin, in each case rising from a minor to a major level, then again declining to minor, and passing through a phase of balance in between (Kohn 2005, 22; see also Graham 1986; Matsumoto and Birch 1985). Rather than leaving the terminology abstract, Han cosmologists linked them with the "five materials," first described in the *Shangshu* 尚書 (Book of Documents), concrete substances or resources used for human livelihood:

minor yang	major yang	yin-yang	minor yin	major yin
wood	fire	earth	metal	water

The "Hongfan" 鴻範 (Great Plan) chapter of the same work treats the five materials in a slightly more abstract manner, establishing particular associations with qualities, processes, and psychological factors. Thus, it links wood with the qualities of bending and straightness, fire with flaming and rising, earth with planting and harvesting, metal with being formable and sharp, and water with wetting and sinking (see Nylan 1992). These, in turn, are further associated with five activities and five attitudes:

wood	fire	earth	metal	water
hearing	seeing	demeanor	thinking	speech
perceptive	clear	respectful	understanding	appropriate

This association laid the foundation for later developments, initializing the complex five-phases cosmology central to Chinese culture that associates every item of life, including body and mind, stars and society with a particular phase, documenting its position in the greater whole while yet emphasizing its transient and fluid quality (Kohn 2005, 23). It shaped discriminating consciousness to work through correlative thinking and formed the foundation of more elaborate forms of logic, still present in the way we acquire language today. For example, to build the plural of *shoe*, we add the letter "s" to get *shoes*. The same applies to cat/cats, stone/stones, etc. But then we learn that this correlative pattern when applied to the word *foot* is wrong and instead of *foots* we use another pattern and go from *foot* to *feet*, then apply the same to get goose/geese, and so on. In all cases, the organization of language follows a simple pattern that is correlated and repeated in different concrete cases, then moulds the mind and shapes consciousness (see Graham 1986; Pinker 2007, 94).

Even the idea of mental awareness is subject to this model and comes to be seen as an integrated network of various energetic properties moving around the body. Thus, the ancient medical work *Huangdi neijing suwen* 皇帝內經素文 (Yellow Emperor's Inner Classic, Simple Questions), divides it into five different forms, associated with the five inner organs:

> Blood is stored in the liver—the residence of the spirit soul.
> Constructive energy is stored in the spleen—the residence of the intention.
> The pulse is stored in the heart—the residence of the spirit.
> Life energy is stored in the lungs—the residence of the material soul.
> Essence is stored in the kidneys—the residence of the will. (ch. 2)

Each inner organ, thus, has its own particular body form of *qi*, matching a specific mental or psychological energy that continuously transforms and mutates into another according to the cycle of the five phases. In other words, consciousness—from basic awareness to complex abstraction and discrimination—is both deeply rooted in the physical reality of the body and an active participant in the ongoing flow of cosmic *qi* through its rising and falling cycles, yet increasingly shaped by organizational structures and language patterns.

Culture and Society

Discriminating consciousness, moreover, is deeply linked with the growth of social structures and the cultural development of humanity—i.e., genes channel learning and learning channels genes (Jolly 1999, 276; Dor and Jablonka 2010, 147)—which follows a similar overall pattern of increasing complexity. As the medieval *Kaitian jing* outlines, in the state of Great Antecedence (*taichu* 太初), under the guidance of Lord Lao as Dao, after the planet had come into being and life first arose,

> All species of life were without sign or shape. Each received just one bit of *qi* and life was complete. Those with raw *qi* were stones and mountains; those with moving *qi* were birds and beasts; those with essential *qi* were human beings. Among all the myriad beings, humans are the highest. (2b; Kohn 1993, 37; see also Schafer 1997)

At this stage, neither discriminating consciousness nor language existed; humans lived for extended periods, subsisting on sweet dew and wine brought forth from heaven and earth. "Upon death they would not bury the corpse, but abandon it in a distant wilderness" (3a).

From here, the world evolved into a state called Hundun 混沌 (Chaos), known best from the *Zhuangzi* as the emperor of the center whose friendly colleagues of the north and south decide to repay his hospitality by boring him sensory openings and killing him in the process (see Girardot 2009). "In the time of Chaos," the *Kaitian jing* says, "for the first time there were mountains and streams," i.e., the continents shifted to give rise to high ranges and low valleys. This is also the time when "high and low, noble and humble arose for the first time" (3a; Kohn 1993, 39).

This in due course gave rise to political structures and cultural achievements, described commonly as the rule of the Three Sovereigns (*sanhuang* 三皇) and Five Thearchs (*wudi* 五帝). The first sovereign Fuxi 伏羲 (Hidden Vapor) observed the patterns of the stars and created the trigrams of the *Yijing* gave clan names and personal appellations to the people.

> Fuxi also taught the people how to make nets and traps to catch birds and beasts to eat. They all wore furs and lived on blood, smelling rancid and putrid. Men and women were not separated, there was no jealousy between them. In winter they lived in caves; in summer they made their homes on trees. . . . People were simple and straightforward; they did not yet have the five grains. (4b; Kohn 1993, 42)

This changed under the rulership of the third sovereign Shennong 神農 (Divine Farmer), who learned about the hundred plants and the five grains from Lord Lao, then "ordered the people to plant and reap them so that they could eat them instead of taking the lives of birds and beasts." This was a time of peace and harmonious integration. As the *Zhuangzi* describes it,

> In the age of the Divine Farmer, the people slept in peace at night and got up to proceed with calm. They knew their mothers but not their fathers, and lived side by side with the elk and the deer. They tilled the soil to eat, wove fabrics to dress themselves, and in their hearts and minds were utterly free from ideas of doing each other harm. This is the epitome of perfect virtue. (ch. 29)

After Divine Farmer, the first the Five Thearchs was the ruler Suiren 燧人 (Fire Drill), who "taught the people to drill wood and make fire, which would give light for several days and allowed the cooking of raw meat, bringing an end to rancid and bloody smells" (5a). After Fire Drill, there was Zhurong 祝融 (Blessed Melter) who developed firing kilns and advanced pottery, followed by several lesser figures. Eventually, Huangdi 黃帝 (Yellow Emperor) came to power. His rule saw further expansion and development of culture: the invention of writing, the building of wagons and roads, the institution of markets, and the first war in human history, in his battle against Chiyu 蚩尤 (Wormy Rebel). Still, the time was one of overall goodness. While people had a sense of social stratification and increased cultural activity and but the increased complexity of life caused various difficulties so that they began to have shortened life expectancies, they still lacked discriminating consciousness (5b; Kohn 1993, 43). The latter only arose under later dynasties, predicated by further cultural development, such as notions of formal ritual and morality.

While the *Kaitian jing* reflects the position of the Celestial Masters, the Numinous Treasure (Lingbao 靈寶) school, which arose in the late 4th century under the impact of Han cosmology and the increasing popularity of Buddhism, expanded this understanding of world development by adopting the Indian notion of kalpa cycles or *yugas*. Here the perfect age, Krta Yuga, is followed by a time of slight decline in the TretaYuga, which proceeds to a time of shortened life-spans and advanced culture in the Dvapara Yuga, and finally ends in a dark age of evil and corruption, the Kali Yuga (see Eliade 1957). After the world has passed through an entire cycle of four phases (*mahayuga*), it is destroyed completely and begins anew.

Numinous Treasure Daoists redefined these four *yugas*—reminiscent also of Hesiod's four ages (gold, silver, bronze, and iron) of primordiality, timelessness, history, and decay (Colavito 1992, 88)—into four kalpas (*jie* 劫). As outlined in the *Shangpin dajie* 上品大戒 (Great Precepts of the Highest Ranks, DZ 177; trl. Kohn 2004b, 100-15), the *Zhihui zuigen pin* 智慧罪根品 (Precepts Regarding the Roots of Wisdom and Sin, DZ 457; trl. Kohn 2004b, 72-88), and other medieval scriptures, they are:

1. Dragon Country (*longhan* 龍漢): Living beings were pure and free from evil and led a simple life. The Heavenly Worthy of Primordial Beginning (Yuanshi tianzun 元始天尊) helped them live in perfect accordance with the rule of Dao. There was no sin. At the end of this kalpa the world collapsed.

2. Red Radiance (*chiming* 赤明): There was a trace of impurity and evil among living beings; karma and retribution first began. The Heavenly Worthy saved as many as he could and established the first colonies of celestial beings above. Again, the kalpa ended with the complete destruction of everything.

3. Opening Sovereign (*kaihuang* 開皇): People still lived simply, but culture and civilization began, exemplified in the knotting of cords for reckoning. Since the minds of people were simple and still largely unconscious, their life spans were as long as 36,000 years. Again, the Heavenly Worthy supported the age.

4. Highest Sovereign (*shanghuang* 上皇): Culture developed fully and the world declined seriously. Having attained discriminating consciousness, humanity was torn apart by strife and jealousy, hatred and war, bringing about a dark age that still continues. To the present, the Heavenly Worthy has handed down precepts, rules, and practices to ensure the survival and salvation of at least a few (2a–3a; Kohn 1998a, 209-10; 2004, 168; 1995, 55).

Each kalpa, then, is a full world cycle that ends with the utter annihilation of all concrete existence. Complete cultural disintegration happens over several cycles, each one bringing more discriminating consciousness and greater corruption. Heavenly beings help to a certain degree, but the world as a whole is in decline. Still, there remains a continuous and permanent level beyond created existence, located both in the highest heavens above and the deepest primordial life energy inside. It survives no matter how pervasive the destruction on earth and offers refuge, providing immunity to all disasters.

The Growth of Consciousness

The most focused Daoist discussion of the evolution of consciousness appears in chapter 2 of the *Zhuangzi*. It begins by pointing out that "people of old had perfect knowledge," then explains that this meant, "they thought in a way that matched the stage before things existed." Their minds matching the time before the division of the cosmos into yin and yang, "their knowledge was perfect and exhaustive; nothing could possibly be added to it." Guo Xiang 郭象 (d. 312), the main *Zhuangzi* editor and commentator (Kohn 2014, 89), calls this first stage Chaos Complete (*huncheng* 混成) and explains it as follows:

> This is the state of complete oblivion of heaven and earth, of total abandonment of the myriad beings. On the outside never examining time and space, inside one is never conscious even of the body. Thus, people are boundless and free from all fetters; they go along with beings and are in full accordance with all. (Kohn 2010a, 17; 2011, 27)

Like embryos in the womb, completely part of the flow of universal energy, people in this stage have no awareness of external things as separate and "relate to the world as if nothing had yet come into existence" (Coutinho 2004, 167). They are perfect and whole in their perception, their mind—if one can call it that—at one with all there is.

From here mental awareness evolved to recognizing "beings" (*wu* 物). "They saw things as existing, yet they did not yet make any distinctions among them," as Zhuangzi describes it. That is to say, people perceive things as separate from themselves, yet they make no distinctions between them and do not attach value to one over the other. "There is more now than undifferentiated mush—there is some kind of plurality of differentiable things, but these things are not grouped into bounded regions" (Coutinho 2004, 166). Guo Xiang describes this as a kind of loss, saying that "oblivion is no longer complete," but gives it a positive tinge in that, despite the fact that "now beings are recognized as existing, there is still the oblivion of distinctions between this and that" (Slingerland 2003, 177). At this time, people were primitive, but they "knew how to live":

> I have heard that in the most ancient of times birds and beasts were numerous while human beings were few. People built nests in trees to avoid them. During the day, they gathered acorns and chestnuts, at night they climbed back up into the top of the trees. For this reason, they are called the people of the nesting clan.
>
> Following this, in high antiquity, people knew nothing about clothes and garments. In the summertime, they would collect great piles of fire-

wood to burn in the winter to keep warm. For this reason, they are called the people who knew how to live. (*Zhuangzi*, ch. 29)

Distinctions such as those of clothes and living quarters appear in the next stage, described as "boundaries" (*feng* 封), a word that has both political and geographical implications (Coutinho 2004, 166). At this stage, as Guo Xiang says, "there is for the first time a distinction between this and that" (*shibi* 是彼). This means, certain objects and phases of life are clearly separate in people's minds, they use them differently and apply categories in life, getting a sense of "destruction and accomplishment," as Guo Xiang puts it. However, they still do not judge things. As the *Zhuangzi* emphasizes, "they had as yet no sense of right and wrong." In other words, they had names or language but merely used it to "pick at things in the world and left it at that, never overstepping its bounds and letting it become reified into rigid concepts and categories" (Slingerland 2003, 177).

That changed with the arising of "right and wrong" (*shifei* 是非), the last stage of the evolution of discriminating consciousness. Here people reach a point where they become slaves to language, establish fixed patterns in their world, and make dichotomous general judgments. They mark things in relation to each other and create classifications in terms of values. At this point, "Dao was destroyed," as the *Zhuangzi* has it, and this "meant the beginning of personal preference and one-sided love." Guo Xiang echoes this, again returning to his theme of oblivion:

> If [the distinction between] right and wrong were not there, Dao would still be complete. With the destruction of Dao, emotions begin to be partial and love develops. As long as you cannot forget one-sided love and free yourself from egotism, there is no way you can ever find original oneness in yourself or with others.

To sum up, from a state of being one with everything, of flowing acceptance, we evolve to objectification, distinguishing between different things and learning to tell A from B but without evaluating them. Next, we come to delimitation, an awareness of things being different and having a particular impact on our lives. Only after that do we move to judgment, attaching permanent, intellectually justifiable values to things and setting up a firm conception of how the world works (Kohn 2014, 33-34).

The *Daode jing* echoes the same idea:

> When the Great Dao declined,
> There were the ideas of benevolence and social responsibility.
> When knowledge and wisdom appeared, great hypocrisy arose.
> When the six family relationships were no longer in harmony,
> Filial piety and love for children arose. (ch. 18)

In other words, the increasing complexity of consciousness goes hand in hand with a more intricate social structure and more sophisticated levels of culture. As Norman Girardot has shown, Daoists speak essentially about the "sociocultural development when men start to classify themselves into particular lineage groups, into a cosmological system of order that is formally reflected in an honorific language of respect, in systems of potlatching prestation designed to gain the return of social prestige, and in discriminating modes of thought" (1985, 84). Discriminating consciousness, therefore, is only one aspect of a general increase in the complexity of culture and society (Kohn 1998a, 212-13), a function of decision-making in the light of multiple options that models actions, taking into account various sets of variables (Jolly 1999, 281, 285).

Language

Daoists in general are highly skeptical about and critical of language, so much so that the very first line of the *Daode jing* emphasizes that Dao can never be formulated in words. Laozi notes that "who knows does not speak and who speaks does not know" (ch. 56) and insists that his ideas represent a "teaching of no words" (ch. 43), while Zhuangzi emphasizes that there can be no verbalization in a state of integrated cosmic oneness.

> Heaven, earth, and I came along together, and the myriad things and I are one. Since we are all one, how can I ever talk about them? Since I am talking about them, how can there be oneness? Myself and my talking make two; talking and the object make three. (ch. 2)

Once there is a multitude of divisions, debates or disputes (*bian* 辯) arise, where representatives of different positions who have each split the world according to their particular categories present their particular viewpoint in the hope to amass enough evidence to convince the other that they are right (Graham 1969, 144). Each would argue from a "lodged place" (Graham 1981, 25), a perspective deeply rooted in his personal context that represented his particular response to reality, determined by inherent categories that in turn depend on language and are utterly different from that of the opponent, yet equally artificially demarcated (Lai 2006, 367). Zhuangzi as much as other Daoists, in contrast, sees beyond the arguments to the underlying structure of dispute:

> Suppose you and I had an argument. If you have beaten me instead of my beating you, then are you necessarily right and I am necessarily wrong? . . . Is one of us always right and the other wrong? . . . Whom

> shall we get to decide what is right? (ch. 2; Watson 1968, 48; Chan 1963, 189; Kohn 2014, 35)

That is to say, right and wrong are manmade superimpositions on reality that reflect people's thinking but, since they never fully match reality, they cannot be determined with certainty or in permanence. The more rigid and inflexible they get, moreover, the more discriminating consciousness dominates life, the more they result in blind dogmatism and come to derange the world (Wu 1991, 38). Another way of expressing the same idea focuses on the notion of "knowledge" (*zhi* 知), the subjective power of intellectually grasping and consciously processing outside reality. It is a way of discriminating reality and reaching understanding through recognition and representation (Zhang 2002, 423-24), in the process, superimposing a "second coding" on it (Moeller 2003, 119). It is a function of the mind that creates a "limited and often incorrect grasp of the world" (Ivanhoe 1996, 199).

All conceptual knowledge, moreover, is tied closely to language or words, which on the purely experiential level constitute a noise like the twittering of birds. Yet, "words are not just wind; they have something to say" (ch. 2), and by giving specific definition to "this" and "that," they take on a life and power of their own. "The one and what I said about it make two, and two and the original one make three," Zhuangzi says and asks, "Do people say something? Or do they say nothing?" (ch. 2; Kohn 2014, 38).

Later Daoists adopt the Buddhist notion of mental projections (*jing* 境) to make the same point. Based on language classifications established in the mind, they are mental imaginations that are projected outward to create an apparent reality of "being," contrasted with wisdom (*zhi* 智), a function of clear perception and pure awareness representing "nonbeing" (Robinet 1977, 245; Kohn 2010a, 37). Mental projections, moreover, create agitation and restlessness in the mind, since they continuously demand classification and evaluation, then stimulate an emotional response to them. As the great physician and Daoist Sun Simiao 孫思邈 (581-682) in his *Cunshen lianqi ming* 存神煉氣銘(Inscription on Visualizing Spirit and Refining Energy, DZ 834; trl. Kohn 2010a, 174-78) notes,

> There is much agitation and little stillness. Thinking is conditioned by a myriad different projections, accepting this and rejecting that without any constancy whatsoever. Dreads and worries, plans and calculations keep racing on inside like mad horses. This is the normal mind. (1b-2a; Kohn 1989a, 220; 2010, 176)

Levels and Stages

The same dichotomy is also central to Ken Wilber's understanding of the nature and evolution of consciousness based on a combination of ancient Indian wisdom and quantum physics. He distinguishes "two basic modes of knowing, one that has been various termed symbolic, or map, or inferential, or dualistic knowledge; while the other has been called intimate, or direct, or non-dual knowledge" (1993, 31). Referring to the quantum discovery that observer and event, subject and object are forever intricately linked (Penrose 2004, 1031), he cites Erwin Schrödinger's conviction that dualistic thought, however useful in daily life, needs to "be abandoned in philosophical thought" (1969, 137).

Connecting to ancient Indian scriptures, he cites the *Mudaka Upanishad* with its discussion of *paravidya* and *aparavidya*, i.e., immediate and mediated knowledge. The former is intuitive and non-dual, while the latter is "inferential, conceptual, and comparative" (Wilber 1993, 32; Deutsch 1969, 82). In addition, he also refers to Daoism with its distinction of natural and conventional knowledge, the latter being "a matter of social agreement," distant from actual reality (1993, 31; Watts 1957, 4). Adducing further examples of similar positions from Mahayana Buddhism, medieval Christianity, and process philosophy, he concludes, "If we are to know Reality, it is to the second (immediate) mode of knowing that we must eventually turn" (1993, 34).

Reality, moreover, is singular, "essentially eternal and unchangeable and numerically one in all men, nay in all sensitive beings," which also means that "the external worlds and consciousness are one and the same thing" (Schrödinger 1964, 21, 67; Wilber 1993, 47). More than that, human beings were quite happy with living in a state of integrated oneness, before they separated from reality through the creation of dualism and the notion of a separate self. This process of an ascending "dualistic spiral," moreover, went through four stages or levels (Wilber 1993, 94-95).

At first, during the Level of Mind, human beings lived in absolute subjectivity or cosmic consciousness, resting in a state of mind only, at one with reality and all things, fully in fusion yet without confusion. Identified with all and at one with the energy of the universe, they lived in a reality "without duality but not without relations" (1993, 47, 94). "Pure organic consciousness participates fully in the non-dual awareness of absolute subjectivity. . . The world is given to me only once, not one existing and one perceived. Nothing is reflected. The original and the mirror-image are identical" (1993, 115).

From here, described in Indian thought as the increasing dominance of *maya* (illusion) or *avidya* (ignorance) and in Christian theology as the Fall from the Garden of Eden (Wilber 1993, 98, 101), primary dualism arose, distinguishing subject from object, life from death. During this so-called Existential Level, human beings came to identify with their organism and see "things" outside as separate from themselves, developing a sense of time and space, even if "only in the most vividly concrete sense" (1993, 116). Perception remains strictly limited to the personal self. Man at this stage "prehends his being and his immediate duration, without any extra overlay of abstractions and symbolic interpretations" (1993, 117).

This changes in the next stage, the Ego Level, when instead of being an organism, humanity evolves to "have" a body, separating further from organic reality by imagining a mind distinct from physical existence. Complete out of contact with the timelessness of organismic awareness, people think more and more in a dualistic mode, using temporal, instrumental, and linear ways of processing reality, drawing concepts and symbols from memory that they then project into reality and express in art and other forms of external representation (1993, 118-19).

The last of the four stages Wilber calls the Shadow Level, because at this point human beings hold but a shadow of true original oneness. They evolve into critical awareness, discriminating consciousness, and come to find some parts desirable, others undesirable, living fully in the seesaw of likes and dislikes, right and wrong both within the self and in outside reality (1993, 130-31). While human beings still owned part of themselves on the Ego Level, they have now split off in a fourth way, cutting themselves off from aspects of their own selves, pushing away the unwanted parts into the shadow of their psyche and living only in a tiny part of their self (1993, 132).

Another model of the unfolding of consciousness, closely related to evolutionary stages in ancient history, appears in the work of psychologist Merlin Donald. He defines overall consciousness in three ways: as a state of higher or lower awareness, a place in the mind that decides on and controls emotions and physical movement, and a capacity for symbolic representation (2001, 117-19). He then distinguishes four stages of its unfolding, focusing on three transitions (2001, 259-79; see also Donald 1991):

1.	episodic	primates	event perception	senses
2.	mimetic	hominids	actions, imitations	skills
3.	mythic	humans	symbols, language	orality
4.	theoretic	moderns	external theories	literacy

That is to say, when the species *homo* first appeared on earth, they were still part of nature and, much like primates, lived purely by instinct and functioned dominantly through perceptual consciousness (Jolly 1999, 274). While as many as six different kinds of men roamed the earth, their mental life was largely episode-based, essentially "plodding, inflexible, literal, and unimaginative" (Pagel 2012, 34, 44), bound tightly by a group-oriented way of life and fused perception (Donald 2001, 261).

From here, hominids developed a new kind of cognitive capacity, i.e., mimetic skill, "the imaginative enactment of an event" (Bellah 2011, 125). "An extension of conscious control into the domain of action" using skill, mime, gesture, and imitation, it enabled them to communicate through body language, still at the core of all language today (Donald 2001, 269, 283). Transmitted as part of culture and community (Tomasello 1999, 4-5; Greenspan and Shanker 2004, 199), it brought about kinematic imagination as well as the ability to mime, i.e., imaginatively reenact an event or playfully pretending to do something, as well as the phenomenon of precise imitation, allowing hominids to share particular ways of doing things. This, in turn, led to the growth of skill, the result of "rehearsal, systematic improvement, and the chaining of mimetics into hierarchies" and the evolution of systematic gestures as an explicit act of communication (Bellah 2001, 264-65).

During the third stage, then, human beings began to add sounds to gestures and developed an oral culture, complete with music, myths, symbols, and internalized or "imprinted" cultural structures that allowed greater complexity (Pagel 2012, 5; Jolly 1999, 276; Mithen 2006, 154). This came with greater social and political organization, the elementary use of metaphors, the spinning of tales, the oral recording of history as well as with genetic changes that gave rise to brain structures supporting increased conscious discrimination.[1]

Moving further along the co-evolutionary spiral, this eventually led to further advancement and the beginning of writing. A completely different mode of dealing with reality, it enhanced long-term memory and allowed for more refined ways of representing reality in complex theories, further increasing conscious differentiation and facilitating ongoing social change (Donald 2001, 305-07; Pankenier 2013, 151). The result was a discriminating consciousness: it allowed human beings to recognize, monitor, evaluate, encourage, and remind themselves. They could also divide their attention, read others' intentions, imitate on cue, create intentional gestures, invent with the help of symbols, and develop complex skill hierarchies—all domain-generated skills that rely on the executive brain and make up the major characteristics of the modern mind (2001, 139-46). While this can be seen as the "great hominid escape from the nervous system" (2001, 305) and certainly provided the basis for unheard-of advancement in culture and technology, it also drove a wedge between human beings and their instinctual and intuitive connection to reality.

When, then, did all this happen exactly? And how does the unfolding of consciousness match the historical and cultural stages of human evolution?

---

[1] Donald 2001, 285, 316; Dor et al. 2014, 2; Newberg et al. 2001, 55, 65; see also Harris 2015; Dor and Jablonka 2010; 2014; Tomasello 1999. Genes and the environment interact closely in the development of advanced phenogenotypes. See Sinha 2014, 40.

Early Hominins

The earth is 4.6 billion years old. It took about 1.2 billion years before oxygen became widely available in the atmosphere and another 1.4 billion before complex cell organisms evolved, i.e., about 2 billion years ago (Joseph 1993, 1-2). This period is known as the Archean Era. Following the Great Oxygenation Event, a major extinction, multicellular organisms arose about 1 billion years ago, and first simple animals began about half a billion or 500 million years ago, followed by the emergence of complex plants, amphibians, insects, and reptiles. This phase is known as the Proterozoic Era.

The Permian-Triassic mass extinction occurred around 250 million years ago. Caused by the impact of large-scale volcanic eruptions of the Siberian Traps, it was the most dramatic extinction in the history of the earth, wiping out between 80 and 90 percent of all living species and ushering in the age of the dinosaurs in the following Jurassic period (Kwok 2013, 32; Tennesen 2015, 19). Their emergence is followed by the evolution of birds around 150 million years ago and that of flowering plants at 130 (Pagel 2012, 2). The entire period is known as the Mesozoic Era.

It ended around 65 million years ago with the late Cretaceous extinction, cause by an asteroid over seven miles wide and traveling at about 44,640 miles per hour, whose crater is still discernible near Chicxulub on the Yucatán Peninsula (Tennesen 2015, 16-17). Comparative mild, it killed off the dinosaurs and opened the path for the emergence of mammals during the so-called Cenozoic Era, i.e., our time.

These early stages of the planet's development can be related to the differentiation of *qi* from singularity to multiplicity, from simplicity to complexity, in the process bringing forth immeasurable numbers of species, i.e., the myriad beings. Since they come in a set of four, it is tempting to relate them to the four great *yugas* of Indian cosmology, which each ended with the complete destruction of the world. They do not, however, connect well to the Daoist understanding, which took the *yugas* in a more limited way, remaining focused on human development.

The first traces of the species *homo* go back to around 6 million years ago, a tiny drop in the huge bucket of the overall history of earth. The earliest hominins evolved from primates, eventually developing into as many as twenty different species.[2] Known as *Australopithecus*, they were the first to walk upright and develop great throwing capability (Corballis 2011, 183-90; Oatley 2000, 79). With a body height of 1.1 to 1. 4 meters and a brain capacity of about 450 cc,[3]

[2] Corballis 2011, 182; Leakey 1994, 7; Leakey and Lewin 1977; Oppenheimer 2007, 95; Tomasello 1999; Toth and Schick 2005.

[3] Corballis 2011, 198; Franks 2010, 24; Greenspan and Shanker 2004, 139; Nadeau and Kafatos 1999, 143; Ramachandran 2011, 118; ; Van Osterzee 2000, 174.

they shared sensory, bodily, and brain systems with all mammals (Toth and Schick 2005, 59). That is to say, they had affects, but these were not encoded as information, instead being "diffuse global states generated by deep, subcortical brain structures interacting with primitive viscerosomatic body representations" (Panksepp 2008, 48).

Early hominins essentially could feel two basic types of body disturbances—pain or fatigue and pleasure or delight—processed in brain regions homologous in all mammals and comparable in their localized stimulations (Panksepp 2008, 49). In other words, the human repertoire of basic emotional feelings and reactions is commensurate with that of animal sensations and behaviors. Functioning along a basic axis of like and dislike, it consists of instinctual urges that "remain intact even after damage to the neocortex," the thinking part of the brain, and thus work without encoding, conscious processing, or any form of analytical reflection (2008, 50).

Their perception was completely instinctual in the sense that they could feel the impact of the environment. However—as also described in the *Kaitian jing* in terms of Great Antecedence and matching Zhuangzi's Chaos Complete as well as Wilber's Level of Mind—they did not actively recognize things outside of themselves or themselves as separate, living instead in a state of complete unity with all. Their behavior was highly automatized and essentially unconscious, free from restraints or recursive evaluations.

As much as other mammals, they tended to congregate and live in some form of social grouping of about thirty members, formed as "a genetic adaptation for protection against predators" (Jaynes 1990, 126; Franks 2010, 25). Primates clearly show group integration. "A thirsty baboon, for example, does not leave the group and go seeking water; it is the whole group that moves or none. Thirst is satisfied within the patterned activity of the group. And so it is with other needs and situations" (Jaynes 1990, 127).

By the same token, the precursors of humanity as much as wild animals today lived in close harmony with the environment and could feel—and immediately react to—changes as they occurred. Thus, animals are nervous before an earthquake, seek higher ground before a tsunami, gather more food when a particularly cold winter approaches, and so on. Their behavior is instinctual and, in modern terms, highly intuitive. Paying attention largely to the here and now, early hominins too worked on an energetic level of immediacy, bypassing complex processing and without recourse to conscious awareness (Franks 2010, 25).

The first creature generally regarded as human is *Homo habilis*, representing a slightly more technologically advanced group than the Australopithecines that emerged after the receding of an ice age about 2.3 million years ago. They used Oldowan stone tools found over much of Africa, the Near East, Asia, and

Europe.[4] More scavengers than hunters, they stood about 1.5 meters tall, had brains of about 800 cc, and lived in slightly larger groups.[5]

While they continued to plod along, a new evolutionary strain developed at 1.8 million years ago: *Homo ergaster*, the maker of the Acheulean stone tools. Archaeological evidence suggests that these early humans lived as hunter-gathers and had some control over fire.[6] Being able to eat cooked meat, as documented in the Nariokotome hominid (Christian 2008, 95; Noble and Davidson 1996, 174, 213), they gained a great deal of energy and underwent various genetic mutations. Their jaws and teeth grew smaller, they developed greater hand coordination, and their digestive tract shrank (1996, 218). "In fact, modern man has a 60 percent shorter digestive tract than predicted for a great ape of our size" (Gazzaniga 2008, 89; Wrangham 2007, 184).

They also developed a larger brain of 1100 cc, combined with a higher forehead and flatter face (Corballis and Suddendorf 2007, 26; Franks 2010, 27), but were as yet without a prefrontal cortex (Walter 2006, 103; Deacon 1998). They grew to heights of up to two meters (over 6 feet), and their females expanded to allow for giving birth to the larger heads (Greenspan and Shanker 2004, 139). Born earlier, infants were more helpless, requiring more care, so that overall "social connectivity increased" (2004, 218; Franks 2010, 27). This connectivity also opened the path to cooperative breeding, in contrast to apes who never let anyone else handle their infants, opening the path to greater social flexibility and cultural specialization (Power 2014b, 200-01).

Another early group that was human but not a direct forerunner of *Homo sapiens* was the Neanderthals, who lived from about 300,000 to 40,000 years ago, mostly under ice-age conditions. Similarly tall and with a rather large brain, they left the so-called Mousterian stone tools behind, but show little variation or adaptation in technology (Christian 2008, 95; Pettitt 2005, 125).

Mimetic Gestures

Although neither of these early humans had speech (Dediu and Levinson 2014, 193), it is quite likely that they evolved beyond instinctual reactions and created a variety of complex signals, sounds, or memes (Blackmore 2007, 2; 1999; Johansson 2014, 67; Lewis 2014, 84)—not unlike the beginnings of language ac-

---

[4] Christian 2008, 86; Corballis 2010, 115; 2011, 205; Johansson 2014, 63; Klein 2005, 85-89; Tennesen 2015, 55-57; Toth and Schick 2005, 61; Ward et al. 1995, 4.

[5] Franks 2010, 26; Corballis 2010, 116; 2011, 192; Greenspan and Shanker 2004, 128, 141; Oppenheimer 2007, 97; Tattersall 2007, 13; Van Oosterzee 2000, 176; Watts 2014, 211-13.

[6] On early man and fire, see Bellah 2011, 84; Jaynes 1990, 129; Noble and Davidson 1996, 205-06; Pagel 2012,1; Van Oosterzee 2000, 85, 180-84; Walter 2006, 50-51; Watts 2014, 214; Wrangham 2007, 188; 2009.

quisition observed in great apes.[7] Using tactile, visual, vocal, and other means, such as "grinding teeth or beating branches," rhythmic banging or drumming,[8] as well as a variety of facial expressions—made easier due to the increasing loss of body hair—they were able to transmit techniques and methods (Greespan 2004, 144). They also established organizational patterns of dominance and subordination, thereby creating elementary hierarchies and social structures (Joseph 1993, ch. 5).

During this mimetic stage of human development, matching the period of Chaos in the *Kaitian jing* as well as Zhuangzi's second stage of "beings" or object cognition and Wilber's Existential Level, humans developed greatly. They created the first standardization of social signals beyond elementary smiling and crying and began to channel primary emotions into social ones (Jolly 1999, 264; Walter 2006, 149, 165). With their increased brain size came an enhanced capacity of the use of mirror neurons, also found in chimpanzees, exhibiting similar powers of interaction and communication.[9]

First discovered at the University of Padua in the 1990s, mirror neurons are brain cells of the premotor cortex, particularly clustered in Broca's area (F5), that fire when we see or hear an action someone else performs nearby, mirroring the neuron activity in their brain (Keysers 2009, 18; 2011, 15; Iacoboni 2009a, 9, 12).[10] Beyond merely acknowledging their action, these neurons make sure that our brain fully shares in them, so that we see, hear, and feel the movements of others just as if we were doing exactly the same thing (Keysers 2009, 19; 2011, 19). That is to say, if we see someone pick up an apple and bite into it with delight, we feel as if we were doing just that (Iacoboni 2009a, 14; 2009, 122). Action and perception are one in the brain: "Your acts become mine, and my acts become yours" (Keysers 2009, 20; 2011, 19).

Present at birth and activated through social interaction, mirror neurons connect to the limbic system via the insula, rousing instinctual reactions and preconditioned, subconscious emotions, such as smiles or frowns, maternal empathy or existential anxiety (Iacoboni 2009a, 126, 162; Keysers 2011, 94;

---

[7] For studies on language and cognition in bonobos and other great apes, see Byrne 1998; Clay and Zuberbühler 2014; Fouts and Mills 1998; Pika 2014; Savage-Rumbaugh and Levine 1994; Tomasello and Call 1997; Washburn 1961; Washburn and Rumbaugh 2007. While they have the ability to learn an already established language, they lack collaborative creativity and trust needed for more advanced forms (Dor and Jablonka 2014, 29). A vivid fictional treatment appears in Gruen 2010.

[8] Blackmore 2007, 11; Dennett 1991; Jaynes 1990, 127; Mithen 2006, 105.

[9] Walter 2006, 58-60; Greenspan and Shanker 2004, 105-23; Kafatos and Nadeau 1990, 95; Oppenheimer 2007, 109; Pika 2014; Power 2014a, 51.

[10] For discussions of mirror neurons, see also Champoux 2009; Corballis 2010, 119-21; 2011, 60-62; Franks 2010, 88-90; Gallese 2009; Gazzaniga 2008, 63-67, 177-81; Gentilucci and Corballis 2007, 50-53; Hickock 2014; Iacoboni 2008; 2009b; Keysers and Gazzola 2009; Lyons 2009; Oberman and Ramachandran 2009; Pineda et al. 2009; Ramachandran 2011, 117-28; Walter 2006, 58-62, 171-72; Whitehead 2014, 167.

Ramachandran 2011, 127). Their very existence in the depth of the brain shows that we—as much as higher primates—are intersubjective in a primordial sense and essentially born to socialize (Iacoboni 2009a, 155; Keysers 2011, 53). The increased brain size and capacity of *Homo erectus*, then, increased the activation of mirror neurons and enhanced the social intersubjectivity of the species.

In addition, it opened a much greater ability to imitate, that is, not only match movements as in mimicry, replicate actions as in mirroring or simulation, act to reach a particular goal as in emulation, but strictly follow the method used. [11] For example, if I pick a fruit hanging above my left side using my right hand rather than the left, which would be closer, strict imitation means using the same hand. By this test, "monkeys are not true imitators"—they would see the desired goal and reach it in the easiest way, not follow the method applied (Keysers 2011, 61). This does not keep them, or any other animal species, from being able to learn quickly and efficiently, be it in terms of finding food, predation, the construction of artifacts, and even the use of tools and special devices (Giffin 1992, chs. 3-6). However, it prevents them from attaining higher levels of advanced culture, where the specific methodology is essential, since only imitation on the subtlest levels of movement can lead to a highly specialized execution of actions (Keysers 2011, 42).

Early humans achieved this and created increasingly sophisticated systems of mimetics. The foundation of language, this is a form of "attention manipulation" (Tomasello 1999, 133) that can still be observed among Pygmys today as part of an immediate-return society where people use objects and food the very day they produce them (see Lewis 2014). It consists of "a complicated system of signs and symbols held together by the logical structure of syntax and grammar."[12] Moving from presentational to representational communication, i.e., from expressions of immediate experiences to instructional patterns frozen in time, language begins with the stabilization of signals used in experiential-mimetic communication (Dor 2014, 110, 119; Whitehead 2014, 159). Set mime signals, including basic vocalizations as well as gestures (2014, 121), require systematic teaching through careful attention, detailed demonstration, and persistent repetition. They also need subtle motor control in coordinated actions and sounds—screams, hoots, barks, grunts, pants, and squeaks (Clay and Zuberbühler 2014, 145)—that match particular objects or situations, key symbols that involve learned associations, and hierarchical structures, i.e., multiple levels and specific orders of actions (Keysers 2011, 72-73; Gazzaniga 2008, 162-63).

An example of an intricate mimetic system of communication, created from scratch in the 20th century, is the sign language of Nicaraguan school chil-

[11] Keysers 2011, 35; Franks 2010, 177; Pineda at al. 2004, 137; Champoux et al. 2009, 84; Lyons 2009.

[12] Kafatos and Nardeau 1990, 95; see also Corballis 2011, 161-65; Power 2014a; Sinha 2014; Wolpert 2007, 177; Greenspan and Shanker 2004, 163.

dren. Traditionally deaf children remained with their families, however, in the late 1970s the Sandinistas pooled them in a specialized school in Managua, encouraging teachers to speak slowly for lip reading and use simple signs for spelling. Students did not respond to them, but developed their own system of signing, younger children not only picking up the basics from teenagers but developing signs into high complexity (see Polich 2005; Corballis and Suddendorf 2007, 27; Iacoboni 2009a, 174; Keysers 2011, 69; Walter 2006, 78). Studies of these children as well as users of other sign languages show that they activate the same processing centers in the brain for comprehending distinctions and creating meaning as spoken and written language (see Poizener et al. 1987; Pika 2014, 130). These are particularly Broca's area for speech creation (F5) and Wernecke's area for language reception (Joordens 2011, 56; Gentilucci and Corballis 2007, 57; Lieberman 2010, 165). In other words, as early humans, inspired by expanded brain capacity for mirror neurons, developed a complex mimetic system, they also primed themselves for the development of speech (Walter 2006, 89; Ardila 2009, 160).

Orality

Oral communication is the ground layer of separative consciousness and core characteristic of the mythic stage—matching the Three Sovereigns and Five Thearchs of the *Kaitian jing* as well as Zhuangzi's third stage of boundaries and Wilber's Ego Level. It first evolved with *Homo sapiens*, who split from the other hominins about 500,000 years ago and whose first clear manifestation appears in *Homo helmei*, dated to 250,000 years ago, i.e., the beginning of the Upper Paleolithic (Christian 2008, 97). As found in the Blombos cave in South Africa, these humans made delicate stone tools, adapted to their environment by expanding their diet to include shellfish, and used ocher coloring on their bodies, signifying body awareness and possibly ritual activity (Pettitt 2005, 132, 143; McBrearty and Brooks 2000; Watts 2014).

Homo sapiens is the source "from which all modern genetic mitochondria descend."[13] With rounder skulls, higher foreheads, and receding jaws, they also had an enlarged pharynx, a cone-shaped 4.5" long cavity behind the nose and mouth, which allowed the larynx or voice box to drop (Walter 2006, 90).[14] In them, for the first time, "pyramidal cells sent out long axons from the rapidly evolving cerebral cortex to connect directly and deeply with the nerve systems

---

[13] Cavalli-Sforza 2000, 79. See Gazzaniga 2011, 24; Oppenheimer 2007, 102; Greenspan and Shanker 2004, 157; Mithen 2006, 246; Tattersall 2007, 139; Tomasello 1999, 3.

[14] For the dropping of the larynx, which also happens in infants, see also Ardila 2009, 163; Blackmore 2007, 9; Dediu and Levinson 2014, 189; Greenspan and Shanker 2004, 162; Lieberman 1984; 2010; Pasternak 2007, 119, 126; Walter 2006, 93.

that manage the lungs, larynx, face, and tongue," providing increasingly conscious control over the organs of speech production and the hundred-plus muscles necessary for making words (2006, 92).[15]

Oral signals probably arose first from intentional calls in imitation of natural sounds, necessitated by the darkness of the European caves—and of the fourth ice age—which replaced the open of the African savannahs.[16] Specific sounds, expressed in a certain pitch and at a certain level of intensity, would warn of particular dangers, alerting the group and allowing them to create an appropriate response—something also found in animal populations (Joseph 1993, 152; Griffin 1992, chs. 8-9). Within human communities, however, sounds would gradually be modified to signal whether the danger was near or far, big or small; they might indicate immediate or delayed action—creating an early form the imperative. Over thousands of years, these particular calls became standardized within a given group. They also, through epigenetic transmission and biological evolution, established themselves in particular areas in the brain, thus gradually forming part of the fundamental make-up of humanity (Dor and Jablonka 2014, 21; Jaynes 1990, 133; Pagel 2012, 280).

Object recognition is clearly evidenced by the first drawings of animals in caves, such as those in Altamira and Lascaux, dated to around 35,000 BCE and related to the rise of Cro Magnon man. They signal the Human Revolution, a period of great advancement in tool-making, bodily ornamentation, pictorial art, culture, and social stratification.[17] Associated also with the mutation of the FOXP2 gene in chromosome 7, responsible for speech production,[18] this period is marked by the development of proper nouns, using simple universal phonemes such as *ba* or *pa* and onomatopoeias (Ardila 2009, 161; Dediu and Levinson 2014, 190; Ramachandran 2011, 172-73). This not only enhanced the ability to think about things as separate, but also developed initial forms of memory. "A Middle Pleistocene man would forget what he was doing. But lingual man would have language to remind him," Julian Jaynes says, eerily echoing Guo Xiang's description (1990, 134).

---

[15] For more on the origins and development of human language, see Bingham 2010; Bickerton 1990; 2010; Corballis 2002; 2010; Dunbar 1996; Fitch 2010a; Franks 2010, 42-44; Gardner 1968; Jablonka and Rechav 1996; Joseph 1993; Kafatos and Nadeau 1990, 96; Kirby 1999; Mithen 2006; Pinker 1994; 2007; Ruhlen 1994; Greenspan and Shanker 2004, 187-207; Tallerman 2005; Tattersall 2010; Tomasello 1999.

[16] Jaynes 1990, 131-32; Ardila 2009, 160; Mithen 2006, 123; Greenspan and Shanker 2004, 169.

[17] Jaynes 1990, 133; Berman 1989, 65; Greenspan and Shanker 2004, 167-70; Kuijsten 2006, 107-08; Mithen 1998.

[18] Ardila 2009, 167; Cochran and Harpending 2009, 63; Corballis 2010, 122-23; 2011, 70-72; Gentilucci and Corballis 2007, 62; Lieberman 2010, 170-72; Pagel 2012, 277; Piattelli-Palmarini 2010.

Verbs, the use of words for specific actions, as well as syntax and grammar, the ability to put words together in structure, came later[19]—although some linguists, connecting to the evolutionary development (Evo Devo) revolution in biology, see syntax as primary, necessary even for mimetics, and words as secondary (e.g., Chomsky 2002; 2010). Still, the likelihood is that the identification of people by proper names began at this time. Naming a person makes him different, special, unique—a particular entity beyond just being part of the tribe and one who deserves special care. The named one is a "he" or a "she" who can be brought to mind even while absent or after death.

With the recognition of objects, actions, and persons, memory transited into more long-term modes, activating parts of the brain such as the hippocampus, underdeveloped and dormant before. Also, gradually certain aptic structures of the brain with specific speech areas evolved further by natural and human selection (Jaynes 1990, 417). These include the supplementary motor area at the top of the frontal lobe, mostly involved in articulation; Broca's area to the side and back of the frontal lobe, used for articulation, vocabulary, inflection, and grammar; and Wernicke's area in the posterior part of the temporal lobe, dealing with vocabulary, syntax, meaning, and understanding (Jaynes 1990, 101; Walter 2006, 61; Dor and Jablonka 2010, 143).

More intricate language structures facilitated and enhanced social interaction. "Language dramatically extends the possibility-space for interaction, facilitates the profiling and navigation of joint attentional scenes, enables the sharing of situation models and action plans, and mediates experimental the cultural shaping of interacting minds" (Tylen et al. 2010, 3; Dor and Jablonka 2014, 26). This set the stage not only for speech as the "uttering-forth of one's whole meaning of one's whole being" (Sacks 1985, 77), but also for the emergence of tales—myths, legends, sagas, and other oral records.

Orally based thought has ten distinct characteristics. Besides relying heavily on memory, in terms of grammatical organization, it is additive rather than subordinative (using "and" more than "while" or "after"), aggregative rather than analytic, i.e., heavily uses proverbs, formulas, epithets, and parallel constructions, as well as redundant or "copious," with repetition and backlooping. In terms of content, it tends to be close to the human lifeworld, homeostatic and present-oriented, "agonistically toned," i.e., deeply engaged with the issues and struggle of the time, as well as focusing on concrete events rather than general patterns. It is overall situational rather than abstract, empathetic rather than detached. Socially, moreover, an oral mindset tends to be conservative or traditionalist, geared toward maintaining the status-quo (Ong 1982, 36-50).

Practically demonstrated in fieldwork among illiterate peasants in Uzbekistan and Kirghizia in the 1930s (see Luria 1976a), this means that categories of thought are practice and process oriented. For example, when presented with a

---

[19] Ardila 2009, 162-63; Gazzaniga 2008, 55-57; Pinker 1994, 22; Ramachandran 2011, 159.

set of four objects, three of which were tools plus one log of wood, the subjects would class them together since they shared the same use, possibly eliminating one tool as not as practical. When asked whether logically there could be such a thing as white bears, they would take recourse to their own experience. When asked about geometrical shapes, they would answer by pointing to specific objects, and so on (Ong 1982, 50-52). All this shows that in orally based mentation there are object cognition and acknowledgment of boundaries, but no self-analysis or isolation of the self as a separate entity (1982, 54).

Still, even spoken language serves to symbolize sensory experience and related processing (Gardner 1968, 328). It determines how we think, the particular way we conceive and classify the world (Boroditsky 2009, 119; Pinker 2007, 155). As a result, people from different cultures pay attention to different sets of distinctions, see colors differently, and envision the flow of time as vertical or horizontal, thick or thin, small or big (Boroditsky 2000). Some cultures even have no words for "right" and "left," using instead geographical directions (Boroditsky 2009, 121-24). Gendered nouns create different perceptions of objects: thus "key" is seen as hard, heavy, and jagged by German speakers and as intricate, lovely, and shiny by Spanish natives (2009, 127).

The Bicameral Mind

About 10,000 BCE, when the last ice age ended and the world became warmer and wetter, the Neolithic Revolution occurred and agriculture began, independently in seven different areas on earth.[20] It signaled "the change from a hunting and gathering economy to a food-producing economy by the domestication of plants and animals," which "made civilization possible" (Jaynes 1990, 137; Diamond 1998, 89). Possibly predicated by an increasing desiccation in the Near East (Toynbee 1962, 1:304), it also came with a further evolution of language in the form of increasingly complex syntax, expressions, and metaphors that increased perception and attention. Causing a major population explosion—despite the reduction in nutritional value that caused a plethora of diseases, an overall shrinking in size, and a reduced life expectancy—agriculture predicated a great increase in genetic change. "Favorable mutations that had previously occurred every 100,000 years or so were now showing up ever 400 years" (Cochran and Harpending 2009, 65), allowing much more rapid developments and increased spread of new genetic components (Pagel 2012, 23).

People came to live in towns with populations of several hundred and eventually established kingdoms and even empires (Scarre 2005, 193; Bellah

[20] Cochran and Harpending 2009, 31; Christian 2008, 118. On the transition from foraging to agriculture, see also Bellwood 2005; Cohen 1997; Cowan and Watson 1992; Mithen 2004; Price and Gebauer 1995; Smith 1998; Yan 2005.

2011). Yet—as outlined in a compelling theory by Julian Jaynes (1920-1997; see Woodward and Tower 2006)—they had as yet no reflective, self-aware, and self-critical consciousness, just as social insects build powerful organizational structures with intricate hierarchies on a purely instinctual basis (Kuijsten 2006, 109-11). "Without analog selves to 'see' themselves in relation to others," they were "signal-bound," i.e., "responding each minute to cues in a stimulus-response manner and controlled by these cues" (Jaynes 1990, 140). They were "a race of man who spoke, judged, reasoned, and so on, but who were not conscious [in our sense] at all" (Norretranders 1998, 310).

Unlike modern man, moreover, whose language processing centers are active in the left hemisphere, they also worked with language in the right hemisphere. The two brain areas presumably communicated via the anterior commissure near the corpus calossum, a "transverse band of fibers that collects information from the temporal lobe cortex, but particularly the middle gyrus, included in Wernicke's area." It then sends it "over the amygdala across the top of the hypothalamus toward the other temporal lobe" (Jaynes 1990, 104). While people then would hear and process regular speech in the left hemisphere, they would also perceive internalized commands from kings, gods, and ancestors—a growing pantheon of divine entities—on the right, in a form of auditory hallucinations not unlike those still found in schizophrenics, nonverbal quadriplegics, and inspired poets today (see Kuijsten 2006; Hamilton 2006; Jaynes 2006a; 2006b). "The speech of the gods was directly organized in what corresponds to Wernicke's area in the right hemisphere and 'spoken' or 'heard' over the anterior commissure to or by the auditory areas of the left temporal lobe" (Jaynes 1990, 105).

While communications received in the right hemisphere were still highly intuitive and formless in nature, they found expression in language—in direct commands and orders perceived as divine. People, being unable to perform any reflective evaluations, just did what the gods ordered them to do, without any perception of or responsibility for individual actions (Norretranders 1998, 311). As a Sumerian proverb says, "Don't think: let there be no time between hearing your inner voice and doing what it tells you" (1998, 315; Jaynes 1990, 204).

The evidence for the existence of this bicameral mind, the key to social control of people at the time, appears in inscriptions and writings of the great empires of early civilization, ruled by god-kings and unified by internal commands. They arise first around 7,000 BCE and include Jericho, Hacilar, and Eridu as well as the better known Hittites, Sumerians, Babylonians, and Egyptians in the Near East, plus—somewhat later in history—the early Mesoamerican civilizations of the Olmecs, Mayas, Aztecs, and Incas (Jaynes 1990, 151-55; Ong 1982, 29).

The greatest literary expression of this early mind is the early Greek epic of the Iliad, written around 1200 BCE, "our window upon the immediate bicameral past" (1990, 257; 2006a, 87; Kuijsten 2006, 114-16). The text is conspicuous for its overall lack of individual consciousness—words that later come to mean mental factors like *psyche*, *thumos*, and *noos* having much more concrete meanings (Greer 2006, 247), such as breath, motion, or watch—not unlike *qi* or *qing* in classical Chinese. The body—echoing Zhuangzi—is not seen as a complete entity—"in Homer, it is always parts that are referred to, and never the body as a whole" (Jaynes 1990, 71). Protagonists, moreover, in the epic have no conscious minds or wills of their own: gods warn them, admonish them, lead them into battle. "It is one god who makes Achilles promise not to go into battle, another who urges him to go, and yet another who then clothes him in a golden fire . . . In fact, the gods take the place of consciousness" (1990, 72; McVeigh 2006, 213).

Human actions at this time, especially under stress or conflict, did not come from personal plans, desires, and motivations; they were the execution of commands issued by the gods. That the Chinese participated in this phase of consciousness development is evidenced by their use of the personator during ancestral sacrifices. This, the *shi* 尸 ceremony, began under the Xia, "when personators would communicate on behalf of the dead" and sacred vessels with powerful eyes facilitated entrance into trance states (Jaynes 2006c, 339; Carr 2006, 398-401). The practice continued under the Shang and Western Zhou, but disintegrated into mere formality and an occasion for drunken revelry under the Eastern Zhou, when people no longer heard the voices of their gods, coinciding with the "timeline for the breakdown of the bicameral mind in other parts of the world" (Carr 2006, 387-88).

Bicamerality in China is also manifest in the use of the word *ming* 命, the later term for "fate" or "destiny," which originally meant "decree," "command," or "mandate." It occurs first in the oracle bones, where it appears as *ling* 令 and indicates a "mission or gift granted by a higher authority to a lower person" and, more specifically, the divine approval or *command* the Shang kings received from a high god or ancestor (Raphals 2003, 540; 2005, 75). Adding the "mouth" radical to *ling* (Schaberg 2005, 24), *ming* is the "official notice of empowerment by the king" (Cook 1997, 260), spoken aloud and using a special, formulaic language during the ceremony of investiture of local nobles (Schaberg 2005, 27). The term thus essentially means the specific mandate, charge, or "allotment granted by a superior arbiter on an occasion of distribution" (Schaberg 2005, 30). *Ming* had to be spoken to be valid, indicating that the Shang kingdom, as much as Mesopotamian empires and later Mesoamerican cultures, was a bicameral civilization.

This civilization, moreover, was generally harmonious with a high degree of social integration. In the various Neolithic kingdoms, "the bicameral mind *was* the social control, not fear or repression or even law. There were no private grudges, no private frustrations, no private anything, since bicameral man had not internal 'space' in which to be private and no analog 'I' to be private with. All initiative was in the voices of the gods" (Jaynes 1990, 205). Chinese thinkers of later centuries have looked back upon this time as the epitome of harmony and peace, and people today still retain "vestiges of the bicameral mind in their longing for absolute guidance and external control that makes them susceptible to charismatic leaders, cults, trends, and persuasive rhetoric" (Kuijsten 2006, 132).

The *Zhuangzi*, moreover, contains various stories where people hear voices and connect to divine or otherworldly entities, commonly described as "dreams." Thus, Zhuangzi addresses a skull he finds on the roadside, asking it how it came to die all by its lonesome; the skull promptly appears to him in a dream, explaining about the delights of the realm of the dead (ch. 18; Watson 1968, 193). Carpenter Shi walks by an ancient, gnarled, practically useless tree, which duly shows up in a dream, chiding him for measuring trees by their use, which only causes them harm (ch. 4; Watson 1968, 64). These dreams all have nonhuman entities speak with reason; they contain a valid and important message, with authority and relevance to real life (Skogeman 1986, 79-80), reflecting a subtler, older, and less divisive stage of more perceptual rather than discriminating consciousness.

Literacy

The transition to the latter occurred through the development of writing, originally a secret or even magical power known to a select few that "conferred privileged access to material and spiritual resources" (Keightley 1996, 89). It was used primarily as a means of record-keeping of economical and political transactions (Ong 1982, 85, 92-93; Scarre 2005, 196). The visible record of spoken words or logophonic script, writing is different from pictorial representations as well as from other forms of record keeping, such as knotted cords, arranged pebbles, carved ivory bones, or pictographic abstractions (Keightley 1996, 70, 87). The first traces of writing go back to about 3500 BCE, when the Babylonians and Sumerians in the Near East developed first cuneiform ideographs, soon followed by the ancient Egyptians (Ong 1982, 83; Cooper 2004, 80; Baines 2004).

Chinese characters appeared about 1500 BCE in conjunction with the greater social complexity of the Bronze Age under the Shang dynasty.[21] Early graphs represented the archaic pronunciation of words and were a phoneticization of early art motives—so that the rounded shape associated with the idea of dragon, for example, came to signify the sound of the word, **kliung* (Keightley 1996, 84-86). This matches the first alphabet developed by Semitic peoples around the same time. The Greek alphabet, more potent due to its inclusion of

---

[21] Keightley 1996, 68; 1989; Boltz 1994, 16-17; Diamond 1998, 330; see also Bagley 2004; Bottéro 2004; Christian 2008,144.

vowels, goes back to about 800 BCE (Trigger 2004, 57). Easier to learn and more flexible in application, it was both more democratic socially and more prone toward abstraction philosophically than the Chinese character script, a "system that, by its very difficulties, limited access to literacy and conferred great status" (Keightley 1996, 89; Pankenier 2013, 151-52; see also Boltz 1994).

By 600, however, use of writing in different parts of the world had spread widely enough among the upper classes to make a difference in thinking (Ong 1982, 88-89). "The most momentous of all human technological inventions," writing eroded auditory authority (1982, 84). No longer subject to the whims of the gods and the manifestation of their voices, people now had them in "a controllable location" (Jaynes 1990, 208; see also Limber 2006). Freeing language from context, standardizing concepts, and creating autonomous discourse, writing gave new powers to the individual (Ong 1982, 77; Robertson 2004, 20).

Completely artificial, writing used cortical areas of the brain more related to visual input and enhanced prefrontal processing, thus raising consciousness to a new level, and opening the path toward the growth of an inner sense of self—characteristic of all philosophies of the Axial Age (Ong 1982, 81). More specifically, it allowed backward scanning of recorded thoughts, challenging logic, increasing the choice of words, and allowing the reduction of inconsistencies. Writing separated the knower from the known, opening the self to introspection and society to abstract concepts, such as justice and morality (Ong 1982, 102-04). For the first time, people became aware of the complexities of their internal motivations and were able to create itemized lists and indexes, gaining a much greater control over the outside world and their inner thinking while being more and more alienated from both (Ong 1982, 148-49).

Discriminating Consciousness

Full self-aware consciousness, then, began around 1200 BCE and first manifested in philosophies of about 600 BCE, a period of great change all over the civilized world that the German thinker Karl Jaspers called the Axial Age, when "man as we know him today came into being" (Jaspers 1953, 1). At this time, in many different cultures new thinkers and religious leaders arose who for the first time placed great emphasis on the individual as opposed to the community of the clan or tribe, creating abstractions and sophisticated forms of criticism (Momigliano 1975, 9). Examples include the Buddha and Mahavira in India, Zoroaster in Persia, Solon and Socrates in ancient Greece, and Confucius and Laozi in China.

As the great bicameral kingdoms disintegrated and smaller states became independent and prosperous, literacy reached wider swathes of society. As a result, itinerant intellectuals not functioning within centralized priesthoods or bureaucracies came to the fore, engaging in criticism and questioning all human activity, including also internal features such as thought and emotion (Bellah 2011, 269). They worked with discriminating consciousness, apparent as the "recursive mind," using a term from computer science and linguistics (see Fitch 2010b), which here indicates the "ability not only to reflect upon our own minds, but also to simulate the minds of others" (Corballis 2011, 1). It also includes "theory of mind," i.e., "the capacity to imagine another individual's mind states." [22] This, like language, precise imitation, and abstraction, is a key feature that distinguishes humans from animals (Shettleworth 2010, 556-58).

The earliest document of this new level of consciousness is the Odyssey, where for the first time people not only distinguish things but evaluate them in terms of black and white, left and right, good and evil (Norretranders 1998, 313). It clearly allows for a space deep within the person and uses key terms in a new way. Thus *thumos*, the word for overall motion, is now used for internal motivation, i.e., basic urges for action (Jaynes 1990, 262). *Noos*, the idea of "watching" or "seeing," now refers to the subjective mind, one's personal way of perceiving and processing the world (Norretranders 1998, 314; Jaynes 1990, 269). *Psyche*, originally indicating "breath" or "life," develops closer toward a concept of the soul (1990, 288; see also Greer 2006).

Matching the fourth stage in Zhuangzi's outline, the phase of right and wrong, which signals the end of cosmic, social, and mental harmony, this development is not merely cultural and philosophical in nature. Rather, it is a biological, evolutionary, and genetic change that came with the expansion of the higher brain and an increased use of the prefrontal cortex. Echoing the *Daode jing*'s outline of the world's decline from small, integrated, and harmonious communities into a state of complexity and confusion, Julian Jaynes describes the transition into consciousness as predicated upon the growth and increasing complexity of bicameral kingdoms as well as on the meeting of individuals from different bicameral cultures.

"Once cities became a certain size," he says, "the bicameral control must be extremely precarious. The hierarchy of priests to sort out the various voices and give them their recognitions must have become a major preoccupation" (1990, 207). A multiplicity of voices would necessitate an arbiter—an arbiter within the individual rather than without. Similarly, multiple voices arise when people from different kingdoms meet who do not know each other's language and are owned by different gods. As long as their theocracies remain unthreatened, their inner directives stay friendly and they can connect and trade with each other (1990, 205-06). As long as they return to their own communities and continue in their traditional ways, no major change occurs.

However, should they interrelate more frequently and learn about each other's gods or—even worse—each other's language, the potential for internal conflict and confusion arises, as reflected in the Biblical record of the tower of

[22] Dunbar 2007, 40; Corballis 2011, 133-38; Whiten 2007, 15; Wellman 1990.

Babel. Language determines consciousness (Boroditsky 2009, 119), and anyone who has worked to acquire another language knows just how much gaining fluency requires a shift in identity—in conception, expression, and body language. Also, if there is any form of threat perceived in either kingdom, the voices may well become aggressive, and hostilities arise. Divinities and royalty are not given to compromise—even today—and more often than not war is the answer (Jaynes 1990, 207). Add to this that the second millennium BCE was subject to geological catastrophes (earthquakes, volcanic eruptions, tsunamis; Jaynes 2006a, 91), displacing entire populations and creating masses of refugees, and the disintegration of the bicameral world becomes obvious.

Discriminating consciousness—"the capability of the brain to become aware of the world" (Tulving and Lepage 2000, 215)—is thus not a biological given but an acquired faculty, the result of a long and complex evolution well into historical times. It has several important characteristics. For one, it thinks in particular spaces, not only on the outside but also internally, creating a subjective mind-space within. We see ourselves as "containing" certain tendencies, feelings, or thought; and we see time along a spatial axis—horizontal (West), vertical (Far East), or directional (Australia) (Boroditsky 2009, 123). For another, the conscious mind excerpts and reduces; paying attention to specific features deemed relevant, it does not see things in their entirety (Jaynes 1990, 61). How and what we focus on depends largely on our feelings about the matter, emotions impacting greatly on cognition (Frijda and Mesquita 2000, 45).

Beyond this, the conscious mind works with an "analog" sense of self, a virtual avatar of who we are, through which we can imagine ourselves doing certain things, then make decisions on the basis of this imagination. This closely connects to a metaphorical self, a created image of "me" that serves both as a point from which to look at the world and as an autoscopic image of who we are. This image, moreover, is upheld and defined by narrative, or rather a continuous process of narratization, the creation of an ongoing story of who, what, why, and wherefore we are. Consciousness means explanation, providing images and giving rationales to events, actions, and feelings. It also means conciliation or assimilation, the ongoing adaptation of experiences into our self-image and repertoire of responses (Jaynes 1990, 62-65).

Childhood Development

While humanity as a whole went from immediate, instinctual reaction to distinguishing conscious awareness over millions of years, each individual human being undergoes a similar development from conception through childhood (Bergounioux 1961, 110-11; see also Whitehead 2014). Already Wilhelm Reich suggested that "our cultural history is encoded in our bodies," leading to what Michael Balint (1968) called "the basic fault," a gap between wholeness and reality as well as a sense that there is something essentially wrong with us (Berman 1989, 23-24).

We all come into being as zygotes, single-cell organisms created through the merging of the sperm of the father and egg of the mother, and are fully at one with our mother's body for the ten months of pregnancy (Berman 1989, 34). The initial oneness is a state of complete symbiosis, variously called cosmic anonymity (Neumann 1976), infant-world unity (Goldstein 1957), primary wholeness, and so on (Berman 1989, 25). Pervasive while in utero, it may be disrupted even before birth or continue for some time after into the first few days or weeks of life (Verny 1981, 31). The argument is that we never entirely lose the impact of this wholeness and continue to search for it in some form or another. Mysticism and drug-taking, as well as meditations, yogic exercises, and various forms of hypnosis or rebirthing, then, are ways to recover, at least for short periods, the integrated oneness of prenatal bliss (Berman 1989, 25).

While the embryo has distinct experiences of what goes on beyond the womb and participates in the stress and tension of his mother, kicking and squirming in reaction (Berman 1989, 26), it remains unconscious and undifferentiated, just as primitive man would react to environmental factors and dangers with instinctual immediacy. For the child, this oneness clearly ends at birth, which may lead gently to a phase of object recognition without distinction or, more traumatically, to a radical separation from mother and wholeness, a catapulting into a bright, cold, and harsh world.

There is a distinct difference in birthing practices and the treatment of infants in traditional versus modern Western cultures. "The 20th-century hospital practice of industrial societies is the most barbaric: the fact of separation is seared into the infant body in a way that it will never forget" (Berman 1989, 27). In contrast to this, traditional societies kept the lights low, the distance minimal, and the infant close to the mother—not just for a few weeks but often for years together. Even today, children in cultures that emphasize close physical contact or "exterogestation"—touch itself being the crucial element in maintaining childhood wholeness, so that infants literally die if they are not held (Montagu 1986, 57)—tend to be better integrated, more at ease with themselves, calmer, and altogether more wholesome than those in others. They have a rich sense of self where we only have an abyss (Liedloff 1986, 72). The most prominent recent documentation of the disastrous consequences of a lack of touch comes from the orphans of Romania, who lived in dreadful conditions—separate, isolated, and untouched—until adopted into various other countries, yet never quite able to attain even the fragmented level of self common in the West (www.livescience.com/21778-early-neglect-alters-kids-brains.html).

Ideally, then, while birth is the end of wholeness, "the most fundamental discontinuity of our lives" (Berman 1989, 27), it is not the beginning of radical separation. Rather, it leads to a period where the infant perceives objects but makes no distinctions among them or between them and itself. The world is nothing but a blur of confusing sensual impressions of varying kind and intensity. Using their bodies as templates to understand the world, children primarily experience life as based on the senses, expressing themselves in simple physical needs or desires (Deikman 1982, 56; Tomasello 1999, 56).

Activating mirror neurons in the brain, which humans have in common with monkeys and primates (Keysers 2011, 13; Iacoboni 2008, 136), children see, hear, feel, smell, and taste the world around them, making facial and physical gestures in return (Hood 2012, 39; Greenspan and Shanker 2004, 88, 273). They react instinctually and mirror all they experience, copying and imitating blindly without deeper understanding or goal appreciation as early as forty minutes after birth (Champoux 2009, 84; Iacoboni 2008, 46; Joordens 2011, 47). For infants, as "there is perfect agreement between mind and world, there is no need and no place for a separate concept of mind, or of belief, true or false, beyond the observed states of the real world in the present" (Nelson 2000, 260). Children at this point are open to all experiences and largely unconscious: they cannot recognize themselves in a mirror (Iacoboni 2008, 140; Rothbart 2011, 120). However, they can form memories and learn new things—as many as a new word every two hours (Walter 2006, 100)—creating neurological pathways of understanding and shaping the patterned activation of neurons across networks (Hood 2012, 78).

Gradually, around the third year of life, there is "the definitive emergence of ego-consciousness," the growing awareness of boundaries and a clear distinction of self and others (Pagel 2012, 42). At this point, "the child begins to work out consciously what was imprinted on its tiny body at an earlier time: that it is a separate self" (Berman 1989, 28; Pagel 2012, 5). Language capability increases to the point where children become elementary conversational partners and often have imaginary playmates—quite possibly hearing voices in their heads in an activation of the bicameral phase. By age four, the transition to full narrative occurs (Nelson 2000, 270), and memories are increasingly processed by the hippocampus in more complex and abstract ways to "become part of the self story that we all rehearse and recall" (Hood 2012, 78, 228).

Thus, the self emerges as a coherent, personal narrative, continuously evolving and constructed by memory (Eakin 2000, 293; Sacks 1985, 105; Rothbart 2011, 120). Its main purpose is to make sense of reality: in order to survive, human beings need to create meaning in themselves and their environment (Freeman 1993, 16), which is then acted out in the particular drama of life. "Metaphors govern everyday functioning" (Lakoff and Johnson 1980, 3); "stories guide action, and people construct identities by locating themselves in . . . emplotted stories" (Somers 1994, 613).

After about age six, brain wave patterns shift from theta (4-8 Hz), indicative of a deeply calm yet aware state common in deep meditation and hypnosis, to alpha (8-12 Hz), the prime brainwave level in basic meditation and increased conscious awareness (Beauregard 2012, 79). Gradually the prefrontal cortex takes over and the sense of 'I' stabilizes, usually around age eight (Berman 1989, 35), with the ability to see the body in its entirety as an object in itself (Deikman 1982, 68). Crossing the "catastrophe point into existential awareness," one realizes that we are "an other for other others" (Berman 1989, 33, 36). At this point children have theory of mind. A critical difference between animals and humans, it implies that we have a certain level of awareness about the contents of our minds. Usage of words like believe, know, suppose, intend, want, desire, or wish indicate its activation, reaching second-order intentionality (2007, 41).

At this point, the body, too, becomes just one more object to receive stimuli from and direct wishes toward. Children evaluate it (and through it, the world) in terms of big and small, good and bad, right and wrong (Berman 1989, 37). They begin to make so-called rational decisions as determined by the higher cortical functions rather than intuitive ones as initiated by instinctual reactions or subcortical connections.

Consciousness of the object self can be divided according to three distinct functions: thinking, feeling, and acting. The thinking self contains one's conception of who and what one is. It is a "me" defined by society and culture, it includes all the characteristics one attributes to oneself: tall, ugly, strong, shy, and so on. Thinking is bound by relativity and the dependence of opposites. It is based on measurements and comparisons, on the establishment of categories and classifications (Deikman 1982, 92).

The feeling self contains the emotions: anger, fear, worry, sadness, joy, and so on. All these are reactions of feeling toward a given object or objective. They are intimately linked with desire. I am joyful because something I have desired has actually happened; I am anxious lest something I desire now will not develop; and I am sad or angry because some object of my desire has passed away. The feeling self is the self of desire; it classifies the world according to whether it is desirable or undesirable at any given moment and reacts with feelings and emotions accordingly (1982, 93).

The acting or functional self contains all that we do. It is an awareness of oneself as an acting individual. I know that I do; I realize the capacity I have to act in the world. I feel my body as an instrument of outer activity; I direct my feet and hands, my facial muscles, as well as my vocal chords in a particular direction, producing a particular effect. The acting self manipulates the world around it. It pulls objects and objectives toward it or pushes them away (1982, 94). These three taken together constitute the object self—the manifestation of separate consciousness functioning in the world, the point furthest removed from the initial oneness and wholeness during gestation. It works through the distinct conception of world and self as objects to be evaluated, classified, and manipulated—eternally worked on yet never satisfying since they remain forever split off and separate.

Chapter Four

The Flowing Mind

Senses, Emotions, and Neuroscience

The main factor that causes this split according to Daoism is the mind (*xin* 心), a term that has two meanings. It refers to the various aspects of consciousness and mental activity in general and to the internal force responsible for our evaluation of the world in terms of "right and wrong" specifically. Since according to traditional Chinese understanding all is *qi*, the mind too forms part of universal flow. Deeply anchored in the cosmos, it is a manifestation of spirit (*shen* 神), the primordial, formless, and ever-changing force of life. Firmly rooted in the body, it is a subtle energetic force that vibrates at a faster speed than physical matter.

Mind as spirit is pure *qi* as it flows through the heart, a form of conscious awareness that aids the overall functioning of life. Mind as body energy tends to disintegrate into opinionated and limited thinking due to its involvement with senses and emotions, leading to the emergence of separate discriminating consciousness. Forever partaking of both, spirit and discrimination, mind resides dominantly in the inner organ of the heart, also called *xin*, where it manifests in different, often conflicting aspects of consciousness. One is evaluative and critical, essential for day-to-day survival in the ordinary world, while the other flows smoothly and remains open to all stimuli, the manifestation of Dao within (Enzinger 2002, 96; Jochim 1998, 50). The cosmological structure, moreover, that defines the mind in these different dimensions is the system of the five phases.

The Five Phases

The five phases (*wuxing* 五行), sometimes also called "five elements," because they have a superficial similarity with the Greek or Indian elements—water, fire, earth, and air—are symbolic designations of five minor and major stages in the dynamic interaction of the two fundamental cosmic forces of yin and yang (Johnson 2014a, 164).

minor yang	major yang	yin-yang	minor yin	major yin
wood	fire	earth	metal	water

Historically, the five phases underwent several stages of development. The ancient *Shangshu* has them as the "five materials" (*wucai* 五才), concrete substances or resources used for basic human livelihood. They are, at this stage, not *qi* at all—*qi* is found in sunshine, shade, moonlight, vapors, and other atmospheric conditions—but substances that people actually use. As such, they should be treated with care and used with moderation and wisdom. They are offered to the gods on the altars of soil and grain, and they have to be guarded by rulers to ensure their continued productivity without excess or deficiency.

In their natural rhythm, the five materials produce each other continuously in a harmonious cycle. Thus, water comes about through rainfall. It makes things grow, so that there is lush vegetation and wood arises. Wood dries and becomes fuel for fire, which burns and creates ashes. Ashes become earth, and earth over long periods of consolidation grows metals in its depths. Metals in the depths of mountains, moreover, attract clouds and stimulate rainfall, thus closing the cycle (Kohn 2005, 23).

At the same time, however, the five materials also serve as a system of mutual control or checks and balances, keeping things in their proper order. Thus, water can extinguish fire, fire can melt metal, metal can cut wood, wood can contain earth, earth can dam water, and water can again extinguish fire. Here the inherently dynamic nature of the five materials is not used to increase productivity, but to set boundaries and limit potential excesses. In all cases, the early vision emphasizes that, although the five materials are substances for human use, they are not merely inanimate objects but contain dynamic powers that can be turned to production or control.

In a slightly more abstract manner, the five are further associated with certain qualities, processes, and psychological factors. Wood is linked with the qualities of bending and straightness, fire with flaming and rising, earth with planting and harvesting, metal with being formable and sharp, and water with wetting and sinking. These, in turn, are associated with five activities and five attitudes (Nylan 1992):

phase	activities	attitudes
wood	hearing	perceptive
fire	seeing	clear
earth	demeanor	respectful
metal	thinking	understanding
water	speaking	appropriate

This early association of the five materials with qualities of human psychology laid an important foundation for later developments. It represents the beginning of the mature system as it became central in Chinese culture. Expanding this early model of the five materials, the cosmologist Zou Yan 鄒衍 (4th c. BCE) created the concept of the "five powers" or "virtues" (*wude* 五德) by focusing on the potency inherent in the materials, such as the power of wood to grow and be lush and the power of fire to flare and rise. He then correlated these abstract powers with the political dynamics of succeeding dynasties, linking his own Zhou dynasty with fire, and predicted that it would be overcome by a newly arising ruler who would conquer it through the symbolic power of water—following the controlling cycle of the five materials (Graham 1986).

This system was picked up by later cosmologists who created a great, encompassing scheme of dynastic succession. It also led to extensive predictions and uprisings, during which revolutionaries dressed in colors associated with the rising phase and claimed that their time to rule had come. In addition, ruling dynasties subscribed to their associated "power" by dressing officials in its colors, using the multiples of its numbers as measuring systems, and generally aligning with it (Kohn 2005, 23-24).

Beyond the political sphere, the five powers of Zou Yan became the foundation of the five phases proper, a complex, integrated cosmological system that fully developed in the early Han dynasty around 200 BCE. At this time, the five energetic phases were associated not only with colors, but also with directions, seasons, musical tones, and more (Johnson 2014a, 76).

phase	dir	season	weather	color	animal	planet	metal
wood	east	spring	windy	green	dragon	Jupiter	iron
fire	south	summer	hot	red	phoenix	Mars	copper
earth	center		damp	yellow		Saturn	gold
metal	west	fall	dry	white	tiger	Venus	silver
water	north	winter	cold	black	turtle	Mercury	tin

Within the body, moreover, the five phases came to define the seat of *qi*, described in terms of energy storage organs (*zang* 臟), understood to be yin in nature, and processing viscera (*fu* 腑), defined as yang.

phase	yin organ	yang organ
wood	liver	gall bladder
fire	heart	small intestine
earth	spleen	stomach
metal	lungs	large intestine
water	kidneys	bladder

These organs, moreover, are energetically connected with other bodymind aspects, such as body parts, body fluids, and forms of *qi* (Kohn 2005, 47; 2012, 5)

organ	body parts	fluids	energies
liver	joints	tears	blood
heart	vessels	sweat	defensive *qi*
spleen	muscles	mucus	pulse
lungs	skin	nasal	protective *qi*
kidneys	bones	saliva	essence

Each inner organ matches a particular body part, fluid, and form of *qi*, reflecting the vision of world and body as an intricate network of energy patterns. Each of these dimensions, moreover, continuously transform and mutate into one another, following the basic cycle of the five phases as they move along the directions with the rising and setting of the sun throughout the day and along the seasons with the rising and falling of temperatures throughout the year. The mind, too, is part of this intricate system, flowing along the body and the world as waves of the various energetic aspects move about (Ishida 1989, 53). Mind in the Chinese sense, then, is an integrated network of consciousness that flows in harmonious balance and serves everyone well. How, then, does it turn into the limiting factor of discriminating consciousness?

The Senses

Another major dimension of the five organs is their connection to the five senses and their orifices: liver—eyes and vision, heart—skin and touch, spleen—mouth and taste, lungs—nose and smell, plus kidneys—ears and hearing. They are essential for human functioning, but easily get out of balance and entice people to indulge and become greedy. Already the *Daode jing* points out the dangers of engaging in sensory pleasures. It says:

> The five colors make the eyes go blind.
> The five sounds make the ears go deaf.
> The five flavors make the palate be spoiled.
> Racing and hunting make the mind go mad. (ch. 12)

The *Zhuangzi*, too, warns against the senses, emphasizing that any gratification or good feeling that depends on sensory satisfaction inevitably has serious drawbacks.

> People's greatest suffering occurs when their bodies cannot get comfortable, their mouths cannot feed on rich tastes, their physical form cannot fit into beautiful clothes, their eyes cannot look upon lovely colors, and their ears do not have a chance to listen to great music. When they do not get these things, they are deeply frustrated and develop tremendous anxiety. (ch. 18; Kohn 2011, 3)

As long as people depend on sensory satisfaction for personal happiness, it will elude them. The *Zhuangzi* continues: "When people are born, whatever they do, frustration is born along with them" (ch. 18), always subject to the vicious cycle of sensory strife and frustration, labor and dissatisfaction.

He admits that, if one has a beautiful, healthy body, vigor, and style, and manages to satisfy his physical needs and sensory demands to the fullest, there is a certain degree of happiness. However, not only do the senses continue to demand more and more, but if we enhance and show off our attributes, "they bring nothing but trouble" because they create immense social pressure to perform as well as jealousy and envy in our surroundings (ch. 32).

Another major drawback of sensory satisfaction is that any procurement of property, beauty, and social status requires hard work and continued sacrifices. "To attain wealth, people submit to great suffering and make themselves sick, . . . to attain position, people slave day and night without stopping" (ch. 18). The goods they acquire to satisfy their senses, moreover, turn into a great problem, since they overwhelm the senses, tie up mind and thinking, and take them ever farther away from inner peace, leading to "confusion, suffering, sickness, addiction, trouble, and fear: the greatest evils in the world" (Kohn 2014, 12-13).

> Look at the wealthy: their ears are overwhelmed by the sounds of pipes and drums, winds and strings; their mouths are filled with meat and wine. These rouse their intention for more of the same so they completely forget their real position in the greater [cosmic] scheme of things: this is confusion. . . .
>
> More stuff piled up than they could ever use, grasping for more than they could ever hold, their mind is full of care and close to exhaustion, yet they still keep going after projects and things, not knowing when to stop—this is trouble.
>
> At home suspicious of theft by deceitful servants, in town terrified of attacks by robbers and con-artists, they surround themselves with alarm systems in their houses and dare not walk around by themselves outside—this is fear. (ch. 29; W 338; Kohn 2011, 11)

Later Daoists agree with this assessment and speak of the senses as "robbers" and associate them with five sins of the flesh: sensuality, gossiping, gluttony, greed, and lust. An example appears in the *Shengxuan jing* 昇玄經 (Scripture of Ascension to the Mystery), an early Tang text recovered from Dunhuang. It records the Heavenly Worthy admonishing adepts to gain full control of their senses: harmonize *qi* and inner nature, move away from the ordinary, cut off pleasures and sensuality, and act fully in accordance with Dao (3b; Yamada 1992, 15). They must fully realize that "sensuality and passions are destructive forces" and follow a set of five rules of sensory control:

> 1. If you see sensuous colors woven in enticing patterns and variegated images—use my precept and cover your eyes.
> 2. If you hear words of good and evil or any of the five sounds—use my precept and block your ears.
> 3. If you are tempted by the delicacies of the eight marvels, or by the delights of the five fragrances—use my precept and stop your mouth.
> 4. If you find yourself imagining wealth and riches, the wondrous jewels of the seven treasures, and are drawn into emotions and at the extreme of desires—use my precept and dampen your heart.
> 5. If you hanker after lasciviousness and lust, coveting the pursuit of evil affairs—use my precept and cut off your intention. (36b; Yamada 1992, 21-22; Kohn 2004a, 39)

One major factor, therefore, that leads people away from the pure flow of the mind as cosmic spirit is found in the senses, with their tendency to overwhelm people through feelings of pleasure and displeasure, approval and disapproval, as well as liking and disliking.

Feelings and Emotions

Sensory input in this different forms, moreover, is called *qing* 情, a word that "has a broad semantic range, including such meanings as basic tendencies, inclination, disposition, and fundamental qualities" (Puett 2004, 42; Harbsmeier 2004, 71). The most common translation of *qing* is "feelings" or "emotions" (Tang 2003, 272). A. C. Graham sees it as "what is essential" in the Aristotelian sense (1981, 62; Puett 2004, 37), while Kim-Chong Chong prefers to read it as "facts," indicating the reality of life as it flows through the person (2010, 23; Harbsmeier 2004, 78). Michael Puett renders it as "basic emotional dispositions" (2004, 42) and Chad Hansen understands it as "reality feedback" (1992, 276) or, more precisely, "reality-induced discrimination or distinction-making reactions" (1995, 196). He says,

> *Qing* just crop up; we must deal with them. They come like the alternation of day and night; we just do not know where they come from. And it does not matter where they come from. They shape our lives. Without them, we would have no notion of 'I' (as distinct from the reality outside us). (1992, 277)

The *Zhuangzi* clearly associates *qing* with likes and dislikes (*haowu* 好惡; chs. 5, 31), and specifically indicates "joy, anger, grief, delight, worry, regret, fickleness, inflexibility, modesty, willfulness, candor, and insolence," describing these reactions as "music from empty holes," i.e., pure life energy flowing from heaven through the person (ch. 2; Watson 1968, 37).

Later Daoists follow Chinese medical literature and place the emotions in close relation to the body's organs, matching the system of the five phases. As the *Huangdi neijing suwen* says, "When the *qi* of the liver is too empty, there is fear; when it is too full, there is anger. . . . When the *qi* of the heart is too empty, there is sorrow; when it is too full, there is excessive joy" (ch. 3). The classic system associates anger or aggression with the liver, euphoria or excessive joy with the heart, care and worry with the spleen, sadness and grief with the lungs, and fear and anxiety with the kidneys. Medicine sees the emotions as closely related to the *qi*-body: they can serve either as diagnostic *qi*-flow symptoms or as a way to better health, but are always central in regulating body movements, food intake, breathing, and mental clarity. Perception, respiration, excretion, and all the various physical and psychological functions relating to the body's orifices, are governed by the mental functions, psychological forces, and emotions, as they reside in the five organs and appear in different forms.

In all cases, the emotions signify a flow of life energy in excess—fear is caution gone haywire, anger is enthusiasm turned into impatience and aggression. They lead to a depletion of *qi* in their respective organs, creating energetic disharmony, which in turn increases the intensity of the emotion. Then the emotion may turn on itself and multiply. For example, reacting to fear with fear, a person may become paranoid, sly, and secretive, lying to others and only intent on self-interest. Similarly, someone full of anger may feel upset at being so aggressive and become deeply resentful of himself and others, seething inside while trying to manipulate people around him.

The negative patterns, moreover, are not limited to one emotion or organ. Once one part of the system is affected, the disharmony spills over to the next through the cycle of the five phases, and negative feelings are compounded. Thus, fear and anger (kidneys and liver) are connected, and so are sadness and hatred (lungs and heart). Originating in response to sensory experiences in the organs, the emotions combine various mental and affective functions to convey sensory information that is already colored, presenting "distinction-making reactions" and leading to a particular attitude of the mind—what the Tang master Sun Simiao describes as the "normal mind."

The presence of emotional reactions, moreover, is personality building, leading to a sense of self described as *shen* 身, the lived, relational body, i.e., the sum total of one's inner life and learned conduct manifest in physical presence and visible to others (Jochim 1998, 47; Jullien 2007, 67). Determined by decision making, reflection, and set behavior, it represents the familial and social personhood of the individual (Sommer 2010, 215-16). *Shen* is the way we shape ourselves as embodied persons; while deeply rooted in nature, it is yet artificial and contrived. The *Daode jing* says that this personal body is "the reason why I have great afflictions" (ch. 13), referring to apprehensions about winning or losing, being in favor or disgrace. In other words, the personal body is the self-image the mind creates on the basis of emotional dispositions, which in turn provide reactions to sensory data activated as we experience life. These emotional dispositions, then, take on a life of their own and, in a continuous feedback loop with the mind, create personality boundaries and a stereotyped vision of life that gets more rigid over time.

Temperament

Not all aspects of emotional patterning and identity are learned. Rather, people are born with a certain constitutional type, documented in ancient China in physiognomic texts, i.e., materials on fortune-telling with the help of body shapes and facial complexion. In the West, this system was especially developed in the French school of acupuncture, and described by Yves Réquéna (1989). According to him, each of the five phases corresponds to one constitution, including a particular body shape, which is vulnerable primarily in one specific organ and shows typical childhood symptoms, adult illnesses, and likes and dislikes.

For example, a person of the wood constitution has wide shoulders and good muscles, a greenish complexion, large eyes, wide eyebrows, and well-proportioned limbs. He or she has a natural weakness in the liver and gallbladder, tends toward allergies and nervousness as a child, and shows skin and digestive problems as an adult. A person of the fire constitution similarly has a slender body, reddish complexion, and long, slender hands. He or she has a leaning toward trouble in the heart or small intestine, is prone to psychological instability both as a child and as an adult, dreads the summer heat, but enjoys bitter flavors.

Expanding this system, acupuncturists Jason Elias and Katherine Ketcham created a model where not only physical but also psychological personality patterns are matched with the five phases. According to them, the wood person is commanding and organized; the fire person is vibrant, loving, and full of enthusiasm; the earth person is centered, giving, and a born peacemaker; the metal person is straightforward, mystical, and artistic; and the water person is visionary, thoughtful, and philosophical. In each case, the dominant pattern can appear in excess or deficiency, leading to overly controlling, restless, or dependent forms of behavior. There are certain diets, supplements, exercises, and meditations for each type that will help restore balance (Elias and Ketcham 1998).

Yet a different take on this understanding of the five phases, which also includes the theories of British acupuncturist J. R. Worsley, is presented by Lonny Jarrett. He identifies certain attitudes in life and basic problems that people have to face in order to determine their key area of healing and fulfillment of destiny. He says:

> In general, the foundation of all spiritual development is to first set the will on wanting freedom more than anything else. Once the will is set in this way, our choices in life are clarified. In this regard we should help the patient make a connection between what he complains about (his symptoms) and his dysfunctional beliefs, thoughts, and behaviors. In short, it is important to educate the patient regarding everything else he is choosing other than health. (2003, 63; see also Jarrett 2000; 2006)

For example, in classical Chinese cosmology, the phase water is associated with the kidneys and the bladder. Emotionally it is linked with fear, its main psychological agent is the will, and its key virtue is wisdom. People of this type, then, respond to fear by overusing their wills, which depletes their resources and particularly their essence. This in turn leads to weakness in the bones and the nervous system, which encourages more fear. They vacillate between conformity—the need to go along with the demands of society and to work within the limitations of their physical ability and social position—and their ideal vision of themselves, moving between phases of extreme anxiety and recklessness, between overcoming and denying their fear.

Similarly, fire people with their heart-based constitution face a strong conflict between chaos (a loose heart) and control (a tight heart), the pursuit of pleasure and extreme measures to avoid sorrow. People dominated by wood face issues of belligerence versus timidity, situations where they can move forward aggressively versus times when they hardly dare to set foot out of their house, which leads to times of excessive planning and strong forward pushes versus periods of stagnation and a sense of frustration.

People of dominantly metal constitution face a strong tension between grief for things past and longing for the future. They do not know when to let go and when to hang on, when to move ahead and when to stay put. Earth people, finally, tend to struggle with issues of service versus selfishness, personal needs versus being needed by others (Kohn 2005, 27-29; Johnson 2014a, 170-79). In all cases, resolution of the conflict involves a strengthening of the appropriate virtue and a greater balance of forces, unlike the typical tendency to get mired in emotions and become more and more rigid over time.

The Thinking Mind

This increasing rigidity, moreover, depends to a large extent on the thinking mind, the internal force responsible for our evaluation of the world in terms of "right and wrong." The seat of various cognitive functions (Chong 2011, 428; Wang 2014, 189)—thought (*si* 思), knowledge (*zhi* 知), recall (*nian* 念), will (*zhi* 志), and intention (*yi* 意)—it is a structuring force within the person that can be open and fluid or regulating and tight, working with preference and aversion, approval and disapproval (Fraser 2011, 104).

In Chinese medical understanding, will and intention function in close relation to the kidneys and spleen, representing specific aspects of the mind: the general power of planning in the will and the more focused focus on a specific objective in the intention. They emerge from pure spirit associated with the heart and receive direction from two overarching mind dimensions essential for survival. The three spirit souls (*hun* 魂) are yang in nature, connect to the liver, and guide people toward cultural, intellectual, artistic, and spiritual endeavors. The seven material souls (*po* 魄) are yin in quality, connect to the lungs, and manage people's instinctual reflexes, making sure the organism receives enough food, water, sleep, and the like.

The thinking mind, then, is the result of the constant dynamic interaction of all these dimensions. It is the chief of the inner organs and functions of the body. As the ancient *Guanzi* 管子 (Book of Master Guan) says in its chapter "Xinshu" 心術 (Arts of the Mind),

> In the body, the mind holds the position of the ruler. The functions of the nine orifices correspond to the separate responsibilities of officials. The ears and eyes are the organs for seeing and hearing. If the mind does not interfere with the activities of seeing and hearing, the organs can maintain their separate functions.
>
> But if the mind is full of desires, the eyes will not see when things pass by nor will the ears hear when there are sounds. Therefore, it is said, "If the person on high departs from Dao, those below will be lax in their work." Therefore, it is said, "The art of the mind lies in controlling the orifices in nonaction." (Rickett 1998, 75; Moeller 2004, 74)

The mind interacts with the senses and emotions like the prime minister managing the officials (*guan* 官) in a ranked administration. The more it leaves them to do their thing, the better they work. However, when it gets into micromanagement or superimposes its particular tendencies or preferences, i.e., socially determined, induced desires (*yu* 欲) (Kupperman 1996, 190-91; Puett 2004, 39), the senses will stop functioning fully and only report pertinent information. "Imposing overnice forms" on the body's functions that are as extraneous as a sixth finger or webbed toes (*Zhuangzi* 8), the mind comes to predispose sensory data, limiting perception of reality in favor of preconditioned responses, and leading to a state Zhuangzi describes as the "fixed mind," "prejudiced mind," or "constructed self" (*chengxin* 成心). As Chad Hansen says,

> *Cheng* (success, completion) is just what wins given the prior commitments. However, these patterns get *cheng* (fixed) in the heart; they persist and accumulate. Discrimination patterns (language) are easy to learn in youth. When we grow old, our commitments to settled patterns begin to weigh us down. (1992, 276)

Being weighed down by settled patterns creates rote responses, inflexibility, and stereotypes. In terms of judgment, it means predictability and prejudices; in terms of personality, it means stiffness and set ways (Enzinger 2002, 136), notions fossilized into *idées fixe* that percolate in the mind without stopping and determine one's behavior (Diamond 1986, 2:160). The fixed mind is no longer free and easy, but covered by weeds and brambles (*youpeng* 有蓬; *Zhuangzi* 1; Chong 2011, 438). Or it becomes machine-centered, a "mechanical mind" (*jixin* 機心) that sees the world in terms of personal gain and loss and strives to impose its own preferences on life (ch. 12).

The source of all errors (Billeter 2010, 50), this kind of mind holds on tight to its set patterns and particularly to established norms, such as the classic Confucian values benevolence and righteousness, loyalty and filial piety. Rather than expressions of spontaneous goodwill and joyful relationships that change over time, they become restrictive, stifling corsets of mind and life (Sommer 2010, 215).

In terms of physical expression, this state matches the *gong* 躬 body: the ritual, sanctimonious body that occurs mainly in Confucian literature. "The *gong* body is that aspect of the human body or person most closely associated with the ritualized performance and public, visual display of character, conduct, and values" (Sommer 2008; 2010, 213). Written with the combination of "body" and "bend," *gong* graphically illustrates the ritual action of bending at the waist and bowing in formal ceremony. Reflecting the fixed mind within and linked with ritual life, it provides an outward presentation of the person on ceremonial display, controlled and constrained, unyielding and inflexible (Kohn 2014, 58).

The *Zhuangzi* as much as later Daoists, not surprisingly, have only contempt and criticism for this kind of body and mind. "With likes and dislikes, sounds and colors you cripple what is on the inside; with leather caps and snipe-feathered bonnets, batons stuck in belts and sashes trailing, you cramp what is on the outside" (ch. 12; Watson 1968, 141). What is seen in Confucian sources as the "purveyor of ideal conduct is conceived here as exhibiting little more than artifice" (Sommer 2010, 215).

Overall, then, the Daoist mind is intimately linked to the body and social persona, each particular way of thinking and feeling not only arising from physical reality but also having a direct impact on it. The fundamental understanding is that the human bodymind forms an intricate part of the cosmos and is geared naturally to work just fine, responding with the right sensations and perceptions, instincts and intuitions. However, as sensory data are being processed in a variety of ways, certain set patterns emerge that eventually take over its entire functioning, until both body and mind are fixed and rigid, twisted and overgrown. How then, does this understanding of bodymind as undergoing an increasing process toward complexity and artificiality translate into modern science?

The Brain

Western science places the seat of all these forms of mind in the brain, an organ hidden in the vault of the skull and deeply encased in darkness and silence. 6½" long, 5½" wide, 3½" tall, it weighs approximately three pounds, i.e., makes up about 2 percent of body weight. Despite its small size, it uses a great deal of the body's resources, requiring a constant flow of oxygen and nutrients, carried by the equivalent of three soda cans of blood every minute, and using 21 percent of all glucose or body energy (Joordens 2011, 55-56; Segerstrom et al. 2011, 26).

The brain consists of a hundred billion cells or neurons (sacks of chemicals in a sea of chemicals) that come in different forms and are unconnected at birth.[1] Gradually they come to talk to each other electrically (impulses) and chemically (neurotransmitters) via threadlike fibers—dense and twiggy thickets called dendrites as well as long and sinuous transmission cables known as axoms.[2]

They also interact energetically through the intercellular matrix, the framework that holds each cell in space (Penrose 1994, 357). It consists of microtubules, i.e., filamentous intercellular structures that, like strings, exist in all living cells and are responsible for its internal movements; plus the cytoskeleton, i.e., a series of intercellular proteins that help cells with shape, support, and movement, as well as the stabilization of tissues.[3] Communication through the intercellular matrix occurs on the quantum level, i.e., works nonlocally and holographically through brain-wide entanglement (Woolf 2006, 85-87; Mershin 2006, 159; Zeh 2004, 110), and is accordingly vastly faster. While the 10^{11} neurons in the brain with 10^{4} synapses per neuron and 10^{3} switches per second work at a speed of 10^{18} operations per second, the 10^{7} microtubule-tubulin

[1] Gazzaniga 2011, 37-39; Harth 1993, 45; Joordens 2011, 47; Woolf 2006, 52.

[2] Ramachandran 2011, 14; Cooke 2009, 134; Frith 2007, 10-12, 93; see also Zeki 1993.

[3] Mershin et al. 2006, 97-100, 164; Priel et al. 2006, 299; Tuszynski and Woolf 2006, 58; Woolf 2006, 69.

dimers in each neuron with 10^{16} operations each run at 10^{27} operations per second. If, moreover, "each tubulin dimer functions as a qubit"—a quantum bit or unit of quantum information, i.e., a bit functioning in two or more states simultaneously (Deutsch 2004, 92)—"not as a classical bit processor, the computing power becomes unimaginable vast" (Tuszynski and Woolf 2006, 8-9). After all, 300 qubits make up the power of a standard computer today—a tiny fraction of what the brain is able to do.

Beyond the immediacy of nonlocal quantum communication, each neuron also has between one and ten thousand contacts or synapses, making for a total of a hundred trillion or even quadrillion connections for the electrical and chemical transmission of information. [4] Synapses can be in different states: on or off, that is actively functioning or not; as well as excitatory or inhibitory, i.e., transmitting and enhancing a given stimulus or preventing it from going any further. They form systematic networks that process information; joined in complex circuits, they build the brain architecture that makes us unique individuals (Ramachandran 2011, 14).

Sensory information that comes in along these highways is processed at different speeds by different neural architectures (Penfield 1975, 14). The brain always waits for the slowest information to arrive, then unifies this polysensory perception by combining all the data into an integrated pattern, continuously constructing an ongoing narrative about the outside world (Eagleman 2009, 155, 157, 165). The technical term for this is cognition. "Cognition is the ability of the brain and the nervous system to attend, identify, and act on complex stimuli" (Restak 2009, 19).

To do this most efficiently, the brain divides into two hemispheres, the right and the left, which control the left and right sides of the body, respectively. Matching the Daoist division into yin and yang (Ornstein 1980, 282), they specialize to a certain degree—the right being more sensory and integrative, the left more abstract and analytical (Gazzaniga 2011, 56-57). Thus, for example, the right parietal lobe manages our physical relationship to our bodies and the world, creating a mental model of spatial layout as well as an appropriate body image, while the left parietal lobe (the left angular gyrus) is in charge of abstractions, such as mathematical calculations, finding the right words, and thinking in metaphors (Ramachandran 2011, 20).

However, the two hemispheres also work closely together, connected by the corpus calossum and the anterior comissure, the large tracts in the middle of the brain that divides its two sides—having gotten smaller in the course of evolution as the brain as a whole got bigger (Pribram 1991, 207; Joordens 2011, 5; Gazzaniga 2011, 34-35). In addition, as numerous cases of various one-sided brain injuries have shown, the healthy side can pick up the tasks of the dam-

---

[4] Cooke 2009, 139; DeSalle and Tattersall 2012, 57-58; Iacoboni 2008, 9; Joordens 2011, 47; Keysers 2011, 140; Woolf 2006, 83.

aged parts, showing that our brains are highly flexible and have a great deal of plasticity, i.e., the ability to learn and unlearn set patterns.[5]

This flexibility, furthermore, has much to do with memory. While the brain with its trillions of connections is overall "pretty awful at storage and retrieval," being "hostage to history and chance" over three and a half billion years of evolution (DeSalle and Tattersall 2012, 5; Tipler 1994, 237), it still encodes and retains all our thinking and acting. To do so, it works with rather intricate and multilayered patterns that involve dual or even triple encoding via the "orchestrated interaction of several brain systems" (Joordens 2011, 5). Memory happens every time when past experience has an effect on present or future attitudes or actions; it is a vehicle that transports experience over time and creates systematic patters of being (2011, 6).

Not all events are processed or stored equally. Most minor impulses received from the senses lead to a direct reaction in the autonomic nervous system and are immediately forgotten (Gazzaniga 2011, 78). Stronger impulses make it into short-term memory, but this is limited to seven bits or items of information at a time, which means that weaker and less excitatory impulses are thrown out from the start. Unless repeated frequently and made part of an experience pattern, thereby becoming a set of encoded structures specifically linked to certain sensory stimuli, information in short-term memory is soon forgotten and does not become part of long-term memory. The latter is processed by the hippocampus, the agency that binds the appropriate coactivation of brain areas into coherent information loops.[6] Such loops, and the habits that come with them, take between three and thirty-six weeks to develop, the most common being about nine weeks (Joordens 2011, 41). Still, short-term memory is essential, because it serves to create specific patterns of memorization known as "chunking" (DeSalle and Tattersall 2012, 180; see also Panksepp 1998).

Chunking is characterized by "feature-binding," the gradual consolidation of initial encoding patterns, located largely in the medial-temporal structures of the brain, which in turn connect to strategic or executive functions in the prefrontal cortex (Eagleman 2009, 162; Johnson and Raye 2000, 52). Here, moreover, as neuroimaging shows, the left—and particularly the left parahippocampal gyrus—is responsible for storage, while the right—notably the right inferior parietal cortex—is in charge of retrieval.[7]

Encoding patterns change over time, being overlaid by new experiences or habituation, as well as by information repeated often enough. Since the brain can also process things it has never actually seen or heard, fantasy can become reality (Joordens 2011, 74; Dill 2009). In addition, memories can be intentional-

---

[5] Beauregard 2012, ch. 2; Newberg and Waldman 2009, 29; Ramachandran 2011, 37; Restak 2009, 20; Woolf 2006, 65.

[6] Joordens 2011, 57; Gould 2007, 263; Eichenbaum and Bodkin 2000, 182; Pekala and Cardeña 2000, 52.

[7] Gould 2007, 278; Nyberg and Cabeza 2000, 504; Tulving and Lepage 2000, 218.

ly cleansed—a feature particularly useful in cases of post-traumatic stress syndrome (PTDS) (Cooke 2009, 135)—or artificially designed, leading to the creation of "a sanitized internal life through selective memory-reconstruction technology" (2009, 141-42)—as depicted in the movie, *The Eternal Sunshine of the Spotless Mind.*

Memory comes in three major levels or types: muscle, episodic, and semantic, also known as procedural, or implicit (emotional, nondeclarative), and declarative.[8] This matches the organization of the triune brain in three major levels or sections, lower, middle, and upper. These are not only the result of its unfolding from older to newer dimensions through evolution, but they also grow in children in this order (Childre et al. 1999, 9). They include the reptilian, proto-mammalian, and neo-mammalian brains, located in the brainstem, the mid-brain, and the prefrontal cortex, respectively, representing the seat of instincts and reflexes, emotions and subconscious responses, as well as of higher consciousness, language, and decision-making (Gazzaniga 2011, 30).

Instincts and Reflexes

What Daoists would call the primordial level of mentation matches the instinctual and most integrative section, i.e., the lowest and oldest part of the brain. Located in the brainstem, the cerebellum, and next to the limbic system, it has been active since the first vertebrates crawled over the planet and is present among all creatures, allowing for the ancient understanding of organismic being. The seat of instinct and basic physical functioning, its nuclei relate to affective processing and generate autonomic output, thereby regulating the body's temperature, its vasculature, and the visceral organs (Wager et al. 2008, 250; Ford and Wortman 2013, 43). It is responsible for basic movement coordination, gait, and posture control as well as the urges that keep us fed and watered, satisfied and rested (Ramachandran 2011, 18). In addition, it manages the autonomic nervous system that controls the inner organs, the breathing apparatus, as well as all cycles of activity and rest (Burrow 1964; Ratey 2002, 160-63).

The midbrain, next, often called the limbic system after the Latin word *limbus* for "ring," includes the paleo-mammalian brain as well as the subcortical system (Murphy 1963; Ratey 2002, 163-64; Ford and Wortman 2013, 43). Some of its areas are essential for instinctual and reflex actions, notably the periaqueductal gray and the diencephalon. The periaqueductal gray receives input from numerous brain areas and coordinates coherent physiological and behavioral responses to threat, i.e., is in charge of the organism's defense mechanism (McCraty and Rees 2009, 530). It thus impacts related aspects of the autonomic

[8] Cooke 2009, 140; Corballis 2011, 112-13; Corballis and Suddendorf 2007, 19; Eichenbaum and Bodkin 2000, 196; Nyberg and Cabeza 2000, 502.

nervous system, such as blood pressure, blood flow, and analgesia (Wager et al. 2008, 250). The diencephalon consists of the hypothalamus and the thalamus. The hypothalamus governs the pituitary gland and manages the endocrine hormonal system; it is in charge of regulating motivated behavior and homeostatic processes, releasing cortisol under stress (2008, 251; Dienstbier and Zillig 2009, 538; Newberg et al. 2001, 43). The thalamus, on the other hand, consisting of thirty-plus nuclei and various loops, is a key "sensory relay station in the middle of the brain," combining and sending signals from the senses (Frith 2007, 24; Gazzaniga 2011, 76).

From all these areas the brain connects to the outside world with the help of electrical signals that enter and exit along superhighways of nerve bundles. Sensory information that comes in along these highways is processed at different speeds by different neural architectures (Penfield 1975, 14). From these, the brain continuously creates perception by constructing a story about the outside world, more or less conscious and more or less verbal, depending on the level of processing (Eagleman 2009, 155, 157). Perception, "the internal representation of the environment" (Pribram 1971, 211; see also Miller 1960), moreover, always works with the principle of relativity. "Everything we experience is a relative process. Every change in the environment registers as a change in neural activity, that is, as the relative change in the rate of impulses firing. Relativity calibrates all our senses," keeping our brain in a state of constant adaptation (Hood 2012, 171; see also Ariely 2008). This is why, for example, an alligator dozing in the sun will rise to instant alertness if something moves in its line of vision—a relative change occurred that immediately translates into neurons firing. The more frequently a certain reaction occurs, moreover, the faster the neuron response and the thicker the resulting dendrites. "Nerves that fire together wire together," as Donald Hebb put it,[9] creating pathways of instinctual reaction, emotional patterns, and conscious evaluation and classification, which ultimately determine personality and identity, potentially leading to rigidity and the "fixed mind."

The Sensory-Motor System

The senses are our "doors of perception" (Huxley 1954), forming the foundation of our individual being while yet deeply connected to nature. Closely linked to the body as physical reality, they establish our primary link between world and mind (Frith 2007, 21; Cameron 2002, 267). In essence, they are bodily receptors that obtain a given stimulus and "initiate a wave of excitation in associated sensory nerve fibers, which in turn convey specific impulses to the central nervous system, where they are interpreted as corresponding sensa-

[9] Joordens 2011, 61; Gazzaniga 2011, 13; Keysers 2011, 140; see also Hebb 1949.

tions" (Henshaw 2012, 6). These, then, transmit information to the brain, to which it responds by sending orders via motor neurons from the motor cortex in the precentral gyrus, basal ganglia, and cerebellum (Pribram 1971, 238) to the different parts of the body, passing through nerves and neuromuscular synapses. This eventually reaches the various muscles, leading to appropriate action (Gardner 1968, 144-46; Gallistel and King 2009; Newberg et al. 2001, 24).

In other words, perception—the experience resulting from sensory activation, as opposed to sensation, the activation of sensory receptors (Cameron 2002, 107)—only happens once impulses reach the brain (Gardner 1968, 175; Gazzaniga 2011, 23). Generally, moreover, we can say that "sensory neurons move from body to brain while motor neurons move from brain to body" (Frith 2007, 61; Dehaene 2014, 139). As pathways grow, muscle memory arises. It is nonintentional and manifests in smooth motor movements, acquired through systematic practice, extensive repetition, and careful training that coordinates muscle actions in set sequences, leading through habituation and automatization to proficiency and performative excellence. Obvious, popular examples include riding a bike or driving a car, but the system is also responsible for language acquisition, which requires learning how to use the vocal muscles in just this and no other way (Joordens 2011, 6; Gazzaniga 2011, 78).

Shared by all mammals, the sensory-motor world of perception and muscle memory works through three distinct venues: (1) general senses, i.e., sensations aroused by stimuli action on or within the body, notably touch (exteroception), pain and temperature (interoception), and self-awareness (proprioception); (2) special senses, transmitting data from a distance from the body (teleceptive) via the standard senses of vision, hearing, smell, taste, and balance (Gardner 1968, 174; 190; Henshaw 2012, 6; Cameron 2002, 106); and (3) exceptional sensory abilities, know particularly from the animal kingdom. The latter include echolocation, a form of specialized hearing that allows orientation in space (bats); electroception, the ability to detect electrical fields (eels, sharks, rays); magnetoception, the faculty to sense magnetic fields (pigeons, sea turtles, bees, lobsters); the perception of infrared radiation, the power to see low-spectrum colors with a special organ such as the pit hole (snakes); the perception of ultraviolet radiation, the ability to see high-spectrum colors with multi-faceted eyes (bees); as well as the sensory power to evaluate the concentration of salt in the ocean via a long tusk, unique to the narwhal (Henshaw 2012, 9-12; see also Shettleworth 2010).

The four general senses work through the myelin sheath and fibers that control and carry various impulses as well as glands that secrete neuropeptides, leading to all sorts of sensations. Stimuli to the skin (exteroception) work through the spine, reaching three different levels. For one, they can remain instinctual, engaging immediate reflexes, fully automated and never reaching the brain. Second, they can link to synapses in the gray dorsal matter, unmyelinated neurons of the central nervous system, present throughout the spinal column as well as the brainstem and cerebral hemispheres, evoking subconscious reactions. Third, they travel via established axions to the higher level of the brain, crossing its midline via the anterior funiculi and head for the thalamus, where they are processed and, if severe enough, sent on to evaluation in the prefrontal cortex (Gardner 1968, 175). Information from the skin to the cerebral cortex travels quite fast, at 1 to 30 meters per second (1968, 177).

Both pain and temperature, i.e., interoception, which include common sensations such as hunger and thirst, heat and cold, work along very similar lines (Sacks 1985, 59; Pineda et al. 2009, 143), as does proprioception, the sense of our position in space (and time), our body image, and the strength of muscular effort, which we feel dominantly through pressure and vibration (Cameron 2002, 212, 218; Sacks 1985, 47). Following specific neural pathways, involving the spinaldorsal horn, the thalamocortical relay nucleus, and the posterior dorsal insula (Pineda et al. 2009, 144), their functions and effects are shared by all living organisms.

Transmitted via neuropeptides—hormones that also function as neurotransmitters such as insulin, angiotensin, bradykinin, enkephalin, and dynorphin (Panksepp 1998, 101)—along non- or thinly myelinated fibers whose cell bodies are in the spinal and cranial ganglia, they impact the autonomous nervous and endocrine systems while remaining largely below conscious awareness (Cameron 2002, 108-09; Gardner 1968, 180-83; Pineda et al. 2009,143). They are subject to delay, since it can take 0.35 to 0.50 seconds before a sensory event reaches the level of conscious perception (Cameron 2002, 265), forming the foundation of tactile or haptic memory (Joordens 2011, 17). The most important sources of interoception are the cardiovascular, respiratory, and gastrointestinal systems, whose activity rises to clear perception mainly in times of acute threat (e.g., butterflies in the stomach). Yet, we can also become more aware and learn to regulate them through biofeedback and other techniques of relaxation (Cameron 2002, 48-50, 91-100).

Special Senses

The five special senses, in contrast, extend strongly into conscious awareness. To begin, vision is the result of the complex interaction of light—charged particles combined with electromagnetic radiation (DeSalle and Tattersall 2012, 104; Harth 1993, 57)—cells, and brain functions, determined by a long evolutionary development. The human eye, specifically, evolved through twenty-five different kinds of eyes from that of sea creatures, which saw light first filtered through water. As a result, it cannot see the full spectrum. Rather, when we see sunlight, we only perceive 46 percent of it, the remainder being below and above our spectrum: 46 percent infrared and 8 percent ultraviolet (Henshaw 2012, 23). The human light spectrum overall is between 400 to 700 millimicrons (mn), which represents a considerably smaller frequency than that of sound—matching the equivalent of only one octave in a total of thirty-seven that the human ear can perceive.[10]

Light enters the human body through the corneal surfaces of the retina, then undergoes refraction that allows us to shape pictures at different distances, changing lens curvature through muscle fibers. The retina is already part of the brain, equipped with specialized nerve endings; its optical disk signals the end of the optic nerve, while its cells are arranged in layers and consist of rods and cones sensitive to radiation. The human eye has 115 to 130 million rods and cones as well as one million optic nerve fibers, allowing it to adapt to light and darkness as well as distinguish different colors, i.e., light waves of different length (Gardner 1968, 191-99; Henshaw 2012, 28). Humans and primates are trichromatic, unlike other mammals that see only in one color or can distinguish two at the most (Ramachandran 2011, 51; LaSalle and Tattersall 2012, 112).

Rather than in the eye, vision happens in the brain (http://glial.psych.wisc.edu/vision/research.php; McTaggart 2011, 150). The retina processes imprinted images by relaying them at twenty-millisecond bursts in so-called soccides or snapshots of parts. After passing through the optic chiasma to the left hemisphere (Barlow 1990, 11), they cause motion detection in the middle temporal area and color processing in the temporal lobe (Ramachandran 2011, 41, 60-63). Once they reach different parts of the cortex through complex synaptic connections, the brain fits them together like a mosaic, first analyzing the relation of the items within the image, then interpreting it within the greater world in a process known as "grouping" (Barlow 1990, 21). Thereby it creates the symbolic representations and classifications we take for reality (Ramachandran 2011, 62-64; Frith 2007, 23; Joordens 2011, 17). This process is most obvious in deceptive images, such as Necker's cube, the Ames room illusion, and the well-known images that could be either a vase or two faces, an old or a young woman (see below; Ramachandran 2011, 48; Frith 2007, 50, 133).

This means that visual as much as all sense perception involves drawing inferences from all the stimuli we acquire through sensation, i.e., the evidence of outside reality as transmitted through the senses and systematically first filtered and differentiated from the bottom up, then integrated from the top down (Henshaw 2012, 215). In other words, "the red of a STOP sign is something that exists only inside our brains," all so-called seeing being the result of neural connections (2012, 226). In addition, each eye has its own blind spot, necessitating perceptual completion and often leading to false perception (2012, 216). This means that sensory perception is never immediate or pure or even fully in the present moment, but always subject to subconscious editing: based on past experiences and established neural pathways, we either fill in or leave

[10] Henshaw 2012, 25; Gardner 1968, 191; DeSalle and Tattersall 2012, 105.

out information, as anybody who has ever done any proof reading will readily acknowledge (Gardner 1968, 332).

Typically, visual stimuli with their fast firing mechanism override those of the other senses—so that a person listening to the sound *ba* while watching someone lip-synch the sound *ga* will hear the latter, a pattern know as the McGurk effect.[11] This overarching power of vision also means that it occupies the largest area in the brain, the visual cortex containing ten times as many nerve cells as that used for hearing (Henshaw 2012, 191).

Hearing is the reception of air-conducted sound waves. First they hit the outer ear, which collects them and funnels them through the ear canal to the middle ear, composed of three bones. Firing approximately every four or five seconds, that is, considerably slower than visual action, they transmit the waves to the oval window in the inner ear. Receiving this mechanical energy, it responds by giving forth different vibrations, creating pressure waves in the fluid of the inner ear (DeSalle and Tattersall 2012, 115). This pressure, in turn, excites the membranes of the cochlea, a part of the inner ear shaped like the shell of snail. The tiny hair cells on its basilar membrane, next, transform the mechanical pressure waves into nerve impulses and transmit them to the brain, where they are decoded and interpreted as sound (Henshaw 2012, 49)—music and language ultilizing different neural pathways (Mithen 2006, 63). The rate of transmission is between 20 and 20,000 cycles per second, with the human ear

[11] Dehaene 2014, 62; Henshaw 2012, 236; Hickock 2014, 87; Iacoboni 2008, 102; Joordens 2011, 17.

being most sensitive around 2048 cycles (Gardner 1968, 208-12; http://mcdermottlab.mit.edu/research.html).

The kinesthetic sense of balance and equilibrium, too, centers in the ear. Receptors in the labyrinth, small membraneous tubes filled with a slightly viscous fluid, respond to all movement, especially of the head, through a pressure change in the epithelial layer at the end of the ear canal. Like water in a rotating glass, they continue to move even after the outside stimulus stops, creating a sense of presence in space (Gardner 1968, 215-16; DeSalle and Tattersall 2012, 115; Sacks 1985, 68).

The remaining two senses are taste and smell, both closely related to visceral function and thus impacting the general sense of interoception (Cameron 2002, 189). Taste, a form of contact chemoreception (DeSalle and Tattersall 2012, 118), occurs through specific buds in the mucous membrane of the mouth, stimulated by food substances as they dissolve in saliva. The membrane initiates impulses in nerve fibers on the tongue and larynx (Gardner 1968, 220), leading to the three dominant flavors of sweet, salty, and bitter (DeSalle and Tattersall 2012, 118). The sense of smell, the oldest of all of them, happens through about 350 chemoreceptors in the upper part of the nasal mucous membrane. It transmits incoming data to the olfactory bulbs in the brain, located in widely different areas and not just in one primary receptive section, allowing for the perception of as many as ten thousand different smells (Gardner 1968, 221-22; Henshaw 2012, 41).

Response Centers

In all cases, the brain is the main location of sensory perception. While certain responses to the taste and smell of food, such as salivation or choking, are unconditioned reflexes, the cerebral cortex also modifies them, resulting in conditioned responses, such as anticipatory salivation (Gardner 1968, 332). This means that sense perception, while working through our instinctual and reflexive systems, is a brain activity and as such culturally determined through learning, memory, and the establishment of set neural pathways.

The same also holds true for the next level of human functioning, reactions to sensory stimuli as determined by arousal, attention, motivation, and emotions—"underlying homeostatic mechanisms tuned by prior experience" (Pribram 1971, 198), over time leading to habituation and automatization, that is, identity formation as described in Daoism. To define these four, (1) arousal is the state of being excited or stirred to activity on the basis of sensory input, while (2) attention is the process of focusing on a single object or thought with the purpose of improving clarity (Cameron 2002, 30; Gross 2008, 503). (3) Motivation is the sense of being oriented toward a particular goal., the mechanism of extending or reducing the available repertoire of behavior, responding to a lack or excess of stimuli in the environment and accordingly leading to excitement and growth or boredom and stagnation (Pribram 1971, 212). After all, biological organisms are open systems, requiring a steady input of stimulation via energy and matter to maintain their activities (Scott 2006, 185). (4) Emotions, finally, are "affective, valenced, positive or negative reactions to meaningful stimuli directed at particular objects" (Larsen et al. 2008, 181).

In terms of brain architecture, the emotional centers are located in the midbrain, in core limbic structures that overlay the brainstem and the diencephalon. Essential for building our identity, they center most importantly on the amygdala (lit. "almond"), the early warning center of the brain, which alerts us to approaching danger (Eagleman 2009, 161). Critical for the evaluation of all sensory cues in terms of threat, it is particularly the seat of fear and defense.[12] It closely connects to the basal forebrain, which manages levels of anxiety and is in charge of the motivational modulation of attention, especially with regard to reward and pleasure (Wager et al. 2008, 252; Franks 2010, 45-46).

The amygdala is a small, almond shaped entity in the midbrain, above the brain stem and in front of the hippocampus. A complex structure consisting of a dozen nuclei and various subdivisions, "densely innervated by serotonergic neurons and abundant in serotonin receptors" (Hariri and Forbes 2007, 119), it is the key player "in the assignment of reward value to stimuli" (LeDoux and Phelps 2008, 160). It gives direction to affectively salient sensory events and issues a call for further processing of those of great significance for the individual, being overall "critical for recruiting and coordinating cortical arousal and vigilant attention" (Davidson, Fox, and Kalin 2007, 50). Especially the lateral amygdala is first site in the ascending sensory stream to have massive convergence of inputs (Quirk 2007, 29). It receives data from the senses via the thalamus, is activated particularly by potential dangers, raises the alarm, and sends information on to its central nucleus, which is the "origin of outputs to fear-generating structures in the hypothalamus and the brainstem."[13]

Thus, for example, a strong warning signal sent from here to the central gray area of the brain will result in freezing; fear information transmitted to the lateral hypothalamus leads to strong responses in the autonomic nervous system; and alarm picked up by the paraventricular hypothalamus initiates an endocrine or hormonal reaction, triggering the release of the classical stress hormones noradrenaline, norepinephrine, and cortisol in a molecular cascade.[14] While the lateral amygdala is thus the seat of fear memory, its central nucleus is the locus of fear expression (Quirk 2007, 30; Pribram 1991, 205). This becomes evident through pathologies. People with a malfunctioning amygdala may have

---

[12] Amodie and Lieberman 2009, 350; Devine and Sharp 2009, 78; Goleman 2011, 14, 30; Newberg et al. 2001, 44; Pineda et al. 2009, 147

[13] Quirk 2007, 29; Eichenbaum and Bodkin 2000, 196; Markowitsch 2000, 476.

[14] Dienstbier and Villig 2009, 538; Goleman 2011, 34; LeDoux and Phelps 2008, 162; Panksepp 1998, 107; Rothbart 2011, 70-71; Beversdorf 2013, 156.

Kluver-Bucy syndrome, the inability to feel disgust and fear (LeDoux and Phelps 2008, 160), the latter being particularly linked to damage to the lateral or central amygdala, while issues in its basal part tend to eliminate the escape reaction (2008, 165).

A functioning amygdala creates automatic subcortical responses that combine into what we commonly know as stress or "flight or fight" (see Lazarus 1966; 1991). While the inherent neuron activation is a hard-wired, natural defense reflex against danger that is essential for survival, exactly what stimulates it and to what degree is a learned response.[15] To about 40 to 70 percent, the excitability of the amygdala is genetic and "reflects a stable, heritable trait," making some people more prone to strong emotional reactions than others (Hariri and Forbes 2007, 111). However, this "does not in itself predict the development of affective disorders" or mean that the pattern cannot be alleviated and the emotional response controlled (2007, 123).

All emotions, but particulary fear—"the expectation based on familiarity of the situation that aversive stimulation will occur" (Pribram 1991, 205)—direct and constrain perception. As few as three to ten repetitions of a stimulus that creates a negative, painful, or unpleasant response will lead to familiarization and temporary stability, "characterized by an inner shape, the structure of redundancy, of a processing holoscope" (Pribram 1991, 217). Such conditioning creates a contour map in the brain that guides perception: in other words, if we are driving down a street while hungry, we tend to notice restaurant signs; if in need of gas for the car, gas stations (1991, 217). In the long run, this gives shape to our brain: the different configurations of values display different hills and valleys in the polarization contour map—making us more likely to react to specific stimuli in pre-set patterns (Pribram 1991, 218; Frith 2007, 96).

Stress, especially chronic stress increases the number and density of dendrites in the amygdala and thus its "ability to learn and express fear associations," while reducing the prefrontal cortex ability to control fear (Quirk 2007, 39). Increased amygdala activity thus potentiates the stress response and has "a deleterious effect on the medial prefrontal cortex, similar to lesions" (LeDoux and Phelps 2008, 165). It leads to a state of selective attention on stress factors, an interpretative bias that causes threats to appear where there are none, and a memory overload that wallows vividly in bad situations (Eysenck 2000, 175; Eichenbaum and Bodkin 2000, 181; see also Eysenck 1997). Influencing cortical areas, including centers of cognition, attention, and perception, it thus modulates the strength of memories, causing highly traumatic events to be played over and over again in the brain. It also tends to project information into the cognitive networks, increasing anticipation through the cholinergic system (LeDoux and Phelps 2008, 166). Increased avoidance continues and exacerbates the syndrome, since it deepens the neural pathways.

---

[15] Quirk 2007, 30; Goleman 2011, 21; Harman and Rheingold 1984, 95-95; Ochsner and Gross 2007, 103; Selye 1984.

This leads to a vicious cycle of increasing fear patterns and enhances a type of thinking that keeps people focused on perceived threats. "This type of thinking is self-centered, absolute, biased, black and white, dichotomous (win or lose; die or survive; right or wrong; good or bad; etc.), inflexible, mechanical, and automatic. . . It is called primal thinking" (Santee 2008, 99). Primal thinking, usually combined with shallow breathing and high adrenaline and cortisol levels, perpetuates stress, leading to a permanent state of hyper-vigilance, hyper-arousal, anger and anxiety. As the *Zhuangzi* describes it, "With everything people encounter, they become entangled; day after day, they use their minds in strife . . . sweating and laboring to the end of their days" (ch. 2; Watson 1968, 37, 38). They create an image of the world as difficult and threatening; rooted in their minds as real, this sets the limitations in which they navigate their lives (Kohn 2014, 34).

Another important structure in this area, located behind the amygdala, is the hippocampus (lit. "sea horse"), the seat of long-term memory formation. It coordinates contextual fear, perception, and the processing of emotional stimuli into set response patterns, thus making survival easier. It also works closely with the basal ganglia, in charge of planning and initiating relevant behavior, not only by computing the affective value of stimuli but also by managing the motor control necessary for appropriate responses (Newberg et al. 2001, 45). Also in this area are the stratium, the nucleus accumbens, and the globus pallidus—essential for our reward perception, motivation, and learning. This area is particularly rich in pleasure-inducing neurotransmitters, such as dopamine, acetylcholine, serotonin, and other endogenous opioids (Wager et al. 2008, 253; Frith 2007, 94).

The perception and reaction patterns established in this midbrain region make us who we are, determining our relation to the outside world. As DeSalle and Tattersall note, "All your joys and sorrows, your memories and ambitions, your sense of personal identity and free will are in fact no more than the behavior of a vast assembly of nerve cells and their associated molecules." What we call self is, thus, in fact merely "a critical mass of brain signals" (2012, 29). Or, as Weger puts it, "People experience conscious will when they interpret their own thought as the cause of their action—quite independently of any actual causal connection between their thoughts and their actions" (2002, 64).

Emotions

Emotions are "multicomponent response tendencies incorporating muscle tension, hormone release, cardiovascular changes, facial expressions, attention, cognition, and more."[16] Unlike moods, which are low-intensity, diffuse, enduring affective states, often without a salient object (Forgas 2000, 111; Clore and Gasper 2000, 11), they are short-lived "powerful waves of affects that can overwhelm the sense of self" (Panksepp 1998, 47). A "primordial form of consciousness," emotions arose in living organisms as a way "for the brain to represent biological survival values to the evolutionarily emergent cognitive deliberation," presenting "survival compass bearings for the cognitive apparatus" and "facilitating rapid decision-making and empathy plus group-sharing and cohesion" (Panksepp 2008, 59-60; DeSalle and Tattersall 2012, 177; Gross 2008, 498).

Emotions come in two major forms: withdrawal and approach, i.e., defensive and inviting or negative and positive—closely related to the presence (increase) or absence (withdrawal) of pleasure-giving opioids and stress-enhancing oxytocinergics (Panksepp 2008, 54-55) as well as a lower or higher activation of the autonomic nervous system (Larsen et al. 2008, 184-85). Matching the universal tendency to seek comfort and avoid discomfort (2008, 51), they are essentially validating reactions to three major "cognitive eliciting conditions," i.e., occurrence of events, actions of agents, and aspects of objects, under the impact of three "sources of value," i.e., goals, standards, and attitudes (Clore and Gasper 2000, 13, 27). They manifest in pleasure and displeasure, approval and disapproval, as well as liking and disliking, reflecting how "the individual imbues the situation with a certain kind of meaning."[17]

Possessing inherent cognitive structure, emotions form an essential part of the organic makeup of all living beings. Animals, and particularly mammals, as much as human beings are affective creatures. They all have specific brain regions that create emotions, notably in the medial subneocortical area plus higher medial limbic system, with structures that are homologous throughout the mammalian kingdom, so that fear, for example, manifests the same way in rats, cats, and primates. Their localized stimulations are comparable, their affective experiences congruent, and their forms of emotional arousal identical (Panksepp 2008, 49-50).

Neuroimaging through PET (positron emission tomography) and fMRI (functional magnetic resonance imaging) scans has provided solid evidence for the presence of seven basic emotional operating systems in the mammalian

---

[16] Fredrickson and Cohn 2008, 778; Cohn and Fredrickson 2009, 14; Elfenbein et al. 2002, 38.

[17] Gross 2008, 504; Fredrickson and Cohn 2008, 778; Clore and Gasper 2000, 15. See also Frijda 1986.

brain (Panksepp 2008, 54).[18] They consist first of three approach reactions, i.e., seeking (desire), lust (sexuality), and play (joy), which facilitate engagement with the environment, broaden people's momentary thought-action repertoires, and lead to actions that build enduring personal resources (Fredrickson and Cohn 2008, 779, 782). Next, there are three matching withdrawal reactions, i.e., the negative emotions of anger (rage), fear (anxiety), and panic (sadness), plus the variable attitude of caring (nurturing, worry) (Watson and Naragon 2009, 208). Altogether they roughly match the ancient Daoist understanding, where emotions form part of the comprehensive "desires and emotions" (*yuqing* 欲情). These include approach reactions such as seeking, greed, and lust as part of "desires" as well as the standard five key emotions, anger, fear, sadness, worry and excessive joy, i.e., euphoria or strong enthusiasm (see also DeSalle and Tattersall 2012, 176).

Seeking or desire in Western understanding, then, signifies a foundational, general-purpose, appetitive-motivational system, driven by mesolimbic dopamine and processed in the medial frontal cortex to result in directed mentation and energy. It manifests as interest, enthusiasm, exhilaration, euphoria, curiosity, exploration, and an overall openness to life and world (Panksepp 2011, 58).

Lust, second, includes all the sexual urges and reproductive system, whose arousal depends on various sex hormones and neuropeptides, such as vasopressin, testosterone, vasopressin, oxycotin, and estrogen. They run in distinct circuits and create biologically founded yet uniquely individual patterns of behavior (2011, 62; McCraty and Rees 2009, 531).

Play, third, including joy, smiles, and laughter, signifies the physical and social engagement system (Oatley 2000, 88). It helps predator avoidance, builds enduring social, enhances physical resources, increases levels of creativity, and fuels brain development. It also encourages novel thoughts and allows experimentation with new activities, enhancing resilience, social support, skills, and knowledge while reducing the impact of stress, pain, and disability (Fredrickson and Cohn 2008, 782-83). A fundamental way of acquiring social and survival skills and exploring intersubjective spaces, playfulness—a major positive factor in Daoism as already formulated in the *Zhuangzi* (Kohn 2014, 256-58)—is a major source of joy, empathy, imitation, and learning (Panksepp 2011, 64-65; 2008, 57).

The first among the major withdrawal reactions serves as a defense system (Lemerise and Dodge 2008, 730; Oatley 2000, 95). Anger with its correlates impatience, annoyance, irritation, frustration, resentment, fury, and rage is the opposite of seeking, a reaction geared to secure resources (Stein 2007, 128). Stimulating especially the medial amygdala and hypothalamus and activating the neuropeptides Substance P and glutamate, it invigorates aggressive behavior

---

[18] On the technology, see Devine and Sharp 2009, 79; Gould 2007, 262; Kaku 2008, 77; Tulving and Lepage 2000, 208.

and enhances mastery over the physical environment (Panksepp 2008, 60; Lemerise and Dodge 2008, 732). Part of a limbic system program that activates automatically, physiologically "it takes less than ninety seconds to be triggered, surge through our body, and be completely flushed out of our blood stream . . . If, however, I remain angry after those ninety seconds have passed, then it is because I have *chosen* to let that circuit continue to run" (Taylor 2006, 146). This choice, then, intensifies the circuitry and causes higher blood pressure, an increased heart rate, and more vascular activity (Larsen et al. 2008, 184), in the long run leading to chronic cardiovascular and other ailments (see Redford 1993).

The second negative emotion works for self-preservation (Parrott 2002, 154). Fear, the complement of lust, ranges from unease through disgust, anxiety, nervousness, fright, and scare to terror and even horror. It serves to reduce pain and the possibility of destruction (Oatley 2000, 99). Neurophysiologically centered in the amygdala, a low-level free-floating anxiety is accompanied by rapid eye shifts, tightened brows, body shivers, and changes in blood pressure (Larsen et al. 2008, 186). As stimulation increases, the organism freezes in fright, then runs away in terror. Key neurotransmitters include neuropeptide Y and corticotrophin releasing factor (CRF). A chronic state of fear arousal leads to neurosis and depression (Panksepp 2011, 61).

The third withdrawal reaction centers on social togetherness and signals being in need of care. The panic reaction finds major expression in sadness, bereavement, and grief, different degrees of the loss of social connection (Bonnanno et al. 2008, 798). Its correlates include gloom, misery, heartbreak, sorrow, melancholy, depression, and despair, all fundamentally signals of separation distress and thus the opposite of play. An inward-turning of attention, sadness is marked by drooping eyelids, lips, cheeks, and jaw as well as tightness in the chest and constricted breathing (Larsen et al. 2008, 184; Bonnanno et al. 2008, 799). Matching low brain opioid activity or withdrawal, it is inhibited especially by oxytocin and prolactin as well as other comfort-providing opioids released particularly through touch (Panksepp 2011, 63-64; 2008, 55).

Care, nurturance and social bonding, the seventh emotional operating system, manifests also in worry and concern. Particularly related to maternal devotion, it links to hormones at the end of pregnancy, but is generally both a rewarding and frustrating emotion that carries social and family ties, enhancing and supporting the social network, within which all the other emotions arise (2011, 63).

Personality

Emotions, then, are reaction patterns that increase chances of survival and success in three major areas of life: material supplies (object acquisition), physical integrity (reproduction), and social connection (interaction with others). Socially activated and influenced by community structures and beliefs (Clark and Brissette 2000, 212), they are shared easily and often contagious, partly through mirror neurons that enhance motor synchrony, partly through nonlocal energy activation (Iacoboni 2008, 110; see also Hatfield et al. 1994). Especially facial muscles are essential in the expression and transmission of emotions (see Ekman et al. 1972; Pineda et al. 2009, 148). Thus, people with Moebius syndrome or a high level of botox injections, who cannot move their facial muscles, are unable to communicate felt emotions or read those of others, failing to achieve any form of emotional interaction (Iacoboni 2008, 115).

While emotions are inborn tendencies, their particular shape and strength differ in each individual. The distinction is particularly clear in the context of fear, which is both an "innate, unconditioned, genetically based response" and also a learned form of avoidance behavior, part of "second-order conditioning of neuroanatomical circuits" (Cameron 2002, 48). While the former, best called "fright," is a gift, an early warning system of impending danger that often saves lives (see De Becker 1997), the latter is an acquired pattern of reactions to often imaginary scenarios or opponents, and thus form part of the stress response centered in the amygdala (Gazzaniga 2011, 97).

The degree, moreover, to which individuals are prone to activate one or the other emotional circuit constitutes their temperament, what ancient Daoists describe in terms of inner nature or inherent tendencies (*xing* 性), an essential component of one's personal identity (*shen* 身). Inner nature, like a genetic blueprint, defines our inborn, genetically determined uniqueness, expressed physically in our fingerprints, retina, hand lines, and all the various physical characteristics that make us who we are. Psychologically it is our predisposition toward certain preferences, behaviors, and skills, i.e., our temperament (Zhang 2002, 368; Kohn 2014, 102).

Temperament is a "set of hypothetical constructs describing individual differences in reactivity and self-regulation" (Bates et al. 2008, 486, 494; Rothbart 2011, 10). Already a common concept among the ancient Romans, it then divided into four major emotional types related to different body fluids: melancholic, i.e., given to fear and sadness (black bile); choleric, i.e., active and tending toward anger (yellow bile); sanguine, i.e., sociable and easy-going (blood); and phlegmatic, i.e., calm and even-tempered (phlegm) (Rothbarth 2011, 15).

Modern psychologists distinguish nine contributing factors or personality styles, evaluating activity level, rhythmicity, emotionality, adaptability, threshold, intensity, mood, distractability, and attention span (Rothbart 2011, 46; Chess and Thomas 1986, 380). On this basis, they classify temperament according to three types: self-confident, introverted, and impulsive—the latter two tending toward fear and anger, respectively (Rothbart 2011, 59). While temperament determines the degree to which we activate and intensify emotional circuits, the resulting reaction patterns form an essential part of our core personality, defined as the organization of "systems that determine one's unique adjustments to the environment," i.e., patterns of thought, emotion, and behavior that show consistency across situations and stability over time (Rothbart 2011, 12; Bates et al. 2008, 486; see also Allport 1961).

In addition, the formation of personality also depends on episodic memory. More conscious and supraliminal than muscle memory, it relates closely to temperament and emotions, and finds particular expression through language. Episodic memory grows from experience and is largely autobiographic: autonoetic in nature, it consists of the various "episodes" we pass through as we live, involving people, places, food, and the like, and is remembered like little movies (Joordens 2011, 5). Backward looking or "palinscopic," it chunks episodes together into groups of similar neuron pathways, creating expectation patterns for the future through sensitization and gradual habituation—enhancing temperament fixtures and emotional modules—as well as developing implicit structures of perception, evaluation, and behavior (DeSalle and Tattersall 2012, 181). It is also responsible for the particular personal narrative we develop that forms the foundation of our perceived self, our personal uniqueness (Tulving and Lepage 2000, 212; Sacks 1985, 105). Our current goals and knowledge influence our recollection as much as social beliefs impact our understanding of the world, so that all autobiography is a continuous, constructive, and creative process (Ross and Wilson 2000, 232).

As Luis Bunuel says, "You have to begin to lose your memory, if only in bits and pieces, to realize that memory is what makes our lives. Life without memory is no life at all . . . Our memory is our coherence, our reason, our feeling, even our actions" (Sacks 1985, 22). Or, in the words of Alexander Luria, "Each of us is a singular narrative, which is constructed continually and unconsciously by, through, and in us—through our perception, our feelings, our thoughts, our actions, and—not least—our discourse, our spoken narrations. Biologically, physiologically, we are not so different from each other; historically, as narratives, we are each of us unique" (1976b; Sacks 1985, 105).

The Prefrontal Cortex

This uniqueness is further reinforced by semantic memory, its most conscious form, the root of "right and wrong" in our thinking. Noetic in nature, it includes general cultural knowledge, what society considers facts about the world (Joordens 2011, 5; Dehaene 2014, 101; Markowitsch 2000, 473). Forward looking or "proscopic," it develops from theoretical patterns through intentional learning and memorization, and forms the root of all critical evaluations, decision-making, and theoretical visions. It also lays the foundation of sets of stereotypes and prejudices we often do not even know we have (Joordens 2011, 36) and creates the illusion of free will (DeSalle and Tattersall 2012, 181; Wegner 2002, 265). Just like the instincts nature gave us, it aids survival by providing us with the means of behaving more effectively and with better adaptation to circumstances (Tulving and Lepage 2000, 211; Markowitsch 2000, 478), but at the high cost of an often rather rigid view of the world.

Its seat is the newest and highest portion of the brain, commonly called the cerebral cortex, neocortex, or neo-mammalian brain.[19] A large area in humans, unlike in other mammals where it is flat, it is folded over itself and therefore looks like a walnut, cauliflower, or "large wrinkled napkin," (Gazzaniga 2011, 34). It divides into four lobes: the occipital lobe at the back, essential for visual processing of color, form, and motion; the temporal lobe on the side above the ears, responsible for higher perception such as objects and faces; the parietal lobe at the top, where touch, muscle, and joint information is processed and from where we maintain ownership of our arms and legs; and the frontal lobe above the forehead, which includes the motor cortex, various areas of language processing, and the prefrontal cortex (PFC).[20]

The frontal lobe and PFC are our centers of "memory and planning, cognitive flexibility, abstract thinking, initiating and inhibiting behavior as appropriate, learning rules, and picking out relevant information perceived through the senses" (Gazzaniga 2011, 32; Stein 2007, 8). Although it makes up 82 percent of the brain's overall mass, it possesses only 19 percent of its neurons, due to the increased number of their connections (axons, dendrites, and synapses) and the space between them (Gazzaniga 2011, 32)—the microtubules and cytoskeleton that greatly enhance connectivity and processing power. Also, it tends to have more pyramidal neurons, allowing it to "receive a larger number of more diverse inputs over a bigger region of the cortex than their counterparts in other parts of the brain" (2011, 38-39).

The area processes information in various ways. Thus, the left PFC centers on single events and activates feelings of enthusiasm and high energy, while the right integrates occurrences into narratives and lights up in times of stress and tension (Goleman 2011, 35). The lateral PFC deals with events that are frequently modified and require specific attention, while the medial PFC works on common patterns that have predictable relationships with sensory-motor sequences. The dorsolateral PFC, not very social, holds things in the mental landscape, directs attention, manages logical reasoning, and interacts with the parietal lobe; the ventromedial PFC, more social, processes pleasurable responses to beauty and provides a sense of embodiment, interacting with the

---

[19] Ford and Wortman 2013, 44; Johnson and Raye 2000, 72; Newberg et al. 2001, 19.

[20] Ramachandran 2011, 19-20; Joordens 2011, 56; Nyberg and Cabeza 2000, 507; Wegner 2002, 179.

anterior cingulate cortex. Generally, the anterior PFC processes more and longer events, while the posterior works on events of shorter duration (Ramachandran 2011, 264-67; Stein 2007, 31-35).

More specifically, conceptual priming occurs in the temporal cortex and left PFC, while bias detection and conflict monitoring takes place in the anterior cingulate gyrus. Response inhibition is a function of the ventral left, regulative control of the dorsal left, and theory of mind of the dorsal medial PFC. Ingroup perception through processing of self and similar others occurs in the medial PFC, while detecting external cues for engaging control and regulating behavior toward social cues centers here and also in the rostral paracingulate (Amodie and Lieberman 2009, 350).

The overall command center of the PFC forms a presence, variously called homunculus (Stein 2007, 7), inner adviser (Harman and Rheingold 1984, 109), decider, or interpreter (Gazzaniga 2011, 75). It represents a complex information-processing system that manages information, acknowledges dangers, promotes tested responses, and rejects ideas that seem impossible or useless. Fundamentally critical, it is goal-oriented; in terms of function and energy use, it is the most expensive part of the brain (Segerstrom et al. 2011, 26). It includes our ability to focus intelligently on one issue or the other, enabling us to think clearly and make positive decisions (Farthing 1992). The locus of ambition, empathy, foresight, and morality, it is the core of our personality, and has been called the "seat of humanity" (Ramachandran 2011, 21; Shettleworth 2010, 556).

Habituating to set patterns and actively construed forms of cognition, the interpreter module creates a set framework for understanding and processing information. "As new experiences largely confirm the existing framework and add less and less new information, requiring less and less modification, the framework becomes more rigid and less amenable to major changes based on new or contradictory information" (Eichenbaum and Bodkin 2000, 202). A fully belief-driven process, it then works with the presumption that new information "must" fit into exiting schemata. As a result, all disconcerting aspects are either forgotten or changed, i.e., subject to memory loss or false memory.[21] This becomes a vicious cycle: the stronger the structure and the more it works with judgments and beliefs, i.e., projections of ideal or threatening situations, the more limited is the interpretation of new information (2000, 203; Fiedler and Bless 2000, 144; Clore and Gasper 2000, 13).

---

[21] A powerful and prominent example of false memory is the extensive narration of her experiences in New York during 9/11 by Tania Head—when, in fact, she was nowhere near the place (Hood 2012, 220-24).

Creating Reality

As we, therefore, create the reality we live in, we hold a number of specific beliefs, defined as the subconscious or implicit operation of assumptions and preferences. In many ways they like possessions: we acquire, inherit, and adopt them; we may lose, disown, or abandon them (Abelson 1986; Banaji and Bhashar 2000, 141). "The port through which emotions exert their influence upon human life" (Frijda, Manstead,and Bem 2000, 1), beliefs constitute the meaning attached to events. Closely related to cultural standards, social modeling, and family expectations, they involve generalizations and get truer as they are repeated, yet often distort actual facts or reflect fictions created by the brain (Frijda and Mesquita 2000, 52-57; Frith 2007, 98). The prefrontal cortex works with them either by assimilation, i.e., it imposes internal cognitive structures and schemata on new problems, or by accommodation, i.e., it remains stimulus-driven and responds automatically to perceived external demands (Fiedler and Bless 2000, 145).

Inconsistencies are anathema to this system. The interpreter continuously searches for structured patterns and, with the help of stored memory information, synthesizes input into an ongoing meaningful narrative to explain our perceptions, emotions, and actions. It is constantly "grasping the gist of situations, interpreting inputs and the body's physiological reactions, and inferring cause and effect" (Gazzaniga 2011, 86). This is clearly evident from experiments with split-brain patients whose left side did not know what the right was doing. No matter what they do, their PFC comes up with a logical explanation, each hemisphere working in its area of dominant specialization (2011, 82-83, 91; Ramachandran 2000, 88-90). If there is insufficient information, therefore, the interpreter "uses what it has and ad-libs the rest," creating a vision of the world unique to each individual (Gazzaniga 2011, 88).

If there is excessive information that leads to major inconsistencies, the interpreter is stymied and a negative emotional state results, commonly known as cognitive dissonance. It motivates cognitive work to reduce emotional discomfort, leading to sometimes absurd beliefs in the goodness of cult leaders or the likelihood of apocalyptic states (see Festinger 1957; Sherrill 2000). These beliefs, in turn, create values and contribute to emotional reactions, which duly lead to adaptations in discriminating consciousness and cause further modification of beliefs (Harmon-Jones 2000, 185; Eysenck 2000, 172).

In other words, the loop between sensory input, emotions, and beliefs as processed in the different sections of the triune brain is an ongoing process, and the interpreter updates our worldview constantly as we receive new evidence through the senses (Frith 2007, 121-25). The interpreter in each one of us incessantly monitors the adequacy of accessible beliefs, expectations, and abilities versus the need for new information, leading to a hierarchy of smaller and larger goals and creating a processing agenda, so that one attends to urgent things first (Clore and Gasper 2000, 34). Positive affects, then, lead to a reliance on one's own impulses, habits, prior beliefs, or expectations; negative attitudes create more outside focus, blind reactions, and stress patterns (2000, 21).

Everything we experience, our so-called reality, in other words, depends on cognition and is a construction of the brain—and not even in real time, but lagging behind by half a second, although it presents the world to us *as if* it experienced it in real time.[22] "Actions are over, done, kaput, before your brain is conscious of them. Your left-hemisphere interpretive system is what pushes the advent of consciousness back in time to account for the cause of action" (Gazzaniga 2011, 112). Experiments have shown that after the command to lift a finger, it takes the brain 300 milliseconds before it activates the urge and another 200 before it initiates movement, that is, a total of 500 milliseconds or half a second elapse between the internal decision and the actual movement (Frith 2007, 66; Libet 2004, 51, 71). Similarly, words flashed at experimental subjects elicited immediate activation in the visual cortex, but for conscious words only, at about 300 milliseconds, the wave of activity amplified and flowed into the prefrontal cortex (Dehaene 2014, 123). In other words, the brain adapts before conscious awareness has had a chance to arise (Frith 2007, 78; Penrose 1989, 439). Consciousness, an emergent property arising as needed (Gazzaniga 2011, 135), is never fully in the present but always delayed: "awareness is always postdictive" (Eagleman 2009, 164).

> After the execution of a spontaneous action, the *perceived* onset of the *intention* to act, that moment when you became conscious that you intend to act, is shifted *backward* in time on the temporal map, and the *perceived* time of the actual *action*, the moment when you are conscious that you are acting, is shifted *forward* in time. (Gazzaniga 2011, 113)
>
> Setting a course of action is automatic, deterministic, modularized, and driven not by one physical system at any time but by hundreds, thousands, and even millions. The course of action taken appears to us as a matter of choice, but the fact is, it is the result of a particular emergent state being selected by the complex interacting surrounding milieu. (2011, 141)

In other words, the brain with its trillions of neurons connected nonlocally and embedded in automated circuits decides and acts long before consciousness can kick in. This means, "we have no immediate conscious contact with the world or even with our own bodies" and "our experience of the world can be completely false" (Frith 2007, 81). Any notion of conscious choice and thus

[22] Norretranders 1998, 215-25; Frith 2007, 41; Libet 2004, 51; Penrose 1989, 439.

free will is essentially an illusion.[23] However, once discriminating consciousness arises, it does have the power and the time to select and control volitional outcomes, discard information, and reject alternatives. In other words, it can stop the flow of actions and emotional patterns the brain set in motion automatically and veto its activities. This means that, while we do not have free will, we most definitely have "free won't," an essential feature in all efforts of self-cultivation (Norretranders 1998, 243). It also means that we posssess an immensely powerful system that works amazingly well. "Our body [and brain] can interact perfectly well even if you don't know what it is doing, even when what you think about the world is actually wrong" (Frith 2007, 69-70).

Stereotypes and Prejudices

Many things we think about the world are in fact wrong, created by sensory and emotional stimuli as well as ingrained cultural beliefs that influence our judgment without ever reaching conscious awareness. The process by which this happens is "priming" (Clore and Gasper 2000, 13), i.e., habit learning, cognitive tuning, or conditioning, the encoding of structures not explicitly presented or the creation of pathways for subliminal perception.[24] It consists of "a variety of ways in which experiences can lead to altered dispositions, preferences, and judgments without providing any conscious memory content" (Zola and Square 2000, 488). A form of implicit stereotyping that relies on representation of conceptual knowledge and association, priming happens constantly, supported by neurocognitive systems for implicit semantic memory in the neocortex and lateral temporal lobe as well as the left lateral PFC (Amodie and Lieberman 2009, 353).

Priming forms an essential part of socialization: other people are contagious, and we cannot help imitating them, automatically mirroring their patterns, synchronizing our breathing and actions, and sharing their emotions and ideas (Frith 2007, 170). We always model the mind of the person we are talking to and alter our way of communication to match their capabilities—the most obvious example being baby talk, when we use a higher pitch and simpler words (2007, 171). We also conform to the expectations of others, a fact demonstrated by Robert Rosenthal and Lenore Jacobson in experiments on teachers' expectations in the 1960s. They describe their results in terms of the Pygmalion and Golem effects: students whose teachers expected enhanced

---

[23] Dehaene 2014, 264; Frith 2007, 67; Gazzaniga 2011, 108; Masicampo and Baumeister 2011, 178; Penrose 1989, 443.

[24] Hood 2012, 152; Joordens 2011, 74; Norretranders 1998, 302; Robinson and Compton 2008, 224; Schwarz 2002, 154.

performance did better, while those whose teachers thought poorly of them did worse (Rosenthal and Jacobson 1968).

Language, too, is a major source of priming. Experiments have shown that students who were given various words to arrange, when confronted with the word "elderly" started to walk more slowly (Frith 2007, 170). Used deliberately by skilled orators and in advertising to manipulate specific knowledge structures (Fiedler and Bless 2000, 155), priming is the key factor in the creation of set patterns of thought and beliefs: what Daoists describe in terms of the "fixed mind" and psychologists today call "stereotypes and prejudices."

Unlike earlier thinkers like Theodor Adorno (1950), who believed that stereotypes and prejudices were rooted deeply in the personality structure and afflicted only selected individuals, we now know that every one is a potential fascist. As Gordon Allport notes, prejudice reflects "man's normal and natural tendency to form generalizations, concepts, and categories where content represents an oversimplification of his world of experience" (1954, 26; Ward et al. 1995, 27-35). Stereotyping and scapegoating as "culturally determined fallacies" (Banaji and Bhashar 2000, 145) are ubiquitous phenomena (Bodenhausen, Todd, and Richeson 2009, 113), a variant of natural belief formation that stems from propaganda, reflects cultural determinants, and is activated by the emotions (Frijda and Mesquita 2000, 48). Everyone of us—although not as strongly in culturally mixed societies (Hood 2012, 218)—tends to form fuzzy stereotypes by uninsightfully soaking up correlations among properties, matching the natural tendency of the brain toward simplification and the creation of meaning (Pinker 2007, 127).

Often seriously different from our professed and acknowledged views, mental associations based on stereotypes and prejudices are triggered independently of our conscious beliefs and bear little or no relation to facts, validity, or truth (Bodenhausen et al. 2009, 112). Maintained through rationalization, justification, denial, or just plain ignoring and avoiding outgroups (Monteith and Mark 2009, 507), they function automatically, characterized by spontaneity, efficiency, uncontrollability, and unconsciousness. That is to say, they happen without specific intention, do not require attentional resources, operate in ballistic fashion, are hard to stop, and remain independent of awareness or conscious monitoring (Bodenhausen et al. 2009, 112).

Their main source is the society we live in, fueled by the fundamental human need to belong, to be normal, to be part of the group. How far people are willing to go to satisfy this need is evident from various experiments.

For example, psychologist Solomon Asch (1907-1996) in the Conformity Experiments of the 1950s showed various subjects a graph of three lines of uneven length and asked them to determine with among them matched a separate ine. Even though the correct answer was A, if the majority of people said B or C, most subjects would doubt their own perception and join group thinking (Hood 2012, 196).

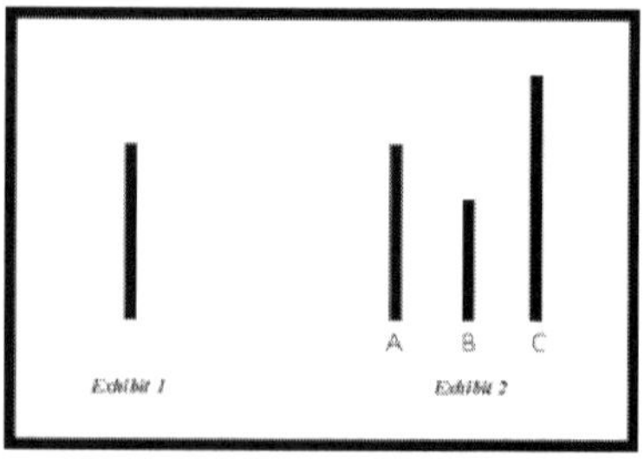

Similarly, Stanley Migram in the Yale Electroshock Experiment on obedience to authority figures, showed that perfectly ordinary people would zap subjects to the point of torture just because someone in a white coat told them to do so (Blass 2004; Miller 1986). Philip Zimbardo, in the infamous Standford Prison Experiment of 1971, randomly assigned twenty-four male students roles of guards and inmates in a mock prison. Participants adapted to their roles so well, guards enforcing authoritarian measures and even resorting to torture, that the experiment had to be cut short (Hood 2012, 199-201; www.prisonexp.org).

Anybody or any institution or media outlet with authority thus has tremendous power in creating fixed ideas, set patterns of thinking, stereotypes, and prejudices, facilitating the so-called chameleon effect, i.e., the adaptation of people's thinking in accordance with dominant figures and groups (Hood 2012, 210; Iacoboni 2008, 113).

Closely linked to the fear responses rooted in the amygdala—more strongly activated when viewing out-group faces and evident on brain scans within 100 milliseconds (Devine and Sharp 2009, 78)—stereotypes and prejudices always go hand in hand with stigmatization, the exclusion and demonization of certain groups of people, resulting in mistrust, discomfort, anxiety, avoidance, and withdrawal (Crocker and Garcia 2009, 233). Being stigmatized is a strong negative experience related to social identity, leading to ego threats that affect cognitive capacity and processes and intense levels of arousal that can disrupt thinking and behavior. The threat activates the fight or flight response in the lower parts of the brain, while its higher cognitive functions of abstract thinking and self-reflection shut down, leading to poorer performance, further rejection, and increased fear. In other words, it leads to a continuous and mutually reinforcing downward spiral that ranges from threat through physiological response and less thinking to poor performance, increased fear and more perceived threat (Crocker and Garcia 2009, 233-34).

Stereotypes and prejudices, as much as the "fixed mind" of ancient Daoism, are an inevitable byproduct of discriminating consciousness with its inherent need to streamline information, simplify facts, and create easily accessible structures. Just as emotions are biological shortcuts toward efficient responses in service of survival in the three areas of physical integrity, object acquisition, and social connection, so stereotypes and prejudices are mental shortcuts determined by socially established classifications and categories. Once set up, it takes the brain only 300 milliseconds to stereotype a social network, then create behavior patterns based on the resulting belief (Banaji and Bhashar 2000, 155). It only takes 100 milliseconds to judge someone we meet for the first time, absorbing and classifying impressions according to a wide variety of categories, including race, culture, language, gender, physical appearance, accent, posture, voice, and so on. Highly useful for survival in primitive times, today this may lead to grave errors in judgment and cause all sorts of complications—as much as the strong reaction to stimuli with particular emotions, especially anxiety and anger, may lead to psychological, physical, and social problems.

While we, therefore, now understand how we got here from cosmic consciousness and the pure Dao at the beginning of creation, we also realize that, as Daoists have claimed for millennia, the development of discriminating consciousness in the PFC and the ingrained survival responses of emotions and the fixed mind contain seeds of alienation and dehumanization. They have served us well in terms of survival—unlike many animal species that are close to extinction or already gone, human beings vastly expanded and now occupy every corner of the globe—and the advances of science and technology. On the other hand, they have also given us an exploitative relationship to the environment and other beings, stratified and often antagonistic social structures, as well as innumerable physical and psychological problems, ranging from stress and anxiety to a host of degenerative diseases. Where, then, do we go from here? How can we move forward to recover bodily health, emotional ease, social harmony, and an overall connection with the universe at large?

Chapter Five

Breathing to the Heels

Body Cultivation and Behavioral Kinesiology

The answer Daoists give to this question is to start with the conscious mind. Thus, the Tang master Sima Chengzhen 司馬承禎 (647-735), in his *Zuowang lun* 坐忘論 (Discourse on Sitting in Oblivion, DZ 1036; trl. Kohn 2010a, 137-58), begins his discussion with the necessity to develop the conscious qualities of "respect and faith." To set out for the ascent to Dao, he says, one must first have realized that one's current state is not ideal, have heard about such things as Daoist practice, and have embraced the belief that it is possible to attain Dao (Kohn 2010a, 60).

The *Zhuangzi* similarly begins the quest with the conscious questioning of knowledge—"How do I know that I know?" (ch. 2)—targeting the discriminating function of the mind that creates a "limited and often incorrect grasp of the world" (Ivanhoe 1996, 199). Knowledge here is the subjective power of intellectually grasping and consciously processing outside reality, reaching understanding through recognition and representation and in the process superimposing a "second coding" on it (Moeller 2003, 119; Zhang 2002, 423-24; Kohn 2014, 38).

That is to say, before we can take even the first step toward recovering a more cosmic way of being, we have to realize that our very own thinking and evaluating are at the root of the problem. Once we accept that, we can actively reorganize our perception and understanding, beginning with the realization that the cosmos is present in our very own bodies, constantly and without limit flowing as *qi* through breath, organs, meridians and energy centers.

Breathing

The most elementary and most fundamental way Daoists suggest that we become aware of the cosmic flow of energy in and through our bodies is by turning the conscious mind to the function of breathing. A major manifestation of *qi*, breath is always there, always unlimited, never failing. One of the few functions of the body that is both automatic and voluntary, breathing offers a bridge to the mind and closely reflects our overall state. Shortness and rapidity of breath show mental agitation, while length and depth reveal serenity within (Loehr and Migdow 1986). For example, watching a scary movie, people hold their breath. Engaged in passionate embrace, they pant with excitement. At times of fear, tension, worry, sorrow, or stress, breathing becomes tight, shallow, and rapid. On the other hand, when we lie down to relax or sleep, we breathe deeply and slowly (Kohn 2008b, 28).

An obvious and easily accessible tool for appreciating our intimate connection to the cosmos, breathing appears already in the *Zhuangzi*, which notes that "the perfected breathe all the way to their heels, unlike ordinary folk who breathe only as far as their throats" (ch. 6; Kohn 2014, 119). Han-dynasty medical manuscripts similarly emphasize that deep breathing is the first step toward the restoration and continued health of the body. Thus, the Mawangdui manuscript *Shiwen* 十問 (Ten Questions) notes that the breath, "must be deep and long, so that pure *qi* is easily held" and stale *qi* can be thoroughly cleansed. "Stale *qi* is that of old age; pure *qi* is that of longevity. He who is skilled at cultivating *qi* lets the stale *qi* disperse at night and the new, pure *qi* gather at dawn, thereby allowing it to penetrate all orifices and organs of the body" (Harper 1998, 395).

Having gained *qi* through breathing deeply, at the right times, and in the right manner, practitioners circulate it through the body, hold it for some time, move it mentally to certain regions, and guide it purposely to relieve ailments and open blockages. They can also use it to stimulate or calm the body, depending on the need. For example, before going to sleep, one might practice "dusk breathing by breathing deeply, long and slow, causing the ears to not hear; thus becoming tranquil, go to bed" (Harper 1998, 396). Integrating deep breathing into their daily life, people can maintain health and vigor well into old age (Kohn 2008a, 40).

Inheriting this ancient wisdom, Daoists emphasize that one should breathe naturally, through the abdomen, allowing it to expand on inhalation and contract on exhalation. This will provide maximum flow of *qi* as breath to the organs. Next, one should gradually lengthen and deepen the breath, increasing abdominal strength and settling the abdominal center in a low position. Following this, one can allow the respiration to grow subtler and finer until the entering and leaving of the breath is very soft. This leads to a state where the mind is deeply focused and one feels as if one were not breathing at all, with the *qi* subtly pervading the entire body (Kohn 2008b, 35).

The breath should enter through the nose, the organ associated with the lungs. Already Heshang gong 河上公 (Master on the River), the Han-dynasty commentator to the *Daode jing*, says that the five *qi* of heaven enter the body through the nose (ch. 10; Kohn 2009, 163). It should exit through the mouth, smoothly and softly to calm the mind, or with specific lip positions and throat movements that bring forth certain sounds to stabilize the related organs. Already mentioned in the *Zhuangzi* and Han manuscripts, these were later systematized into a set called the Six Breaths or Six Healing Sounds (*liuzi jue* 六字訣). They are:

> 1. *Si*, a gentle, relaxed exhalation that lets the breath escape between slightly opened lips; it is associated with the lungs.
> 2. *He*, a strong breath with open mouth accompanied by a guttural rasping through tightening of the throat at the base of the tongue; it expels heat and aids the heart.
> 3. *Hu*, the standard term for "exhale," is a blowing out of breath with rounded lips; it supports the spleen.
> 4. *Xu*, a gentle expulsion of breath with open mouth; it balances the liver.
> 5. *Chui*, a sharp expulsion of air with almost closed lips; it, expels cold and aids the kidneys.
> 6. *Xi*, traditionally the sound of sighing, is a soft exhalation with the mouth slightly open; it supports the Triple Heater, a uniquely Chinese organ that absorbs *qi* from food and breath and directs it to the vital organs. (Kohn 2009a, 57; Chia and Chia 1993, 104-05; Despeux 2006)

Becoming aware of the breath and increasingly using it consciously to enhance peace of mind and the functioning of the inner organs is thus a first step toward breaking the power of the fixed mind and opening to the cosmic flow of universal energy.

Healing Exercises

Another way Daoists connect with the greater universe is by becoming more conscious of how we use the body and invite *qi*-flow into our lives through particularly ways of moving. Always in close conjunction with deep, conscious breathing, this forms the foundation of the traditional practice of *daoyin* 導引, literally "guiding [the qi] and stretching [the muscles]," as well as the modern system of *qigong* 氣功, literally the "effort" or "merit" of *qi* (Kohn 2008a, 11, 198; 2012, 95; see also Johnson 2014b, sect. iii; Phillips and Mroz 2016).

Daoyin arose as part of Han-dynasty medicine, which encouraged people to relish the world in all its aspects, find greater health, and enjoy their physical and social pleasures. As a result, the earliest works are immensely practical in nature and can be precisely dated. Found among manuscripts unearthed from southern China, they include the silk manuscript *Daoyin tu* 導引圖 (Exercise Chart) and the bamboo tablets of the *Yinshu* 引書 (Stretch Book).

The *Daoyin tu* was found at Mawangdui 馬王堆, in the tomb of the Marchioness of Dai, the wife of a local lord who died in 168 BCE. The text consists of 44 color illustrations of human figures performing therapeutic exercises that are explained in brief captions. The figures are of different sex and age, variously clothed or bare-chested, and shown in different postures (mostly standing) from a variety of angles. Many of them have their arms wide open, reaching up or down, while bending or twisting in different directions (Harper 1998, 132). The captions are often illegible, but among them are the well-known "bear amble" and "bird stretch," showing a figure walking in a stately fashion with arms swinging and one bending forward with hands on the floor and head raised, respectively (Kohn 2008a, 36).

The lack of written explanations is somewhat alleviated by the *Yinshu*, which consists entirely of text. It was found in a manuscript at Zhangjiashan 張家山, also in Hunan, in a tomb that was closed in 186 BCE. The text contains a general introduction on seasonal health regimens, a series of about a hundred exercises, and a presentation on the etiology of disease and ways of prevention (Harper 1998, 110-11; Engelhardt 2001, 215). Executed in all different positions of the body, many of its practices imitate animals and emphasize wide, open movements in combination with bends and stretches (Kohn 2008a, 43).

In the middle ages, daoyin practice advanced into integrated sequences and was associated with famous immortals of old, such as Chisongzi 赤松子 (Master Redpine) and the long-lived Pengzu 彭祖, as well as with medical masters, such as the physician Hua Tuo 華佗 (3rd c.). The latter, in particular, is famous for creating a series of movements known as the Five Animals' Frolic (*wuqin xi* 五禽戲), a form that matches body movements to motions typical for cranes, bears, tigers, monkeys, and deer, and is still popular today (Kohn 2008a, 164-68; see also Miura 1989; Wang and Barrett 2006).

Further standardized and expanded throughout the Tang and later dynasties (see Kohn 2008a), daoyin today survives in qigong, a system developed in the late 1940s on the basis of Daoist exercises (see Palmer 2007). It includes numerous traditional as well as newly developed forms, including movements that, in conjunction with the breath, imitate the key characteristics of the five phases, connect actively to heaven, earth, and the stars, work with various animal models, and increasingly combine healing exercises with martial practice, notably taiji quan (Kohn 2012, 204-13).

Meridians

In yet another dimension of body cultivation, Daoists also undertake conscious "*qi* guiding" (*xingqi* 行氣), a way of intentionally moving *qi* through the body via the meridians—channels connecting the inner organs with the hands and feet and providing communication between the upper and lower, interior and exterior body. As it flows through them, *qi* moistens the bones and tendons, provides nutrition to the joints, and balances yin and yang (see Maciocia 1989; Seem 1990).

There are twelve pairs of organ-based meridians in the human body, documented since the Han dynasty, that match the five yin and yang organs plus a sixth set, the pericardium (yin) and the Triple Heater (yang). A uniquely Chinese entity, it provides a connection between heaven (upper heater, lungs), humanity (middle heater, stomach), and earth (lower heater, intestines) and is responsible for integrating the nourishment extracted from air and food as well as its transport, utilization, and excretion (Kohn 2005, 31-32). The six yin meridians store and process essential *qi*, connect to spirit and souls, and are a function of overall health; they can be full or empty. The six yang meridians process active *qi* and run closer to the surface than their yin counterparts; they digest food, transmit fluids, and can be replete or exhausted due to pathological conditions (Kaptchuk 1983; Kendall 2002).

Beyond the twelve paired meridians, Daoists also work with four single energy lines that traditionally form part of the so-called eight extraordinary vessels. Called "vessels" (*mai* 脈) rather than "meridians" (*luo* 絡), these are functional containers of primordial *qi* that arise at early stages of embryonic development before the organs are formed (see Larre and Rochat 1996; Matsumoto and Birch 1986; Johnson 2014a, ch. 6).

Most important and most primordial among them is the Penetrating Vessel (*chongmai* 沖脈), which runs right through the center of the body. It begins at the perineum, a small cluster of muscles located between the anus and the genital organs, passes through the central torso, and ends at the crown of the head, a point known as Hundred Meeting (*baihui* 百會; GV-20) in Chinese medicine and as Heavenly Pass (*tianguan* 天關) in Daoism. Connecting the kidneys and stomach, as well as the main energy centers, it is considered the main conduit of primordial *qi*. Adepts use it to send healing and spiritual intention into the depth of the elixir fields, thus opening their centers and connecting to the primordiality of the cosmos.

The second major energy line is the Belt Vessel (*daimai* 帶脈). It runs around the abdomen a few inches below the navel, connecting the Ocean of *Qi* in front with the Gate of Destiny in the back and linking the vertical meridians and the major storehouses of *qi*. Next are the Conception (*renmai* 任脈, yin) and Governing Vessels (*dumai* 督脈, yang), which run along the front and back of the torso respectively, reaching from the pelvic floor to the head. They are of great importance both in all levels of Daoist practice, serving to mix *qi* and blood and to guide the *qi* along the major centers of the body.

The Conception Vessel begins at Meeting of Yin (*huiyin* 會陰) at the perineum, passes through the front of the body along its central line, and ends at the mouth. A carrier and major supporter of yin-*qi*, it supports urogenital, digestive, and thoracic aspects of the body and, together with the spleen meridian, controls pregnancy and menstruation. The Ocean of *Qi* in the lower abdomen is actually one of its points (CV-6) as is the navel known as Spirit Tower (*shenque* 神闕) and the center of the chest, here known as the Ocean of Stillness (*jinghai* 靜海). Two further points of Daoist importance are Central Court (*zhongting* 中庭; CV-16,) which matches the solar plexus and thus the middle elixir field, and Purple Palace (*zigong* 紫宮; CV-18), i.e., the heart.

The Governing Vessel also begins at the pelvic floor, then passes along the back of the body, moves across the top of the head, and ends inside the mouth at the upper gums. It transports and aids yang-*qi* and has many points connecting to channels and inner organs. Its twenty-eight points include also the more spiritual points Gate of Life (GV-4) at the 2nd and 3rd lumbar vertebrae, Numinous Terrace (*lingtai* 靈台; GV-10) at the 6th thoracic vertebra, as well as the Jade Pillow (*yuzhen* 玉枕; GV-17) at the back of the skull (see Kaptchuk 1983; Larre and Rochat 1996).

The two meridians connect at the mouth, with Fluid Receptacle (*chengjiang* 承漿; CV-24) located at the lower lip and Gum Intersection (*yinjiao* 齦交; GV-28) found at the upper gums. They also both continue internally, descending back to the pelvic floor and forming a continuous, intricate inner loop. Rather than using this path, however, adepts tend to activate them as one straight circle of *qi*-flow. They place the tongue at the roof of the mouth as a bridge between the meridians, then inhale deeply into the abdomen to enhance their Ocean of *Qi* or lower elixir field. From there, they breathe out, envisioning their *qi* flowing downward to the pelvic floor and reaching the perineum.

Focusing on the coccyx (*changqiang* 長強, GV-1), they inhale the *qi* up along the spine, passing through all the various points along the Governing

Vessel. At Great Hammer (*dazhui* 大椎; GV-15) below the neck, they begin to exhale, carrying the *qi* further up along the back of the skull, across Hundred Meeting, along the forehead and to the nostrils. From here they inhale again, envisioning the *qi* flowing down along the Conception Vessel and through the Ocean of *Qi* into the pelvic floor, thus establishing a cycle of *qi* throughout the torso, which is known in Daoist practice as the microcosmic orbit (*xiao zhoutian* 小周天) (Neswald 2009, 35-37; Chia and Chia 1993, 253).

Elixir Fields

While the twelve paired meridians with their various yin and yang organs represent the horizontal dimension of the human body and its connection to earth, the extraordinary vessels feature its verticality and connect it to heaven in conjunction with three major energy centers. Commonly known as cinnabar or elixir fields (*dantian* 丹田), they are located in the head, solar plexus, and lower abdomen, and house the three treasures: spirit, energy, and essence (Jahnke 2002, 67). Matching the three cosmic levels of heaven, humanity, and earth, they are also known as Heavenly Palace (*qiangong* 乾宫), Scarlet Palace (*jianggong* 絳宫), and Earth Palace (*kungong* 坤宫), using the appellations of the *Yijing* trigrams for heaven and earth. Serving as the residence of body gods, they have also more mythological names: Niwan Palace (*niwan gong* 泥丸宫), Purple Palace (*zigong* 紫宫), and Yellow Court (*huangting* 黃庭) (Neswald 2009, 37-38).

The upper elixir field in the head is the place from where celestial energies are accessed or through which, at the stage of immortality, the spirit embryo passes to ascend to the otherworld. It is the central chamber or palace among a total of Nine Palaces (*jiugong* 九宫) that house a host of deities central to traditional Daoist body cosmology.[1]

The main entrances to this cluster of palaces, moreover, are the Heavenly Pass, at the very top of the head, in acupuncture known as Hundred Meeting, which furnishes the major doorway to heaven; and the Hall of Yin (*yintang* 陰堂) between the eyebrows, often described as the third eye, a passage way to the world of humanity (Johnson 2014a, 307-08). A major center of energetic processing, the upper elixir field thus houses divine entities as representatives of spirit, managing the close connection of humanity to heaven.

The middle elixir field, next, is in the solar plexus, between the nipples. Called the Cavity of *Qi* (*qixue* 氣穴), it is the center of humanity and seat of pure energy within the body, collecting *qi* and holding it for dispersal either through ordinary activity or for immortality cultivation. The heart is its primary

[1] See Homann 1971, 72-74; Kalinowski 1985; Kohn 1991; Réquéna 2012, 149-51; Johnson 2014a, 310

organ, seconded closely by the lungs, thus relating to both emotions and breathing (Johnson 2014a, 295). Governing also fire and the blood circulation in the body as well as controlling the major yin organs, it plays also a key role especially in women's cultivation.

Centrally located in to torso, the middle elixir field further centers on a point known as Platform Central (*shanzhong* 膻中, CV-17). Here the Conception Vessel meets the meridians of the spleen, kidneys, small intestine, and the Triple Heater, thus presenting a major control center of the body.

The lower elixir field is commonly placed about 1.3 inches beneath the navel, in the center of the abdomen. Also called Ocean of *Qi* and identical with the *hara* in Zen, it is the point where adepts find their center of gravity, their reproductive power, and their stability in the world (Kohn 2005, 11). The home of primordial *qi*, the original life force of the world, it is closely connected to earth and linked with the reproductive energy known as "essence" (*jing* 精), the indeterminate aspect of *qi* or *qi* in transition from one determinate form to another, and thus also described as semen (Porkert 1974; Kohn 2005, 33).

An important energy point related to this is the Gate of Life (*mingmen* 命門, GV-4) toward the back, in the kidney area—the kidneys, too, being associated with primordial *qi* and reproductive potency. Another point is Spirit Watchtower (*shenque* 神闕, CV-8), located in the front of the torso, the place where the mother's energy and spirit enter the embryo through the umbilical cord (Johnson 2014a, 290). The lower elixir field, moreover, also housed the universe at large, its center equal to the celestial Pole Star with constellations spinning all around it (2014a, 291).

One key goal of Daoist body cultivation, then, is to promote full energetic presence and harmony in the organs, meridians, and elixir fields, ultimately reaching for natural perfection. In the words of T. L. Nichols, "When a man is perfect in his own nature, body, and soul, perfect in his harmonious adaptations and action, and living in perfect harmony with nature, with his fellow man, and with God, he may be said to be in a state of health" (1853, 227). Or, more recently, as formulated by Walt Whitman, "In that condition the whole body is elevated to a higher state—inwardly and outwardly illuminated, purified, made solid, strong, yet buoyant" (1954, 513).

Environmental Adjustments

Once the inner body closely connects to cosmic energy through deep breathing, intentional movement, guiding *qi* along the meridians, and spiritual empowerment of the elixir fields, Daoists bring this to bear on the environment. Seeing their lives as playing out in the constant energetic interaction with things and features on the outside, they pay close attention to how they relate to them, most importantly to in terms of food, personal items, and living space.

To create a living space well conducive to energy flow, they apply the traditional Chinese system of *fengshui* 風水, literally "wind and water," which like Chinese medicine depends on a doctrine of macrocosm-microcosm correspondence and seeks to channel or alter natural processes for purposes of curing sickness and securing general well-being (Seaman 1992, 75-76). To do so, it distinguishes two major forms of *qi*-flow: killing *qi* (*shaqi* 殺氣), which rushes along straight lines, pointed arrows, and angular forms; and dead *qi* (*siqi* 死氣), that is stiff and obstructed, found in all types of clutter, dirt, and blockages (Kohn 2005, 130)

Qi best flows smoothly and in balance. As already the Tang work *Tianyinzi* 天隱子 (Master of Heavenly Seclusion, DZ 1026; trl. Kohn 2010a, 188-97) says,

> The room I live in has windows on all four sides. When wind arises, I close them; as soon as the wind has died down, I open them again. In front of my meditation seat, a curtain is suspended; behind it, a screen has been placed. When it is too light, I draw the curtain to adjust the brightness inside. When it gets too dark, I roll the curtain up again to let light in from outside. (sect. 5; Kohn 2010a, 192)

Overall, the house should be in a natural setting, surrounded by hills and water as well as plenty of greenery and wildlife. It should have a regular shape and rounded driveway, and be pleasing to behold. Inside, room divisions and furniture should be arranged to allow for rounded shapes, open corners, and a pleasant atmosphere, ideally also including the presence of all the colors of the five phases and the various aspects of yin and yang—heavy and light, dark and bright, soft and hard. When all aspects are represented in every room, *qi* can flow harmoniously, and one will find health and good fortune (see Rossbach 1983; Lip 1995).

On the basis of a healthy and well-adjusted lifestyle, practitioners then conform to a Daoist diet, which essentially means eating moderately, never to complete satiation, and in natural balance by partaking of all the food groups—grain, vegetables, fruit, and meat—as they are associated with the five organs and their flavors. They include,

organ	flavor	grains	greens	fruits	meat
liver	sour	wheat	onions	plum	mutton
heart	bitter	beans	lettuce	apricot	poultry
spleen	sweet	rice	cabbage	date	beef
lungs	spicy	corn	watercress	peach	venison
kidneys	salty	millet	kale. chard	chestnut	pork

As described by Sun Simiao in his *Sheyang lun* 慑養論 (On Preserving and Nourishing [Life], DZ 841; trl. Kohn 2012, 149-59), one should eat warming foods in winter and cooling foods in summer and prepare foods in accordance with the celestial constellations. One should also, as much as possible, use locally grown and organic ingredients and systematically, in accordance with one's personal constitution, supplement regular foodstuffs with herbal and mineral substances (Kohn 2010b, 46-47; 2012, 122-27).

All base materials and utensils, moreover, should match the requirements of naturalness and clarity. Thus, Daoist cooks prefer cold-pressed oils, whole grains, and organic produce as bases and use as much as possible natural cooking gear, such as unglazed pottery or earthenware, wooden spatulas and strainers (Kohn 2010b, 75). Other items of daily use, too, should be made from natural materials with minimum processing, including furniture, dishes, clothes, soaps, and more. That is to say, body cultivation extends to the overall way of living, matching the seasons of the year and the circadian rhythm of the day, integrating the basic wisdom of chronobiology (McTaggart 2011, 39). It aims to create a well-adjusted body in an organic environment, where *qi* flows smoothly and in a regular rhythm, allowing cosmic awareness to pervade everyday life.

Kinesiology

Independent of the Chinese and Daoist understanding of body and *qi*, the Western science of kinesiology has developed a system that is surprisingly similar and equally as valid. It supports everything Daoists say about the nature of body, self, and society, and emphasizes the very same measures—social, physical, and psychological—people should take to enhance their well-being and find perfection within this world. As F. M. Alexander (1869-1955), the Australian actor who developed the widely effective Alexander Technique of physical integration and forerunner of Moshe Feldenkrais (1904-1984; see Feldenkrais 1970) and Thomas Hanna (1928-1990), the founder of Somatics (see Hanna 1988), puts it, "Every man, woman, and child holds the possibility of physical perfection: it rests with each of us to attain it by personal understanding and effort" (1989, 3).

Kinesiology, also known as biomechanics, is originally the science of human movement—how to move the body and use its joints, tendons, and muscles to create maximum efficiency and best performance (see Starkes and Ericcson 2003). The term derives from the Greek *kinesis*, meaning "motion," combined with *logos*, meaning "word" or "knowledge." The field of study involves anatomy, physiology, physics, and geometry to explore human biomechanics, musculoskeletal anatomy, and neuromuscular physiology (Jensen and Schultz 1977, 1). Kinesiology works to a large extent with mechanics to demonstrate the physical principles and laws governing bodily movement (Spence 1975, 1).

Using various technological devices (video, EMG, etc), students measure the ways bones and muscles move under various conditions, examine the principles involved (gravity, synergism, alternation), and develop ways of improvement. The latter range from healing major and minor injuries through designing sports equipment to efficient training for the Olympics (see Spence 1975; Yessis 1992). Kinesiology thus forms and important part of sports culture; it is studied widely in departments of physical education at universities and colleges (Luttgens and Wells 1989).

Its use for diagnostic purposes and more subtle forms of healing, involving a wider understanding of well-being, began in the 1950s when the chiropractic physician George J. Goodheart (1918-2008) made a fascinating diagnostic observation. When any part of the body is out of balance, or a noxious substance comes close to it, he found, all its muscles weaken. Beginning in 1964, he gave lectures and wrote articles about his understanding of the musculature of the body as closely connected to internal organs and overall health (see Goodheart 1989).

Goodheart's system is known as Applied Kinesiology (AK). It centers on muscle testing, which typically involves the subject standing with one arm held out straight to the side or to the front while a tester pushes on it. When the immune system is working well and health is strong, or when the examined substance—either held by the subject in his other hand or by the tester close to the subject's body—is beneficial, there will be a solidness or spring in the arm and it will not budge. In the opposite case, the muscles are weak and the arm is easily pushed down.[2]

Applied Kinesiology, expanded by Goodheart's student, the chiropractor Alan G. Beardall, into Clinical Kinesiology in the late 1960s (Levy and Lehr 1996, 5), goes beyond classical kinesiology. It does not merely see the mechanics of physical movement but understands the body's muscular system as a closely interconnected network that has a direct relationship to the entire body, including organs, glands, and nerves. The body itself has its own wisdom and method of appreciation or rejection (1996, 9, 15). Using muscle testing, practitioners can diagnose and determine most efficient treatment for all sorts of

---

[2] Diamond 1979, 14-21; Levy and Lehr 1996, 22-24; Valentine and Valentine 1989; Walther 1981. See also www.AppliedKinesiology.com.

issues, from physical diseases through nutritional deficiencies or excesses to imbalances in lifestyle and problems in the nervous system.

Goodheart, Beardall, and many natural health practitioners in their wake, have been using Applied Kinesiology successfully for chiropractic "therapy localization," also testing physical stimulants such as food, medications, herbs, vitamins, as well as environmental factors. The method is common in naturopathic circles today, and numerous health care practitioners use it to establish diagnoses and prescribe kinds and amounts of medication (see Levy and Lehr 1996; Weil 1983; 1995).

Today, its main organization is the International College of Applied Kinesiology (ICAK), which seeks to promote the advancement of AK. Founded in 1973, it now has chapters in the United States, Canada, Europe, Japan, Russia, and Australasia. The organization awards certification to applicants with 300 or more hours of instruction, after proficiency examinations and the submission of original research papers (www.icakusa.com).

Behavioral Kinesiology

In the 1970s, the Australian psychiatrist John Diamond (b. 1934) realized that the body's musculature also responds to emotional states and thoughts and expanded Applied into Behavioral Kinesiology (BK). Using muscle testing to access the subconscious mind, he added the dimension of personal perfection as a goal of treatment: the attainment of complete health, the extension of life expectancy, and the realization of virtues and inherent goodness in self and society. In other words, Behavioral Kinesiology, moving beyond biomechanics and therapy localization, takes the field into the realm of personal perfection—how we can realize ideal health and harmony by using our bodies and minds most efficiently (www.DrJohnDiamond.com).

The musculature of the entire body being in immediate contact with, and responsive to, any energy changes in the system makes it possible to measure subtle modifications not only in the physical and psychological sphere of the individual, but also—since we are energetically connected to the entire universe—in the greater cosmos. That is to say, the inherent health or disease of any particular section of the bodymind as well as the truth or falseness of any given statement or fact can be evaluated through muscle testing (Diamond 1979, 25).

Since, as shown in the work of cell biology, moreover, the body's cells respond to mental and emotional impulses, we can instantaneously change our energy flow and thereby control our internal health and harmony. Thus, for example, if someone experiences anger, he or she needs to recognize that it hurts himself and others and that he can transmute it by saying the appropriate affirmation. "You will then activate your will to be well and you will overcome the anger with positive emotions. Your anger no longer exists. It has been transformed, transmuted, into something positive and productive, and your life energy has been stimulated" (Diamond 1985, 227).

The focus of John Diamond's work, then, as much as traditional Daoist practice, centers on the intentional guiding and active restructuring of the flow of this life energy, both a spiritual and material force. He describes it as "*love and humanity* which is within," the *love energy* in people and world, and—closely echoing Daoist sentiments—concludes,

> Perhaps the best word of all is *spirit*. It *is* spirit that enters our bodies when we so desire, when we so wish it, when our hearts are open to love. It *is* spirit that courses through the acupuncture channels of the body and is then transformed into physical energy, which then activates the totality of the physical aspects. (1986, 3:32)

Using kinesiological muscle testing, Diamond not only measured the mental, psychological, emotional, and subconscious dimensions of people's health, but also correlated specific positive and negative emotions, central pressure points, and appropriate affirmations for each acupuncture meridian, establishing an objective analysis of their functioning, in many ways confirming traditional Chinese claims yet also going beyond them.

Power Lines

Behavioral Kinesiology claims that all illness starts at the energy level (Diamond 1979, 25). This matches the traditional Chinese contention that an imbalance in the body's system manifests on three levels. First, there are the initial signs of an illness, which may be very subtle and perceived merely as a slight irregularity by the patient. Second, these signs grow into specific "symptoms," detected by the physician in a thorough examination. If left unchecked, these may further develop into a full-fledged "syndrome," which creates invasive disharmony both in the body and the social life of the patient (Kohn 2005, 63).

Behavioral Kinesiology also claims that the musculature of the body is immediately in contact with, and responsive to, any energy changes in the entire system and that, therefore, health and well-being—and, by extension, the benefits or harm of certain substances and the truth or falseness of a given statement—can be verified through muscle testing. Just as a weak muscle signals energetic imbalance in this system, so the traditional Chinese understanding claims that strong, vibrant muscles mean the presence of proper *qi*-flow (*zhengqi* 正氣) and health in the body (Diamond 1979, 32). The practice of acupuncture, meridian-based massages, and tapping accordingly serves to enhance energy flow and immunological strengthening as well as an increase in harmonious living in self and society.

Using muscle testing, John Diamond identifies twelve core meridians in close approximation of the classical Chinese system. Unlike the latter, though, he does not divide them into yin and yang lines of storage and transformation, but links them with the right and left hemispheres of the brain. He describes their functions as centering on "ordered, logical relationships, semantics, and arithmetic" for the left hemisphere; and "fantasy, imagination, intuition, dreams, visual imagery, rhythm, rhyme, spatial relationships, humor, syntax, and music" for the right (1985, 83).

He also identifies specific points on the torso related to each meridian. The subject touches the point with two fingers of his or her right hand while holding the left arm out straight. As the practitioner pushes on the extended arm, muscle testing reveals whether the meridian is strong or weak at this time. Meridians that relate to the left hemisphere have test points in the body located along the central front axis, while those related to the right have bilateral test points on the side of the torso. In some cases, the test points are located on the meridian as known from traditional Chinese medicine; in others, they are completely different. For example, the test point of the lung meridian is in the front of the shoulder, close to the traditional energy line (1985, 102); that for the large intestine is about two inches below and to the side of the navel, nowhere near the established meridian (1985, 133).

Each meridian, moreover, has a core emotion, both positive and negative, as well as a set of positive affirmations that, if recited with conviction and a sense of emotional activation, instantaneously changes the energy flow from weak to strong (1985, 100). They are as follows:

Right Hemisphere | | | | *Left Hemisphere*

Meridian	**Negative**	**Positive**		**Meridian**	**Negative**	**Positive**
Lung	contempt	humility		Thyroid	depression	lightness
Liver	unhappiness	happiness		Stomach	greed	contentment
Gall	rage	love		Heart	anger	love
Spleen	anxiety	confidence		Bladder	impatience	peace
Kidney	indecision	security		Circulation	jealousy	generosity
Lg. Intest	guilt	self-worth		Sm. Intest	sadness	joy

(Diamond 1985, 99-202)

Typical affirmations include: "I am humble;" "I am happy;" "I reach out with love;" "I have faith and confidence in my future;" "My sexual energies are balanced;" "I am worthy of being loved;" and "I have forgiveness in my heart" (1985, 220-21).

The meridians as listed here match, that is, each pair on the right and left is closely connected, sharing a similar place in the overall energy system of the human being (Diamond 1985, 199). Thus, for example, the lung and thyroid lines—the latter traditionally known as the Triple Heater—are paired, since life energy enters the human body first in the form of breath and is processed in the upper region of the torso (1985, 103). By the same token, the other pairs connect to highly similar emotions, which moreover also tend to match those associated with them in the traditional Chinese system. Thus, both liver and stomach encourage happiness and contentment (benevolence); the gall bladder and heart meridians center on anger and love; spleen and bladder promote an inner centeredness and harmony (honesty, trust), while the two intestines relate to feelings of inadequacy and/or personal worth.

In addition, the meridian connected to the kidneys as well as the one Diamond calls "circulation-sex" have to do with sexuality—again echoing traditional Chinese medicine, according to which sexual energy or "essence" is stored in and managed by the kidneys. Diamond's kidney line particularly centers on sexual indecision versus sexual security, notably in conjunction with the future, involving questions of whether or not one should enter a relationship with a specific person. The circulation channel, on the other hand, physiologically present in the adrenal glands, connects to sexual tension most strongly as related to activities and relationships of the past, thus it finds expression not only in jealousy but also in regret and remorse.

Another feature that Diamond's system has in common with traditional Chinese medicine is the layered interconnection of the meridians. That is to say, traditionally the organs and meridians interact on the basis of five phases, using the productive or control sequence in an integrated chain. If one part in this chain is weak, the weakness passes on to the next, which explains why, for example, someone with symptoms typically associated with the lungs has in fact a weakness of the spleen. To treat the condition, one begins by stimulating and harmonizing the organ showing the symptoms, then gradually moves back toward the organ of origin until the entire structure is cleared (Kohn 2005, 26).

In the same manner, John Diamond shows how energy moves in layers of different depths. For example, a person with great anxiety about the future reveals a weak spleen meridian, while all others test strong. She repeats the positive affirmation, "I have faith and confidence in my future," and soon the meridian tests strong. However, upon closer inspection, now the liver meridian is weak, showing an underlying tendency toward unhappiness from where the insecurity about the future sprang in the first place. After remedying this by repeating the appropriate affirmation, "I am happy," the next layer may be a weakness in the thyroid meridian, signaling a pervasive feeling of depression and lack of hope. Once this, too, is addressed, the entire system tests strong.

Just as acupuncture physicians recommend a quarterly check-up and regular qigong practice to keep the energy system humming along smoothly, so John Diamond suggests daily repetition of positive affirmations for the meridians, while lying down with back and neck supported and feet firmly planted on the floor (knees pointing to the ceiling). The session should close with, "My life energy is high. I am in the state of love," and always pay particular attention to the thymus gland, the central control of the entire energy system. [3]

Energy Centers

Closely corresponding to the three elixir fields in Daoism, Behavioral Kinesiology acknowledges three major centers in the human body. The most important among them, and the key factor in the entire system, is the thymus gland, matching the central elixir field (Diamond 1979, 10; 1985, 15).

Located in the solar plexus, the thymus gland was known already to the ancient Greeks as the central seat of vitality. "Thymus is the stuff of life, vaporous breath, active, energetic feeling and thinking, material very much related to blood" (Spencer 1993, 47). The gland, although known to exist, was ignored in Western medicine until the 1950s as not having a specific function, since it grows during puberty, is reduced in adulthood, shrinks to a miniscule size during sickness, and shrivels up completely after death (Diamond 1979, 10; 1985, 15-16). This in many ways matches the Chinese description of the rise and fall of kidney *qi*, i.e., sexual or vital essence, in the body. It moves in an eight-year cycles in males and a seven-year cycle in females. As the *Huangdi neijing suwen* has it,

> When a girl is seven years old, she has abundant kidney *qi* for the growth of permanent teeth as well as body hair. At 14, heavenly stock begins to be produced which ensures active functioning of the Conception and Penetrating Vessels: she starts to menstruate and is able to conceive.
>
> At 21, the level of kidney *qi* attains its peak and her body's development stops and her wisdom teeth grow. At 28, her body is at its peak and she has strong muscles and bones, and thick, luxurious hair. At 35, she starts to decline: initial aging signs such as a sallow face, wrinkles, or hair loss are usually due to the degeneration of the yang meridian.
>
> At 42, the three yang meridians in the upper body begin to decline, which leads to facial sagging, and graying hair, which eventually turns white. At 49, due to declining heavenly stock, the Conception and Penetrating Vessels are empty and collapse. Her body deteriorates, and her ability to menstruate and give birth ceases. (ch. 1; Veith 1972, 99)

---

[3] John Diamond has found the extraordinary meridians, activated in the Daoist meditation of the microcosmic orbit, related to second-order emotional states such as embarrassment and shame (1985, 187-89). He notes that the Daoist practice of placing the tongue at the roof of the mouth to connect the two centrla vessels activates the "centering button," a place that opens the body's central power lines and releases stress (1979, 31).

Recent biomedical studies have shown that the thymus gland functions as the center of human vitality, is thus in many ways connected to vital essence. It is also the seat of the will to live, the fundamental energy force that keeps people going in life and the opposite of what Freud describes as the death drive or death wish, sometimes called *thanatos* after the Greek word for "death" (Freud 1961). Psychiatrist Arnold Hutschnecker studied the will to live in detail, finding that it is engaged in a constant battle with the death wish in every human being, health or disease resulting as one or the other gains the upper hand (1978). Naomi Remen similarly finds that, however sick some people may get, when there is a strong will to live they can recover or hang on considerably longer than normally expected (2001).

Losing or lessening the will to live, i.e., the integrity of the thymus gland, creates a fundamental distortion of life energy. Once distorted at this level, it is twisted throughout the entire system, making everything in life more difficult and less effective. The will to live thus affects all else: medicine, counseling, weight issues, peak performance, alternative therapies, and all other endeavors aimed at living a healthy life—physically, mentally, emotionally, and spiritually (Carlson and Kohn 2012, 120).

Like the central elixir field in Daoism, the thymus gland as the seat of the will to live is the center of immunological surveyance and works to produce lymphocytes, i.e., the white blood cells responsible for the immunological reaction in the body (Diamond 1979, 11). Connected energetically to all the different organs and meridians, it reacts immediately to stress (see Selye 1984), but prevents disease and cancer if kept strong (Diamond 1979, 28-29).

The test point for the thymus gland is in the center of the breastbone, between the chest and the throat (1985, 19). It responds to massages, tapping, and positive affirmations, connecting particularly to the emotional attitudes of love, faith, trust, gratitude, and courage (1985, 33-38, 221). Physically we can strengthen it by opening our arms wide, like the Madonna offering a blessing; we weaken it by crossing our arms over our chest, like an Egyptian mummy (1985, 31-32). Fundamental negative emotions include fear, hate, and envy (see Klein 1957), which may be deeply rooted in the person and go back all the way to the birth trauma (see Leboyer 1975). However, they can be overcome through the creation of energetic immunity by clearing the meridians, repeating affirmations, and building the will to live, thus systematically strengthening the thymus gland (Diamond 1985, 49).

Not only the central, but also the upper and lower elixir fields of Daoist physiology have a match in the West. The upper field is obviously the brain with its major center of mental and emotional processing. Reactions in the brain divide into two types: good and bad, pleasant and unpleasant. Usually the bad, unpleasant emotions are afflictive, negative, and destructive; they tend to cause people to withdraw or move away from the object or circumstance that caused them. Good, pleasant emotions are beneficial, positive, and engaging;

they make people approach and seek out the object or circumstance that caused them (Goleman 1997, 34).

In terms of brain chemistry, withdrawal reactions are located in the right frontal cortex, while approach reactions are activated in the left frontal cortex. People are born with a tendency toward one or the other dominant activation. Those with more right frontal cortex activity are more emotionally volatile, get sick more easily, have a harder time recovering, suffer from numerous ailments, find much difficulty in their communities, and die earlier. People with dominantly left frontal cortex activity are more positive, do not submit to stress, will not catch colds even if exposed to germs, and live longer and happier lives. The dominant mode of reaction can be changed through learning and systematic training, notably through detached awareness and mindfulness practice, such as advocated by traditional Buddhists and Daoists alike.[4]

After giving prevalence to the brain for the longest time, modern scientists increasingly recognize that personality and mental activity also happen in other parts of the body. For example, more and more findings show that heart-transplant patients are taking on certain characteristics of their organ donors, such as a predilection for certain foods or a fascination with motor cycles (Sylvia and Novak 1997; Pearsall 1998; Schwartz and Russek 1999), indicating the importance of the central elixir field.

By the same token, the lower elixir field is now recognized as the seat presence of the "abdominal brain," where the body produces 95 percent of its serotonin (McMillin et al. 1999). "The gut," as Nora Gedgaudas notes, "has more neurons than the brain" (2009, 67). These neurons make up their own center of personality, holding inherent, spontaneous intelligence, in the vernacular described as gut feelings or intuition (Diamond 1979, 10). The "psychic center of the body," the enteric brain, as already described in the 19th century (see Bedell 1885), is the optimal source of creativity and productivity, so that top-energy musicians play entirely from here (Diamond 1986, 3:6).

Traditionally its activation is best known from Zen Buddhist and Daoist meditation, which both require a tightly held upright posture as well as conscious breathing and control over the diaphragm. Using the diaphragm to control the abdomen through breathing, practitioners activate the lower elixir field. As Katsuki Sekida says, "Mental action is exercised through the oscillation [of energy] from the brain to the [abdominal muscles] and from the muscles to the brain" (1975, 84). Much of Zen and Daoist practice thus serves to activate gut consciousness and interior energies while requiring complete overcoming of the conscious mind and ego-based reaction structures.

---

[4] Davidson 2003; Beauregard 2012, 74-75; Goleman 1997, 68-69; 2011, 35; Begley 2007, 226-33. Mindfulness practice is used increasingly for healing and emotional stabilization, helping people to live fuller lives and become more supportive members of society. See Kabat-Zinn 2005. Behavioral kinesiology, too, emphasizes the replacement of negative with pleasant feelings, loving thoughts and generosity (Diamond 1979, 45-46).

Practices

Behavioral kinesiologists recommend a number of practices to stimulate the thymus gland and increase individual vitality. Closely matching the repertoire of traditional Daoists, they include first of all forms of breathing that focus on the abdomen and engage the diaphragm as well as an active stimulation of the thymus area through tapping of major energy centers, especially in the chest, as well as self-massages along the Conception Vessel.

In terms of healing exercises, they insist on a straight and upright posture that allows an even flow of energy in all parts of the body and strongly recommend conscious and careful movements. They also suggest that movements should be three-dimensional and include lateral space, not just forward and back (Diamond 1986, 3:24) and alternate between the body's two sides and cross over the body at various times to stimulate energy flow in different areas (Diamond 1979). This reflects the kinesiological discovery that, when there is too much synchronous activity on either side of the body, it will suffer a cerebral-hemisphere imbalance and weakened muscles, a state Diamond describes as "switching" (1979, 40; 1985, 88).

In other words, the subtle energy lines of the body need to be activated by using the opposite arm and leg as much as possible, creating a sense of good body coordination. The lines are also impacted by any kind of metal that may be placed in the body's center and prevent proper energetic integration (1979, 43). Positive energy is further enhanced by wide, open gestures, such as the spreading of arms in a blessing or the welcoming of loved ones at a reunion (1979, 49; 1985, 32)—movements often seen in Chinese exercises where the *qi* is gathered or spread by opening the arms wide. In other words, the muscles of the body provide a clear indication of well-being and serve as a major way of enhancing health and longevity, which in turn have an immediate impact on social and political harmony in the community.

Movement, moreover, can be undertaken to melodious music—"a communication of love" (Diamond 1986, 3:19) and thus a powerful source of heightened energy. As John Diamond says,

> Its effects can be extraordinary. For example, we play music into acupuncture points on the body as an anesthetic.[5] We use music to help people overcome phobias, to love their mothers, to stop hating their spouses, and so on. (1986, 3:8)

---

[5] This is reminiscent of the incantations Daoist acupuncturists use to connect to the heavens and enhance their treatments (see Jackowicz 2011).

Music and rhythm being part of the human experience from before birth, they are closely connected to breath and thus part of the elementary experience of life energy (1986, 3:12).

A key factor in this context is the underlying feeling of love and care. We should refine this as well as cultivate the virtues, do good deeds, and create community at home and in society. Good energy emerges in the volition to increase peace in the world and support the creation of a harmonious society. After all, energy flows constantly between people so that, for example in music, "the listener picks up the precise negative or positive emotional state of the performer and even of the composer" (1986, 2:158). Depending on people's unique personality and energy management, they enhance or reduce its flow as they project it outward. The highest and most potent energy power, moreover, they achieve from an inner position of cosmic oneness—feeling deep love and a sense of unity with our family, friends, strangers, society, and nature (1986, 2:68, 71-73).

Besides interpersonal flow, kinesiologists note that environmental care plays an essential part in "energy hygiene" (Carlson and Kohn 2012, 158), providing good air, light, housing, and natural settings, closely matching the Chinese art of *fengshui*. It is similarly important to be careful about the selection of food, avoiding processed, preserved, or chemically altered items, which—as numerous studies have shown—denature foods and create imbalances in the body's chemistry. This goes closely together with the suggestion to wear loose and pure clothes, using natural fibers. More specifically, John Diamond suggests avoiding the use of sunglasses, wrist watches, nylon hats, wigs, high heels, and metal chairs, as well as seat cushions, mattresses, sheets, and clothing made from synthetic fabrics (1979, 74-77; 1985, 47).

In addition to widely recognized pollutants, such as denatured food, neon lights, smoking, and various irritating chemicals, he advises against contact with ugly sights and shrill or intensely pulsing sounds since they lead to "therapeutic weakening" (1979, 62). This, too, matches traditional Daoist rules against energetic pollution through encounters with dirt, death, or violence (Kohn 2004a, 23). Diamond especially singles out the weakening agents of aggressive art work and advertising as well as noise pollution through traffic, television, and modern atonal or rock music (1979, 65-66; 1986, 2:107-15).

Instead, we should take advantage of the energetic benefits of beauty, as found in poetry, music, painting, art, and natural landscapes and regularly take "energy breaks" by reciting poetry, looking at nature, viewing a painting, singing a song, or walking about with the arms swinging (Diamond 1979, 39; 1986, 3:51). All these are practices Daoists have embraced for centuries, living in beautiful natural settings, pursuing arts and music, and practicing visualizations such as the Inner Smile, where the facial muscles are relaxed and the internal organs viewed with sympathy and kindness (1979, 124).

To round all this off, John Diamond strongly recommends that we find a "homing thought"—what Ed Carlson calls Perfect Moment (Carlson and Kohn 2012, 116-17). This is a memory or mental vision of oneself in a pleasant and stress-free situation, such as in nature, on a beach, or with loved ones, and practice smiling both inwardly and to others, to create an internal harmony and relax the facial muscles (Diamond 1979, 47, 49; 1985, 71-82).

To sum up, the modern scientific examination of the body's musculature and essential glands in Behavioral Kinesiology shows that, as Chinese physicians and Daoists have contended for millennia, it is a finely tuned energetic system consisting of key power lines and energy centers, described traditionally as meridians, organs, and elixir fields. This system can be used to best advantage and enhanced in performance and longevity by taking certain basic precautions and following a few key daily practices. These include living in a healthy environment while maintaining careful awareness of energy imbalances and practicing deep breathing, open-armed movements, and the meditative repetition of positive affirmations.

The overall result of such practices, which are neither difficult to learn nor hard to do, is the realization of what F. M. Alexander has called "the possibility of physical perfection." This is a state of complete health, much more than the mere absence of illness or symptoms. Health here means an integrated balance of physical well-being, personal happiness, good fortune, and harmony, a state of overall wholeness, in which people go beyond being discreet entities separate from the outside world and instead become active participants in the triad of heaven, earth, and humanity. Physical and energetic perfection as pursued in Daoist body cultivation as well as in Behavioral Kinesiology is thus key not only to greater well-being and personal satisfaction, but also to the realization of a harmonious society and new world order.

Energy Psychology

One mode of treatment that has embraced this model is energy psychology, a development of energy medicine, which understands the body as a living matrix, simultaneously a mechanical, vibrational, energetic, electronic, photonic, and informational network, a complex, linked "tensegrity" system of pathways and molecules.[6] "Various interrelated energy systems, such as the aura, chakras, and

[6] For more details on energy medicine, see www.energy-medicine.info. Relevant works include Becker 1982; Becker and Sheldon 1985; Coghill 2000; Durlacher 1995; Filshie and White 1998; Foss and Rothenberg 1987; Gerber 2004; Oschman 2000; 2003' 2004; Philpott et al. 2000; Rosch 2009; Shealy 2011; Thomas et al. 2010. Other modalities that make use of energy psychology include Brain Gym and Educational Kinesiology (EduK), developed by Paul and Gail Dennison (www.braingym.org); PSYCH-K created by Rob Williams (www.psych-k.com); Eye Movement Desensitization and Reprocessing (EMDR)

meridians, each serve specific functions" (Feinstein et al. 2005, 197).[7] Supported increasingly by electromagnetic measurements, practitioners distinguish seven major aspects of the body's network:

—energy channels, e.g., acupuncture meridians and Ayurvedic channels (*nadis*);
—energy centers , e.g., chakras in yoga and elixir fields in Daoism;
—an energy shield up to a foot beyond the skin, i.e., the aura;[8]
—an energy grid, a sturdy fundamental network that underlies all;
—energy struts in the form of the Celtic Weave, a spinning, spiraling, twisting, and curving flow that holds it all together;
—an energy pulsation of five rhythms which match the five phases of Chinese cosmology and establish a person's primary functioning;
—the Triple Heater, which "networks the energies of the immune system to attack an invader and mobilizes the body's energies in emergencies;"
—and the radiant circuits, an adaptation of the eight extraordinary vessels in acupuncture, "operating like fluid fields and embodying a distinct spontaneous intelligence" (Feinstein et al. 2005, 201-03).[9]

On the basis of this essentially Asian-based vision of the human body, energy psychologists propose that people should (1) enhance their "energy aptitude," (2) perform daily exercises to harmonize their energies, and (3) use specific tapping techniques to release tensions, emotional trauma, and even physical ailments.

The first, energy aptitude, means the ability to work effectively with one's internal energies, along the lines of Daoist and kinesiological recommendations . It has four components: a fundamental careful awareness of energetic patterns, the ability to influence these patterns in a beneficial way, the faculty to perceive energies in other people and outside objects, and to join or transform these outside energies in a beneficial way (Feinstein et al. 2005, 204-5).

Daily exercises, next, include many moves familiar from yoga and qigong: they involve pressing key acupuncture points while breathing deeply and visualizing energies flowing through the body. Like Chinese healing exercises, they make use of various bodily postures and involve self-massages of key areas, such as the face, the scalp, and the abdomen. In some cases, meridian lines are

---

(www.emdr.com); Neuro Emotional Technique (NET) developed by Scott Walker (www.netmind-body.com); Core Health created by Ed Carlson (www.core health.us; Carlson and Kohn 2012) . For more, see the website of the Association for Comprehensive Energy Psychology, www.energypsych.org.

[7] This section also draws on Brennan 1987; Callahan and Trubo 2001; Eden and Feinstein 1998; Feinstein 2003; Gach and Henning 2004; Gallo 2000; 2004; Gallo and Vincenci 2000; King 2011; Lambrou and Pratt 2000.

[8] The aura is a single or multiple-colored layer of energy surrounding the body that reflects the person's inherent nature and that can be photographed with the help of Kirlian photography. See Krippner and Rubin 1974; Kunz 1991. See also www.kirlian.org.

[9] For more details on the various energy lines and centers in Chinese medicine, see Diamond 1990; Kaptchuk 2000; Kohn 2005; Seem 1990.

opened through placing the hands at either end and allowing the energies to flow. In others, simple bends and stretches in conjunction with conscious breathing and mental release serve the purpose (Cohen 1997).

The third and most important clinical application of energy psychology lies in tapping techniques—found both in Daoism and kinesiology—that ease stress, release trauma, and heal ailments. Developed into various modalities, such as Thought Field Therapy and Emotional Self Management (Lambrou and Pratt 2000) as well as Emotional Freedom Technique (Craig 2011; Salomon 2011), the method has patients measure a problem on a scale of "subjective units of distress" (SUDS) from 1 to 10. Preparing with a two-minute exercise in balanced breathing, they then imagine the feeling associated with the issue, create a positive affirmation ("Even though I have . . ., I deeply and completely accept myself"), and repeat it while tapping a set of acupuncture points.

The points range from the center of the forehead through the face, neck, and upper torso to the sides of the hands. Following completion of one round, they anchor the new energy pattern into their system. After this, they subjectively reassess their feeling and repeat the technique as needed—often with a slightly modified affirmation ("Even though I still have a remnant of . . .")—until their distress reaches zero. Not only are urgent and psychological issues relieved, but even long-standing physical conditions resolve with persistent tapping.

In a one-year study, a group of 2,500 patients received Energy Psychology, and another group of 2,500 patients received traditional Cognitive Behavioral Therapy (CBT) with prescription medications. Energy Psychology proved 43 percent more effective in reduction of symptoms (90% vs. 63%) and 49 percent more effective in total remission (76% vs. 51%), their participants needing 80 percent fewer visits (3 vs. 15) (Feinstein 2003, 20).

The Daoist-style approach to the human body and health central to Behavioral Kinesiology and energy psychology is still beyond acceptance in the established scientific community. This is partly because it requires a major paradigm shift: no longer seeing the structure of the body and its different aspects as mechanical but, matching quantum physics and string theory, as energetic, inherently alive, nonlocal, and holographic. It accordingly changes the modes of treatment away from outside intervention and toward personal acknowledgment and self-healing, increasing personal responsibility and individual autonomy, coming closer to the traditional system of Chinese longevity techniques and Daoist body cultivation.

Chapter Six

Way to Sit

The Neuropsychology of Meditation

On the basis of an energetically integrated and empowered body, Daoists further proceed to stabilize the mind, transform the senses, forget the self, and develop true observation and a positive approach to being in the world. They do so with different forms of meditation, the inward focus of attention in a state of mind where ego-related concerns and critical evaluations are suspended in favor of perceiving a deeper, subtler, and possibly divine flow of consciousness (Kohn 2008b, 1). Daoists use this in different ways to attain a subtler and more harmonious energy, sublimating the bodymind further while connecting to Dao on the sensory, emotional, and thinking levels in their overall quest to recover the cosmic potentiality of the universe within.

Stabilizing the Mind

The most fundamental form of Daoist meditation is a practice of concentration or mental focus that stabilizes the mind. It appears first in the *Daode jing* in the expression "embracing the One" (*baoyi* 抱一) as part of a general effort at "balancing life energy" (ch. 10). The Han commentator Heshang gong explains,

> If you can embrace the One and cause it to never leave the body, you will live forever. The One is the first product of Dao and virtue, the essential energy [*qi*] of Great Harmony. Therefore, we call it the One.
>
> The One pervades everything in the world. Heaven attains it to become clear; earth attains it to become solid; princes and kings attain it to become upright and just. Entering people, it forms their mind; emerging

> from people, it forms their activities; spreading through people, it forms their virtue. All this is simply called the One. What it ultimately means in practice is that one makes the will one and not two. (Kohn 2009, 164-65)

The One or "oneness" (*yi* 一) is highest unity, the "ultimate ancestor of everything" (Puett 2002, 318), the formless omnipresent integration of the cosmos (Capra 1975, 131). Unifying all things that exist, it is not a material or visible entity like heaven and earth or a single phenomenon as opposed to the many (Ames 1998, 228). Rather, signifying the number "one," overall unity, uniformity, and non-duality, it is a fundamental quality of Dao, designating togetherness, integration, the sum-total of all things, the origin of beings, the unity and coherence Dao gives to the world (Gu 2009, 162; Wang 2012, 48). It is the not-quite-something all things have in common that binds the universe together (Kohn 1989b, 127).

Adjectives associated with the One include all-round (*zhou* 周), whole (*quan* 全), combined (*he* 和), equal (*qi* 齊), together (*tong* 同) and pervasive or open (*tong* 通) (Shang 2002, 243). Oneness is the spontaneous activity that makes all things what they are (*zisheng* 自生), "the infinite flux of the ever-becoming nature in which everything comes to be and ceases to be and cannot help but be what it is" (2002, 248). The One thus means commonality but not uniformity, togetherness but not identity (2002, 244). All beings obtain the One to be just what they are (*Daode jing* 39; *Zhuangzi* 6; Kohn 2014, 83-84).

A more formalized way of oneness meditation is "guarding the One" (*shouyi* 守一), an expression that first occurs in the *Zhuangzi* as part of the later commonly cited catchphrase, "Once knowing how to guard the One, the myriad affairs are done" (*zhi shouyi wanshi bi* 知守一萬事畢) (ch. 12; Kohn 1989b, 131). Medieval Daoists describe it as a practice of inward attention and one-pointedness of mind, using breath, body, inner lights, or body gods as their main object of focus (1989b, 137-41; in Pregadio 2008, 575).

The resulting state is one of stillness, quietude, or tranquility (*jing* 靜), described in the *Zhuangzi* as "the body like dried wood and the mind like dead ashes" (ch. 2) and already in the *Daode jing* associated with "guarding stillness" (*shoujing* 守靜), an empty and open mind (ch. 16), as well as with inner peace and freedom from desires (ch. 37). Also a key feature in the "Neiye" 內業 (Inward Training) chapter of the *Guanzi* (Roth 1999, 109-12), stillness plays a central role. The word forms part of the general Chinese term for meditation, "quiet sitting" (*jingzuo* 靜坐), used in Confucian texts for calm reflection in a formal kneeling posture (see Taylor 1988; Kohn in Pregadio 2008, 902). It also occurs in the technical Daoist term for meditation hut, "quiet chamber" or "oratory" (*jingshi* 靜室), a separate, sparsely furnished structure not unlike a Japanese tea house (Kohn 2003, 107-09; Boltz in Pregadio 2008, 573).

Stillness is the quality of clear water in its most aligned, even state—transposed into the natural and human realm as "uprightness" (*zheng* 正), the best and most proper way of being (Roth 1999, 110). It also comes with a deep inner solidity, described as "stability" (*ding* 定), later used to translate the Buddhist term for highly focused mental absorption, *samādhi* (Kohn 2010a, 49). And it gives rise to a soft radiance (*guang* 光) or luminous clarity (*qing* 清), in later Daoism associated with the bright light of wisdom (*zhi* 智). Already the *Zhuangzi* says, "He whose inner being rests in peaceful stability will spread a heavenly radiance" (ch. 22), while the *Daode jing* emphasizes that "clarity and stillness provide uprightness in all under heaven" (ch. 45).

A completely focused mind, then, is stable and radiant. As Sun Simiao says in his *Cunshen lianqi ming*,

> The mind is turned entirely toward clarity and stillness. Whether involved in affairs or free from them, there is no agitation at all. From an efficiently controlled mind, firmness and solidity arise and full stability develops. (2a; Kohn 2010a, 176)

The contemporaneous *Dingguan jing* 定觀經 (Scripture of Stability and Observation, DZ 400; trl. Kohn 2010a, 163-73) adds,

> Serene yet steadily radiant, radiant yet constantly serene, empty yet steadily functioning, functioning yet constantly empty—this is the attainment of original and primordial serenity, thus described as "perfect stability." (10a; Kohn 2010a, 168)

Also, the *Wuchu jing* 五廚經 (The Five Kitchens, DZ 76; trl. Kohn 2010a, 198-206) notes,

> Upright wisdom is deeply luminous. It mirrors universal light, and the world's dust and grime have no place to stick. Like a deep abyss and unadulterated, it regards the myriad phenomena equally. Seeing all phenomena equally without a perceiving agent: this is the constant mind. (3b; 2010a, 202; see also Mollier 2000)

The constant or stable mind, then, is the root condition for all other meditative explorations. From here, adepts move on to transform sensory perception, release emotional affects, and reorganize their conscious thinking.

Sensory Transformation

The first description of sensory transformation appears in the *Zhuangzi* in a practice called "mind-fasting" (*xinzhai* 心齋).

> Unify your will and don't listen with your ears but listen with your mind. No, don't listen with your mind, but listen with your *qi*. Listening stops with the ears, the mind stops with matching [perception], but *qi* is empty and waits on all things. Dao gathers in emptiness alone. Emptiness is mind-fasting. (ch. 4; Graham 1981, 68; Kohn 2011, 107; 2014, 125)

This involves the systematic release of sensory processing until, instead of hearing with the ears and the mind, one is only aware of the steady flow of *qi* manifesting as sounds in a state of immobile, empty, open, nonjudging awareness (Jochim 1998, 52; Santee 2011, 52-53). To reach the inner emptiness of Dao, one begins with an act of will and intention, turns one's attention inward, stabilizes the mind, and withdraws the senses. Then one relaxes into a more fluid state, letting the senses and emotions go, and allowing pure cosmic energy to move, impartial and open, eventually reaching emptiness and no-mind (Kohn 2010a, 25; Santee 2008, 114-15). The *Zhuangzi* also describes the same process in Guangchengzi's instructions to the Huangdi, the Yellow Emperor,

> The essence of perfect Dao is serene and dark; the ultimate of perfect Dao is dim and silent. Don't look, don't listen, but embrace spirit in stillness, and your body will right itself. . . . Take care of inner [power], close off outer [impact]. (ch. 11; Roth 1997b, 59-60)

As this state of stillness develops, as the mind increasingly becomes "like dead ashes," the senses and their effects are increasingly experienced as cosmic flow, to the point of complete freedom from sensory-based reactions and emotional dispositions (*wuqing* 無情). As the *Zhuangzi* says: "What I mean when I say a person is free from dispositions is that he does not allow likes and dislikes entering him and burdening his body, but always goes along with his inherent naturalness, never trying to improve on life" (ch. 5). This is illustrated vividly in several episodes concerning death and mourning. While Zhuangzi feels sadness at the loss of his wife, for example, "his grief being unexceptional and its origin obvious," he expresses it by drumming and singing, showing that there is no need for "sorrow of greater duration" (ch. 18; Olberding 2007, 342).

Rather than placing particular values and attaching specific interpretations to sensory and emotional patterns, creating a sense of identity and personal body, one's self becomes part of the natural world and the body is just that: a physical vessel of survival. A vibrant, living entity, this body is pure physical form (*xing* 形). As such, it serves as the lodge or residence of the spirit (ch. 6;

Pregadio 2004, 108), allowing cosmic energy to flow through it freely. The more we keep the spirit whole, retaining innocence and wonder, the more "the form stays whole, so that it can live forever" (ch. 11) (Billeter 2010, 63). Not only that, but the senses, part of the flow of pure spirit, can be heightened toward enhanced perception.

Later Daoists, too, place high emphasis on the control and withdrawal of the senses as part of the overall effort of retaining and enhancing *qi* as part of the immortality process. For example, the early Numinous Treasure text *Shangpin dajie* presents a set of "Six Precepts of Wisdom" as essential blocks against the six passions and the basis for future transformation. For example,

> 1. Let not your eyes gaze widely or be confused by flowery colors lest you lose their clarity and diminish your pupils, their radiance no longer bright and penetrating.
>
> 2. Let not your ears be confused in their hearing or obscured by the five sounds lest you harm spirit and destroy uprightness, hearing bad sounds everywhere. (6a)

These precepts contain warnings against overindulgence in the senses, which cause turbidity in the body and loss of *qi* (6ab). They merge the *Daode jing* warning against overloading the senses with the medical understanding of moral action, while also adjusting the number to match the Buddhist system of the five precepts and adding the mind as a sixth sense (Kohn 2004a, 32).

Beyond curbing harmful tendencies, however, these precepts also encourage sensory transformation toward purity and cosmic openness. As the bright radiance of wisdom shines forth from the stable mind, each sensory organ shifts its focus from passion to compassion, from separation to oneness, attaining psychic perception, classically called "spirit pervasion" (*shentong* 神通). For example, the eyes transform from human sense organs into heavenly potencies as concrete sight turns into universal vision. "With the eyes of heaven, one's understanding is lofty and wisdom pervades all without limits. Above and below, in the four corners and eight directions, nothing is not illumined, nothing is not radiantly bright" (10b).

That is to say, by avoiding the intricacies of worldly vision and being shaded against the enticing patterns of outside life, practitioners transform the potency of their eyes, making them susceptible to the subtler and more brilliant vibrations of the light of heaven. The inner eye joins with cosmic radiance, and their merged vibrations obliterate blockages to expose all to a pervading, penetrating light. "As long as people pattern themselves on heaven, the bright pupils in the eyes can freely follow the radiance of the five colors" (10b). Similarly, the other senses transform from a mundane to a cosmic level, so that the Daoist becomes able to see, hear, and feel with the *qi* of Dao rather than through the limited agents of the body (Kohn 2004a, 33-34).

Oblivion

To further liberate themselves from the limiting sense of a human-bound self, Daoists also practice oblivion (*zuowang* 坐忘), literally "sit and forget." The practice is first mentioned in the *Zhuangzi*, in a dialogue between Confucius and his disciple Yan Hui 顏回, during which the latter reports that he is "getting better" at attaining Dao.

When Confucius asks what he means, Yan Hui says that he has "forgotten benevolence and righteousness," two essential Confucian virtues that, according to the *Daode jing* (ch. 18), form part of the superimposition of culture on human life and thus represent a step away from Dao. Confucius tells him that this is good, but that he has not gone far enough. At their next meeting Yan Hui says he has now "forgotten rites and music," taking aim at the fundamental Confucian ways of relating to the world, which are similarly denounced as betraying true humanity in the *Daode jing*. When Confucius tells Yan Hui that he still has a ways to go, he leaves, then reports again:

> "I'm getting there!" — "How so?" — "I sit and forget!"
> Confucius was startled: "What do you mean, you sit and forget?"
> "I let my limbs and physical structure fall away, do away with perception and intellect, separate myself from my bodily form, and let go of all knowledge, thus joining Great Pervasion. This is what I mean by sit and forget."
> (ch. 6; Kohn 2010a, 7; 2015, 162; Watson 1968, 90)

Used sparingly in the early middle ages, oblivion became the general appellation of Daoist meditative transformation in the Tang dynasty, when the Highest Clarity patriarch Sima Chengzhen used it in his *Zuowang lun*. Beginning with strong "respect and faith" in Dao, practitioners leave the world (at least temporarily) to "intercept karma," then practice concentration to "tame the mind" and gain one-pointed focus. In the fourth step, "detachment from affairs," they reevaluate the way they live in the world and the development of a sense of inner flow and connection to Dao. After that, they come to see the world differently by practicing "true observation." Eventually they reach the "stability of cosmic peace" and from there "attain Dao" (see Kohn 2010a).

Today "sit and forget" denotes a practice that involves a loss of self and conscious mentation. For example, the Shaanxi Daoist master Liu Xingdi says,

> *Zuowang* is allowing everything to slip from the mind, not dwelling on thoughts, allowing them to come and go, simply being at rest. It is important to take a good posture to still the body and calm the mind. Otherwise *qi* disperses, attention wanders, and the natural process is disturbed. Just remain empty and there is no separation from Dao.

> Then wisdom will arise and bring forth light, with is the clear *qi* of the person. Do not think too much about the theory of this, otherwise you are sure to disturb the mind. It is like the sun rising in the east and setting in the west. To think about stopping it halfway is a futile exercise. Just trust the inherent natural process. (Shi 2005, 6)

While this sees oblivion more of a state that is natural and not separated from Dao, Eva Wong, renowned author and long-term practitioner of Complete Perfection (Quanzhen 全真) Daoism, finds it more of an active method:

> *Zuowang* is a dropping of conceptions. When we drop conceptions, what we have is the natural emergence of the natural self, the natural celestial mind, which has been with us all the time. It is only because of our conceptions that we cannot experience it. So when we practice zuowang, we are simply saying that here is a method where we can begin to drop conceptions. . . .
>
> Everything is meditation—walking, sitting, standing—and when we begin to realize this, then that is true meditation. There is no longer a distinction between non-meditation and meditation. (Shi 2007, 8)

Part of Daoist training everywhere, *zuowang* is actively taught in the West today by the British Taoist Association (BTA) under their leader Shi Jing, in Da Yuan Circle founded by Liu Ming (see Phillips 2008), in the Qigong and Daoist Training Center by Michael Rinaldini (Rinaldini 2008; 2013), as well as in other Daoist institutions.

Formally undertaken in a seated position, it requires a stable physical alignment. As Liu Ming points out: legs crossed or folded (solid like a mountain), back straight but light, stomach empty, head drawn upward, eyes holding a relaxed gaze, tongue touching the roof of the mouth, hands resting comfortably in the lap, and the breath flowing gently and in complete silence (Kohn 2010a, 15; 2015, 162). The stability of the body allows the release of the mind and the self. As Shi Jing notes: "*Zuowang* is to sit and forget. What we forget is the thing we hold most dearly: self, with all its opinions, beliefs, and ideals . . . personal ambitions and desires" (2006, 11; see also Rinaldini 2008, 187).

The meditative procedure of oblivion, then, involves various forms of release. Already the *Zhuangzi* uses terms like "let fall away" or "drop" (*duo* 墮), "do away" (*chu* 黜), "separate from" (*li* 離), and "let go of" (*qu* 去). The same holds also true for other, related *Zhuangzi* passages that use terms like "fast" (*zhai* 齋; ch. 5), "put outside" (*wai* 外) and "not have" (*wu* 無; ch. 6), and various verses of the *Daode jing*, which speak of "emptying" (*xu* 虛; ch. 3), "abandoning" (*que* 絕, ch. 18), "diminishing" (sun 損; ch. 48) , and so on.

The core notion that emerges from these descriptions, both ancient and modern, then, is of a relatively rigid self—a cluster of perceptions, emotions, intentions, intellect, responses, actions, and more—that needs to be released, diminished, unfurled, emptied, or opened, so that we can attain Dao and "join Great Pervasion." Ultimately this will lead to the desired state of leisurely resting in nonaction, flowing through life in free and easy wandering, and finding perfect happiness—to use *Zhuangzi* terms; or be fluid and gentle like water, weak and soft, deep and still, simple and tranquil—in the vision of the *Daode jing* (Kohn 2015, 163). Free from emotional reactions and mental judgments and classifications, the cumbersome burdens of the personal self, one can take life as it comes and relate to the world with ease and flexibility.

Observation

This ease and flexibility, moreover, develop further through yet another form of meditative practice: "observation" (*guan* 觀). The Chinese first used the term to describe insight, mindfulness, or awareness practice (*vipāsyana*) as adopted from Buddhism. It works with developing a new dimension of the conscious mind, establishing a detached, objective observer or "witness consciousness," a mental position of distanced observation.

Anyone with discriminating consciousness and theory of mind inevitably can see himself as an object and thus naturally has this detached observer, most obvious in the ability to laugh at oneself when in a strange situation. Insight or observation practice enhances it and makes it accessible at all times. Learning to both feel an experience immediately and see it from a distance, practitioners begin to identify, observe, and cleanse negative reactions while cultivating positive thoughts and states, such as compassion and kindness, calmness and equanimity, peace and joy. They also come to see the world increasingly in the perspective of the religion, understanding that neither mind nor self or life are immutable, firm entities but constantly changing (Kohn 2008b, 73).

The earliest Daoist record of the practice appears in the *Zhuangzi*:

> The hundred joints, the nine openings, the six organs, all come together and exist here [as my body]. But which part should I feel closest to? I should delight in all parts, you say? But there must be one I ought to favor more. If not are they all of them mere servants? . . . There must be some true lord among them, yet try as I may, I cannot find him. (ch. 2; Watson 1968, 38; Kohn 2008b, 85)

Medieval Daoists continue this in a practice called "inner observation" (*neiguan* 內觀). As documented in the Tang-dynasty *Neiguan jing* 內觀經 (Scripture of Inner Observation, DZ 641; trl. Kohn 2010a, 179-87), this refers to a practice of turning one's eyes inward and seeing the interior state of one's body and mind. The term can indicate the seeing of colors in the inner organs, the visualization of deities, the observation of the movements of life energy, the detached analysis of mental activities, and the development of a non-judgmental attitude toward all things. Coming to see the body is a microcosmic replica of the starry heavens above, full of palaces and chambers, gods and deities, Daoists increase awareness of their heavenly nature, rest in their original cosmic nature, and let the intuition of the spirit(s) guide them through life (Kohn 1989a).

The late-Tang *Qingjing jing* 清靜經 (Scripture of Clarity and Stillness, DZ 620; trl. Kohn 1993, 24-29; Wong 1992), details this further, contrasting inner (*neiguan*) with outer (*waiguan* 外觀) and far observation (*yuanguan* 遠觀). By this, it means observation first of the mind, then of the body, and finally of outside objects and other beings, in each case encouraging practitioners to recognize through the practice that none of the objects is there in reality as a firm, solid, material entity but dissolves upon closer scrutiny into vibrations of cosmic energy and pure Dao. The practice then culminates in "observation of emptiness" (*kongguan* 空觀), the perfect way of looking at the world in a pervasive openness to cosmic power.

Another dimension of "observation," more closely related to Buddhist insight practice is "perfect observation" (*zhenguan* 真觀), the title of Section 5 of the *Zuowang lun*. The text guides adepts to view their life as a manifestation of Dao and *qi*, loosening attachments to self, life, and body, and eliminating all critical evaluations of the world and its objects.

> Someone who is horrified by death, for example, should think of his personal body as the lodge of spirit. As the body grows old and sick, as *qi* and strength decline day by day, it will just be like a house with rotting walls. Once it becomes uninhabitable, it is best to abandon it and look for another place to stay. The death of the body-self and the departure of spirit are then a mere change of residence. (Kohn 2010a, 152)

Similarly, "poverty and diseases, irritations and troubles" should be seen in a larger karmic and cosmic context, examining them in wisdom and observing them with detachment. "Realizing that smell and taste are to be given up as nothing but a steady flow of craving and desires, how could you regard the fishmonger's shop as stinking?" (2010a, 153).

To further strengthen this Dao-based outlook, Daoists also practice affirmations or resolutions (*yuan* 願), declarations of positive intent based on a cosmic mindset. Found first in the *Benyuan dajie* 本願大戒 (Great Precepts of Original Resolutions, DZ 344), a Numinous Treasure text of the fifth century, they include specific prayers or good wishes. For example, "When I encounter clouds and rain, I pray that all may be soaked with kindness and be full to overflowing, so there is nothing that does not grow." Or, "I will constantly practice a compassionate mind and pray and be mindful that all beings equally get to see the divine law" (6a; Kohn 2004a, 198).

Not just generally lofty thoughts during encounters with others, affirmations also raise the awareness of ordinary, daily functions with the help of special verses. First documented in the *Huayan jing* (e.g., Cleary 1984, 318), they accompany all daily activities of Daoists, creating a sense of cosmic connection and universal well-wishing even during the most mundane of acts. They appear variously in medieval texts, are prominent in the rules of Complete Perfection, and still play an important role today (Kohn 2004a, 106). For example, opening the eyes after a night's sleep, Daoists think, "I pray that all living beings leave the path of error and enter awakening, clear and open like this bright morning." Upon hearing the bell that orders them to rise, they reflect, "May the great sound of the bell wake all to truth and perfection!" (Min 1990, 107).

Concentrative Meditation

Following the Buddhist model, contemporary researchers frequently divide meditation into two types: concentrative and insight (Shapiro 1984, 6; Dalai Lama 2002, 118-19; Goleman 1988). Called cessation (*samathā*) or mindfulness of breathing (*ānapānasati*), concentration here is a one-pointedness of mind that involves complete control of attention and the absorption in a single object to the exclusion of all else. Its counterpart is insight (*vipāsyana*), an openness to all sorts of sensory stimuli, a sense of free-flowing awareness with detached observation (Wilber 2004, 125).

The object of concentration can be a sound, a visual diagram, or a concrete object. Most commonly, however, it is the breath, either intentionally lengthened or observed as a natural process. If the latter, practitioners typically anchor the mind with the help of kinesthetic, visual, or auditory awareness. That is to say, they observe the breath as they feel it in the body, either as it enters and leaves the nostrils or as it expands and flattens the abdomen. Alternatively, they link it with a simple and steady image, such as of a flame, vase, or deity. They may also associate it with certain words matching inhalation and exhalation, such as "in-out" or "one-two," or count the length or number of respirations (see Rosenberg 1999).

In all cases, the basic goal is to still the conscious mind. Called elementary or access concentration, what Daoists describe as "stillness," this creates a basic level of mental focus and sensory calm necessary for further pursuits (Kohn 2008b, 40). In neurophysiogical terms, it signals a state of hyperquiescence of the autonomic nervous system (Newberg et al. 2001, 40). Full or attainment concentration, on the other hand, in Daoism described as "perfect stability," happens when there is a breakthrough from quiescence into arousal (2001, 42). Complete one-pointedness of attention, it is the utter absorption in a single object, a state of inner bliss and the release of the ego—in Buddhism formulated in a series of stages of absorption (*dhyānas*; King 1980, 41-54), in mysticism studies described as the introvertive or enstatic experience.[1]

In the modern West, concentrative meditation has been widely studied in medical and psychological settings and today is accepted generally as an efficient means to reduce stress and enhance inner calm. It first appeared in the 1960s when Transcendental Meditation under the leadership of Maharishi Mahesh Yogi made major inroads in Western societies, inspiring the Beatles and Rolling Stones to meditate in India and making converts among professionals, businessmen, and hippies alike (Roth 1987). Soon the practice inspired experimental research into altered states of consciousness (Tart 1969) and first scientific studies were undertaken, consisting largely of EEG brain wave measurements as well as various forms of psychological assessments (see Shapiro and Walsh 1984, 363-534).

Fundamentally, concentration works by lengthening and deepening the breath (Newberg and O'Leary 2009, 179). Breathing is intimately connected to the autonomic nervous system, which "oversees the body's vital functions through subconscious signals that originate in the anterior cyngulate gyrus and are relayed to the hypothalamus and spinal cord" (Ratey 2002, 171). Its sympathetic part puts us into a state of readiness to meet challenges or danger, causing nerve endings to emit neurotransmitters that stimulate the adrenal glands to secrete powerful hormones that increase the heartbeat and the rate of breathing. Its parasympathetic aspect, on the other hand, activates neurotransmitters like acetylcholine that lower the pulse and breathing rate. Its responses are comfort, relaxation, and sleep (2002, 173; Newberg et al. 2001, 38; see also Selye 1984).

Both, moreover, connect closely to the endocrine system in charge of the hormones that control growth, activity levels, and sexuality. Notably endorphins and enkephalins modulate reactions to stress and pain, affect moods and appetite, and support abilities of learning and memory. The more one is in the parasympathetic mode, i.e., the deeper and slower the breath, the better the endocrine system can do its work. The same holds also true for the immune system, which explains why so many people today are suffering from stress related ailments (Loehr and Migdow 1986, 20-26; Kohn 2008a, 30). While it is physiologically impossible to breathe deeply and be stressed at the same time, people under stress breathe only into their chests, gasping out air as if they were pushing a heavy load (Kohn 2008b, 32). As Zhuangzi puts it, "The multitude breathe just to the throat—bent over and submissive, they croak out words as if they were retching" (ch. 6; Watson 1968, 77-78).

The best known and most prominent Western study and adaptation of concentration practice is the Relaxation Response, developed by Herbert Benson of Harvard University. Its practice involves sitting or lying comfortably, closing the eyes, and breathing deeply through the nostrils while repeating a

---

[1] James 1936, 380-81; Underhill 1911, 416-20; Roth 2000, 33; Beauregard 2012, 185.

word or phrase of choice—often inspired by religious beliefs—either vocally or mentally. The practice should be continued for twenty minutes while maintaining a receptive, passive attitude and permitting relaxation to occur at its own pace. The Relaxation Response is effective in relieving pain and anxiety, enhancing an inner state that encourages natural healing or allows a gradual drifting into death.[2] In the 1980s, Joan Borysenko and Ilan Kutz developed it further in their Mind/Body Clinic, using deep breathing and gentle stretches to alleviate anxiety and also working with mindfulness to restructure thinking (Borysenko and Rothstein 1987, 36-52).

With prolonged concentration efforts, moreover, breathing slows down even more, to as few as two respirations per minute, and the brain moves into slower rhythms, such as alpha waves commonly observed in Zen practitioners. More advanced disciples may also enter states dominated by theta waves that indicate a deeply calm, yet conscious state unique to meditation. Less frequent but also observed were delta waves, usually associated with deep sleep and hypnotic somnambulism. People in this state appear unconscious yet can perceive sensory stimuli (Davidson 1984), opening to the vista of the inner mind and more divine levels of life.

Sensory Modification

One effect of concentration is the reduction of sensory input, setting the stage for a modification of the senses, i.e., changing the inner workings of the brain, the main location of sensory perception. While certain responses to the taste and smell of food, such as salivation or choking, are unconditioned reflexes, the cerebral cortex also modifies them, resulting in conditioned responses, such as anticipatory salivation (Gardner 1968, 332). This, through culture and over time, may significantly alter human needs.

A drastic example is the continuously increasing desire for sweet flavors in the modern world. In the 1700s, after the introduction of sugar from sugar cane, people consumed about four pounds per person per year. By 1800, this number had risen to eighteen; by 1900, to ninety; and by 2005, especially in the United States, to 140. Today, Americans consume twice the sugar Europeans do, and nine times more than the Chinese. By the same token, taste potentiators, i.e., chemicals for flavor enhancement, have increased exponentially, American using twelve pounds of artificial sweetener per person in 1980 and 24 pounds in 2005 (Henshaw 2012, 131-34).

All this goes to show that sense perception, while working through our instinctual and reflexive systems, is a brain activity and as such culturally de-

---

[2] Fried 1993, 240-42; Newberg and Waldman 2009, 184; see also Benson 1976; 1996; Benson and Proctor 1985.

termined through learning, memory, and the establishment of set neural pathways. This means that there really is no such thing as "pure experience," a common catch phrase in Zen and other mystical traditions (e.g., Nishida 1990). Rather, as Aldous Huxley famously noted, "The function of the brain and the nervous system is to protect us from being overwhelmed and confused by masses of largely useless and irrelevant knowledge" (1954, 22; Norretranders 1998, 293). Or, as Eben Alexander puts it, "Our brains work hard every moment of our waking lives to filter out the barrage of sensory information coming at us from our physical surrounding, selecting the material we actually need in order to survive" (2012, 81), a process technically known as "latent inhibition" (Stein 2007, 225).

Huxley personally experienced just how far this protection goes when, in May 1953, he underwent an experiment later replicated by Timothy Leary (1970), Huston Smith, and others (Beauregard 2012, 200; Prince 1980, 344; Sacks 2012, 110). He took a dose of lysergic acid or mescaline, a chemically synthesized version of peyote, a Mexican cactus with strong hallucinogenic properties, which "inhibits the production of enzymes that regulate the supply of glucose to the brain" (Huxley 1954, 9-11, 24). Within a half hour, he started to see a "dance of golden lights, red surfaces swelling, nodes of energy vibrating in continuously changing patterns" rather than faces or landscapes (1954, 16). As his perception slowed down drastically, he saw all objects in great detail, noticing how the flowers breathed and appreciating the intrinsic aliveness of everything (1954, 17-19).

Space and spatial relationships no longer mattered; time and temporal relationships became irrelevant. He had no more sense of self and others, but rather experienced a sacramental vision of reality and a sense of being one with all things (1954, 20-22)—matching Daoist ideas of perceiving through *qi* and opening to cosmic flow. "Mescaline," he says, eerily echoing Daoist contentions, "delivers us from the world of selves, of time, of moral judgments, and utilitarian considerations, the world of self-assertion, of cocksureness, of overvalued words, and idolatrously worshiped notions" (1954, 36), taking us on a "chemical vacation from intolerable selfhood" (1954, 64).

A less intense but more permanent state of sensory alteration also emerges in deep hypnotic trance (see Erickson and Havens 1985) and through the intensification of perception. This can be intentionally developed in ordinary life. For example, as commonly known, artists who work with a full palette tend to see more colors, possessing a greater subtlety of perception and the ability to distinguish hues that would look the same to others (www.colourlovers.com). Trained musicians can hear subtle differences in pitch, tone, and rhythm that elude others who lost this ability—after all, infants tend to have perfect pitch, which only one in 10,000 retains after the first few years of life (Mithen 2006, 77). World-class "noses" in the perfume and wine business can detect and identify hundreds, if not thousands, of different odors, a skill developed through years of rigorous training (http://phys.org/news/ 2011-03-super-innate.html).

Beyond that, some people with deficiency in one of their senses develop a heightened perception in others. Typically, deaf people learn how to lip read and use sign language, expanding both their visual and kinesthetic powers. Blind people regularly train to use their hands to read via Braille; some also learn to see colors by sensing their electromagnetic radiation (Panati 1974, 159). More recently, they can also train in echolocation, the ability known from bats "to build a representation of the environment from information carried by echo returns, which lays the foundation for auditory spatial memory" (http://pbs.jhu.edu/research/moss/research). The best-known representative of human echolocation is Daniel Kish (b. 1966), who lost the sight of both eyes at the age of 13 months. Now he uses his ears to see, clicking his tongue and then listening as the sound bounces off nearby objects. Having perfected this skill, he has developed a training system called FlashSonar, instructing blind people worldwide and thereby opening them to a full life with no limitations (www.worldaccessfortheblind.org).

Yet another form of sensory modification is synesthesia, literally "union of the senses," where "images or qualities of one sensory modality are transferred to another" (Marks 2000, 121; Panati 1974, 41). Found in about one person in 25,000, it occurs when the stimulation of one sensory or cognitive pathway leads to automatic, involuntary experiences of a second one, enhancing one sense through another and activating overlapping neural networks (2000, 132). For example, people may see colors or shapes when hearing words or sounds, envision dates or numeral sequences in certain locations in space, or have particular tactile sensations or tastes when they hear specific sounds.[3] While this comes naturally to some people, it is also possible to learn the application of multiple senses. For example, in brain enhancement and memory training, people who want to improve their ability to remember names are taught to create an association with the name and link it to a visual cue.

As the senses are sharpened and made subtler, they not only merge but also allow perception on a subtler level. Thus, some people are able to sense electrical currents, feel magnetic fields, or detect subterranean water (e.g., dowsers); others become sensitive to emotional states or even thoughts in others. Developing a sort of sixth sense, they work with hunches, instincts, and intuitions, navigating the world on a subtler and more potent level, activating the enteric in addition to the head brain. This closely matches the subtle combination or even merging of the senses in ancient Daoism, where it is a sign of advanced spiritual attainment. As the *Liezi* records in the words of Laozi's disciple Gengsangzi,

---

[3] Frith 2007, 51; Henshaw 2012, 225; Marks 2000, 128; Ramachandran 2011, 75-116.

> Whenever the minutest existing thing or the faintest sound affects me, whether it is far away beyond the eight borderlands or close at hand between my eyebrows and eyelashes, I am bound to know it. However, I do not know whether I perceived it with the seven holes in my head and my four limbs, or knew it through my heart and belly and internal organs. It is simple spontaneous knowledge. (ch. 4; Graham 1960, 77-78)

Forgetting

In order to fully experience this subtle state, moreover, we must silence the conscious mind with its constant judgments, evaluations, and criticisms or, as the *Zhuangzi* describes it, do away with "body and mind, perception and intellect," forget all prior knowledge and establish ourselves fully in the present moment. Neurophysiologically this would involve the prevention of long-term memory formation through a major inhibition of the hippocampus. There are people who have experienced this, a condition medically known as Korsakov's syndrome, often caused by extensive alcoholic degeneration. People in this state have no conscious memories but are still functioning socially, typically showing faint amusement and indifference (Sacks 1985, 26).

"Isolated in a single moment of time, with a moat of forgetting all around them" (Sacks 1985, 28), they have no day before, no awareness of self, and no future. "I have no memory of the present. I do not know what I have just done or from where I just came," a patient says (1985, 33-34). A prominent recent example is Clive Wearing, a musicologist at Cambridge University who had a herpes infection that hit the hippocampus. Living in the eternal present, he was permanently trapped in the here and now, "under the constant impression that he had just emerged from unconsciousness" and forgetting the existence of everything and everyone, most notably his wife: every time she returned after leaving the room, he discovered her anew (Hood 2012, 77; Joordens 2011, 61; Wearing 2005).

A fictional treatment of the same topic appears in the movie, *Fifty First Dates*. Susan, a pretty young art teacher, has suffered an injury to her temporal lobe and is stuck on the day of the accident, going through exactly the same motions from morning to night. Her father and brother recreate the day as much as possible but then Bill, a local animal trainer, meets her at her regular breakfast diner and falls in love with her. After a lot of resistance from family and friends, and after she wakes up screaming when she finds him in her bed, he hits upon the ingenious method of showing her a videotape every morning that familiarizes her with the fact of her accident and memory loss and updates her to the present day. They marry and have a little girl. Susan retains her youthful, sunny disposition but she never gets better, meeting her husband and daughter anew every day.

An ancient Daoist version of this rather radical forgetfulness appears in the story of Master Hua 華子, a man of Song who was constantly forgetting everything. "He would receive a present in the morning and forget it by evening, give a present in the evening and forget it by morning. On the road, he would forget to walk; in the house he would forget to sit down. Today he would not remember yesterday; tomorrow he would not remember today" (*Liezi* 4; Graham 1960, 70).

However, unlike modern sufferers, he managed to recover his faculties. His family, deeply upset by his condition, consulted various specialists, all to no avail, until a Confucian of Lu came and offered to do an early version of psychotherapy. "He tried stripping Hua, so that he looked for clothes. He tried starving him, so that he looked for food. He tried shutting him up in the dark, so that he looked for light." Encouraged by these signs that there was a survival instinct still at work, the Confucian asked to be left alone with Hua and, literally overnight, jerked him out of his memory loss—to the latter's great regret: "Formerly, when I was forgetting everything, I was boundless. I did not notice whether heaven and earth existed or not. Now suddenly I remember: all the disasters and recoveries, gains and losses, joys and sorrows, loves and hates of twenty or thirty years rise up in a thousand tangled threads. . . . Shall I never again find a moment of peace?" (Graham 1960, 71; Kohn 2014, 150).

This case is highly illuminating. The mental state outlined here matches the descriptions in passages on sitting in oblivion and is close to the ancient Daoist ideal. The behavior, the radical forgetting of all social connections and personal episodes combined with complete helplessness in daily functioning, on the other hand, is extreme and not at all like that of the perfected in the *Zhuangzi* or later Daoist mystics, who have practiced oblivion yet live successfully and even excelling in the world. Also, unlike modern sufferers, Master Hua was able to recover his memories—however much he disliked doing do. He, therefore, was not suffering from a severely impaired hippocampus, but had found a way to block all conscious memory formation for a limited time.

In that respect, he is like the drunken man in the *Zhuangzi*, "who falls off a carriage and may get hurt but won't die. He has the same bones and joints as everyone else, but his injury is different because his spirit is whole. He never knew he was riding, he never knew he fell" (ch. 19; Watson 1968, 198; Graham 1981, 137; Mair 1994, 176; Kohn 2010a, 22). Drunkenness, as modern science shows, interferes greatly with memory (Joordens 2011, 41). Like betablockers, it prevents long-term storage of information and can lead to amnesia, preventing the formation of memories as built from new proteins (Cooke 2009, 136-37).

A drunk person is "happy go lucky," with no particular sense of body or self, yet possessed of continued proprioception, i.e., the ability to automatically respond to physical stimuli and a discreet but unconscious sense of where one is in space (Sacks 1985, 30, 47). Drunks are particularly immune to fear; as the *Zhuangzi* says, "Life and death, alarm and terror never enter his breast, so he meets peril with no fear" (ch. 19). Similarly the *Liezi* tells the story of Shangqiu Kai 商丘開 who performed amazing feats of jumping down a steep cliff, diving into a deep river, and walking through a burning storehouse. He was able to do so because he was free from fear and self-conscious awareness. "I forgot where my body was going; I forgot which things benefit and which things harm me" (ch. 2; Graham 1960, 41).

Rather than in the hippocampus, the filing system of the brain and seat of long-term memory formation, the key to unlock the neurology of oblivion, therefore, lies in its early warning system and locus of fear, the amygdala. Practitioners reprogram the way their amygdala works not by releasing fear and letting go of stress reactions, "not by passive forgetting but through an active process, often involving new learning," the formation and consolidation of new and different response patterns that takes "multistage learning" (LeDoux and Phelps 2008, 164).

This again requires the active involvement of the prefrontal cortex, especially the dorsolateral PFC with its power to override other areas, our "free won't," and the rostral PFC in charge of "weighting priority between internally generated, stimulus-independent input versus stimulus-oriented thought or current sensory input" (Davidson et al. 2007, 49). The higher the activation of the baseline left prefrontal cortex, the more skilled the person becomes in "down-regulating negative affect" (2007, 50). In other words, rather than forget and let go, we reach the desired state through intention and control.

Emotion Regulation

Psychologists today speak of intention and control with regard to amygdala-centered stress responses in terms of emotion regulation, particularly as applied to cases of PTSD, anxiety, phobias, and mood disorders (Quirk 2007, 38; Beauregard 2004). The key to their control is the power of attention, described as the "gatekeeper" that "allows goal-relevant information" to enter specific areas "for further processing" (Ochsner and Gross 2007, 93; Nelson and Bouton 2002).

Various ways of modifying intention have been found useful. Thus, selective attention limits the processing of stimuli (e.g., focusing on the breath when confronting the boss), distraction of attention redirects it to non-threatening areas (e.g., counting when getting angry), and shifting attention creates a cognitive change by altering the evaluation of the situation (e.g., being grateful for a flat tire now and not last night) (2007, 93-96; Goleman 2013, 76; Gross 2008, 503; Gross and John 2002, 301). In addition, one may work with reappraisal, the active reinterpretation of a stimulus, i.e., the classic attitude described as "look on the bright side;" or one can set out to learn new and different responses through classical conditioning techniques (Ochsner and Gross 2007, 98-99).

Removing attention from the threatening stimulus by "taking the position of a detached observer" allows the dorsal anterior cingulate cortex to inhibit strong emotional responses while nourishing the ability to think and plan—even in split-seconds—under great pressure (Davidson, Fox, and Kalin 2007, 51). The strongest way, in turn, to maintain observer status is by focusing on something higher than oneself. "Think about what life really means to you, what is most important in your life" (Ford and Wortman 2013, 24).

That is to say, find an inner, conscious center, like a key spiritual focus or other high value—something like heaven or life in the *Zhuangzi*. Doing so, you place reality in perspective: the high office becomes a prison compared to relaxing by the riverside (ch. 17). At this point, "you know when your thinking center is really working. You're aware that somehow what you're doing right at that moment is totally worthwhile" (Ford and Wortman 2013, 25). Radically focusing attention switches core concerns from survival to learning and trains the conscious mind to notice alarm signals from the amygdala, then intentionally activate the learning brain and deal with them in focus. Memory remains unimpaired, but the automatization of responses is inhibited.

Once in this mode, people stop and think before taking action, distinguish between facts and assumptions, evaluate situations clearly even under pressure, respond rapidly and competently, solve problems creatively, and change worry into plans. They come to enjoy life as a series of challenges, are able to savor quiet times without the need for new stimulation, and continue to reflect on what they want to gain from a particular experience (Ford and Wortman 2013, 36).

This state can be described as the optimal brain, when one makes strong use of all capabilities, unhindered by fear, emotional reactions, and primal thinking. It is the root of peak performance, when body, skills, emotions, and thinking all work together as cooperative partners. All seems to flow intuitively and effortlessly—quite like what *Zhuangzi* calls free and easy wandering, the state that makes the amazing feats of the skilled craftsmen possible, what the skater Michelle Kwan experienced when she won a gold medal: "I didn't skate for gold. I went out and had a good time" (Ford and Wortman 2013, 47).

From a neurological perspective, the key to oblivion is thus not forgetting but inhibiting, not letting go but learning to control, not doing away with body and mind but centering in the thinking center of the brain. The word *wang* 忘 is thus best read not in its transmitted meaning of "forget," but in its literal graph as "perish" (*wang* 亡) plus "mind" (*xin* 心). Rather than "forget" danger signals and cultural norms, sitting in oblivion allows us to "never mind" them, actively and consciously override them by focusing on more important and more powerful core values. In other words, Yan Hui, rather than having "forgotten rites and music," now "no longer minds" them: he still knows they are there and what they are, he may even use them when socially required, but in his inner being, he has gone beyond them. By the same token, rather than forgetting who and what he is, he no longer minds his "limbs and physical structure, perception and intellect, bodily form and knowledge." He can do so, moreover, by establishing himself actively and consciously in a position of Dao, by "joining Great Pervasion," from there engaging in the world powerfully yet with detachment.

Conscious Reprogramming

A further level of enhancing the new mind is by reprogramming it toward the increased development of a detached witness consciousness with the help of mindfulness, the practice of "receptive attention" that encourages disengagement from habitually evaluative and conceptual processing" (Brown and Holt 2011, 150; Goleman 2011, 37; Siegel 2007). Described variously in Western psychology, it most prominently appears in Arthur Deikman's understanding of the observing self. Unlike the object self, which is left-brain centered and sees body and self as strictly separate from inner perceptions and feelings, providing us with clear recognition of friend and foe, a good sense of time, and all the various faculties of remembering and planning (1982, 68), the observing self integrates encompassing right-brain perception. Neither part of the subjective oneness of the right hemisphere nor objectified as an outside entity, it represents a totally subjective answer to the question, "Who am I?" yet also has the detachment and distance needed for critical awareness and decision-making (Kohn 1992, 125).

Matching the witness consciousness developed in observation and insight meditation, the observing self stands apart from the content of consciousness and cannot be affected by outside world. Featureless and formless, it has no limits. It allows people to be deeply involved in the activities of life while at the same time maintaining distance and creating a sense of detachment to thoughts and feelings. It can be activated by noting thoughts, feelings, and reactions, as well as by encouraging awareness of automated responses that have replaced the choices of truly autonomous individuals (1982, 96; Wilber 2004, 13). Once one realizes these, one can go about changing them, replacing the way one used to do things with new patterns, centered in Great Pervasion.

A key new pattern, then is the "receptive mode" of consciousness, a way of perception that diminishes the boundaries between self and world and gives people a sense of merging with the environment (1982, 71; 1980b, 263). An example for this would be the appreciation of a piece of music or a work of art. Looking upon anything artistic as a mere object one is bound to be bored by it, left cold and untouched. In order to really appreciate art, people must open themselves to it and merge with it to a certain degree. The same holds true for more intense relationships among people. No true understanding can take place if individuals keep themselves shut into a world of mere objects.

The observing self, then, is the fulfillment of the receptive mode. Originally at the center of one's being, this self is the deep inner root of one's existence, an ultimate and transcendent sense of being alive within. It is there, yet cannot be consciously known, felt, or manipulated: it cannot be objectified in any way. Rather than thinking, feeling, and doing things actively and with regard to an object, the observing self allows things to happen spontaneously. Instead of as objects, people then see themselves and the world as flowing streams of energy, intensely alive and perfectly individual, yet ultimately interconnected in a cosmic whole. The observing self has no limits; it is transcendent and yet most deeply immanent in all (Deikman 1982, 122).

A very similar mode of transformation also appears in the work of Abraham Maslow, who speaks about the contrast of object and observing self in terms of Deficiency-cognition versus Being-cognition (1964, 73, 97). To think in terms of deficiency means to concentrate primarily on outside objectives. It leads subjectively to such emotions as anxiety, fear, worry, and anger. Being-cognition, on the contrary, is self-justifying, cheerful, and compassionate. People moving in that direction often experience times of complete happiness called peak-experiences. The most thrilling moments of life, such peak-experiences are also times of greatest maturity, individuation, and selflessness. Similar to John Diamond's notion of the "homing thought" (1979, 47), Ed Carlson's concept of the Perfect Moment (2012, 116), and Deepak Chopra's admonition to "have a higher purpose that goes beyond yourself" (Chopra and Tanzi 2015, 237), peak-experiences are full of joy and meaning, transcending the ego and giving people a sense of unity with all-that-is.

Another way to enhance the observing self and reprogram the subconscious is through affirmations, simple sentences that make a positive statement about oneself (Harman and Rheingold 1984, 89), used in a highly ritualized manner in Daoism and Buddhism. A form of hypnotic suggestion, they can be formulated as facts in the present tense or as orders in the imperative mode. Examples include, "I am at peace," "I am filled with love," or "I am healed." Through their constant repetition, either vocalized or silent, they not only create a certain sound vibration but more importantly a mental attitude that reflects the desired state of the practitioner and help rewire the brain (McGill 1979, 188-90).

"Affirmations," Robert Gass says, "are a form of conscious reprogramming in which we seek to counterbalance some of our less-useful beliefs and habits of mind" (1999, 35). He then tells the story of his experience with cancer in the left eye that he combated with the affirmation "I choose life." He practiced it everywhere, walking in the hills, taking a shower, holding his child, undergoing tests at the hospital. Like a mantra, the phrase came to reside in the depth of his mind, forming a subconscious background to all his experiences and. "It permeated my mind and heart and filled me with the energy I needed to face my fears and engage with my struggle for physical survival and spiritual awakening" (1999, 36).

Affirmations are also used successfully in hypnosis, cognitive therapy, and with cancer patients. Working directly with people's thoughts, they serve to replace a negative inner voice with positive reinforcements. Therapy begins with patients writing down negative thoughts, such as "I am a bad person" or "I can never do anything right." They then consciously create counter-thoughts, such as "I take things one step at a time" or "I have valuable strengths." They keep the affirmations in their minds continuously for at least twenty minutes a day, in fact practicing a form of mantra recitation. Over time, the practice changes the pattern of negative thinking and people gain a more positive attitude and better self-esteem, which in turn leads to changes in their lives (see Blair 2004; Beck 2004; Simonton 1978).

All the various modes of traditional Daoist meditation—from basic concentration through stillness, oblivion, and observation to mental resolutions—therefore, have in common that they center in the conscious mind, the prefrontal cortex of the brain. Beginning with the conscious qualities of respect and faith, combined with the realization that there is a better way of being in this life and living in the world, they reprogram their breathing habitss, sensory experiences, reaction patterns, decision-making, and overall attitudes toward a cosmic, Dao-based position. In doing so, they make active use of what we today call neuroplasticity, the brain's ability to change neuronal circuits through focused effort and constant repetition (Gould 2007, 279; Taylor 2006, 111). As animal studies have shown, 400 to 600 repetitions per day of a challenging functional task, such as fine motor grasping, lead to the brain rewiring for the new task. Similarly, people who suffered a stroke can cause cortical changes and functional improvement with large numbers of task repetition (Schwartz and Begley 2002). Always slow and gradual, the Daoist attainment of the cosmic mind through meditation thus in many ways echoes modern methods and our understanding of neuropsychological functioning

Chapter Seven

Smile at Your Heart

Visualization and Cell Biology

Going to a yet subtler level of the bodymind, Daoist further restructure their entire internal system on the cellular level, making use especially of visualization, the active, intentional use of imagery to alter or transform mind and emotions. Objects of visualization can be colors or colored energies imagined to pervade parts of the body; they can involve static objects, such as a vase, a diagram, a landscape, or the statue of a deity; and they can be focused on an entire sequence of activities and events, almost in movie fashion, either for detached viewing or active engagement. Since the brain does not distinguish outside stimuli from imagined ones, visualization is a powerful mode of accessing the subconscious mind to retrain brain mechanisms and transform emotional reactions.[1]

In traditional Daoist meditation, visualization tends to focus strongly on the five inner organs. Going back as far as Heshang gong's commentary to the *Daode jing* and formalized as the Five Sprouts in the school of Highest Clarity, it is best known today as the Inner Smile. In all these and other modes, it utilizes colors, transforms emotions into virtues, and optimizes health and well-being. Its practice increases immune resistance and enhances vigor, eases tensions and opens the person to happiness and limitless abundance.

---

[1] Kohn 2008b, 128 on the basis of Begley 2007, 9, 151-52; Ratey 2002, 147; Samuels and Samuels 1975, 56-63. The best documentation of the efficacy of visualization as a form of mental rehearsal is in sports: athletes of all kinds vastly improve their performance by experiencing their best performance through focused attention in a quasi-meditative state (McTaggart 2007, 127-35; Newberg and Waldman 2009, 187).

The Inner Smile

The Inner Smile transforms *qi* stored in the inner organs both through color visualization and the clearing of negative emotions. It is best undertaken in a quiet place, a simple room, made comfortable with pillows and maybe with candles or incense. Practitioners dress comfortably and sit on the edge of a chair, their legs hip-distance apart, their feet flat on the floor. The back is straight, the head up, shoulders back and down, chin tucked in slightly. The hands rest comfortably in the lap, right palm on left. Close or lower the eyes and breathe normally.

The first step is to relax the forehead and envision a smiling energy flowing between the eyebrows to the nose and cheeks, allowing it to warm the whole face. Practitioners place the tongue on the roof of the mouth to connect the Governing and Conception Vessels and allow the jaw to release all tension. Taking the smiling feeling lower along the face, they smile into the throat area to the thyroid and parathyroid glands, which frees the ability to speak and communicate. From here, they let the *qi* flow down to the thymus gland, the seat of love and enlightenment, and allow it to moisten and grow bigger (Chia and Chia 1986, 145).

After this preparatory smiling, practitioners allow the *qi* to flow to the five inner organs in turn, envisioning them with their respective colors, appreciating them for their work, and allowing negative emotions to leave and positive virtues to enter. For example,

> Focus your attention on the area of your lungs. Feel them expand with inhalation and deflate with exhalation. Get a sense of fullness and strength in the lungs. Now envision a radiant white energy filling them. Let the lungs be rich and strong with the white energy. Smile at your lungs and develop a sense of appreciation for their continuous good work. Mentally thank them for their efforts and encourage them to be healthy and vigorous. Note that sadness and melancholy tend to manifest in the lungs. Let go of all sadness and melancholy, and instead invite in righteousness or social responsibility, the virtue associated with the lungs (see Chia and Chia 1993, 94; www.healing dao.com).

Continuing through all the organs, the practice follows the classical body model of Chinese medicine, using the system of the five phases and envisioning each organ with its specific color: liver—green, heart—red, spleen—yellow, lungs—white, and kidneys—black. Practitioners take their smiling attitude to each organ in turn, feel it physically and in its energetic vibration, then visualize it in its respective color and send positive thoughts and intentions toward it. They further allow its psychological dimension to activate, becoming conscious of any emotional feelings, then let those go and replace them with a particular virtue (Chia and Chia 1993, 64-66).

Emotions and virtues in this understanding utilize the same *qi*, but in different direction and intensity. Emotions, negative in outlook, are excessive manifestations of natural and appropriate attitudes, directed strongly toward one's own personal gain and benefit—born from egotistic strife and in reaction to potentially threatening situations. Virtues, fundamentally positive, are directed toward others and universal well-being—expressions of altruistic consideration and a feeling of connectedness with all beings. Neutral between the two are general attitudes that are appropriate for the particular organ in its respective season:

organ	season	emotion	attitude	virtue
liver	spring	anger	assertive	compassion
heart	summer	euphoria	enthusiastic	respect
spleen	Indian summer	worry	planning	empathy
lungs	fall	sadness	concerned	care
kidneys	winter	fear	cautious	understanding

After having connected to each organ in turn, practitioners move on to smile into the digestive tract to activate the yang organs, gathering saliva and swallowing *qi* into their area, then smile into the endocrine system, glands, nerves, and bones. They conclude by collecting and storing the smiling energy in the lower elixir field, centering it by spiraling it 36 six times in an outward direction (women counter-clockwise, men clockwise), then 24 four times the other way (Chia and Chia 1993, 103).

The Inner Smile should be practiced daily, preferably upon waking up in the morning. In addition to enhancing physical health by allowing the organs to relax and expand, as they feel appreciated and enriched in vitality, its regular application also energizes people as a whole and makes them more loving toward themselves and kinder toward others, giving them a sense of connection to all beings and the universe at large.

Historical Unfolding

The earliest mention of nourishing the inner organs through meditation appears in a commentary to the *Daode jing* associated with the legendary Heshang gong, a mysterious saint of magical abilities under Emperor Wen of Han (r. 179-165 BCE) (see Chan 1991). Chapter 6, "Image Complete," contains the line, "Valley spirit [there is] no dying," which Heshang gong interprets:

> "Valley" means "nourish." Nourish the spirits, and you do not die. The "spirits" are the spirits of the five organs. The spirit soul in the liver, the material soul in the lungs, the spirit in the heart, the intention in the spleen, and the essence in the kidneys. If the five organs are exhausted or harmed, the five spirits will leave and one dies. (Kohn 2009, 163)

He connects the spiritual with the physical, psychological factors with bodily organs, and encourages readers to "nourish" these. Commenting on the following line, "This is called the mysterious and the female," he says how:

> This means that the Dao of no-death lies in the mysterious and the female. The mysterious is heaven; in the human body, it is the nose. The female is earth; in the human body, it is the mouth.
>
> Heaven feeds people with the five *qi*, which enter the organs through the nose and settle in the heart. The five *qi* are pure and subtle, they cause people to have sentience and spirituality, intelligence and perception, sound and voice, as well as the five kinds of inner nature. They are represented in the spirit soul. It is male and leaves and enters the human body through the nose in order to interact with heaven. Therefore, the nose is the mysterious.
>
> Earth feeds people with the five tastes, which enter the organs through the mouth and settle in the stomach. The five tastes are turbid and heavy; they cause people to have body and skeleton, bones and flesh, blood and pulses, and the six kinds of emotional passions. They are represented in the material soul. It is female and leaves and enters the human body through the mouth in order to interact with earth. Therefore the mouth is the female. (Kohn 2009, 64)

To nourish the inner organs, one should consciously practice breathing exercises, bringing cosmic *qi* into the specific organs of the body to vitalize and enhance them while also being aware of the food one takes and the emotions that arise from the organs. This early passage thus contains the elementary rudiments of the Inner Smile practice, the activation of *qi* within the self on both the physical and psychological levels in conjunction with heaven and earth.

A more specific practice of bringing colors into the organs appears first in the *Taiping jing shengjun bizhi* 太平經聖君秘旨 (Secret Instructions of the Holy Lord on the Scripture of Great Peace, DZ 1102), a short redaction of meditation methods of the *Taiping jing* 太平經 (Scripture of Great Peace), the first revealed Daoist scripture known from the literature. Dated to the 2nd century CE, it was instrumental in organizing a major Daoist community in eastern China and inspired the Yellow Turban rebellion of 184 (see Hendrischke 2006). The text was lost in the process and later reconstituted; its meditation methods were presented separately.

According to this, human beings consist of the triad of essence (*jing* 精), energy (*qi* 氣), and spirit (*shen*), the core factors in later internal alchemy (see Johnson 2014b, ch. 14), which they receive from heaven, earth, and the "middle harmony" of the two (1a). "Spirit revolves and light is born," thus opening the path to visualization. Practitioners here focus on their inner core, sitting quietly with their eyes closed. After some time, "a brilliant light will arise," shooting up like fire. Red at first, it later turns white, then green, matching different phases of yin and yang—green being the light of lesser yang, white of lesser yin, and black, "shimmering like deep water," that of greater yin (2a). The organs radiating in these colors, "you may see your entire abdomen pervaded by light while the four directions are utterly in darkness. This is the light of great harmony, the Dao of great accordance" (2b) (Kohn 1989b, 139; 1993, 195; Nicholson 2004, 5).

To enhance this inner empowerment, practitioners imagine their bodies as pervaded by white light and activate the emptiness, nonbeing, and spontaneity of Dao by seeing "a white radiance both above and below, pure like jade without the smallest flaw" (3a). They systematically move through their bodies, both seeing and feeling its constantly shifting features as well as "visualize the spirits residing in the five organs and observe how they come and go, carefully watching their movements." Next, they should "let the spirits emerge from your body and mingle with the five phases and four seasons, thus letting the green, yellow, white, and black be equally stored within" (3b). The instructions continue by encouraging practitioners to also connect to various outside forces, such as earth deities and ancestors, creating a close connection to all spiritual forces while remaining in a central position of power (Kohn 1993, 196-97). The core motif, however, again is the enhancement of internal energies in relation to the larger cosmos, through the energies of heaven and earth.

Another set of visualization instructions appears in the *Daoyin jing* 導引經 (Scripture on Healing Exercises, DZ 818; trl. Kohn 2012, 95-116), a collection of physical and meditation methods geared toward strengthening the body and prolonging life. In particular, it contains a set of eight exercises associated with the classical immortal Wangzi Qiao 王子蹻 which "extend the years and increase longevity by eliminating the hundred diseases" (7b).

Here adepts lie on their back in a relaxed posture, then practice conscious breathing, allowing the breath to become soft and slow, then swallow the *qi* to enhance the inner organs. From here, they mentally move through the body, seeing each organ in its respective color and characteristic shape:

> The windpipe is like a succession of white silver rings, stacked twelve levels deep. Going downwards, one reaches the lungs, white and glossy. They have two leaves reaching tall in front, and two leaves hanging low in the back.

The heart connects to them underneath. It is large up top and pointed below. All over it is shining red like an unopened lotus bud hanging down from the lungs.

The liver rests below. Its color is a clear green like a male mallard's head. It has six leaves that envelop the stomach. The two leaves in front reach up tall, while the four leaves in the back hang down low. The gall bladder connects to it underneath, like a green silk bag.

The spleen is in the very center of the belly, enwrapped from all sides. It is bright yellow like gold, lustrous and radiant.

The kidneys look like two sleeping rats lying back to back, curled up with elbow to navel and as if they wanted to stretch out. Their color is a thick, glossy black. Fat streaks run through them, so that the white and black glow jointly. (8a; Kohn 2008a, 124-25; 2012, 109-10)

The text continues by noting how the five organs house the various psychological forces, as already outlined by Heshang gong, making them "containers of spirit" and the root of all physical and spiritual harmony (8b). It provides a more physical dimension to the practice and presents the first systematic procedure of moving from one organ to the next—not in the order of the five phases but as they are placed within the body.

Body Gods

Another dimension of visualization appears in the understanding that the various organs and energy centers of the body are the home of divinities, commonly known as body gods.

For example, the inner organs are inhabited by the heraldic animals, massive constellations in the cardinal directions of the night sky that comprise a number of stars not unlike Western zodiac images (Major 1986; Csikszentmihalyi in Pregadio 2008, 908-11l). Thus, the immense constellation of the cerulean (green or blue) dragon (*qinglong* 青龍), representative of the east, includes stars from *Virgo* to *Scorpio* (Pankenier 2013, 45).

The vermilion bird (*chiniao* 赤鳥) in the south "extends from lunar mansion *Willow* (δ Hya) to *Chariot Platform* (β Crv)" (2013, 196). They further include the white tiger (*baihu* 白虎) in the west and the turtle, later combined with a snake and known as the Dark Warrior (*xuanwu* 玄武), in the north. They appear first as mussel shell mosaics in a Neolithic tomb of the Yangshao 仰韶 culture, dating from the late fourth millennium BCE (Pankenier 2013, 337).

In the Daoist system, they not only serve as the celestial guardians of Lord Lao but also rule the inner organs. For example, the 9th-century *Huangting neijing wuzang liufu buxie tu* 黄庭内景五臟六腑補瀉圖 (Illustrated Manual on the Tonification and Dispersal [of Qi] in the Five Organs and Six Viscera According to the Inner Yellow Court Scripture, DZ 432) notes that the white tiger is the resident body god of the lungs, which belong to the phase metal and are shaped like a hanging chime. The deity controls the person's material soul and can transform into a jade lad seven inches in height, who comes and goes in the body, creating various reactions and emotions (2b; Despeux 2006, 58).

Body gods in human shape appear first in the *Huangting jing*. It places particular emphasis on Lord Lao as the chief resident of the body's center in the Yellow Court, aided powerfully by the deities of the three elixir fields, the Three Ones. Visualizing them ensures a successful celestial connection, matching a practice described in the Highest Clarity work, *Jinque dijun sanyuan zhenyi jing* 金闕帝君三元真一經 (Scripture of the Three Primordial Perfect Ones by Lord Goldtower, DZ 253; trl. Andersen 1980; Kohn 1993, 204-14).

According to this, to activate the centers, adepts visualize the Three Ones as manifestations of three kinds of primordial *qi* in the elixir fields. These govern the twenty-four fundamental powers of the human body, which correspond to the twenty-four *qi* of the year and the twenty-four major constellations in the sky. The exact procedure of the meditation varies according to season but, if at all possible should be performed at the solstices and the equinoxes.

To prepare for the practice, adepts have to purify themselves by bathing and fasting. They enter the meditation chamber at midnight, the hour of rising yang. Then they light incense, and click their teeth thirty times. Facing east, they close their eyes and visualize the Northern Dipper slowly descending toward them until it rests right above their heads with the handle pointing straight east. This preliminary measure serves to protect adepts from evil influences during the practice.

Then they start with the Upper One. They visualize a ball of red *qi* in the Niwan Palace, the upper elixir field in the center of the head. Within this, a red sun about nine inches in radius will appear. Its brilliance envelops practitioners to such a degree that they enter a state of utter oblivion. As soon as they have reached this state, the god Red Child becomes visible. The ruler of the Niwan Palace, he holds a talisman of the white tiger, the sacred animal of the west. He is accompanied by an attendant, the god of the subtle essences of the teeth, the tongue, and the skull, who holds a sacred scripture in his hands.

The Middle and Lower Ones are similarly imagined as residing in the other elixir fields, the Scarlet Palace of the heart and the Ocean of Qi in the abdomen and are accompanied by assistants who govern the five inner organs as well as the extremities, senses, and fluids of the body. Through visualization, adepts keep them securely in the body. Over time, they learn to communicate with them, resulting in the attainment of yet higher stages. At this point, adepts transpose the visualized gods back to their true realm in the stars and paradises and themselves take flight to visit those extraterrestrial realms, which in due course become their true home.

Reorienting the body to be the container of heavenly palaces and deities, to be in fact a cosmos in itself, adepts attain oneness in body and spirit with the cosmic dimensions of the universe. As all parts of the body transform into divine entities, firmly guarded by their responsible gods, the very physicality of the adept turns into a cosmic network and becomes the celestial realm in which the gods reside.

The Five Sprouts

A yet different method of visualization links the internal observation with the five directions on earth and various stars and deities in the heavens. It appears first in the *Lingbao wufuxu* 靈寶五符序 (Explanation of the Five Talismans of Numinous Treasure, DZ 183). A complex text, its content goes back to the magical practitioners of the later Han, while its final form was edited under the auspices of Numinous Treasure around the year 400 (see Arthur 2013; Yamada 2000). Its first scroll contains various methods of visualization and talisman practice (see Yamada 1989), including a set called "The Five Initial Methods of Great Clarity."

Adepts connect to the seasons and the directions by practicing at a particular time and by facing in a particular direction, then visualize their internal organs in the appropriate color. Not only allowing this color to radiate through the entire body, they also empower the organ by seeing a celestial deity within, often the representative of a starry constellation. The practice, besides enhancing the adept's health and vitality, also creates a positive energy impact in the greater universe. For example,

> To practice Dao of the east, focus on the *qi* of wood and the organ of the liver, which rules over the heart as its higher master. Enter the meditation chamber on Spring Beginning and Spring Equinox, then rest your head and lie down. Close your eyes and visualize the inside of your body.
>
> See your liver *qi* perfectly green, with a red spirit attending on it and yellow *qi* nourishing it. Then see your whole body being filled with green *qi*, above reaching out to heaven to penetrate primordial energy, below

> entering deep into the body, making the god Goumang appear, serving Lord Lao as his ruler.
>
> Practice like this and you will find unicorns arriving, soaring phoenixes coming toward you, and the myriad beings blossoming and flourishing around you. Jupiter will move in its proper rhythm, the world's essence will penetrate Great Tenuity, and the southern barbarians will come to court, bringing numerous auspicious gifts.
>
> Remember: the east corresponds to benevolence and to wood; it governs fire and matches earth; it is killed by metal and imprisoned by water. If stagnant, imprisoned, or dead, you must nurture the son to revenge the father. (1.17a)

Continuing this method, followers of Highest Clarity (Shangqing 上清), a school beginning in the mid-4th century on the basis of extensive revelations from immortals and deities of the higher Daoist heavens (see Robinet 2000; Strickmann 1978; 1981), developed a version of organ visualization known as the Five Sprouts (*wuya* 五芽). It is described in the *Taishang yangsheng taixi qi jing* 太上養生胎息氣經 (Highest *Qi* Scripture on Nourishing Life Through Embryo Respiration, DZ 819) and later summarized in Sima Chengzhen's *Fuqi jingyi lun* 服氣精義論 (How to Absorb *Qi* and Penetrate [Ultimate] Meaning, DZ 830, *Yunji qiqian* 57; trl. Engelhardt 1987; Kohn 2012, 204-29). According to this, the practice opens the body to the cosmos through the ingestion of the *qi* of the five directions and is also known as the "method of mist absorption" (Robinet 1989, 165-66). As the *Fuqi jingyi lun* says, it serves "to take in cloud sprouts to enrich the body fluids, inhale misty radiances to nurture spirit power within" (2b).

A ritualized version of organ visualization in conjunction with the invocation of celestial deities, the Five Sprouts should always be undertaken at midnight, the hour when yang energy first begins to rise. Rather than sitting (as today) or lying down (as in the *Daoyin jing*), practitioners should "stand upright, dressed in proper cap and gown, then activate your golden bridge [tongue] and waken the jade radiance [breath] to balance the flowery pond [mouth]. Rinse with the sweet spring [saliva] and numinous fluids. Contract your nose and make the *qi* return, going up to the head and sinking down inside the mouth. There it can transform into jade spring [refined saliva]. From here, pull the *qi* to the root of the tongue, swallow, and send it off" (3b; Jackowicz 2006, 85; Johnson 2014a, 78).

The practice thus begins by swallowing saliva. The next step is to face each of the five major directions while chanting incanations to its spirit, here called "sprout." As the *Fuqi jingyi lun* has:

> Green Sprout of the East: Be absorbed to feed my green sprout [liver].
> I drink you through the Morning Flower [upper teeth].
> Vermilion Elixir of the South: Be absorbed to feed my vermilion elixir

[heart].
I drink you through the Elixir Lake [lower teeth].
Lofty Great Mountain of the Center: Be absorbed to feed my essence and *qi*.
I drink you through the Sweet Spring [molars].
Radiant Stone of the West: Be absorbed to feed my radiant stone [lungs].
I drink you through the Numinous Liquid [lip saliva].
Mysterious Sap of the North: Be absorbed to feed my mysterious sap [kidneys].
I drink you through the Jade Sweetness [tongue saliva].
(3ab; Jackowicz 2006, 84; Kohn 2012, 206-07)

In each case, adepts pass the tongue along a certain part of the lips and teeth, matching the incantation. They should then lick the lips, rinse the mouth by filling it with saliva, and swallow—three times for each sprout. In all cases, one's full attention should be focused on the direction in question, while inhaling deeply and exhaling slowly through the nose. It is best to breathe according to the appropriate number: nine times east, three times south, twelve times center, seven times west, and five times north (3b).

Next, adepts face each direction and visualize its *qi* in its appropriate color. A vague haze at first, the *qi* gradually forms into a round ball, and then is condensed into a pill (Kohn 2008a, 156). They thereby ingest the sprout and guide it mentally to its appropriate organ, again in the order of physical location rather than five-phases sequencing. Practice begins with the lungs, the Flowery Canopy, described as having "six leaves, their color a silky, shiny pink" (4a). Next comes the heart, with its silky, shiny red color, followed by the liver which consists of four leaves on the right and three on the left, and in this case is not associated with the color green but with "a silky, shiny violet" (4b). Following this, adepts turn to the spleen, which "rests right above the navel, close to and slightly in front of the stomach, its color a silky, shiny yellow" (4b).

Last but not least are the left and right kidneys, facing the navel area and resting on the pelvis, "their color a silky, shiny purple." The right kidney, moreover, is the location of the acupuncture point and Daoist center known as the Gate of Destiny, where "males store their semen and females harbor the ability to get pregnant," i.e., the reproductive center of the body, where primordial *qi* resides and new life begins.

Undertaken over a prolonged period, the Five Sprouts strengthen and cosmicize the organs to the point where a spirit or numinous embryo (*lingtai* 靈胎) begins to grow inside the practitioner, a supernatural alter ego that is able to draw in the primordial *qi* of the universe and is directly nourished by it. "This method of absorbing *qi* involves visualizing the heart as if it contained a baby in the mother's womb. After ten months it is complete, its tendons and bones harmonized and supple" (*Taixi jing* 1a). The spirit embryo develops as and when the practitioner reconnects with his numinous root (*linggen* 靈根), the last remnant of the connection the individual had with the universe while in the womb and often identified with the tongue, thus explaining the extensive tongue movements of the practice (Jackowicz 2006, 86).

As practitioners progress, they are permeated with the essence of the five phases as absorbed from the five directions, so that the meeting ground in the center of their bodies becomes a microcosm of Dao and they themselves mere manifestations of cosmic flow. "Effectively dissolving the distinction between self and universe through Five Sprouts practice, the person's body becomes as integrally whole as the universe itself" (Jackowicz 2006, 86). The practitioner carries an embryo but is not pregnant; he is the universe but remains himself. Unlike in the Heshang gong and *Daoyin jing* version of organ visualization where personal energy is enhanced and also quite different from the *Taiping jing* practice where the practitioner connects to spirits outside himself, here *qi* is personal as well as divine yet not other: it is cosmic *qi* made one's own.

Chakras

A rather similar way of looking at the body combined with energy-enhancing practices appears in India in the chakra system. Chakras, literally "whirling wheels" or "vortexes," are energy centers located in the torso and grouped along the spine. Like Chinese organs, they are "superphysical centers or organs through which the energies of different fields are synchronized and distributed to the physical body" (Karagulla and Kunz 1989, 33), "specific areas of the body that seem best to contain the different degrees of 'freed up' bliss, . . . located to specific areas or organs but not identical with those areas" (Wilber 1979, 126, 128). "Sense organs for the astral body that pick up vibrational information" (Tiller et al. 2005, 236), they are both abstract energetic representations of spiritual growth and physical locations in the body that may knot up with tensions and provide release when opened. This, again like the Daoist organs, links them to emotions: orgasmic ecstasy in the genitals; joy, vitality, and laughter in the belly; sadness, openness, and love in the chest; intellect and insight in the eyes and head; and spirituality in the crown (Wilber 1979, 127).

The standard system acknowledges seven chakras, located between the pelvic floor and the top of the head. Each of them is formally named, precisely located, and associated with colors, geometric forms (*yantras*), and personality aspects.[2] They are:

---

[2] This list and description of the chakras are based on Khalsa and Stauth 2001, 177-265 in consultation with Breaux, 1989, 174-93; Feuerstein 1998, 150-59; Johnson 2014, 259-72; Karagulla and Kunz 1989, 39-45, 98; Larson 2003, 97-100; Leadbeater 1972, 11-15; Selby and Zelig 1992.

Name	Location	Color	Yantra	Aspect
Root	Perineum	red	square	survival
Sacral	Abdomen	orange	semi-circle	creativity
Central	solar plexus	yellow	triangle	ego/confidence
Heart	chest/thyroid	pink	star	love/compassion
Throat	throat/pineal	blue	triangle	logic/thought
Brow	third eye	violet	circle	intuition
Crown	top of head	gold	triangle	spirituality

In addition, the chakras also connect to major elements, represent psychological tendencies and physical organ systems, and may be responsible for particular physical conditions.

Name	Elem	Psychology	Organ	Glands	Conditions
Root	earth	greed, jealousy	colon	testicles, ovaries	constipation
Sacral	water	desire, creativity	kidneys	adrenals	infertility
Central	fire	ambition, fear	spleen	pancreas	ulcers, heartburn
Heart	air	grief, joy	heart	thymus	asthma
Throat	ether	pride	lungs	thyroid	voice issues
Brow		intuition	liver	pituitary	memory loss
Crown		cosmic vastness	brain	pineal	limitation

More specifically, the Root Chakra is located at the perineum between the genitals and the anus, matching the acupuncture point Meeting Yin and beginning of the Conception Vessel in Chinese medicine. It helps maintain the energies in the body and contains the seed of dissipating passions and greed (Silburn 1988, 27; Khalsa and Stauth 2001, 178). The Sacral Chakra, second, matches the lower elixir field and Ocean of *Qi* in Daoism and links to the kidneys among the five organs. It controls sexuality and creativity, thrives in contact and collaboration with others, and can give rise to great anxiety and fear. The Central Chakra, next, is located at the upper end of the stomach, near the solar plexus; relating to stomach and spleen, the Daoist residence of Lord Lao in the body known as the Yellow Court and central seat of honesty and trust. It controls digestion and the thinking mind, giving rise to ego, ambition, and worry (2001, 189, 197).

The Heart Chakra, fourth, matches the middle elixir field or Cavity of *Qi* . as well as the heart among the five organs. It is full of subtle energy and connected closely to all energy lines and centers (Silburn 1988, 28). The nexus of spirit and an emotional sense of self, it can be blocked by sadness or opened to great joy. The Throat Chakra connects to the thyroid gland and the vocal cords and relates to the lungs in the Chinese system. Part of the grief response, it governs all vocal actions and can give rise to encouragement and praise as much as to slander, gossip, and lying (Khalsa and Stauth 2001, 225-26). The sixth chakra, often called the Third Eye, governs the intuition and is a major area of spiritual opening. It matches the upper elixir field in the Chinese system, located inside the head at eye level. Related to the eyes, by extension it also connects to the liver among the five organs; it represents the cosmic spark in the self and is a center of truth and dignity as well as caring and compassion (2001, 244).

The seventh and highest center, the Crown Chakra, is also called the Abode of Light. Located at the top of the head, it is a classical exit gate for the spirit and as such matches the Hundred Meeting point in acupuncture and the Heavenly Gate in Daoism. The passage to eternal power and a cosmic sense of self, it represents personal vastness and infinity, the ultimate connection to cosmic energy, the point where the immortal embryo takes birth (Khalsa and Stauth 2001, 262).

The chakras are pervaded by two major energy forms, *kundalini* and *prāna. Kundalini* like primordial *qi* is celestial or cosmic, divine energy; it lies dormant in the Root Chakra at the base of the spine. If awakened properly, it begins to move upward, rising along the spine through three major energy channels (*nadis*). Along the way it opens the chakras until it reaches the top of the head where it unifies with the overarching consciousness of the universe and exits the body (Worthington 1982, 100-02).

Prāna, on the other hand, is the inner life force that smoothes out irregularities and preserves health, the power of gravity, attraction, repulsion, electricity, and radioactivity (Yasudian and Haich 1965, 30, 53). *Prāna* is more concrete and more tangible than *kundalini*: present in everything, it does not need to be awakened. Like *qi*, it is omnipresent, flows through energy channels, and is activated through conscious breathing, controlled physical movements, and visualizations. People tend to neglect and waste their *prāna*, straining it through exhausting labor, excessive sexuality, and draining mental work—a position that Daoists would heartily endorse. Indian yoga, like qigong, accordingly teaches to use and store life energy to the maximum, thereby enhancing health and extending long life (Yasudian and Haich 1965, 36, 31).

Prāna, moreover, is described as moving in five distinct ways or *vāyus*, i.e., rays of vitality that come in distinct colors and move in particular ways through the body (Leadbeater 1972, 60-61; Karagulla and Kunz 1989, 50)—closely matching the Chinese system of the five organs and their colors. Thus, a green ray fills the abdomen from the solar plexus and vivifies the liver and digestive system, while a red or rose-colored ray, "known as the nucleus or life-source of the nervous system," spreads through the body and centers in the heart.

A yellow-golden ray activates the lower abdomen (spleen) and also has a branch to the brain, while a deep orange, even purplish ray "flows into the base of the spine and activates the urogenital organs (kidneys), acting as a stimulant to the desires of the flesh and also helps to maintain body heat" (Tiller et al.

2005, 235). A light blue or soft violet ray naturally flows to the throat (lungs) and invigorates the force center at the top of the head (2005, 233).

As in the Inner Smile, practitioners enhance the chakras through a mixture of physical practices, breathing exercises, and visualizations, working toward perfect balance in their energy system for health, vigor, and long life as well as complete transcendence and their true self. In the process, they overcome and eventually eliminate all sorts of harmful emotions, such as rage, fear, grief, sorrow, fright, jealousy, despondency, and pessimism (Yasudian and Haich 1965, 37), reaching full control over body and mind and the ability to counteract various outside influences. Beyond enhancing altruistic tendencies, the practice leads to the opening of "a reservoir of peace and generates abundant energy for human uplift," leading eventually to a state of universal oneness, where "the seer, the sight, and the seen have no separate existence from each other" (Iyengar 1976, 20, 22).

The Aura

The power of the chakras, moreover, is also visible in the aura, a haze of energetic atmosphere or field of subtle luminous radiation intimately connected to the body of all living things that represents our energy body in visible, palpable form (Kilner 1965, 1; Larson 2003, 1). Long associated with religious, spiritual, and mystical traditions, with names in numerous languages (2003, 15-16), it came to the attention of scientists in the 19th century in conjunction with the craze about Mesmerism and hypnotism.[3]

In the early 20th century, Walter John Kilner (1847-1920), a medical electrician in London, conducted a series of experiments involving glass slides containing alcoholic solutions of variously colored dyes, including a blue dye called "dicyanin." They would allow perception outside the normal spectrum of visible light, enhancing human vision so it could detect auras to discern health issues (Kilner 1965, 60). He divides the aura into three layers: the etheric double, a dark band of about 1/8 of an inch around the body; the inner aura, a denser and more granular field about three inches wide, which bulges in locations of injury or illness; and the outer aura without particular boundaries that gradually dissolves into space (1965, 37-47).

All three layers are subject to change, most commonly perceived as rays that, too, come in three forms: rays proceeding from one part of the body to another; streams issuing straight into space; and brighter patches entirely surrounded by the aura in close proximity to the body (1965, 52). Experimenting further, Kilner found that there is no magnetic polarity in the aura, but that it

---

[3] Moss 1974, 69; Panati 1974, 40; Targ and Harary 1989, 73; see also Johnson 2014c, 36-40; www.historyofhypnotism.org.

may relate somewhat to electrical charges on the surface of the body (1965, 89, 103). Auras also come with colors, visible upon training (Ambrose 2011, 110; Brennan 1987, 9; Larson 2003, 96) or by inborn ability. Thus, the mystic and healer Edgar Cayce (1877-1945) says,

> The aura emanates from the whole body, but usually it is most heavy and most easily seen around the shoulders and head, probably because of the many glandular and nervous centers located in these parts of the body. The dark shades generally denote more application, more will power, more spirit. The basic color changes as the person develops or retards, but the lighter shades and pastels blend and shift more rapidly as the temperament expresses itself. The mind, builder of the soul, is the essential governing factor in the aura; but food, environment, and other conditions also have their effect. (Todeschi and Liaros 2011, 104)

These effects became physically visible with the discovery of Kirlian photography in 1939, named after the Russian scientist couple who first developed it. They placed photographic film on top of a conducting plate and attached a second conductor to a hand, a leaf, or other living entity, then energized the conductors by a high-frequency high-voltage power source, producing photographic images typically showing a silhouette of the object surrounded by an aura of light. The Kirlians published their discovery in 1958. It reached the West in 1970 with the publication of *Psychic Discoveries Behind the Iron Curtain* (Ostrander and Schroeder 1970, 198-205; Targ and Harary 1984, 160).

In the U.S., neuropsychiatrist Thelma Moss replicated its workings and expanded its application, obtaining many photos of something she suspected was an unknown form of radiation (Larson 2003, 71-73; Moss 1974, 23-61; Williams 2007). In her wake, William Tiller proposed that Kirlian photos exhibit an electrical phenomenon known as corona discharge (Tiller, Boyers, and Dakin 1974), while Kendall Johnson expanded the technology to include circuitry for radiation field devices (1975, 30). Healers today link it to the universal energy field (Brannon 1987, 39) and various kinds of radiation, from extremely low frequencies to gamma and higher heavenly rays (Johnson 2014a, 217).

Integrating the Indian chakra system, spiritual seekers today understand the aura as consisting of seven layers rather than three, including the following (Ambrose 2011, 36-44; Brennan 1987, 47-54; 1993, 92; Larson 2003, 60-78):

Body	**Size**	**Color**	**Power**	**Needs**
Etheric	2 in.	blue, gray	life-force	physical comfort
Emotional	4 in.	multicolor	emotions	self-acceptance
Mental	6 in.	yellow	intuition	clarity of thought
Astral	1 ft.	rose	caring	loving relationships
Etheric Template	2 ft.	blueprint	openness	divine alignment
Celestial	4 ft.	opalescent	love	spiritual ecstasy
Ketheric / Causal	4 ft.	gold	spirituality	cosmic consciousness

Moving further away from the physical body, these layers are increasingly subtler and more luminescent, opening flowing connections horizontally to other people and beings in the world as well as vertically to the greater universe and ultimate creative power. The colors associated with the organs in Daoism and with the chakras in India typically represent the activities and tendencies of the emotional body, consisting of "colored clouds of fine substance in continual fluid motion" (Brennan 1987, 50). Typically—and closely matching the Daoist system—the darker colors, such as blue, relate to spirituality and wisdom. Lighter blues and green indicate healing and altruism, while red is associated with energy, force, passion, and vigor. White shows purity, innocence, holiness, and perfection; and gold or yellow stands for personal and spiritual truth, integrity and self-realization (Todeschi and Liaros 2011,133-39; Brennan 1993, 115).

Usually people will radiate in darker, bluish-purple hues when their aura is quiescent, with vibrating waves at a rate of about 15 pulses per minute (Ambrose 2011, 126; Brennan 1987, 89). If emotionally engaged, reddish and orange streams or bolts will emerge at great speed, darker if there is anger, brighter if there is enthusiasm and engagement. A whitish-gray color signals anxiety or fear, while envy looks like a dark, dirty green (Brennan 1987, 91-92). In all cases, color constitutes a fundamental aspect of our being, both expressing who we are and allowing us to enhance certain patterns and characteristics.

Working with Colors

Biologically colors are the reflection of light in the human retina. It contains receptor cells that consist of rods and cones; they number in the hundreds of millions and are interconnected by a million optic nerve fibers (Johnson 2014a, 218). Retina cells are sensitive to radiation and connect to bipolar cells, which in turn synapse with ganglion cells (Gardner 1968, 196-97). In other words, light rays hit the sensory layer of the retina, then enter through the corneal surfaces, undergo refraction, and shape pictures at different distances, changing with the lens curvature (Gardner 1968, 191-92). The different waves of light are then integrated in the brain, as complex synaptic connections relay information to different parts of the cortex (Barlow 1990, 12).

Light enters equally through both eyes, but processing depends on the location of the object. Thus, an object on the viewer's right side is processed in the left hemisphere of the brain, and vice versa. Information entering through the left eye is transmitted directly to the left side, while data coming through the right eye cross over at the optic chiasma, located in front of the corpus calossum. The same holds true for objects on the left, which are integrated into full images in the right hemisphere (Barlow 1990, 11).

The human eye has four light sensors: three for color with cones for short, medium, and long waves plus one for low light. Very long light waves appear red; very short ones look violet, but we can see neither of these. Instead, human vision is essentially trichromatic, seeing only three primary colors: blue (400-500), green (500-600), and yellow (600-700) (Henshaw 2012, 28, 32). Our vision mixes the rays and adds the different colors together, creating the full spectrum of the rainbow—which is significantly different from mixing paint, when we subtract colors (2012, 32). White in this context is the combination of all colors, the ultimate joining of all light; while black means the complete absence of all color, the state of no light at all (Henshaw 2012, 35).

The kind of color activation found in Daoist visualization and yogic chakra meditations is known as chromotherapy; it is essentially a way of directing energy of a particular wavelength into specific areas of the bodymind. It has proved quite effective in cancer treatment: visualizing cancer cells as little soldiers in a color that is felt invasive or negative plus good, nurturing, healing cells as troops in another, more positive, life-enhancing hue, patients are guided to engage them visually in an internal battle. As they see and feel the good guys win, they spread wholesome, soothing, nurturing color—and thereby healing energy—through their bodies. This can actively reduce the size and presence of tumors (Beauregard 2012, 101; Simonton 1978).

Beyond health, chromotherapy finds application in interior design as well as in sales and advertising. Studies have shown that red tones are warming and energizing, while blue hues tend to be cool and calming. Thus, blue-colored pills tend to be less effective than red ones; blue-colored streetlights contribute to a reduction in crime; dark green walls calm down hyperactive children. Red, on the other hand, increases speed and excitement and causes subjects to do less well on exams. Moreover, the combination of blue and yellow in advertising attracts more buyers than other color variants.

The color associations in Daoist visualization have a firm foundation in nature. Red, for example, is the color of fire and blood; the most physical and of the greatest wavelength, it represents energy, power, love, passion, and joy. Yellow is the color of sunshine and food; still very long in waves, it is warm and cheerful, associated with happiness and clear thinking as well as with positive, outgoing energy and openness. Green is the color of nature and growth; in the middle of the spectrum, it symbolizes safety, fertility, and abundance, and is overall restful and caring. Blue, especially a deep blue, is the color of the sky and the sea as well as of overall health and vigor; shorter in wavelength, it symbolizes depth, stability, trust, wisdom, and confidence and is generally beneficial to body and mind. White, finally, at the short-wave end of the spectrum, near the violet, is the power of light as such, symbolizing purity, innocence, goodness, success, and perfection (www.color-wheel-pro.com).

Bringing energy of these different wavelengths into the central sections of the body, practitioners of Daoist visualization as well as of chakra meditation activate the subtle energies of their bodymind and enhance overall functioning and general well-being. They also make sure that they are fully pervaded by energies of all different lengths, bringing the full breadth of the spectrum to bear on their constitution and raising their being to more celestial levels. The radiance of heaven and earth spreads through them in its full power.

Cell Biology

Besides color visualization, which Daoist visualization shares with chakra meditation, it is unique in that it also works with smiling at, and communicating with, the organs. How this works is best understood in terms of modern cell biology and epigenetics, "the study of the molecular mechanisms by which environment controls gene activity" (Lipton 2008, xxiv, 37; McTaggart 2011, 29). That is to say, as the "the epigenome is always interacting with life," "genes react to experience. . . and when you subject your genes to a healthy lifestyle, you're creating supergenes" (Chopra and Tanzi 2015, 31). This means that by sending a particular intention or emotion (smile) into the direction of a certain cell cluster in the body (organs), we activate the positive genetic properties in our cells and thereby shape how we function in the world (Beauregard 2012, 95; see also Pert 1997).

The human body consists of about 50 trillion cells, of which 3 million die and are born anew in every second. 260 billion of these cells are replaced every single day. We have an all new gastro-intestinal lining every three days, and all new red blood cells every 120 days. Each cell of the human body is an elaborate chemical computer, using power that corresponds to 10^7 chemical reactions per second. Containing a nucleus, membrane, and various other parts, it has its own power management structures as well as read-only and random-access memory, and communicates with its neighbors (Karp 2014).

Each cell, moreover, is an individual organism with the ability to survive, multiply, and act independently. For the first 300 billion years of the earth's existence, single-cell organisms such as amoebas were the only life form on the planet. 700 million years ago, they first clustered into more complex forms, building plants and animals. Cells began to live in communities and specialize, matching the overall tendency of evolution to favor efficient survival less through alpha leadership and more through cooperation, networking, specialization, and complex organizational structures (Lipton 2008, 99). Cells contain inherent wisdom, being acutely aware of their environment, functioning with the least possible expenditure of energy, communicating closely with other cells, and bonding tightly ro make up a particular tissue or organ. In addition, they recognize each other as equally important and combine in ever more complex and creative ways, knowing how to be while remaining in a constant interchange of give and take (Chopra and Tanzi 2015, 234-35).

The human bodymind functions very much like this complex cell organization. Like a computer, it is managed by its CPU, the brain, through various signals sent out to community members that activate their specific functions. Like computer chips, cells receive signals through their semiconductor-like membranes—powerful amplifiers for electromagnetic and other subtle energies (Rosch 2009, 300; Oschman 2000, 45; 2004)—and act on them. They have receptor and effector proteins that function like sense organs or antennas, on the one hand, and provide life-sustaining responses, on the other. Receptors known as Integral Membrane Proteins can be chemicals (hormones), energetic vibrations (light, sound), or mental activities (thoughts, imagination). Effectors can be sodium-potassium connections that generate energy, cytoskeletal proteins that regulate the shape and motility of cells, or enzymes that synthesize or break down molecules (Lipton 2008, 53-55).

Brain impulses sent to the cells come in three types: instinctual patterns hardwired into the reptilian part and thus largely unconscious; repeated, habituated patterns originally learned then automatized and made subconscious in the mammalian part; and conscious, higher-level commands from the prefrontal cortex. The conscious mind picks up only one in 40 million bits of information perceived and processed by the subconscious, making the latter dramatically more powerful (Lipton 2008, 136-38). Nevertheless, impulses sent from the conscious mind have a pervasive impact on cell reality and reactions.

It is, moreover, also the conscious mind that makes decisions on which patterns and attitudes to habituate. 95 percent of the way we live depend on such learned patterns of behavior—which can be modified, unlearned, and reprogrammed. Rather than being inborn or natural, the large majority of our responses are thus determined by what and how we think. We actively create our cell responses, and a single conscious change may result in tremendous transformation (Lipton 2008, 39, 4).

Cell responses come in two major forms: protection and growth. Protection means shutting down certain functions in favor of those essential for survival: it works along the hypothalamus-pituitary-adrenal (HPA) axis and is best known as the "fight or flight" response, aka stress (Lipton 2008, 117; see also Selye 1984). Unlike primitive man who was often faced with life-threatening situations, people today activate the stress response in quite ordinary situations, perceiving threats as more dangerous than they really are. They then get used to being in high alert, with increased adrenaline and intense mental capabilities, causing large numbers of cells to be in protection for prolonged periods. Like people under threat of war never emerging from their air raid shelter, the body under constant stress shuts down and gradually disintegrates (Lipton 2008, 122-24).

Cells in growth, on the other hand, enhance life and work toward the continuous renewal of the bodymind, always growing new cells and maintaining close cooperation within their community. They are responsible for health, which can essentially be defined as the majority of our cells being fully in growth (Carlson and Kohn 2012, 53). Unlike chemicals which move about half an inch per second, energy is instantaneous, so that impulses along the lines of Daoist visualization—initially conscious, then habituated and subconscious—affect the cells instantly, creating health, longevity, and a spiritual connection to the cosmos with amazing efficiency.

Perception and attitude are thus essential in how our cells respond. Rather than our lives being determined by genes, genes are subject to environment and mentation. "Epigenetic changes occur in response to our environment, the food we eat, the pollutants to which we are exposed, even our social [and emotional] interactions" (Francis 2011, xi). Each gene blueprint creates 30,000 variations of protein: it can correct a mutant gene by reading it in a healthy way or, vice versa, transform a healthy gene into a cancerous one—all provided the mental attitude or intention is consistent and the message is repeated often enough. In other words, a gene is merely potential: how it will work depends on which protein variation is activated, which in turn depends on how we respond to our environment, what attitudes, emotions, and virtues we project.

By visualizing our organs, glands, and bones in a positive, life-enhancing manner, we thus instantaneously shift our cells from a protection to a growth response, optimizing health and emotional well-being. By consciously releasing negative emotions and intentionally inviting positive virtues, we release endorphins into our system that are 700 times more powerful than morphine. Practicing focused visualization puts us firmly in the growth response, increasing our immune resistance and enhancing health. It also connects us to the greater universe, allowing the ever-flowing energy of the cosmos to pervade and enrich us with limitless abundance

Chapter Eight

I Alone Survive

The Physics of Immortality

Becoming fully one with the ever-flowing energy of the cosmos in Daoism means the attainment of immortality (*xian* 仙). The culmination of the various practices, this is an advanced spiritual state of profound transformation on earth, followed by ascension into heaven (Kohn 1990a, 1). Ge Hong's 葛洪 (283-343) *Baopuzi* 抱朴子 (Book of the Master Who Embraces Simplicity, DZ 1185; trl. Ware 1966) divides immortals according to their ascensions: prior or post, directly or indirectly. The highest type, celestial immortals (*tianxian* 天仙), ascend directly to the heavens to serve in the celestial administration. Earth immortals (*dixian* 地仙), second, are ready for ascension any moment, but still remain on this earth. A yet lower group are those liberated by simulated corpse (*shijie xian* 尸解仙), who leave a substitute such as a sword or staff behind (see Robinet 1979; Cedcich 2001; Campany 2014, 39-43). In addition to these three major groups, there are child immortals, recent immortals, and numerous other categories of divine beings (2.9a; Ware 1966, 47).

The aim is to develop the body from an individual entity to being part of the larger universe; no longer a means of sensory gratification, it becomes a vehicle of perfection. Similarly, human emotions become powerless: the immortal sees and feels at one with the deep truth of perfection, able to dismiss the surface waves of passions and desires. The conscious mind, too, undergoes a change through rigorous control of all mental projections, so that the socially and emotionally defined personality dissolves in favor of a wider sense of oneness with the universe. A being of eternal life, more at home in heaven than on earth, the immortal has complete control of *qi* both within and without. Able to manipulate both mind and matter at will, he or she not only becomes a beacon of energy and catalyst of change in society, but also possesses a plethora of supersensory powers, contributing actively to the transformation of life.

Transfiguration

As described variously in medieval literature, notably by the great Tang masters Sun Simiao and Sima Chengzhen, aspiring immortals begins by curing acute physical diseases and take good care to spot latent ones (Kohn 1990a, 6; 2008a, 150; 2012, 205). They use various longevity techniques—*fengshui*, breathing, exercises, dietetics, etc.—to attain harmony of all physical actions.[1]

They set themselves up in a properly ventilated and brightly lit space, control their diets, and use herbal concoctions to replace the five grains, cleansing both their environment and their body of harmful and extraneous matter to achieve greater purity and energetic openness. They undertake healing and breathing exercises, frequently imitating the movements and habits of animals, relax the body and shake off old tensions, thus gaining new flexibility and higher suppleness. Not only stimulating digestion and blood circulation, healing exercises harmonize *qi* in the body and allow a greater sense of control (Kohn 2008a; 2012).

Moving on to control the mind, adepts practice concentration. They focus their attention on the lower elixir field in the abdomen until they attain full control over the conscious mind, i.e., until they can fixate it on whatever object they wish for any length of time. Reaching perfect stability of will and intention, they attain the highest of the five phases of the mind.

> The mind is turned entirely toward clarity and stillness. Whether involved in affairs or at leisure, there is no agitation at all. From an efficiently controlled mind, firmness and solidity of concentration develop. (*Cunshen lianqi ming* 2a; Kohn 2010a, 176)

This stability of mind is then used for a critical examination of their psychological constitution. Adepts come to understand that their conscious mind is originally spirit. Spirit works through the human mind and governs life perfectly, but—due to delusion—it is wasted on sensory amusements and the uncontrolled exertions of the senses.

> Spirit is neither black nor white, neither red nor yellow, neither big nor small, neither short nor long, neither crooked nor straight, neither soft nor hard, neither thick nor thin, neither round nor square. It goes on changing and transforming without measure, merges with yin and yang, greatly encompasses heaven and earth, and subtly enters the tiniest blade of grass.
>
> Controlled it is straightforward, let loose it goes mad. Clarity and stillness make it live, defilements and nervousness cause it to perish.

---

[1] These practices are very similar to a set of methods recommended by naturopathic physicians today for the creation of "supergenes." See Chopra and Tanzi 2015, 119-227.

> When shining it can illuminate the eight ends of the universe; when darkened it will go wrong even in one single direction. You need only keep it empty and still, then life and the Dao will spontaneously be permanent. (*Neiguan jing* 2b; Kohn 1989a, 207)

To control the senses and be liberated from their dictates, one must realize the impermanent nature of the personal body or socially determined identity. This, rather than the body of flesh and bones, is the body that one identifies with on the psychological level, one's personality or selfness. Adepts come to understand that this is nothing permanent, but forms merely part of the continuous natural transformations of *qi*.

Eventually they reach a level where they can absorb *qi* directly by visualizing the five *qi* of the directions in their respective colors, seeing them enter the body from heaven through the nose and from earth through the mouth, then circulating and storing it. Eventually the practitioner becomes independent of outer air and the normal act of breathing (Engelhardt 1987, 91; Kohn 1990a, 9).

Internal *qi*, the pure seed of immortality within the body, develops once a certain amount of outer *qi* has been absorbed. Thereby the adept's physical constitution reorganizes from a profane to a sacred level; the flesh and bones of the body are no longer of individual solidity but only pure, cosmic *qi*. Similarly, personal identity dissolves as emotions are controlled through the experiential understanding that all sensory impressions are fleeting and that all selfhood is an illusion. The fluidity of *qi* enters into one's very personal core of being, eliminating the dependency on outer stimuli and emotional patterns (1990a, 14).

Only when the negative aspects of the self, all strong feelings of identity, and one's captivity in the clutches of the senses are realized fully and accordingly have begun to wane, can one turn attention to the heavenly qualities inherent in oneself. One's true self, i.e., the physical yet cosmic body and the sensory yet unemotional and well-controlled mind, are now seen as the storehouse of inner nature, the habitation of the spirit(s), and the vehicle or host of Dao. The spirit shines forth from the body like the light from the lamp.

> The presence of the spirit light in the self can be compared with the light in a basin lamp. Light arises from fire, fire arises from burning. Burning in turn arises because of the oil, and the oil needs the wick and the basin lamp proper. Once those four [fire, burning, oil, and lamp] are gone, how could there be light?
>
> The same pattern holds true in that spirit radiates through human action. But spirit is only present when it resides in the mind. The mind exists only within the body, and the body is only complete through the Dao. (*Neiguan jing* 5b; Kohn 1989a, 217)

Advanced States

Immortals in training increasingly identify with Dao as it guides and inhabits the body and thereby loosen attachments to their limited physical and personal selves. They begin to develop a new and wider identity as part of the universe at large, coming to see themselves truly as beings of spirit that are merely housed in this fragile physical framework subject to all the transformations the spirit transcends. All ordinary fear of death is dissolved.

The resulting personality remains unbound by physical limitations, by emotional engagements, intellectual divisions, and arguments of reason. Any conscious ego identity that was there before is lost, and it is hard to determine at what point exactly the individual ends and the Dao begins. All is in continuous flux, moving along smoothly with the changes of the greater universe.

First, there is the "stability of cosmic peace," a trancelike or enstatic state of complete immersion in the Dao to the exclusion of all else. This state is characterized by unconsciousness and immobility: "The body is like rotten wood, the mind is like dead ashes. There are no more impulses, there is no more search: one has reached perfect serenity" (*Zuowanglun*, sect. 6; Kohn 2010a, 154).

Descriptions of this state speak of "preserving," "embracing," "harmonizing," and "recovering. " Rather than in terms of flux and going along, it is a state of fullness and stability; an intense tranquility and restfulness pervade the adept. The imagery used is accordingly one of union, oneness, and merging; it is full of darkness and the shading of light, showing a mind here characterized by innocence and simplicity, purity and restfulness in the origins of the Dao. People in this state are like an uncut block of wood; their time has stopped and there is no more progress and no more decay. They have fully joined the One at the source of creation, the deep underlying root on whose basis change takes place, the center from which all universal development springs. This source of the universe is what is truly permanent, it is "being" in its truest form. Unless this is recovered and preserved, unless one has made oneself completely one with this, immortality cannot be had. The underlying ground is static—and so in this phase of realization is the immortal state (Kohn 1990b, 630).

In a second phase, adepts emerge from their deep absorption and refine themselves to a yet higher level of purity. Coming out of enstatic immersion and the complete cessation of all physical, sensual, and mental functions, they go off and transcend all in ecstatic pervasion. This state is described as a gradual increase in movement, openness, joy, light, even ecstasy, until the successful adept of immortality takes up a position next to the Jade Emperor of the Great Dao.

> Going beyond all beings in one's body, one whirls out of normal relations and comes to reside next to the Jade Emperor of the Great Dao

in the Numinous Realm. Here the wise and sagely gather, at the farthest shore and in perfect truth.

In creative change, in numinous pervasion, all beings are reached. Only one who has attained this level of cultivation has truly reached the source of the Dao. Here the myriad paths come to an end. This is called the final ultimate. (*Cunshen lianqi ming* 3a; Kohn 2010a, 177)

The imagery of this ecstatic level is strongly shamanistic: the flight into higher realms, the experience of an altered state of consciousness, the freedom from the limits of this world—all are present in the descriptions. The process of attaining ultimate freedom is depicted as one of getting lighter and brighter; the higher one ascends, the purer the spirit becomes, the more light one will radiate. The worldview that underlies this model of eternal life is one of "becoming:" the universe is in a constant flux, and nothing stands ever still or stops for a moment. Timc is conceived as cyclical, eternity can only take place in an eternal return (Kohn 1990b, 635). By attaining both, the immortal has become one with the Dao in both its key aspects, as the quiescent, underlying power of all and as the creative power of the world, continuously moving and forever transforming.

Ascension

Ascension is the strongest symbol of the going-beyond of individual personality and social context. Whether a given immortal observes his or her own funeral, whether a high Daoist master exhibits his "transformation" to his disciples, or whether the person just vanishes—in all cases the break with normalcy is complete, the transcendence of all individuality and social integration is demonstrated. The transition from a perfected life on earth to an eternal existence in the glory and delight of the heavens is the process of ascension. Ascension is the key phase that separates immortals as true human being from immortals as members of the administration of heaven and attendants on the higher deities of the Dao.

Ascension comes in different forms (Kohn 1990a, 18-20). The highest way to ascend is by celestial chariot. Receiving a summons to office among the heavenly bureaucrats, the immortal readies himself or herself and, on the day appointed, is formally met by a dragon-drawn cloudy chariot and escorted up to heaven by a large entourage of celestial guards, supernatural horsemen, and divine lads. The most famous ascension of this kind is that of Huangdi, who mounted on a huge celestial dragon together with seventy of his followers, some people trying to cling to the dragon's beard and claws in a desperate effort at eternal life.

The second most powerful way of ascension is by vanishing completely. Again, a divine invitation is received, but rather than in a formal reception, the immortal ascends upward on his own, using clouds and streams of air for support. Here, too, the celestial-to-be announces his or her supernatural state and gets ready for departure, but the entire setting is decidedly less formal. This form of ascension, not as celebrated and rather less well prepared, often leaves friends and family in a state of confusion. How can one be sure there was not foul play by some nasty demon?

A third form to ascend is through "liberation by simulated corpse." This is a rather crude way, since it requires that the immortal leave some physical token of his or her worldly presence behind. This shows that he or she is not quite able to dissolve completely into the heavenly spheres. If there is a corpse, it does not decay, unlike that of an ordinary dead person. Far from smelling offensive, the corpse is fragrant, pink clouds come to hover, and strands of celestial music sound. Most classically, this is the way Daoist masters go, announcing their transformation and leaving the world sitting upright in deep meditation (Campany 2014; Cedzich 2001; Robinet 1979).

In terms of methods, there are several ways to undertake an ascension. The most effective and immediate is by swallowing a cinnabar elixir, a concoction of various metals and minerals, but ultimately identifiable as a mercury compound. The stronger the elixir, the more instantaneous is the transformation. Operative alchemy in traditional China is not only a formalized and ritualized process of replicating the creation of the universe and an attempt to find the philosophers' stone, but the safest way to be ready for the celestial summons at the moment it comes. Elixirs are highly poisonous, but ascending immortals knew where they were going.

Another way is to produce an inner elixir by way of internal alchemy. Here an immortal embryo is created, an agent that combines all the celestial elements of the practitioner and who will travel freely through the otherworldly realms. When the summons comes or the natural lifespan of this body ends, the embryo ascends once more, this time for good. Then again, there is the way of dissolution, a more meditative method in which the adept transforms his or her self and body to ever subtler energies and eventually loses himself completely in Dao. Rather a gradual process, ascension here is the opening of the earth-bound body and mind to a more subtle being, the gradual floating away of the self and merging into the nothingness of Dao.

Among the most famous ascensions is that of Huangdi. According to *Shiji* 28, he was received into the heavenly host by a divine dragon. He mounted it with seventy of his followers, and with people still trying to cling to the dragon's beard and claws, was taken off into the empyrean (Le Blanc 1986). Another famous case is Liu An's 劉安 of the Han, who, as Ge Hong's *Shenxian zhuan* 神仙傳 (Biographies of Spirit Immortals; trl. Campany 2002) tells it, took an immortality elixir and ascended into heaven on a cloud, followed by the dogs and chickens of his court that lapped up the dregs of the elixir left behind (Kohn 1993, 296; Campany 2002, 238).

A case from the late 8th century involves Lad Qu, aka Qu Baiting 瞿白庭, who ascended to heaven in broad daylight in a public occurrence in the fifth month of the year 773. He was at that time eighteen years of age and apprenticed to the 15th patriarch of the Shangqing school of Daoism. The event took place in the courtyard of Peach Blossom Monastery (Taohua guan 桃花觀) in full view of monastic and lay onlookers: while holding on to a chestnut tree, Qu's physical form dissolved completely and he vanished into thin air (Kohn 1993, 328-32).

Many Daoist masters show their transfiguration in a ritual way. Thus, Sima Chengzhen reportedly announced that he would shortly take up a position in the heavenly administration. On the date specified a pink cloud surrounded him and he rose up as a full immortal to the sound of heavenly music. His disciples duly proceeded to bury his robe and cap (Engelhardt 1987, 52).

Whichever form the ascension takes, it expresses the complete dissolution of mundane ties and forms of identity. In all cases, ordinary life is sacrificed for the attainment of perfection. The coming realm of immortality is greater and higher than the mundane world left behind. Throughout, there is a strong sense of purpose and of duty to Dao, a going-along with the needs of the universe, of which even the immortal is but a part.

The fully accomplished immortal, easy traveler to the stars and companion of the perfected in the realm of Dao, is still human. For the time being, he or she has still to come back to the world of humanity to live among ordinary people, to deal with life in its various forms. Only after the life expectancy decreed at this time has ended or when a summons to celestial office arrives, do immortals finally leave this world and ascend off and away for good. They then become one of the heavenly host, receive a rank in the hierarchy above, and serve in the celestial administration of this and the other world.

As long as they are still with ordinary mortals, however much their heads and minds and feelings might rest above the clouds, immortals are human beings with particular characteristics, people with extensive minds, superior powers, and extraordinary behavior patterns (Kohn 1990a, 3).

Immortal Personality

Definitions and descriptions of this immortal personality differ. Most commonly, living immortals are described as perfected (*zhenren* 真人). They are realized ones in that they have fulfilled their full potential, true persons in that they have become truly human. Such people maintain unshakable equanimity in all situations, never rushing after gain, taking pride in achievements, worry about ventures, or despair in failure. As the *Zhuangzi* already says,

> The perfected of old did not resent being humble, did not take pride in success, and never plotted their affairs. From this basis, they could be without regret if things went wrong, remain free from self-congratulations when they went right.
>
> For this reason, they could climb high places without getting scared, dive into water without getting soaked, and pass through fire without getting hot. Their understanding was such that they could rise up and join Dao at all times.
>
> The perfected of old slept without dreaming and woke without concerns. Their food was plain and their breath deep: in fact, the perfected breathes all the way to the heels while the multitude breathe just to the throat—bent over and submissive, they croak out words as if they were retching; full of intense passions and desires, they have only the thinnest connection to heaven.
>
> The perfected of old had no clue about loving life and hating death. They came to life without celebration, they left again without messiness. Calmly they came, calmly they went—and that is all. They never forgot where they came from, they never inquired about where they would end. They received whatever came and enjoyed it; they lost whatever went and just let it go. (ch. 6; Kohn 2011, 139)

Living immortals are calm and uninvolved, yet take action in just the way that is best for any given situation. With their hands on the pulse of nature, they can be compassionate and understanding, compliant and gentle, helpful and upright. They seem to do the most outstanding feats with ease and no particular effort, fully in control of themselves, yet charming in their interaction with others.

Immortals tend not to have much patience with the constrictions of ordinary social life and on occasion appear weird and eccentric. They come across as happy-go-lucky fellows who hang out drinking and playing games, writing silly verses on the walls of taverns, and shocking contemporary citizens with their unconventional behavior. Gone far beyond the "normal" mind, they may sing at funerals, pinch wine and meat from the gods at sacrifices, drink and make merry, and laugh at anything and everything.

Accepting life and death as a single flow, they take neither seriously and make the best of all they meet. Their happy attitude, their playful way of being is characteristic of the popular image of the immortal today, frequently expressed in pictures of the Eight Immortals (*baxian* 八仙), playing and drinking in merry company, found on good-luck cards and in restaurants.

Immortals are completely at one in their personalities. Oblivious of physical needs, emotional upheavals, and mental patterns, their minds merge with

Dao and harmonize with nature. Should one or the other, despite the tendency to live either in seclusion or at ease, take up an active social role, he or she may well become a catalyst of change in society. Whether in a prominent position or just in an ordinary place, such a person does not need to do much to make the world a better place. In fact, the more he remains in nonaction, the more Dao that is concentrated in him can freely radiate and thereby create harmony and openness for all.

One with Dao, they also have all sorts of supersensory or paranormal powers, ways in which they intentionally exercise their oneness with and control over *qi*. For example,

> Ge Yue 葛越, also known as Master Yellow Hut [Huangluzi 黃盧子] was good at curing and healing. Even at a distance of one thousand miles, if he only knew the name of the sick person, he could cure him. All would get well, even if he never saw the patient's body.
>
> He also excelled at exorcising with the help of *qi*. He would get rid of tigers, wolves, and all kinds of nasty insects. None of them would dare to move when he was around. And he could make rivers flow backwards as far as a mile.
>
> Easily reaching the age of 280, he was able to lift a ton without any trouble and walked as fast as other people rode on horseback. Around his head there always was a five-colored halo, which made him look about ten feet tall.
>
> At times of drought, he could enter deep into the springs and summon forth dragons. Controlling them, he ordered them to ascend to the sky and produce rain. Numerous times, he worked miracles like that. One day he said farewell to his family and friends, mounted a dragon and ascended, never to return. (Kohn 1993, 290-91; Campany 2002, 303)

Another immortal of multiple powers described in the *Shenxian zhuan* is Taixuan nü 太玄女 (Lady of Great Mystery). She possessed complete immunity to the elements, could enter water and not get wet, sit in a blazing fire and not burn. Able to travel far distances in an instant and adept at bilocation, "she could change her appearance at will: one moment she was an old man, then again a small child." She also transformed material objects. "Whatever she pointed at would vanish into thin air: doors, windows, boxes, or caskets that were securely locked needed only a short flexing of her finger to break wide open. Mountains would tumble and trees would fall at the pointing of her hand. Another gesture would resurrect them to their former state" (Kohn 1993, 291).

The powers of immortals divide into two different dimensions: those applying to themselves and those working transformations in the outside world. Having full control over their own *qi*, they are shape-changers who can appear in any form they please. They can multiply themselves into many different people, bilocate to be present in more than one place at once, become visible and invisible at will, travel thousands of miles in an instant, see through walls and into distant locations, read the minds of others, and predict the future. They have complete mastery over their appearance, health, and vitality, and are able to live for as long as they like, eventually ascending smoothly to the subtler realms of the heavenly spheres.

Controlling not only themselves, immortals also have power over nature and the outside world—an integral part of the unified world of *qi*. They can make rivers flow backward and mountains tumble. Plants, animals, and people die at their command and come back to life if they tell them to do so. They transport buildings to far-off places, open up mountains to reveal grottoes. They heal the sick, exorcise demons or beasts, make rain or stop it, foretell or prevent disasters, and call upon wild animals as helpers. They have full integration of *qi*, manifest in control over the body, a subtle harmony with the forces of nature, as well as an easy relationship with gods and spirits, ghosts and demons (Kohn 1993, 279-81).

Energy Gauge Symmetry

In terms of modern physics, Daoist immortals are human beings who have attained a higher level of energy gauge symmetry. As described by physicist William Tiller, a specialist in crystallization, the universe began in state of compression to infinite density at the Big Bang, and has been expanding ever since. Originally one hot fireball, it evolved to successively lower thermodynamic free energy states through an ongoing cooling process.

First it reached a state described as "special unitary" (SU) (2) symmetry state, which involves an infinite number of infinitesimal strings engaged in continuous integrated transformation, moving in non-relativistic spin due to double covering of the rotational grouping of space (Tiller et al. 2005, 106; 2001, 352-54; Steinkirch 2011, 37). In this high, subtle energy state, magnetic charges coexist with electric poles along two inner symmetry parameters, energy is exchanged via both photons (light) and phonons (sound), and it works with magnetoelectric (ME) rather than electromagnetic (EM) forces, i.e., carrier waves faster than light (Tiller et al. 2005, 107; Steinkirch 2011, 1).

From here the universe continued to evolve into a "unitary" (U) (1) symmetry state, matching the evolution from plasma to gaseous, liquid, and eventually solid states. The mixed solids, liquids, and gases reached an approximate thermodynamic balance called "unitary," and the world as we know it emerged: unconditioned and conventional, consisting of a finite number of elements in a particular order of grouping in unitary matrices (Tiller et al. 2005, 106). Determined by electromagnetic forces, it divides into magnetic dipoles, positive and negative, with fields and vectors defined by a single inner symmetry parameter. The physical reality thus created is relatively coarse and particulate, its electric monopole constructing types of substance that move at velocities below the speed of light (2005, 107, 110). This is our world. However, the SU (2) level remains active beneath it.

Experiments have shown that fine, information-wave generated patterns from magnetic monopole types and substances can move faster than the speed of light in a coarse physical vacuum, working at a higher electromagnetic gauge symmetry level (McTaggart 2007, 113-20; see also Pagels 1982). Tiller describes this subtle substance that can move both below and above the speed of light and acts as a coupling agent between the coarse and fine levels of physical reality as deltrons. In other words, deltrons constitute mediator fields within the different levels of energy symmetry (Tiller et al. 2005, 110). Human consciousness as intention—defined as "a purposeful plan to perform an action that will lead to a desired outcome" (McTaggart 2007, xxv)—when concentrated and focused to a very high degree, can activate the deltron population and modulate substances in a measurable and meaningful way (Tiller et al. 2005, 114).

All human beings participate in these different energy gauge symmetry states. They consist of three different selves, each with two layers. The most basic is the body or personality self with a visible, material interface defined through the five senses plus a subtle sensory system described in terms of energy conduits (meridians, chakras). The second is the mind or soul self with emotion and mentation plus intuition and soul domains. The third is the spirit or God self with the two dimensions of higher personal or spiritual self plus cosmic consciousness, attainment of oneness with the universe, i.e., God or Dao (Tiller et al. 2005, 8-10). Powerfully concentrated and focused intention originates at the level of spirit and then manifests as a unique radiation pattern of consciousness and energy waves at the level of mind, from where its conjugate pattern is diffracted to reciprocal lattice spaces in the body and physical environment (Tiller et al. 2005, 110, 126; 2001, 336).

Immortals according to this understanding are highly developed human beings who have reached a sustained higher energy gauge symmetry state close to SU (2). Their cortical neurons act like strong receiving antennas in a large array, easily converting spacetime information into a diffraction pattern. They are thus able to process vast amounts of information at an immensely high speed (Tiller et al. 2005, 127). They have also reached a high degree of coherence within their brains and a strong entrainment of brain and heart—the latter being the largest antenna, the biggest electrical system, and a major "brain" in the body (McTaggart 2007, 54-55; 2011, 41; Childre et al. 1999, 38; Chopra and Tanzi 2015, 239see also Gowin 2001).

The heart works without interruption for seventy to ninety years, without care or cleaning, without repair or replacement. It beats 100,000 times a day, 40 million times a year, three billion pulsations all told. It pumps two gallons of blood per minute—well over one hundred gallons per hour—through a vascular system about sixty thousand miles in length, i.e., over two times the circumference of the earth (Childre et al. 1999, 9). Autorhythmic, i.e., with self-initiated beat, the heart has own independent nervous system and contains at least 40,000 neurons, whose signals connect to the brain neurologically through nerve impulses, biochemically via hormones, biophysically through pressure waves, and energetically via the electromagnetic field: they are instantly obeyed. In contrast, the brain may send orders to the heart through the autonomic nervous system, but the heart will not necessarily follow them (1999, 10, 28).

The heart beats in certain rhythms and patterns, described technically as heart rate variability (HRV), which clearly match emotional states and affect the electrical activity of the brain.[2] An emotional intelligence, it can be controlled with meditation, energy work, and biofeedback. Most powerful steadying means are attitudes of spirit: appreciation or gratitude, nonjudgment or tolerance as well as anger release or forgiveness (Childre et al. 1999, 105-30; McCraty and Rees 2011). These come forth most strongly after setting up a conditioned space and calming the mind by focusing on breathing or another steady object (McTaggart 2007, 200-01). The steadier the heart rhythm, the better integrated the inner teamwork, the stronger the immune system, the more potent the parasympathetic response (Childre et al. 1999, 15, 25), the closer one comes to a higher energy gauge symmetry state (Tiller 2004b).

This high symmetry state, then, explains how immortals and qigong masters transform objects or shift people just by directing their intention at them: in a SU (2) state, they have highly synchronized heart and brain waves they can emit energy at will and point toward any person, object, or goal they envision (McTaggart 2007, 53). From a state of meditative concentration, typically characterized by alpha and theta waves, they can raise the intensity of emissions to extremely fast frequency waves of the gamma level, i.e., 25-70 hertz, signifying a state of rapt attention, "when the brain works the hardest" and creates a powerful level of synchrony. This phenomenon also occurs, and has been studied in some detail, among experienced yogis and Buddhist meditators, whose "neural processing had been permanently altered by years of intensive meditation" (2007, 67-70; see also Murphy et al. 1997; Shapiro and Walsh 1984). More than that, it is also part of everyday life, except that ordinary people are not aware of it and use it to a much lesser degree. However, they, too, can harness it and influence their bodies and the world around them by focused, directional thinking. "Experiments indicate that there is a profound connectivity between any part of nature and another. Everyone of us—including even animals—can influence all biological life forms around us via our biofield emissions and the information they carry, whether one consciously intends to or not" (Tiller et al. 2005, 92; McTaggart 2007, xxvii, 155-56, 200-06).

---

[2] Oschman 2000, 27; Tiller et al. 2005, 14; McCraty and Rees 2009, 528; McCraty 2004; Rosch 2009, 304.

The Power of Intention

Part of self-help culture, e.g., Wayne Dyer's *The Power of Intention* (2004), human biofield emissions have long been acknowledged as underlying the power of prayer. Prayer, as Larry Dossey says, "uses the nonlocal mind to affect self, others, and the world. Intention sends energy everywhere. . . . Once distant objects have come into contact, a change thereafter in one causes an immediate change in the other—no matter how far apart they are" (1993, 84). Numerous trials—such as Lynne McTaggart's "Intention Experiment"—have shown that ailing people who receive intentional support through a prayer chain—even if anonymous and far apart—heal better, faster, and more permanently than control groups.[3]

While this evidence is largely circumstantial, if statistically significant, the question of the physics of intention, the problem of actually showing and measuring how thought affects physical reality, led William Tiller to discover the different energy symmetry states. In 1997, a California company hired him to improve a simple device to eliminate electromagnetic pollution. About the size of a remote control, it contained three quartz oscillators plus a read-only memory and was able to screen incoming energy. Fascinated by questions of thought and intention (see Tiller 1997), he decided to find out if he could imprint this device with thought (McTaggart 2007, 113-14).

His method was simple: he and several co-experimenters would sit down together next to the device and enter a meditative state, creating a sense of loving attunement with it while holding their particular intention in the heart. After fifteen minutes, one would read a formal imprint statement: "We intend to activate our indwelling consciousness in order to condition the device to a significantly higher electromagnetic gauge symmetry state. And so be it. Thy will be done" (Tiller et al. 2001, 23-25; 2005, 52-53). This procedure echoes the general recommendation of intention workers to be specific and state the intention clearly, visualizing the outcome with all senses in real time, followed by moving aside, i.e., surrender to the power of the universe, what Daoist traditionally call nonaction (McTaggart 2007, 208, 212).

Protecting against energy leakage, Tiller and his partners repeated the process several times. They found that their "intention infused electrical device" (IIED) would not only move into the higher state as demanded, but also that there was no limit in terms of physical distance between the intention-generating meditators and the machine. It would receive imprints even over long distances. Physics measurements, such as the spontaneous appearance of material property oscillations of very large amplitude, clearly demonstrated that it was in a higher electromagnetic gauge symmetry state. The device, moreover,

---

[3] McTaggart 2007, 83-98; 199-212; see also Benson 1996; Benor 2001; Braud 2003; Dossey 1994; 2001.

did not keep this charge to itself. Over time, the entire room and area around it would come to be in a higher charged state. Even an untreated device (UED), electrically turned off, at a distance of a hundred meters, would receive the imprint in the course of a week. Removing the source of imprinting, the device would gradually lose its conditioning, returning to "normal" after about a week. On the other hand, wrapping it in aluminum foil and storing it in an electrically grounded cage prolonged the imprint for months and even years (Tiller et al. 2005, 36-37).

This experiment shows that human consciousness as specific information pattern can modulate a subtle energy carrier wave and be stored in a simple electronic device as well as broadcast into space to condition it (2005, 104). The implications are far-reaching. For one, it serves as the model for a new paradigm in medicine. Tiller demonstrates this with a glass of water containing bacteria. Using chemical drugs of biomedicine, the dominant mode of treatment today, he added a spoon of silver collodial, which killed the bacteria through physical contact. Using energy medicine, the system at the root of acupuncture and other traditional modes, he placed a piece of silver in a separate fluorescent glass tube next to the infected water; its focus emitted light on the water through electromagnetic waves and eliminated the bacteria. Using the new dimension of quantum-based information medicine, he applied the power of subtle energies as directed by intention, creating a higher gauge symmetry state and thereby purifying the water (2005, 106-07).

This understanding is also at the root of Bruce Lipton's approach to disease in four steps: inform, conform, unform, and reform. That is to say, we inform ourselves about what is going on, accepting the fact that we have a certain condition and acknowledge its presence; we do not reject, deny, or denigrate it nor do we scold ourselves for being in this situation. Next, we conform to it: we love it as it is and resonate energetically with its form, accepting it as part of our being; this is usually the hardest part, where traditional conditioning is overcome. Third, we unform it by consciously and gently releasing it into the greater energy stream of the universe, allowing particles to shift into waves and thus making active use of the quantum world. And finally, we reform it: we shape the condition to new purpose and direct it into the greater universe without attachment (Lipton and Bhaerman 2009, 286-87).

Higher Levels

To reach this new level of energy being, we must gain full control over our mental functioning, so we can send out powerfully focused intention. As William Tiller puts it, "Just as physical exercise leads to muscle development in the outer layer of the personality self, inner self-management exercises like meditation, qigong, taichi, remote viewing, local and nonlocal healing, etc. lead to the development of key structural features of the inner layer of the personality self" (Tiller et al. 2005, 91).

Similarly, David R. Hawkins (1927-2012), mystic, psychiatrist, spiritual teacher, and expert in behavioral kinesiology, noticed that, as human beings react to stimuli or feelings in a predictably strong or weak energy mode, they produce certain types of attractor patterns or morphogenetic (M) fields. Entraining with positive attractor fields, people create their reality in a complex process that involves traditional causality as well as nonlinear, karmic dynamics and nondual, holographic interaction as described in chaos theory and quantum physics (see Hawkins 2006; 2008; Larson 2003, 127; McTaggart 2007, 164). Hawkins says,

> The individual human mind is like a computer terminal connected to a giant database. The database is human consciousness itself, of which our own cognizance is merely an individual expression, but with its roots in the common consciousness of all humankind. This database is the realm of genius; because to be human is to participate in the database, everyone, by virtue of his or her birth, has access to genius. The unlimited information contained in the database has now been shown to be readily available to anyone in a few seconds, at any time and in any place. (2002, 34)

In other words, rather than being victims to the whims of the cosmic super-computer, people can be in-powered by it. Not everybody reacts negatively to all potentially harmful stimuli or is completely subject to influences of the environment. People of high energy gauge symmetry can control their energy fields and gain immunity from negative patterns. This creates a major shift in awareness: rather than limiting exposure to energetic pollutants or changing the environment, we now can enhance our personal potency and create health from the inside-out (Hawkins 2002, 195).

The sustained application of intention and training in meditative practices such as those of Daoism and other traditional religions eventually leads to superlative energy development. Over time, the practices render people, whose lives are determined by withdrawing emotions and stress, immune to negative energy flows, turning normal folks increasingly into adepts of a raised energy gauge symmetry state, i.e., immortals (Tiller et al. 2005, 92).

A numerical way of demonstrating this progress appears in David Hawkins's scale of the "levels of human consciousness," developed on the basis of behavioral kinesiology. Within a range from 1 to 1,000, the dividing line between testing weak and strong is at 200, the number associated with the level of "courage." Below is the field of "force" where violence and aggression dominate: shame, guilt, apathy, grief, fear, desire, anger, and pride. Above is the realm of "power" with the positive attitudes of neutrality, willingness, acceptance, reason, love, joy, and peace.

Clinically Proven "Map of Consciousness"

View on God	View on Life	Level Name	Level #	Emotions	Process
Self	Is	Enlightenment	700-1000	Ineffable	Pure Consciousness
All-Being	Perfect	Peace	600	Bliss	Illumination
		Spontaneous Healing			
One	Complete	Joy	540	Serenity	Transfiguration
Loving	Benign	Love	500	Reverence	Revelation
Wise	Meaningful	Reason	400	Understanding	Abstraction
Merciful	Harmonious	Acceptance	350	Forgiveness	Transcendence
Inspiring	Hopeful	Willingness	310	Optimism	Intention
Enabling	Satisfactory	Neutrality	250	Trust	Release
Permitting	Feasible	Courage	200	Affirmation	Empowerment

POWER ↑ — STRONG ↑

Levels at or above 200 have Truth, Integrity and support life. — *CREATIVE*

Levels below 200 are False, lack Integrity, do not support life. — *DESTRUCTIVE*

FORCE ↓ — WEAK ↓

View on God	View on Life	Level Name	Level #	Emotions	Process
Indifferent	Demanding	Pride	175	Scorn	Inflation
Vengeful	Antagonistic	Anger	150	Hate	Aggression
Denying	Disappointing	Desire	125	Craving	Enslavement
Punitive	Frightening	Fear	100	Anxiety	Withdrawl
Disdainful	Tragic	Grief	75	Regret	Despondence
Condemning	Hopeless	Apathy	50	Despair	Abdication
Vindictive	Evil	Guilt	30	Blame	Destruction
Despising	Miserable	Shame	20	Humiliation	Elimination

POWER is self-sustaining, permanent, stationary, and invincible.
FORCE is temporary, consumes energy, and moves from location to location.

Logarithmic *Energy Field* Increases: 1 = 1; 2 = 10; 3 = 100; 4 = 1,000; 5 = 10,000; 6 = 100,000 ...etc.

All levels below 500 are "objective" and all levels from 500 to 1,000 are "subjective."

Highest among all is the sphere of "enlightenment," which divides into further levels to culminate at 1,000 with the great spiritual teachers of the planet, such as Krishna, Buddha, Laozi, and Jesus. Here "all the dualities have been transcended . . . and the self disappears into the Self. . . All the vicissitudes of life disappear and now, free of even death itself, there is the remembrance that one always has been and always will be, and that survival was never a problem at all" (Hawkins 2001, 60).

This clearly matches the traditional description of Daoist immortals, beings of very high energy gauge symmetry expanding universal purity everywhere. While the world as a whole stands currently at 207, having just moved into the "strong" realm of power after being in the 190s for millennia, 85 percent of human beings are still below 200, living in tension, poverty, and primitive conditions. Only 15 percent test higher, with people beyond 600 a tiny minority. Still, a single individual at level 700 counterbalances as many as seventy million below (Hawkins 2001, 75; 2002, 40), reinforcing the ancient Daoist claim of the central importance and catalyzing potency of the sage and enhancing the impact of immortals, even if not active within society.

In addition, all human beings are capable of experiencing higher levels of consciousness in what traditions call mystical experiences, characterized by oneness, beingness, timelessness, and knowingness.[4] Anytime we enter a mental state of fully focused intention and connect to the higher energy gauge symmetry of the universe, we leap into the higher ranges of the consciousness scale with tremendous impact. "Just one instant in a very high state can completely change a person's orientation to life, as well as his goals and values. It can be said that the previous individual who was is no more, and a new person is born out of the experience," an intensely charged energy bundle of tremendous power (Hawkins 2002, 106).

Supersensory Powers

This bundle of power, then, typically possesses several abilities that go beyond ordinary senses and abilities. Attaining "spirit pervasion" (*shentong* 神通), immortals are able to make themselves light or heavy, minute or vast, taking on any energetic form or shape while knowing of and controlling various objects and creatures around them (Johnson 2014b, 259; 2014c, 8). Today known as ESP (extrasenory perception), these abilities typically come in three distinct forms. One is an enhanced level of sensory awareness, the ability to connect to the world in more subtle ways or through multiple venues such as in forms of synesthesia. The second is an increase in attention, a powerful focus on, and

[4] See James 1936, 371; Beauregard 2012, ch. 8; Happold 1970, 45; Proudfoot 1985, 124-48; Radin 2013, 46-65; Stace 1966, 44. See also Bucke 1961; Underhill 1911; Wulff 2000.

heightened awareness of, the "nonlocal hyper-dimensional space-time in which we live" (Targ 2012, 209; Katz 2008, 10). It leads to states of nonsensory knowing and the reception of information as manifest in the classic psychic or "psi" phenomena of telepathy, clairvoyance, and precognition—using a term first coined by the British psychologist Robert H. Thouless in 1942 (Alcock 1990, 16; Beauregard 2012, 136). The third is the powerful direction of intention into the holographic, interconnected universe, leading to a direct impact, an active modification of the world in the major psi manifestation known as psychokinesis (PK).

More specifically, telepathy is direct mind-to-mind communication, also known as the perception of the *ganzfeld*, i.e., the "whole field," of mental and physical reality. Clairvoyance is the unmediated knowledge of distant events, today most strongly activated in remote viewing, while precognition is the awareness of future events, also called "feeling the future" (see Dossey 2009). Psychokinesis, moreover, is the power of mind over matter, the ability to influence physical reality by sending focused intention, activated in qigong demonstrations, spoon bending, and—most powerfully—in spiritual healing.[5]

Forming the core of parapsychology, these three are widely credited even in the modern world—by 65 percent of Americans and, due to more general cultural acceptance, by 90 percent of Afro-Brazilians (Targ et al. 2000, 220). They first attracted scholarly attention in the 19th century in conjunction with Mesmerism and underwent extensive if often disparaged studies in the 20th century, notably at the parapsychology lab founded by Joseph Banks Rhine (1895-1980) at Duke University in 1932.[6] Since the founding of the Stanford Research Institute under government auspices in 1972, they have attained a great deal of credibility (Targ 2008, 125; Targ and Harary 1984, 14; Targ and Katra 1998, ch. 2; Kaku 2008, 75). Compelling and meaningful, "the experimental evidence for ESP from a century of research is so strong and over-

---

[5] For definitions, see Alcock 1990, 9; Beauregard 2012, 136; Hansel 1985, 101-04; Katz 2008, 2; McTaggart 2007, xxviii; Nash 1986, 77-80; Panati 1974, 3; Radin 2013, 130-74; Targ 2004; 2012, 7-9; and Harary 1989, 53; et al. 2000, 220; Tiller et al. 2005, 219-28. Spiritual healing comes in many different forms, including absent or distant healing, bioenergy therapy, directed prayer, faith healing, laying-on of hands, mental healing, therapeutic touch, occult medicine, psychic surgery, and more (Krippner and Achterberg 2000, 357; see also Panati 1974, 83). Biomedical explanations involve changes in blood supply and other physiological reactions as well as systems theories of social setting and shared worldview and, most prominently, the placebo effect (2000, 377-81). The latter can be eminently powerful so that, for example people receiving sham knee surgery walk just as well as those really treated (Beauregard 2012, 1-2; see also Benedetti 2014).

[6] For studies of parapsychology, see Alcock 1990; Beauregard 2012; Girden and Girden 1985; Heyman 1985; Irwin 1999; Panati 1974; Mitchell and White 1974. On J. B. Rhine, his institute, and his experiments, see Alcock 1990, 81; Hansel 1985, 109; Heyman 1985, 43-46; Kaku 2008, 73; Radin 2013, 132;

whelming that reasonable people simply should no longer doubt its reality" (Targ 2012, 12; et al. 2000, 223; Beauregard 2012, 149).

The psi phenomena all work due to the nonlocal, holographic nature of the universe, its fundamental characteristic of quantum entanglement, where all is interconnected and separation is an illusion.[7] "Entangled photons are affected jointly by what happens to each twin, even many kilometers away" (Targ 2012, 202). Psychically connected to all existence on a subliminal level, "we are constantly submerged in a sea of telepathic suggestions" and other psi-based phenomena, leading to sympathy pains, mass hysteria, and other linked events (Panati 1974, 105-06, 137). Russell Targ systematizes this fact with the notion of eight dimensions: three dimensions of space plus time in both the real world of matter and the imaginary world of cosmic consciousness. Closely intersecting, each real dimension is paired with its imaginary counterpart, allowing any two locations on the "real" plane to be connected by a path of zero distance (2012, 203, 212; 2004, 5).

Similarly, William Tiller distinguishes two levels of physical reality, the atomic/molecular plus a vacuum, that mirror each other and connect through the subtle energy system of the body, i.e., auras, chakras, and meridians, which in turn are intention modulated (2001, 380; et al. 2005, 131, 137; see also Grof and Bennett 1992, 7-9). They function in a layer of fine information linked through deltrons in a biomagnetic process, which he calls the R-space. Since we are always R-space connected to others, we can both pick up information and broadcast radiation to influence the world around us, provided our intention is focused and we have a willing receiver (Tiller et al. 2005, 207).

For example, if two people, A and B, sit in separate rooms and have their EEG measured and we shine a light on A, creating a particulare signature in his brain, there is nothing equivalent in B. However, if the two focus on each other in a meditative state for ten minutes and we shine a light on A, the exact same brain signature also occurs in B, even though there is no light directly on him. In both cases, the gamma value is increased, which means that their deltron activation level is raised (2005, 209). Similarly, two subjects who placed each other into hypnotic trance continue to interact in synchrony with nonverbal communication, closely linked nonlocally (Panati 1974, 72). In other words, engaged in psi activities, they set their personality self aside, rest in a semi-hypnotic state, and become pure channels of the unseen universe. Residing in the R-space domain, they enhance their gamma waves to a higher gauge symmetry level, making amazing feats possible.

---

[7] The first to link quantum mechanics and parapsychology was Evan Harris Walker, a parapsychologist at Johns Hopkins University; see M. Gardner 1985, 589-95. For more, see also Radin 1997; 2006.

Activation Today

To activate the various psi powers, then, the first requirement is that we learn to quiet the mind, to relieve it from its ongoing chatter and "analytic overlay," i.e., the impact of our memories, imagination, and the tendency to question and analyze data (Targ 2012, 2, 234). Letting go of ego, will, and control, we enter a semi-hypnotic state or "twilight mind" (Panati 1974, 129), hone our attention to receive subtle inputs, and strengthen our intention toward impacting the energy field (Katz 2008, 18). This "loss of self-consciousness, of self-awareness, of self-observation" (Maslow 1971, 269) leads to a freed state of seemingly infinite potential (Panati 1974, 68).

A mono-motivational sense of fusion with the cosmos (1974, 69), this is a form of transcendence consciousness, which allows us to function fully in the R-space, making us invulnerable—not unlike the feats told of Daoist immortals. Modern examples include sky diver Bob Hall who hit the earth at about sixty miles per hour, suffering "nothing more serious than a smashed nose and loosened teeth" (1974, 66); and martial arts grandmaster David Harris, his crew, and his van who remained entirely unscathed when a truck careened into them on the freeway at high speed (personal communcation, April 2014). By the same token, bilocation becomes an entirely normal "physical phenomenon: a person experiencing it feels that they can interact with their surroundings, experience sensations exactly as if they were there, even leave footprints behind" (Dames 2011, 21).

Standardized and demystified by renowned psychic Ingo Swann (1933-2013) as part of military and secret service training, remote viewing—a basically telepathic ability to process pictorial, nonanalytical information garnered from a psychic inspection of distant objects—is open to everyone today.[8] "A natural ability and easy to learn" (Targ 2012, 26), it requires people to open themselves to subtle information, ease out of the body, and travel to far-distant realms on this earth and beyond (Panati 1974, 139-46; see also Monroe 1971)—not unlike Daoists undertaking ecstatic excursions. Instead of dropping off into a meditative state to produce dreamlike images in the mind, Swann's system, known as coordinate remote viewing (CRV) uses a site address and a geographic map coordinate, encoded so that practitioners have no way but telepathy to access the information (Morehouse 2008, 120). Once at the target, they record their quick response in an exact format to cut down on interference from the imagination (Dames 2011, 49). Results lead to documentation in six stages, from initial fragmentary images of the target through basic emotional and kinesthetic sensations, dimensional descriptions, qualitative mental percepts, and specific

[8] Targ and Harary 1989, 17. On Swann, see Panati 1974, 145; Targ 2005, 58; 2012, 68; and Katra 1998, 52. For more on remote viewing, see Dames 2011; Morehouse 2008; Targ 2004, chs. 2-3; 2008, ch. 9; 2012; and Katra 1998, chs. 2-3.

focus to three-dimensional modeling, which frees the mind to obtain increasing amounts of data (Morehouse 2008, chs. 6-11).

All this goes to show that the supersensory faculties exhibited by Daoist immortals are subtle and powerful but not unnatural or beyond innate human abilities. As quantum thinking and string theory make further inroads into different areas of life, these faculties are likely to become more and more prominent in the world. As Russell Targ says, "The exploration of psychic abilities is the essential step in the greatest opportunity we have as a species—the evolution of consciousness" (2012, 13). Charles Panati adds, "Just as a physicist today can convert a material atom into pure energy, a paraphysicist tomorrow would be able to materialize a thought" (1974, 119). This, then, encourages the development of feats that now seem impossible, pushing us closer to the edge of established reality and opening the road to things like instant communication, instantaneous healing, teleportation, time travel, and more (Kaku 2008).

Physical Infinity

Another dimension of traditional Daoism that reverberates powerfully with modern physics is the claim to everlasting life. Looking at the overall history, i.e., ongoing unfolding and decline, of the universe, physicists have determined that all entities, from the largest stars to the minutest microbes, have a particular worldline, i.e., a life expectancy that begins at some point and ends at another. "However, it is possible "to imagine worldlines that have no such endpoint. Such worldlines are called *future-endless*" (Tipler 1994, 131). That is to say, they constitute the physics equivalent of Daoist immortality. Defining life as a form of complexity and, as Frank Tipler says, "using the standard physics measure of complexity, it is possible for an infinite amount of complexity to be produced, and hence an infinite amount of subjective time, between now and the Omega Point, even though there is only a finite amount of proper time. Progress *can* continue forever in a closed universe" (1994, 119).

The Omega Point in this understanding signifies the final state of the universe. The term comes from the work of Jesuit paleontologist Pierre Teilhard de Chardin (1881-1955), whose understanding of body, life, and spirituality has quite a bit in common with medieval Daoism (see Bidlack 2015). His major work, *The Phenomenon of Man*, describes the evolutionary history of the earth and its biosphere, arguing that all life is fundamentally driven by energy. All energy is psychic in nature, but divides into two distinct components. These are "a *tangential energy* which links the element with all others of the same order (that is to say, of the same complexity and the same centricity) as itself in the universe; and a *radial energy* which draws it toward ever greater complexity and centricity—in other words, forwards" (1959, 64-65). Anything consisting only of tangential, i.e., physical energy "must be doomed to extinction in the end, no matter how powerful it becomes" (Tipler 1994, 111). In contrast, radial, spiritual energy becomes more concentrated, more available with time. Ubiquitous and present in all matter, however minutely, it is the vehicle for survival in infinity and thus spirit immortality (1994, 112).

In Teilhard's cosmology, evolution does not end with humankind but moves on to a higher level of life where supersatient beings—the perfected and immortals of Daoism—dwell in a highly cognitive layer, what he calls the *noosphere* (Teilhard 1959, 180). As human science and civilization develop further, this sphere—currently present in a latent state—will grow exponentially and eventually result in "the end and the fulfillment of the spirit of the earth" (1959, 287).

This is the ultimate goal and perfection of existence, the Omega Point. It has four distinct properties. (1) It allows humankind to escape death, preventing all further entropy; (2) it is in the ultimate future, at the limit of time, overcoming all processes of growth and decline; (3) it can be seen as the singularity at the sharp end of a cone, a point rather than a circle, globe, or line; and (4) it requires the finite, bounded system of life for its emergence (Teilhard 1959, 270-71; Tipler 1994, 113-14).

Applying this notion of the Omega Point to modern physics means that "the laws of physics and every entity that exists physically would be generated by the Omega Point and its living properties" (Tipler 1994, 183). In other words, the Omega Point is the universal wave function of the unique field that gives being to all other fields—electromagnetic, quantum, and strings—and thus resides at the root of all existence, a core of perfection in a sea of energetic vibration (1994, 248). In addition, physicists define life as "information preserved by natural selection" (1994, 126; Tiller et al. 2005, 104), noting that in our bodies, we are being annihilated and recreated faster than 10^{23} times per second (1994, 236). That is to say, the substance of the human being is not preserved, only the pattern of information, and even that not perfectly, but with miniscule changes that over time constitute a process we call aging.

Connecting the ubiquity of the Omega Point as energy field with the notion of life as information, which can be expanded indefinitely, it becomes possible to describe infinite worldlines that go all the way to the end of time. Here information processing continues indefinitely, storage capacity is unlimited, and energy is immeasurable, constantly renewed in an everlasting exchange with all existence (1994, 132-33).

This changes the entire concept and apperception of time to an immortal level, overcoming both objective (material) and subjective (personal) forms—matching the distinction of three dimensions of time made by Thomas Aquinas, i.e., *tempus*, *aevum*, and *aeternitas* (Craig 2001), i.e., human time, divine time, and eternity. Living in *aeternitas* is being in the eternal now, duration as experienced by God, in "the complete and perfect possession of unlimited life all at once" (Tipler 1994, 134). As the closed universe ends in a final singularity of infinite density, and the temperature diverges to infinity, it becomes physically possible for life as information processing to continue forever (1994, 135-36).

In addition, "the Omega Point is both transcendent to and yet immanent in every point of spacetime." This means, it is entirely possible for human beings not only to attain a higher-level gauge energy symmetry, but also to elevate their organism ever further to ascend through multiple worlds or layers of the universe (Tipler 1994, 184). Eventually they reach a state of such energetic height and spirit intensity that "the distinction between living and nonliving matter loses its meaning" (1994, 154-55, 185).

In this state, a transfiguration or "emulation" of their ordinary self (1994, 238), they have reached celestial proportions both in terms of information processing and time perception. Connecting actively to everything in the universe, they live fully in the eternity of God or Dao and experience the entirety of time, the whole of universal history, all at once (1994, 157). Possessing an immeasurable level of information processing and storage capacity, they are omniscient and immensely powerful, exhibiting all the various so-called supernatural features Daoists associate with immortals (1994, 270-72). Rather than processing information at 10^{44} bits of information per second, the rate of the human brain, and much more than the largest computer to date, which only makes it up to 10^{14} bits, the Omega Point person would match the total capacity of the universe at 10^{90} bits per second (Vedral 2010, 186; Tiller et al. 2005, 216).

In addition, such a person would be celestial in nature, open to all sorts of higher dimensions, and not limited by one single personality or gender. More than a single encoded, well-defined individual, he or she would be able to adopt any number of *personae*, exhibit multifaceted characteristics, appear and disappear at will, and execute all manner of what ordinary humans consider miracles—not unlike the angels in the Bible, defined as God himself in "earthly manifestation" (Tipler 1994, 157). Like Schrödinger's cat, the immortal is able to be and not to be both at the same time, possessing the wave function of both a living and a non-living entity, simultaneously dead and alive, flowing through the various parallel worlds of the multiverse without hindrance or obstruction (Tipler 1994, 168-69)

Chapter Nine

Be as Gods

Self-Realization and Cognitive Science

While still on earth, this free flow manifests in a variety of ways. Within the individual, it is a feeling of happiness, of flowing along with things, resting in nonaction with the mind in a state of clarity and stillness. Within society, it manifests in virtues such as honesty and benevolence, essentially refined emotional energy transformed to an altruistic level. It also means following admonitory precepts to enhance positive attitudes, remaining free from desires, and knowing when it is enough. All this, in turn, frees the mind to concentrate on what one likes and does best, leading to perfect self-expression and the attainment of superior skills and outstanding excellence. These, in turn, may be highly creative and provide a positive effect on the world, as does the free and easy way of the accomplished Daoist.

Happiness

The classic Daoist description of realized inner well-being occurs in the *Zhuangzi*, expressed as "free and easy wandering" (*xiaoyao you* 逍遙遊; ch. 1) and "perfect happiness" (*zhile* 至樂; ch. 18), describing a vision that impacts all later ideals of the immortal life.

Zhuangzi's "wandering" fundamentally means following one's own natural so-being while adapting to the changes of life. The word *yao* in *xiaoyao* is "related to terms meaning 'to cross over' or 'to go beyond,' and to other words indicating pleasure, agreeableness, and lack of depth. *You* means 'swim' or 'float' and evokes the image of a waving flag" (Robinet 1993, 171; Wu 1990, 85). Wandering thus means being in naturalness: it implies essentially "a laid-back attitude toward life in which one takes things as they come and flows along with Dao" (Mair 1994, 385). Sometimes also rendered "distant excursion," it may be more ecstatic, a "trip" beyond the boundaries of ordinary life (Graham 1981, 8); or it may be more spiritual and profound, a surrender "to the chaos of self-emerging life" (Møllgaard 2007, 22). "It is a self-satisfying movement that fulfills itself" (Wu 1990, 85), a way of being in the world that is "completely open, versatile, and ready to become whatever the hand you are dealt requires" (Levinovitz 2012, 395; Kohn 2014, 17). A more subtle analysis of free and easy wandering shows that it has five features:

> 1. it transcends contingency and is not dependent on circumstances or good fortune;
> 2. it implies no fixed norms or direction but focuses on adaptation to change;
> 3. it is grounded in an understanding of the potential range of alternative forms of life;
> 4. it implies a readiness to transcend limits or boundaries associated with mainstream values and norms;
> 5. and it is associated with an essentially carefree attitude (Fraser 2011).

Flowing along (*shun* 順) with the natural processes engenders a fundamental sense of personal freedom, understood less as political liberty than as intrapsychic harmony (*he* 和) and inner peace (*an* 安). Yet, since it requires a constant response to change, it involves cognitive flexibility, the ability to look at things from multiple perspectives, and the childlike capacity to play: discover, explore, and wonder at the world (Wu 1982, 19; Zaidel 2013, 133). It is "being in phase," a form of "free evolution, proceeding in comfort, without a designated port and without anxiety over the outcome" (Jullien 2007, 09). Like fish in water, people are in Dao: they "swim in this milieu of endless movement," letting "life itself decide how it will go" (Kohn 2014, 18).

Another way to describe this playful "swimming" is as living in nonaction (*wuwei* 無為), the classic ideal of the *Daode jing* that pervades ancient Chinese thought (see Slingerland 2003). Interpreted in numerous ways (Kohn 2014, 13-16), in its spiritual dimension it implies a transcendence of ordinary consciousness, letting heaven take over and moving about the world and the universe in cosmic freedom (Liu 1991, 49). Beyond all standardization, nonaction is a "system of no system," a state of inner spaciousness and personal realization (Wu 2002, 75). Living life from this position allows the realization of each person's perfect potentiality in authentic action: "Authentic action not only realizes the potential to do or be but also the potential to not do or be" (Møllgaard 2007, 55). It is perfect action, "because it is act without activity, action not carried out independently of heaven and earth, in perfect harmony with the whole" (Merton 1969, 28).

Happiness, then, can be defined as the intrinsic quality of the ongoing process of wandering in an attitude of nonaction (Kohn 2014, 18). It is not *eudamonia*, the ancient Greek concept of the good share or good spirit (*daimon*) given by the gods. Nor is it the ultimate fulfillment of human endeavor, the universal end of life, what the American founding fathers implied with the "pursuit of happiness" (Jullien 2007, 110). The trick to realizing it fully is to "bring some heaven into myself," i.e., "to make contact with that part of myself which is pure process (natural and spontaneous) through the liberation from everything superimposed by the 'induced point of view' or bias of an individual ego" (Jullien 2007, 43).

This will also result in heaven providing the best possible situation at all times, a propitious combination of time (*shi* 時), place (*chu* 處), and circumstances (*shi* 勢)—the latter expressing "the particular configuration (disposition, arrangement)," tendency, or "propensity" of reality in an inherently dynamic process (Jullien 1995, 12, 221). Always stepping into good fortune, Daoists naturally remain free from harm. Already the *Zhuangzi* says, "The perfected enter the water and do not get wet; they enter the fire and do not get burned" (ch. 15). This is not so much because they have magical powers, although of course they do, but more because, as Guo Xiang says, "they naturally walk on dry land without, however, purposely avoiding water; they are naturally far away from fire, but never intentionally run away from it" (Kohn 2014, 100). At one with universal flow, from which no wrong can ever come, they live life to the fullest.

Ideal Daoists, therefore, rest in unknowing, remain free from all fixed identity and the imperatives of discriminating consciousness, and are constantly at one with spirit and the pure *qi* of the cosmos. Utterly free agents, they coast through life with ease and playfulness, always linked with the greater universe. As a poem ascribed to the Song immortal Chen Tuan 陳摶 (d. 989) has,

> With spirit, I step on emptiness as if on solid ground,
> Rise up as easy as if falling down.
> Imperceptively, I float around with the gentle winds,
> Whirling, I appear with the easy-going clouds.
> Sitting quiet, I reach the purple realm of Mount Kunlun,
> With ease, I pass through lucky places and the grotto heavens.
> (Kohn 1993, 274)

Virtuous Living

This inner ease, moreover, carries ethical implications and supports specific virtues that Daoists understand as the transformed energy of basic emotions directed toward others and universal well-being. Expressions of altruistic consideration and a feeling of connectedness with all beings, these include the traditional Confucian values of kindness, propriety, honesty, righteousness, and wisdom, as well as gratitude, compassion, tolerance, and respect.

Already the *Zhuangzi* expresses an ethics of difference with the demand that one should accept everyone and everything as unique, acting for their good rather than for personal gain. Rather than "do unto others as you would have them do unto you" (Keysers 2011, 217), the golden rule here is "do for others in not doing for others," encouraging people to connect with heaven and wander beyond the ordinary (Møllgaard 2007, 118-19). Another expression of the same idea is the copper rule, "Do unto others what they would have us do unto them" (Huang 2005, 394), i.e., being virtuous toward nature and all beings while having their best interests at heart (Huang 2010, 73).

Since nature and Dao are inherently whole and complete, and the underlying blueprint of the universe arranges things to perfection, we should not try to double-guess it or change anything. Just as "the acceptance of ethical diversity is part of the larger acceptance of the richness and diversity of the world itself" (Wenzel 2003, 116), our job is to be open-minded, adaptable, and flexible. We should cultivate reciprocal consideration of others, appreciate variety, respect individual uniqueness, and refrain from interfering in anyone else's decisions and actions (Huang 2010, 75-76). Realizing "great benevolence," Daoist thus aim to go beyond the ordinary demands of human society and ethics in a spontaneous sense of cosmic oneness (Kohn 2014, 153).

The *Daode jing*, too, encourages its readers to move away from established cultural norms and become simple and dull when everyone strives for sophistication and wisdom (ch. 20). People should reduce desires when everyone engages in the quest for more and bigger possessions (ch. 37); relax and do nothing when everyone pushes, strives, and works hard (ch. 57). People should realize that their bodies are more important than their reputation (ch. 44), get away from involvement (ch. 56), discard wisdom, and return to simplicity (chs. 19, 48). Controlling the input of the five senses (ch. 12), they should recover the value of emptiness and openness (chs. 11, 45) and the vitality of an infant (ch. 10). Learning when it is enough (chs. 33, 44), they should cultivate weakness and softness (chs. 36, 43), live in nonaction, and always flow along with Dao (ch. 64) (Moeller 2006).

Later Daoists adopted these principles and formulated them in various sets of precepts, the first of which appear in the *Laozi Xiang'er zhu* 老子想爾注 (Xiang'er Commentary to the *Daode jing*, trl. Bokenkamp 1997, 78-148), a text ascribed to the third Celestial Master, Zhang Lu 張魯 (ca. 215) and recovered from Dunhuang. Its precepts are of two kinds: a group of nine that provide positive attitudes based on philosophical concepts of the *Daode jing*, and a set of twenty-seven that present a mixture of general rules, behavioral regulations, and temporal taboos. The nine admonitions specifically encourage to practice:

1. nonaction;
2. being soft and weak;
3. guarding the female and never moving first;
4. being nameless;
5. resting in clarity and stillness;
6. doing only good;
7. having no desires;
8. knowing when it is enough;
9. yielding and withdrawing. (Bokenkamp 1997, 49; Kohn 2004a, 59)

In other words, the accomplished Daoist cherishes his uniqueness and fulfills his particular destiny in relation to heaven, going against the dominant social values if necessary. Relaxed and at ease, yielding and withdrawing, he is at peace within and does good in society, consuming what he need while always knowing what is right for him and never desiring more. As the *Zhuangzi* illustrates in Yan Hui's answer to Confucius's question, "Why don't you get a job?"

> I don't want a job. I have eight acres of fields outside the city wall, enough for vegetables and grain. I also have an acre and a half of farmland nearby, which gives me enough silk and hemp. Strumming my zither is enough to give me pleasure, studying Dao with you is enough to make me happy. I don't want a job. (ch. 28; Kohn 2014, 73)

The same principles are, moreover, at work in a frequently used set of ten precepts of medieval Daoism, first found in the *Zhihui dingzhi jing* 智慧定志經 (Scripture on Setting the Will on Wisdom, DZ 325), a 5th-century work of Numinous Treasure. The rules consist of the five classic precepts against killing, stealing, lying, sexual misconduct, and intoxication, plus five self-admonitions to act in harmony and with compassion, supporting others with joy and dignity (Kohn 2004a, 64).

They are further supplemented by fourteen principles of self-control (*chishen* 持身), personal resolutions to behave graciously and with kindness. For example: "When I speak with another's lord, I shall feel gracious toward his country;" "When I speak with another's father, I shall feel kind toward his son;" "When I speak with a stranger, I shall feel protective about his country's borders;" and "When I speak with a slave, I shall feel concerned about his affairs" (1b). The rules teach practitioners to be empathetic and kind, concerned with the plights and loyalties of others. They create a conscious awareness of the feelings and views of others, encouraging an altruistic mind-set and the creation of harmonious community (2004, 65). This, in turn, frees the individual to concentrate fully on developing his or her unique skills and abilities.

Skillful Spontaneity

Every human being in Daoist understanding is a unique embodiment of universal spirit, each with his or her own inner nature (*xing* 性) and destiny (*ming* 命). Inner nature is the personal share everyone has in the cosmos. Independent of our subjective wishes or concrete hopes, it orders personal existence from within. It encompasses all our inherent tendencies, the abilities we have naturally, our inborn gifts whose full realization brings us perfect happiness. Destiny is what should best happen given our particular circumstances, the movement of forces beyond our control. It is the way heaven "orders" (*ming*) our life to run, the circumstantial trajectories that come our way—both as auspicious coincidences that help our course and as obstacles that strengthen our resolve (Kohn 2014, 96).

As the *Zhuangzi* describes it, using the words of the swimmer at Lüliang, a man who dives into massive water and delights in doing so, the interplay between these two happens in three stages. He says, "I began with my original ground (*gu* 故), grew in accordance with my inherent tendencies (*xing*), and let things come to completion in alignment with circumstantial trajectories (*ming*)" (ch. 19; Billeter 2010, 29). He further explains, "I was born on dry land and felt safe there—this is my original ground. I grew up with water and felt safe there—this constituted my inherent tendencies. I don't know why I do what I do—this is following circumstantial trajectories."

In other words, beginning with being grounded in concrete reality, facing the life we have in this world, we begin to discover what is right for us in accordance with our unique talents and abilities. Inevitably we are attracted to, or strongly resonate with, something we encounter—more so than with other things and more so than other people. Once this affinity is established and a strong inner motivation is found, we receive training in technical knowledge and practical skills, gaining physical coordination, social niceties, elementary and higher education, and professional expertise (Yearley 1996, 168-70). However, this training is not forced or pressured, felt to be a chore or necessary evil. Rather, the expansion of natural skills is a delight, a joy of discovery and exploration—another manifestation of flow. It feels like growing into one's own, mastering an ability deeply rooted within, bringing one's inner truth to fruition, reaching far beyond ordinary skillfulness (Yearley 1996, 164).

Eventually we reach a level of expertise where the inherently anchored and thoroughly trained skill becomes spontaneous. The techniques have become second nature, so deeply mastered and embedded in muscle memory that their motor execution requires no conscious attention (Eno 1996, 136). Flowing right along with inherent *qi*, they manifest easily under different circumstances and situations, far beyond our control and guided by the flow of life as destiny or circumstantial trajectories (Kohn 2014, 214). The *Zhuangzi* illustrates this skillful spontaneity in a series of anecdotes, so-called skill stories or knack passages. They are about craftsmen or sportsmen engaged in ordinary, benign activities, who have reached a level of skillfulness beyond words and knowledge (Ivanhoe 1993, 651).

There is, for example, a hunchback—someone with physical limitations—"catching cicadas with a sticky pole as easily as though he were grabbing them with his hand" (Watson 1968, 199). The ferryman at Goblet Deeps "handles his boat like a spirit," while Ji Xingzi trains fighting cocks to perfection, able to judge by their looks and demeanor how they will do in a fight. Woodworker Qing, moreover, makes bell stands that "seem to be the work of gods or spirits;" and Wheelwright Bian produces perfectly aligned wheels (Graham 1981, 135-42; Kohn 2014, 209).

The most famous master in the *Zhuangzi* is Cook Ding 庖丁, who prepares oxen for the sacrifice (ch. 3; Kohn 2014, 211-13). He moves with rhythm and agility, "his hands touching, his shoulders leaning, his feet stepping, his knees thrusting—each with its own sound, all knife cuts completely in tune" (Møllgaard 2007, 48-49). Asked about his skill, he explains that after decades of training he now flows along with Dao, far beyond ordinary expertise: he no longer sees ordinary, solid reality but works with subtle patterns, moving purely by intuition, feeling the *qi* of things and letting spirit move. "The spirit takes over completely. It lets me follow the natural contours, twisting in the deep hollows, sliding through the great openings" (Kohn 2011, 171). As a result, his knife never gets dull, and he never gets tired or makes a wrong cut.

These virtuosi all follow their inner nature and destiny and undergo years of training. Most importantly, they get themselves—their personal concerns, emotions, and minds—out of the way, allowing cosmic energy and spirit to flow and act through their subconscious, using the brain as a conduit rather than a filter (Billeter 2010, 24, 67). The *Zhuangzi* makes this especially clear with regard to archery:

> If you join a contest and shoot to win a nice brick, you will be skillful. If you shoot for a fancy buckle, you will be nervous. If you shoot for a gold bar, you will be a wreck.
>
> Your shooting skill is the same in all cases, but if there is something you want badly, your focus will be outside. The more your focus is outside, the more you get clumsy on the inside. (Kohn 2011, 169)

Free from the interference of the self-conscious mind, people of skillful spontaneity are like the "drunken man who falls from a carriage" and remains unhurt "because his spirit is whole" (ch. 19). Dao flows as freely through them as they flow along in it. In addition, this skillfulness feels good. It is the most comfortable, natural, and harmonious way of being, the ultimate in health and self-expression. It means that we nourish ourselves to the fullest with what is most appropriate and most delightful to us, while remaining constantly connected to the great, universal flow of life (Kohn 2014, 210).

Immortal Freedom

Later Daoists embrace the same ideal in their vision of living immortals, often represented as reclusive and eccentric, happy-go-lucky bums with no social commitments or cares in the world, yet powerfully skilled and highly creative in their chosen art—be it poetry, calligraphy, chess, martial arts, or drinking. Inherently transmoral beings beyond the social network, they have no concern for social niceties, but relate directly to the greater universe, pursuing their unique artistry for their own pleasure and fulfillment.

Thus, the poet Liu Ling 劉伶 (d. 265), a member of the Seven Sages of the Bamboo Grove, spent much of his time intoxicated, writing great poems. According to the *Shishuo xinyu* 世說新語 (A New Account of Tales of the World; trl. Mather 1976), he was completely free and uninhibited. "Sometimes he would even take off his clothes and sit naked in his room. Once some people came to see him and chided him for this behavior. Liu Ling retorted, 'I take heaven and earth for my pillars and roof, and the rooms of my house for my pants and coat. And now, what are you gentlemen doing in my pants?'" (23.3; Kohn 1993, 301).

Immortals also place little value on material goods or reputation. In one story, Lü Dongbin 呂洞賓, the leader of the Eight Immortals, never hesitates to hand over all the New Year's presents he carries, cash and gifts, to a beggar at his gate (Kohn 1993, 130). Unconcerned with social approval, he and other immortals are generous to a fault and free from the lure of material possessions.

This generosity also plays out in the form of compassion for others. Many stories tell of immortals who appear among mortals and support them by healing diseases, exorcising demons, providing instructions for long life, or merely providing an increased sense of beauty. Thus, Lord Horsemaster cured animals far and wide and once even relieved a celestial dragon of an atrocious toothache. Fei Zhangfang 費長房, after training with the Gourd Master, became a demon-dispeller, reducing frightful monsters to quivering jelly. Li Tieguai 李鐵拐, handicapped by being caught in a beggar's body, yet excelled in the fighting arts. And Zuo Ci 左慈 procured most wonderful foodstuffs from far-off places within an instant.

Rather than out of a sense of obligation, though, immortals act for their own personal enjoyment. Fully partaking in the unlimited freedom of the heavens, they see all worldly striving and ambitions as just so much nervous fluster and tension—a total waste of *qi*. Being as they are, they hold up a mirror to ordinary people from the perspective of the divine, a state of oneness with heaven and earth. They illustrate how one can live with the larger universe as one's home, free from involvements, obligations, and social relationships, yet not unfriendly or harmful.

Themselves part of the core power of the cosmos, immortals present and enhance this power—its virtues and goodness—in the world. Whimsical and unpredictable, they appear out of the blue and do a good turn to an utterly amazed community. They show up and render social institutions ineffectual, making the threatening postures of warlords and demons look ridiculous. Always smiling, full of laughter, and inherently playful, they increase goodness, joy, and fun in the world by being fully who they are, living among humanity yet connected to heaven—in the world yet not of the world. The happiness and joy they radiate spread everywhere, allowing people to become more complete, more cheerful, and better human beings. A Japanese film story illustrates the point:

> Two petty thieves, an old beggar couple, a stuttering idiot, and a prostitute occupy a ramshackle house in an inner-city slum. A wandering monk, a bald old man with only a staff and bowl, asks for shelter, and they agree to put him up as a sign of good luck. He sits down in a corner, while the inhabitants argue about whose turn it is to do the cleaning. As soon as he realizes what the problem is, he gets up and begins to clean.
>
> As time goes on, the monk continues to be present fully in the moment, doing whatever needs to be done. By just being there, polite and friendly, he gradually turns the house around. He helps. When the old invalid dies, the monk holds his hand. When the idiot cannot find his flute, he discovers it for him. He never criticizes, never praises.
>
> When the burglars get jobs as laborers, he says nothing. When the prostitute becomes a housekeeper, he merely smiles. The story ends with a New Year's party. Everyone contributes and all join into the fun. Honesty, harmony, and care prevail where discord and tension nhad been the norm. [1]

---

[1] I first heard this story from a Zen master in Japan. For a full written synopsis, see Wetering 1975, 39-41.

Just by being fully oneself, staying in the present moment, and doing whatever is needed and whatever one is good at without thinking, evaluating, or arguing, one can effect powerful transformations in the world. There is no need for formal rules, regulations, sermons, or punishments. People—inherently nothing but cosmic energy and universal flow—will naturally gravitate toward harmony and peace, toward being in the flow of Dao rather than going against it. But they need to be shown the way, and that is the role of accomplished Daoists, perfected and immortals.

Flow

The closest equivalent to the immortal life-style of free and easy wandering in Western psychology is the concept of "flow" as studied and defined by Mihaly Csikszentmihalyi (1975; 1990). A deep sense of enjoyment and feeling of exhilaration—seemingly effortless movement (1990, 53)—flow is "a state in which people are so deeply involved in an activity that nothing else seems to matter" (1990, 4; Goleman 2011, 51). A state of hyperarousal of the autonomic nervous system (Newberg et al. 2001, 41), it occurs every time when an experience is so enjoyable that it is pursued for its own sake, providing a feeling of "optimal experience." A goal in itself, this is "autotelic" (Csikszentmihalyi 1990, 67; Nakamura and Csikszentmihalyi 2009, 195). Typically an experience of this sort has eight characteristics:

1. a chance of successful completion;
2. the ability to concentrate fully;
3. clearly delimited goals;
4. immediate feedback;
5. oblivion of everyday life;
6. a sense of control;
7. no concern for self;
8. an altered sense of time

(2009, 196; Csikszentmihalyi 1990, 49; Jochim 1998, 63)

Activities that favor the flow state are first of all games, sports, dance, music, art, and leisure, but that list can easily be expanded to include all kinds of activities, including work, housework, and daily chores (Csikszentmihalyi 1990, 59). No matter what one does, the individual is deeply absorbed and transcends his or her limited self. She feels fully engaged—neither bored nor anxious—and fully authentic: "In flow, there is no room for self-scrutiny."[2] Our attention absorbed, we experience an ordered state of consciousness where all our feelings, wishes, and thoughts are in harmony, allowing the emergence of greater levels of skill. In a dynamic equilibriums, we operate at full capacity (Nakamura and Csikszentmihalyi 2009, 197).

Flow is universal: regardless of geography, culture, age, or social standing, people all have and report it (Csikszentmihalyi 1990, 4). Plus, it is not limited in time or scope. Ultimately, we can "turn *all life* into a unified flow experience" (1990, 214). To do so, we need to center ourselves on a coherent overall meaning that goes beyond the playing of a game or the completion of a task, something higher and greater, traditionally offered in religions. Daoists speak of Dao, heaven, spirit, inner nature, and destiny in this context. Others describe it in terms of activating our "key spiritual focus" (Ford and Wortman 2013), centering our minds on a "homing thought" (Diamond 1979), opening ourselves to peak-experiences (Maslow 1964), or being in our Perfect Moment (Carlson and Kohn 2012). Any one of these will afford us "a sense of wholeness and harmony, of being connected to everything, the certainty that life is good and that we are an integral part of that goodness" (2012, 116). Relaxing into the underlying pattern of life, the universal flow of energy we have no control over, we achieve harmony and a dynamic order in consciousness. This, then, allows us to "go with the flow," seeing obstacles as challenges and mistakes as learning opportunities (2012, 148; Goleman et al. 1992, 43).

Another take on this perfection is offered by Gary Zukav, who describes it in terms of "authentic power":

> Authentic power feels good. It is doing what you are supposed to be doing. It is fulfilling. Your life is filled with meaning and purpose. You have no doubts. You have no fears. You are happy to be alive. You have a reason to be alive. Everything you do is joyful. Everything is exciting. You are not worried about doing something wrong, making a mistake, or failing. You do not compare yourself with others. You do not compare what you do with what others do. (2002, 105-06)

Power is also a key concept in the understanding of David R. Hawkins, psychiatrist and master of behavioral kinesiology. Echoing Csikszentmihalyi's emphasis on the importance of meaning, he says:

> Power arises from *meaning*. It has to do with motive, and with principle. Power is always associated with that which supports the significance of

---

[2] Csikszentmihalyi 1990, 63; Diener et al. 2009, 189; Leary and Guadagno 2011, 139; Robinson and Tamir 2011, 161.

> life itself. It appeals to that part of human nature that we call *noble*. . ., to what uplifts, dignifies, and ennobles. . . .
>
> Power is total and complete in itself and requires nothing from outside. It makes no demands; it has no needs. It energizes, gives forth, supplies, and supports. . . . Only power brings joy. (2002, 132, 136)

As we integrate fully with our and universal power, Hawkins emphasizes, we focus our attention away from the limited goals and perspectives of humanity and allow the universe to play a dominant role in our lives, living with courage and dignity as part of a great, heavenly, unseen power (2006, 100). We also enhance positive attractor fields that bring about the increased presence of synchronicity in our lives.

Synchronicity

Developed first by the Swiss psychologist Carl Gustav Jung (1875-1961) in conversations with relativity founder Albert Einstein and the quantum physicist Wolfgang Pauli in the 1930s, synchronicity is a nonlinear and "acausal connecting principle."[3] It manifests in the "simultaneous occurrence of a certain psychic state with one or more external events that appear as meaningful parallels to the momentary subjective state" (Jung 1973, 8; Main 2008, 26; Von Franz 1980). Different objects, events, and intentions congregate to form an overall pattern in space and time (Peat 1987, 65). Examples include the ringing of the telephone just as we are thinking of someone we have not heard from in years, the continued appearance of certain numbers that for some reason have caught our attention, the unexpected presence of a person connected to an earlier acquaintance as one thinks about him, as well as other coincidences (Schwartz 2008, 68; see also Aziz 1990; Jung 1955; Koestler 1972).

Not caused in a discernible way or at any level of existence in terms of a systematic chain of events (Tart 2008, 121; Peat 1987, 41), synchronicity can be thought of as complementary to causality, allowing for both nonlocality and meaningful flow (Mansfield et al. 2008, 131; Von Franz 1992, 231). In some ways similar to telepathy, clairvoyance, and other paranormal phenomena (Storm 2008, 180), it plays a dominant role in traditional sciences such as astrology, alchemy, and divination (Beloff 2008, 102). In its starkest form it appears in the *Yijing*, which works to reveal "the configuration formed by chance events in the moment of observation" (Sabbadini 2008, 79; Peat 1987, 30). Unique to the specific person and the particular moment, and meaningful only

---

[3] Jung and Pauli 1955, 14; Donati 2008, 49; Peat 1987, 14-22; 2008, 19. See also Meier 2001.

to them, it is non-reproducible and hard to test scientifically. Speculation abounds about whether it might be connected to electromagnetic or quantum phenomena (Beloff 2008, 103; Mansfield et al. 2008, 143; Palmer 2008, 187), but agreement persists that a relaxed state of reduced physical arousal and lessened sensory processing, a receptive mode of consciousness and right-hemisphere dominance are conducive to the experience (Storm 2008, 165).

Synchronicity favors being over doing, allowing over making, and emergence over creation. It can be brought about intentionally with a meditative calming of the mind and the activating of lower brain wave frequencies, such as alpha and theta (Stein 2007, 145; Davidson and Harrington 2002), leading to a holistic entrainment with the subtle energetic frequencies of cosmic consciousness. Since we are originally one with the cosmos, we cocreate our reality with it, activating the synchronicity principle to change and modify it in perfect flow (Cannon 2007, 59).

In terms of neurophysiology, perfect flow is the result of the successful integration and cooperation of the two hemispheres of the brain, just as happiness is a state of complete psychophysiological coherence, the full entrainment of all the various rhythms of the body, leading to increased output and optimal exchange (McCraty and Rees 2009, 529). The state allows the perfect functioning of both, the "peaceful consciousness of our right brain and the practical skills of our left" in "dual interpenetrating awareness" (Taylor 2006, 149). It means deautomatizing our focus on left-brain functioning with meditative practices, recognizing the limitations of discriminating consciousness, as well as placing greater value on, and paying more attention to, the signals and visions that emerge from the right, the more inclusive, artistic, and mystical (Deikman 1980a, 247; Newberg, D'Aquili, and Rouse 2001; Newberg 2012).

What the right brain has to offer is most vividly documented by Harvard University brain anatomist Jill Bolte Taylor, who suffered a hemorrhage in her left hemisphere in 1996. She notes that, "when I lost my left hemisphere and its language centers, all concepts of time and space evaporated, leaving me instead feeling open-ended, enormous, and expansive" (2006, 68). Thinking in pictures and resting in the eternal now, her entire self-concept shifted. "I understood that at the most elementary level, I am a fluid"—adding a yet different dimension to the notion of "flow." Recovering the core nature of atomic reality, an essential sense of *qi*-presence, right-brain awareness is a mystical state, where one immediately perceives that "everything around us, about us, among us, within us, and between us is made up of atoms and molecules vibrating in space" (2006, 69)

> My left hemisphere had been trained to perceive myself as a solid, separate from others. Now, released from that restrictive circuitry, my right hemisphere relished in its attachment to the eternal flow. I was no longer

> isolated and alone. My soul was as big as the universe and frolicked with glee in a boundless sea. (Taylor 2006, 69)

While she experienced this freedom and selflessness involuntarily, the key to life in full flow or free and easy wandering is learning to release and relax the left brain and let our right brain have its moments. Through it, we can be fully in the here and now, "bouncing around with unbridled enthusiasm, not having a care in the world" (2006, 139). "Moment by moment we make the choice to either hook into established neurocircuitry or move back into the present moment, allowing [conditioned emotional] reactions to melt away as fleeting physiology" (2006, 146). Doing so, we let the universe play in our lives while we rest in nonaction and flow along in free and easy wandering. Friendly and cheerful, we are no longer dominated by judgment and analysis, but enjoy a deep inner calm, "completely committed to the expression of peace, love, joy, and compassion in the world" (2006, 133).

Positive Values

These values of peace, love, joy, and compassion closely echo the transformed emotions of traditional Daoism. They become active as we choose not to engage the neurological circuits established by strong emotions, the limbic reaction patterns that increase chances of success in terms of material supplies, physical survival, and interpersonal community. Deeply at rest and at one with the universal flow of energy that will always provide, we can be free from all concerns for material supplies. Knowing that we are essentially cosmic beings that live as long as heaven and earth, we can relax about issues of reproduction and physical survival. Always closely linked with all beings, members of an intergalactic community that includes the living as much as the dead, the embodied as much as the spiritual, we can stop worrying about our social connections.

Instead, we can rest in postive values, goodwill and kindness, and allow them to give us a deep sense of peace and rightness. This state, then, enhances vagal nerve tone, steadies the heart beat, calms the nervous system, and gernally increases our ability to meet challenges (Goleman 2011, 39).

No longer facing life-threatening situations, we do not need great focus and the stress response (Cohn and Fredrickson 2009, 15; Tugade and Fredrickson 2002, 320). At ease in the flow of life, we can let go of anger and greed and instead project humanity, benevolence, empathy, and compassion. We can abandon fear and lust, replacing them with gratitude, sufficiency, justice, and wisdom; and we can eliminate schmoozing, sadness, and grief, living instead with courage, righteousness, and social responsibility. We can replace worry and care with honesty, integrity, and inner clarity, as well as euphoria with a sense of temperance and propriety. Rather than being driven by emotions, we are now the living expression of pure cosmic consciousness, described in Buddhism as the four positive attitudes of the enlightened mind (*brahmaviharas*): love, compassion, sympathetic joy, and equanimity.

We can move up in the scale of human behavior, leaving behind automated responses to stimuli, learned habits and dispositions, as well as social norms and expectations. Instead, we can follow the logic of life's inherent necessity, doing what we do "because this is necessary (important) to me" (Leontiev 2006, 53). From here, we can move even further, opening to possibilities and emerging to new dimensions—"the next developmental stage of human maturity" (2006, 53). This, in turn, can open us to the "logic of ultimate understanding," where we act "because this matches the way things are" (2006, 54). Close to the way Daoist sages and perfected live in the world, this means acting in close relation to universal patterns, in the vibrant presence of ultimate truth. Embodying and practicing positive values is to become fully human while at the same time being fully cosmic.

Getting there is a process of acquiring advanced emotional intelligence, the ability to recognize one's own and other people's emotions, to discriminate between different feelings and label them appropriately, and to use emotional information to guide thinking and behavior. Emotional intelligence is the competence for successful adaptation to, and efficient coping with, emotional events.[4] Besides learning to value emotional experience and trusting it in life, using our feelings to interpret events positively and grow from them (Gohm and Clore 2002, 100; Tugade and Fredrickson 2002, 332), an important step to to this higher level is the enhancement of gratitude and empathy (Myers 2008, 328).

To wit, gratitude is a feeling of undeserved merit or of receiving a gift. The more frequently and intensely we feel it—by counting our blessings or writing in a gratitude journal (Emmons 2008, 473, 476)—the more we relate to the greater flow of life. We no longer evaluate an event in our limited personal way, but see it in a larger context, feeling gratitude for whatever is, whatever the universe offers, and whatever life provides (Ochsner and Gross 2007, 96; Emmons and Mishra 2011, 250; see also Klein 1957). Empathy, based on mirror neuron activity and part of our inherent motor response, and strongly enhanced by mindfulness of loving-kindness (*metta*), connects us to our fellow beings. Emotional and cognitive empathy allow us to feel what others go through, thus "promoting social cohesion, feelings of group membership, and inclusive fitness."[5]

---

[4] Matthews et al. 2002, 47; 2007; Larsen and Priznic 2008, 270; Zeidner et al. 2009, 86. For more, see also Gardner 1983; Goleman 1995; 1998; 2011; Bradberry and Greaves 2009.

[5] Pineda et al. 2009, 149; see also Bacharowski and Owren 2002, 16; Frith 2007, 149; Goleman 2011, 38, 61; 2013, 98; Iacoboni 2008, 108; Newberg and O'Leary 2009, 206.

Opening us to the willingness to perform random acts of kindness that have nothing to do with survival or personal gain (McTaggart 2011, 102), empathy and gratitude also support the development of altruism, defined as "the willingness to act in consideration of the interests of other persons, without the need of ulterior motives."[6] Altruism, as much as the other positive values, involves a different way of looking at the world, regarding oneself as a person among others and finding identity as part of a larger whole and seeing other as fellow travelers instead of as strangers or potential threats. As a result, altruists typically state that their unselfish actions are entirely natural and that they do not have a choice over whether or not to help someone (Munroe 1996, 9-14, 197-216; Nagel 1970, 82-83, 100-02). They have a strong will to give and a vivid sense of social interconnectedness (McTaggart 2011, 103).

This attitude, as much as positive values in general, can be intentionally developed. To this end, positive psychology uses an ongoing process of "broaden and build" to facilitate approach behavior and motivate exchanges with the environment.[7] Therapists encourage people to be playful, flexible, creative, and generally open to new information and different ways of doing things.[8] Measured by the five factors of "extroversion, agreeableness, conscientiousness, neuroticism, and openness to experience," this leads to joviality, self-assurance, and open-mindedness, the ability to change one's habits and outlook.[9] These, in turn, enhance health, including a broader perception, an increased sense of wellness, and a greater ability to savor positive experiences, which in turn lets us find life more satisfying and fulfilled, increasing flow and making us "chronically happy" (Diener et al. 2009, 188; Cohn and Fredrickson 2009, 18). Transforming emotions into positive values, as much mindfulness practice, allows the prefrontal cortex to have more resting activity and reprograms the setpoint of happiness levels we all have.[10]

Some people are naturally and inherently happier, notwithstanding good or bad fortune (Stein 2007, 130; Brickman et al. 1978). Still, those training to embrace positivity, turning the relevant genes on or off and enhancing the brain's output of dopamine, no longer return to their setpoint or "hedonic treadmill" (Larsen and Priznic 2008, 268). Rather, they assign positive meanings to sensory stimuli, pay more attention to beneficent information, and generally prime themselves toward what is good in life (Robinson and Compton 2008,

---

[6] Nagel 1970, 79; Munroe 1996, 6; Emmons 2008, 471; Myers 1992; 2008, 331.

[7] Fredrickson 2006, 81; 2008, 450; Cohn and Fredrickson 2009, 15; Tugade and Fredrickson 2002, 320.

[8] Fredrickson 2006, 88, 91; 2008, 450; Isen 2009, 503; Lucas 2008, 185.

[9] Hood 2012, 237; Fredrickson 2008, 452; Watson and Naragon 2009, 209-10; Isen 2009, 503.

[10] Davidson 2003; Fredrickson 2008, 450; Goleman 2011, 37; Larsen and Prizmic 2008, 268; Lucas 2008, 173; Siegel 2007; Watson and Naragon 2009, 210.

221-24). As a result, they come to think happier thoughts and feel more kindness, generosity, and gratitude (Isen 2009, 504). Growing in positive values they enhance their character strengths that in turn provide them with the necessary backbone to flourish within their particular setting, protecting and enhancing their inborn gifts and allowing them to deal efficiently with social issues and situational obstacles.[11]

Creating a deep sense of "authentic happiness" (Seligman 2002; Authentic Happiness.sas.upenn.edu), this leads to positive outcomes in life: happier people who love what they do attract more money, better relationships, and vibrant health (Diener et al. 2009, 191; King 2008, 441). The potential for success, moreover, has less to do with demographics—it makes no difference what gender, age, education income, or work one has (Watson and Naragon 2009, 211)—but depends a great deal on the degree one is embedded in social networks and the greater universe. That is, it depends on one's sense of being part of something greater and more encompassing (Andrews 2009, 58-60; Myers 1992; 2008, 326).

Social Impact

This something greater may be the universe, but it can also be your local community as was made clear in the so-called Roseto effect, named after an Italian-immigrant village in Pennsylvania whose inhabitants remained surprisingly free from heart disease and other common old-age ailments due to their strong community and active neighborhood support.[12] It really is not all that surprising. Being healthy and comfortable in our community, we experience feelings of bliss, joy, elation, contentment, pleasure, and euphoria in the enjoyment of what is (Bok 2012, 11; Segal 2009, 28). This, in turn, leads to the embrace of three positive values with strong social impact that also closely echo the traditional Daoist agenda: simplicity, humility, and sufficiency.

Simplicity is the absence of luxury, pretentiousness, and extraneous ornaments combined with a freedom from deceit and guile, the practice of plainness and clarity (Andrews 2009a, 4). Humility involves an accurate assessment of one's own characteristics and abilities, admitting limitations without downplaying oneself and relishing the ability to just be. Like plainness, humility means being open-minded to new ideas and advice, tentative of one's own be-

---

[11] Duncan 1995, 77; Goleman 2011, 36; King 2008, 437. See also Peterson and Seligman 2004; Seligman 2011; Siegel 2007.

[12] Dickerson and Zoccola 2009, 521; McTaggart 2011, 77; see also Bianco 1974; Gladwell 2008, ch. 1.

liefs, and free from self-focus or self-preoccupation (Leary and Guadagno 2011, 138; see also Libet 1985; Tangney 2009).

Sufficiency is a sense of enoughness, what Swedes call *lagom*, literally being "connected to a team" (AtKisson 2009, 101), the innate feeling how material objects and money move through life in a current, constantly coming and going yet always providing just the right amount (Twist 2003, 103). Numerous studies have shown that, while income contributes to subjective well-being, not much is needed once people have basic security through food and shelter; in fact, "actively wanting money is toxic to happiness" (Biswas-Diener 2008, 315-16; see Maslow 1954, 309). It is, therefore, essential that we get over the urge to accumulate, unveiling the pervasive lie of scarcity with its three toxic myths: that there is not enough, that more is better, and that it is just the way it is (Twist 2003, 49-53). As Lynne Twist says,

> We each have the choice in any setting to step back and let go of the mind-set of scarcity. Once we let go of scarcity, we discover the surprising truth of sufficiency. By sufficiency, I don't mean a quantity of anything. Sufficiency isn't two steps up from poverty or one step short of abundance. It isn't a measure of barely enough or more than enough. Sufficiency isn't an amount at all. It is an experience, a context we generate, a declaration, a knowing that there is enough, and that we are enough. (2003, 74)

In other words, embrace the age-old Daoist principle of knowing when it is enough and stop trying to get more of what you don't need!

This, in turn, leads to deep wisdom and a great sense of personal integrity. "The question of what you want to own is actually the question of how you want to live your life," Marie Kondo says (2014, 182). The way we spend our money makes a statement of what we value most in life. "It takes courage to direct the flow [of money], but with each choice, we invest in the world as we envision it" (Twist 2003, 131), a world with fewer possessions and more happiness. As the Dalai Lama notes, "Those living in the materially developed countries, for all their industry, are in some ways less satisfied, are less happy, and to some extent suffer more than those living in the least developed countries" (Andrews 2009a, 5). Americans in particular tend to be "overfed but undernourished," incomes rising and material goods increasing while happiness is tapering off (Wann 2009, 41). It would be much better to shift from "an emphasis on material wealth to an abundance of time, relationships, and experiences," where values of moderation, frugality, and efficiency create a high quality of life (2009, 43).

These values, moreover, transform our fundamental outlook in relation to others, seeing them as partners rather than competitors. This signals a major game change. In contrast to traditional games that work with the win-lose principle so that the winner takes all, nothing remains in the pot, and the total is a zero sum, the new way of interacting in games, life, and business, works with win-win or non-zero sum. That is to say, all participants benefit in one way or another, nobody leaves empty-handed, and there is overall more to go around and great joy and well-being in togetherness (McTaggart 2011, 120; Wright 2000).

This emphasis on cooperation is also borne out by recent developments in the understanding of evolution. Biology and anthropology still insist that evolution favors the "survival of the fittest." However, the definition of "fittest" no longer includes being the strongest and most aggressive, the alpha-male or the one with the greatest firing power. Rather, the fittest is now the most cooperative, the one who can create the best networks, who garners the most support from the community and furnishes the best living conditions for everyone (Wright 1994).

This, then, places us into what Buckminster Fuller has called "livingry," a greater concern with sharing than with owning, with being than with having, with living than with succeeding, with peace than with defense.

> In nature's own economics, that of ecology, the grass was not obliged to pay the clouds for rain. Regeneration, being comprehensive and interdependent, neither gained nor lost energy and could only grow sum-totally. . . .
>
> Acquiring costly technology for producing national-defense armaments is the politically assumed number-one mandate, a mandate based on national fear. Such a survivalist mentality inadvertently also produces life-supporting technology, but it takes a quarter of a century longer than it would if humanity first recognized the public longing to attain sustainable peace for all humanity and directly used that same high-technology production for livingry rather than weaponry. (1992, 45)

Focusing on community and livingry, moreover, does not mean that we all have to live in shared poverty. On the contrary, sufficiency and integrity are excellent for business. For example, a Swedish transportation company called Green Cargo, originally founded 1889, lost money for 115 years. Then they hired a new CEO, Stefan Falk, who introduced flow and sufficiency principles, focusing on identity strengths, work enjoyment, challenges to workers, good feedback, and community service. The company has been profitable ever since (Nakamura and Csikszentmihalyi 2009, 202). In the US, too, more and more businesses embrace Daoist principles, applying the concept of corporate social responsibility (CSR) and taking an active role in social progress. This echoes the *Daode jing*: "To produce things and to rear them; to produce but not to take possession of them; to act, but not to rely on one's own ability; to lead them, but not to master them—this is called profound and secret virtue" (ch. 10; Egizii 2011, 195).

As a result, we see more and more businesses turning from being profit-based to values-based, using common, universal values to develop and run ethical organizations. Treating their people as whole persons and thinking of their workers and stakeholders as extended family, such businesses concern themselves with their overall impact on society and life as a whole, extending their planning into the future and the environment. Statistics clearly show that employees who are ethical and work in ethical organizations outproduce others, so that positive values enhance profit and well-being on all levels (Mitroff and Denton 1999).

Outstanding Excellence

Being in flow and resting in positive values, with simplicity, integrity, and sufficiency, frees us to develop our innate abilities and best gifts to the fullest. No longer distracted by sensory impacts, immune to emotional turbulence, free from ethical conflicts and social anxieties (Goleman 2013, 14-15), we can turn to our personal development, open to our natural abilities and capacities, discover our deepest calling, pursue our art with single-minded passion, and attain outstanding excellence (Green and Gallwey 1986, 11; Stein 2007, 227).

This requires enormous personal integrity, the strength to resist the temptation to betray our heart and "give the teacher [father, boss] what we believe he wants" (Diamond 1986, 3:129). We have to have an immense confidence in our own guiding values, our inner rudder that steers us toward our deepest sense of purpose and meaning in life—as exemplified in the work of George Lucas and his creation of *Star Wars* against all outside advice and apparently insurmountable odds (Goleman 2013, 61-63). Steve Jobs summarizes it, "Don't let the voice of others' opinions drown out your inner voice. And most important, have the courage to follow your heart and intuition. They somehow already know what you truly want to become" (2013, 65).

To realize our deepest longing and follow our true calling next requires a great deal of attention, defined as a mental muscle that involves various processes, including comprehension, memory, learning, self-awareness, emotional intelligence, and smooth interaction (2013, 3). It comes in three forms: (1) focus, i.e., keeping a representation of a sensory percept zeroed in over short time periods; (2) dedication, that is, the drive that compels a person to persevere, keep striving, maintain discipline, and keep his eyes on the prize, inextricably linked with motivation, will, and desire; and (3) inhibition, the way the mind repels the continuous sensory barrage to which the brain is exposed, runs interference against distracting thoughts and inappropriate behaviors and remarks, and overrides all sorts of habitual old grooves (2013, 79).[13] Another way of describing attention is by way of its direction: focused inward, it attunes us to our intuitions, guiding values, and better decisions; directed toward other people, it smoothes our social connections; and turned outward, it lets us navigate successfully in the larger world (Goleman 2013, 4).

Turning our attention inward to the development of our deepest potential, we amp up the sensitivity of the insula and activate our somatic markers, "the sensations in our body that tell us when a choice feels wrong or right" (Goleman 2013, 66; Damasio 1999). Doing so, we use our minds "bottom up," that is relying dominantly on the lower-brain neural machinery, as opposed to "top down," the mental activity in the neocortex—using a fore that is immensely fast, continuously active, intuitive, impulsive, automatic, and habitual (Goleman 2013, 25; Penrose 1989, 422).

The same idea is also described as Self 2 versus Self 1, i.e., the seat of unlimited resources connected to the entire autonomous nervous system as opposed to the seat of concepts and judgments, of "should and must" (Green and Gallwey 1986, 16). Another way to talk about the same idea is in terms of Me versus I, that is, the person in general who is the nonconscious subject of all bodily actions and mental processes in contrast to the conscious player who is only active when there is time for thought yet takes credit for all decisions and outcomes. The conscious I sees itself as the manager of our lives, but that is pure illusion. The nonconscious Me is the real doer: body-based, it works through the brain circuits and muscle memory, with access to vast amounts of information and enormous speed of connection (Norretranders 1998, 258-59).

All superb accomplishments work through the subconscious part of the brain, but they require extensive periods of practice and the continuous fine-tuning of minute details, always "seeking out training in which the set goal exceeds the current level of performance" (Goleman 2013, 165; Starkes and Ericcson 2003). Starting out with something we deeply want to do and are naturally good at, we love doing it, train with dedication and deep absorption, and get even better at it. Then we love doing it even more, train to greater expertise, and get highly proficient, always learning, always growing (Lykken 1998, 34).

This—as much as the positive values of love, joy, and compassion—sets us up to realize the optimal brain state, where key circuitry in the PFC gets into a synchronized, entrained state or phase lock, marked by "great neural harmony—a rich, well-timed interconnection among diverse brain areas."[14] Working persistently over long periods of time (Kaufman and Baer 2004, 5; Simonton 2004, 91), we reach a level of coordination that can be "performed without bringing consciousness into play" and is triggered without further conscious

---

[13] See also Fuster 2003; Gardner 1994, 144; Goleman 2011, 40-43; Eysenck 1994, 209; Stein 2007, 19; Viscontas and Miller 2013, 125; Zaidel 2013, 135.

[14] Goleman 2011, 45; 2013, 16, 22; McCraty and Rees 2009, 528-29.

decision (Norretranders 1998, 254). This is the core of first-class athletics, great excellence in art, subliminal perfection in music, and all sorts of other amazing skills or knacks as described in the *Zhuangzi*.

We perform to perfection when we act with our entire personality, losing ourselves in the doing, enjoying the working process free from ego, frazzle, and separate thinking, with the brain on autopilot.[15] A pleasant, effortless, fully self-realized state, at the peak of automaticity (Goleman 2013, 28), there is no nervousness or shyness, but only familiarity and tranquility, a sense of being the vehicle or channel of something greater: art unfolds of itself, spirit moves, and perfection results—maker and made are one (Moeller 2004, 114; Green and Gallwey 1986, 64). Neither the instinctual behavior of an animal nor the passive following of circumstances or yet the strange random actions of a madman, this is self-oblivion or unthought spontaneity in a setting of order and discipline (Groves 2006, 102).

As John Diamond notes with regard to an exceptional musical performer:

> There must be no particle of his own ego involved. He must play totally with love, and he must want to communicate this love to the listener and be able to communicate it freely. He must at all times be totally subservient to the composer. He must be totally in phase with the pulse of the music. He must totally surrender his ego . . . and be totally at ease in his relationship with his instrument . . . in every way unstressed. Life energy must be coursing through him, flowing through him in a most balanced way. (1986, 3:134)

Music performed at this level of perfection raises the consciousness and inner aspiration of the audience, transmitting a divine, spiritual potency that enhances cosmic energy flow wherever it is heard (Mithen 2006, 98). By the same token, great art, great literature, great theater, great sports, great science—in short, anything done at this level—inspires and amazes, enhances and transforms, bringing the flow of cosmic energy to bear in the world. At the same time, it also provides the perfect outlet of the individual's unique gifts, allowing him to share his self-realization with the world.

Playfulness

The automated, spontaneous functioning of the bottom-up mind may happen upon extensive practice, when muscle memory is strong and the brain circuits are well primed. However, it can also be jump-started by short-circuiting the

---

[15] Norretranders 1998, 264, 266; Goleman 2011, 47; Lilly 1973, 173.

conscious mind in various ways. We can put it to sleep by keeping it occupied with steady, monotonous repetition of sound or movement, by focused concentration or deep absorption (Green and Gallwey 1986, 96-99). We can also give it an overload of things to deal with, a technique used commonly in the induction of hypnosis (Blair 2004). For example, people asked to play the violin while smiling and singing certain words cannot pay any attention to their fingers. They must let their hands do their thing, and as a result learn amazingly fast (Norretranders 1998, 268). A yet different technique involves play: role-playing to get out of established grooves, surrender to the ridiculous, opening to the impossible, and generally accepting the unpredictable, disorderly, and willful.[16]

A form of behavior that all higher species engage in, play is an affective-behavioral system in its own right that encourages flexibility and opens venues to learning for enhanced survival and greater self-realization (Garvey 1977, 6, 27-28). Defined as a variety of pleasurable activities without extrinsic goals, play is spontaneous and voluntary, effortless and active, undertaken within set parameters and in a nonliteral attitude (Garvey 1977, 4, 7; Huizinga 1955, 5, 7; Olson 2013, 247). Steady to-and-fro movement, play renews itself in constant repetition. Controllable, measurable, and limited, it involves both absorption and lightness. Absorption means that the player loses himself in play, functioning in an "unconscious consciousness" (Crandell 2010, 110). Lightness indicates that the activity is effortless, lighthearted, thoroughly enjoyable, and refreshing (2010, 113).

Associated with fun and enjoyment, play is entirely free from all deviousness and double-guessing. Complete and direct in its expression, it always communicates straight from the heart, is utterly uncontrolled, spontaneous, and free in every gesture, every look, and every sound (Diamond 1986, 3:130). Play is when our bottom-up mind is fully active, opening us to a higher state of being. If maintained beyond the limited time and place of a particular play, moreover, this state becomes *playfulness*, a lasting attitude of mind and personality trait of the individual (Lieberman 1977, 23, 108; Dewey 1933). Also called the "lusory attitude" (Suits 1978, 37), it is a fun way of being, full of enthusiasm and exuberance, humor and laughter, spontaneity and joy.[17]

A "bubbling effervescence" (Lieberman 1977, 116), playfulness means being fully within one's situation yet never entirely of it (Olson 2013, 255), maintaining the ability to joke and fool around, to laugh even—and maybe especially—when things get tough. Humor, notably also gallows humor, is an effective antidote against the useless struggle against ultimate danger (Ramachandran 2011, 40; Hood 2012, 42), shown clearly when Zhuangzi sings at his

---

[16] Norretranders 1998, 274; Green and Gallwey 1986, 104-08; Johnstone 1985, 91.

[17] Bacharowski and Owren 2002, 21; Tugade and Fredrickson 2002, 326; Lieberman 1977, 25.

wife's death, the four friends crack up when faced with terminal illness, or immortals drink and write silly ditties on the walls of taverns (Crandell 2010, 109; Sellmann 1998, 167). A sign of release in the face of an apparent danger or emergency as activated by the amygdala (Ramachandran 2011, 39; Hood 2012, 43), laughter brings more oxygen into the body, releases endorphins in the brain, and thus creates the shift into playfulness (Provine 2000). Signaling conditions of well-being, it enhances good feelings within the person and lubricates social interaction (Garvey 1977, 22; Hood 2012, 42). These good feelings, in turn, allow a joyful way of being in the world and a playful attitude to life.

Engaging with the world in playfulness, it becomes our personal playground, where new and exciting adventures beckon every day, fantastic opportunities arise, and growth and joy never cease (Carlson and Kohn 2012, 162). We find that we are loveable, that there is nothing to fear, and that the world is fun. Seeing that life is not a contest to be won, we fully come to belong to the beneficent universe that protects all, always at peace with who we are in any given moment (Donaldson 1993; www.originalplay.com). Whole, pure, and fun-filled in our spirit, we "respond to the world spontaneously, just as small children do. As to the child, so the world to us is always new and interesting" (Lash 1993). Like Zhuangzi in his butterfly dream and like the accomplished immortals, we are awakened to an ever-present possibility of changing back and forth (Wu 1990, 381). Relishing the transformations of life, we are free of all fear and hesitation, open to continuous journeying into new spheres and ways of being (Olson 2013, 251). Actively engaging in the three factors of divergent thinking, ideational fluency, spontaneous flexibility, and originality, we can set out to explore new shores and ways of being, fully realizing our creative potential (Lieberman 1977, 26, 108; Ward et al. 1995, 40).

Creativity

Creativity is the expression of cosmic oneness through unique individuality. It combines preexisting modes and materials as well as inherent talents and trained skills, i.e., genetically transmitted structures and domain-specific techniques and expertise, with originality and divergent thinking (Stein 2007, 226; de Moor et al. 2013, 97; Simonton 1999, 85). "For creativity to happen, something within us must be brought to life in something outside of us" (Goleman et al. 1992, 8). Through various "ways to jump from the worn grooves of life's daily record" (Wakefield 2001, 7), it leads to the generation of ideas, rules, patterns, relationships, insights, or artifacts that are new and surprising yet also appropriate and valuable for others.[18]

Creativity is universal: all people constantly transform their own reality as the brain updates its data and circuits (Runco 2004, 23; Kaufman and Baer 2004, 11). Jean Piaget says, "To understand is to invent" (1976). As Jacques Derrida puts it with regard to text, "The reader is the creator of meaning, human world-making consists essentially of the "systematic and creative play of differences, or the traces of differences, of the *spacing* by means of which elements are related to each other" (1981, 27).

Utilizing inherent traits and biologically given abilities in combination with skill, motivation, time, effort, and a sense of purpose and meaning, creativity is ubiquitous and relevant in all aspects of daily living.[19] Like flow, it requires an openness to new experiences, an internal locus of evaluation, a sense of psychological safety and freedom, as well as the ability to play with elements and concepts (Harman and Rheingold 1984, 17-19; Kaufman and Baer 2004, 11). It arises best in relaxed, unpressured situations of defocused attention, such as a leisurely walk or play.[20] Unlike during focused attention, with the frontal and parietal circuits in concert, when the mind is "at rest," the various other parts correlate in functional connectivity, allowing subconscious relationships of events or ideas stored deep in the memory to be activated and combined in novel ways.[21] "Freedom and playfulness make it possible for leisurely thinking to come up with original formulations and solutions," leading to unique perceptions, conceptual breakthroughs, unconventional designs, and idiosyncratic combinations (Csikszentmihalyi 1996, 138; Viscontas and Miller 2013, 120).

There are several ways of classifying creativity. One divides it according to its novelty into psychological and historical, i.e., whether something is new to the person or to humanity at large (Boden 1994, 76; 1998). Another looks at how it works and finds three major types: combinational, exploratory, and transformational. That it, it either manifests in the unfamiliar combination of familiar ideas, the exploration of new structures within conceptual space, or in transformative ideas that are new and strange, even impossible (Boden 2013, 6;

---

[18] Boden 2013, 3; Ward et al. 1995,10; Eysenck 1994, 200. For more definitions and discussions of creativity, see also Barron 1969; 1976; 1980; Boden 2004; Dacey and Lennon 1998; Eysenck 1995; Gardner 1983; Glover et al. 1989; Goleman et al. 1992; Harman and Rheingold 1984; Henderson 2004; Hodder 1998; Kaufman and Baer 2004; Kaufman and Sternberg 2006; Lubart and Guignard 2004; Ludwig 1995. Perkins 2013; Plucker and Beghetto 2004; Richards 2007; Simonton 1999, 94-99; Sternberg 1996; Wakefield 2001; Weisberg 2010.

[19] Goleman 2011, 41; Kaufman and Baer 2004, 7; Wakefield 2001, 4; Richards 1999; 2007; Runco 2004, 23.

[20] Boden 2013, 7; Garvey 1977, 5; Goleman et al. 1992, 57; Simonton 1999, 90.

[21] Gabora and Ranjan 2013, 22; Viscontas and Miller 2013, 116. Also Eysenck 1995.

1994, 82). Another way is to distinguish it by results in to five kinds: a novel solution to a well-defined problem; a new, encompassing theory; a set or frozen work that can be exhibited; a formal, ritualized, artistic performance; or a high-stakes performance, such as protests, fasts, and the like (Gardner 1994, 150-51).

The creative process, moreover, typically consists of five stages: preparation, incubation, illumination, verification, and translation. That is to say, individuals begin by immersing themselves in a problem or project, gathering materials and ideas to find out all they can about it, then allow the materials to simmer and churn for a while, connecting to patterns deep in their unconscious. Next come one or several breakthrough "aha" moments when things fall into place, characterized by a spiking of gamma waves in the brain that signal the binding of neurons and indicates the connection of far-flung cells in a new neural network, activated for conscious access in the temporal area and the right neocortex (Goleman 2011, 26). The new insight in turn leads to double-checking and testing, evaluating the new understanding in relation to previous knowledge and the demands of the field. Finally, the creative product is translated into a social setting and offered to an audience.[22]

The process requires skilled and voluntary effort (Kelly and Gasso 2007, 441), may take many years, and commonly involves numerous false starts, dead ends, failures, and frustrations (Perkins 1994, 131). Typically, it requires dealing with several major obstacles. They include "rarity," the fact that, while the options are many, good ideas that actually work are far and few between, as well as "isolation," the tendency that creative innovations are often far out, in areas that are hard to get to and require courageous jumps and extensive exploration. In addition, there is the danger of "oasis," the temptation to linger in areas of promise that ultimately offer no pay-off; and the "plateau" phase when one does not quite know in which direction to look next (1994, 122-24). Creativity being an intrinsically human activity, it is quite different from evolution, which produces generative innovation but, rather than searching for truth or excellence, is only concerned with survival power (1994, 128).

Neurological studies, using various methods of brain imaging during tests that involve alternative uses, utopian situations, and insight tasks (Fink and Benedek 2013, 210; Jung and Haier 2013, 235), have shown that

> the brains of extremely creative people may be more sensitive to the incoming sensations and perceptions than less sensitive individuals tend to discard in a process called 'latent inhibition.' Normally our brain unconsciously screens out objects, sounds, events, and ideas that experience has shown are irrelevant to our needs. Unusually creative individuals may

---

[22] See Csikszentmihalyi 1996, 79-80; Goleman et al. 1992, 18-23; Harman and Rheingold 1984, 21-27; Kelly and Gasso 2007, 426; Runco 2004, 24; Sternberg and Lubart 1995.

> have lower levels of this latent inhibition. . . . The normal person classifies an object, then forgets about it; the creative person, by contrast, is always open to new possibilities. (Stein 2007, 225; Simonton 1999, 90)

Low latent inhibition means that "creative people are not as good at learning to ignore things." They also have a higher dopamine level, signifying a greater degree of being exploratory and open to the environment (Babot et al. 2013, 75). And they tend toward looser associational networks of the PFC, allowing the activation of more neural cliques, i.e., co-spiking neurons, over a greater realm of brain circuitry with overall greater efficiency in brain processing.[23] Not acting in preset patterns or established synchrony, they more easily trigger new ideas and are open to divergent thinking (Goleman et al. 1992, 30).

Tests further have shown that creative people have a high level of neuron activity in the PFC whether the task is rote or challenging, which means they don't get bored as easily (Stein 2007, 228). Their two brain hemispheres work together closely, activating the right side strongly when facing a new task, then transferring learned structures into the left side, where abstracted patterns reside that no longer require full attention (2007, 229-30). As their right PFC network gleans the raw material of a creative event, their left organizes and shape-sculpts it into new dimensions (2007, 233; Kelly and Gasso 2007, 453).

Creativity connects intimately to intelligence—including all seven learning styles identified by Howard Gardner: visual-spatial, musical, linguistic, mathematical, kinesthetic, intrapersonal, and social.[24] Each requires a different set of skills, provides access to a particular domain, and comes with special traits or talents—most people being strong in one and somewhat good at a second (Feist 2004, 62-65). They are to about 50 percent genetically determined or inherited and often appear in family clusters. [25] The other 50 percent are subject to training, involving various techniques of improving working memory and fluid intelligence, the ability to adapt to new situations.[26] In all cases, creativity requires more than giftedness and superb accomplishments—in fact, excessive domain mastery restricts it (Simonton 2004, 91): the individual also needs to be open to other learning styles and less intensely developed brain circuits, allowing them to work in fluid integration and integrating a wide range of ideas and skills (Feist 2004, 74).

---

[23] Stein 2007, 226; Beversdorf 2013, 153; Gabora and Ranjan 2013, 29; Jung and Haier 2013, 238.

[24] Documented in Gardner 1983; 1993; 1994; 1999; Eysenck 1995, 2; Feist 2004, 64; Goleman et al. 1992, 27.

[25] Babot al. 2013, 74; de Moor 2013, 95, 101; Lykken 1998, 26; Simonton 2004, 91.

[26] On ways of training and enhancing creativity, see Keiänen and Gardner 2004, 171; Lubart and Guignard 2004, 51; Vartanian 2013, 258-61; Wakefield 2001, 145.

Successful Adaptation

Creativity does not exist in a social vacuum, but takes place in a wider system, in a potent dynamic between isolation and social connections, leading to products that both resonate with and surprise their audience (Viscontas and Miller 2013, 120; Gardner 1994, 145, 154). That is to say, it works within a specific domain and a particular field, i.e., a set of symbolic rules and procedures in a given area of expertise plus the people involved in it. Creative people, then, endowed with abilities and inclinations suited for his particular area, use the symbols of the domain to make a novel contribution that changes the field (Csikszentmihalyi 1996, 28; see also Amabile 1983; 1996). To attain success, they have to be sociable, practical, and career-driven, exhibiting traits "more characteristic of Wall Street marketing executives than what we have come to associate with artists" (Abuhamdek and Csikszentmihalyi 2004, 39). The social and market dimension, then, is what distinguishes the creative from the merely original—an idea, mechanism, or artwork that has never arisen before yet remains unappreciated and has no impact (Babot et al. 2013, 78; Boden 1994, 78).

Creativity as an innate, boundless, energetic potency is the fruit of minds represented on the far ends of the bell curve. This means that intensely creative individuals walk a tightrope between highly productive lives and debilitating mental illness, most notably bipolar disorder, schizophrenia, and frontotemporal dementia.[27] Often the children of psychiatric patients and open to the depth of the unconscious, they do not fit the dominant social mold, facing the stigma of being different while confronting deep existential questions (Carson 2013, 186). Prone to cognitive overinclusion and reduced inhibitions, they have a vivid imagination and work with primary-process imagery, engaging in fantasies, trances, dreams, and visions, and even incorporating psychotic-like experiences into the matrix.[28]

It is essential, though, that they find the right level. "Too much, and the outcome is highly original but useless variants, such as the crazy thoughts of psychotics . . . Too little, and the result is adaptive, but lacking in originality, as in everyday thinking" (Simonton 1999, 64). Or, as Elmer Green puts it, psychotics may "lock in" on the eidetic imagery and accept this hallucinatory world as real while geniuses "merely dip into the reservoir of reveries for inspiration, then return to beta consciousness to execute their ideas" (Panati 1974, 147).

---

[27] On creativity and madness, see Babot et al. 2013, 76; Claridge 1998; Eysenck 1995, ch. 6; Kelly and Gasso 2007, 473; Kubie 1976; McTaggart 2011, 117; Stein 2007, 225; Viscontas and Miller 2013, 115. A special case are autistic savants. See Lykken 1998, 16; Sacks 1985; 1995.

[28] Barron 1980, 312-16; Harman and Rheingold 1984, 6; Kelly and Gasso 2007, 432, 441.

To reach a happy medium between beta and transcendent consciousness, creative people have to combine various antithetical traits and live in a dynamic state of ongoing dialectical tension (Csikszentmihalyi 1996, 57). Such traits include great physical energy and the need for restful quietude, being both smart and naive, playful and disciplined, imaginative and profoundly realistic, as well as socially engaged and happy in solitude. Creative people are both extroverted and introverted, humble and proud, masculine and feminine, rebellious and rule-bound, independent and domain-trained, passionate and objective, as well as suffering and joyful (1996, 58-76; see also Simonton 1999, 90-92). Contrary to common myths, there are no special demographics to creativity, nor does it require a full-time commitment, solitary living, bad relationships, youth, or alcohol (Wakefield 2001, 31-67). Most of all one needs inherent clarity of mind, body, and spirit, a strong sense of uniqueness, combined with the cultivation of moderate living, meditation exercises, and the release of negative emotions (2001, 71-84).

Genius

The highest level of clarity and openness, then, allows a close connection to divinity, an almost mystical communion in awe and wonder, when we feel as if we are downloading information from the universe by extrasensory perception (Barron 1980, 317-19). This is "genius," using a word that goes back to the Roman term for "beget" and also connected to "genie," an attendant spirit that connects us to the higher realms (Bloom 2002, 7; de Moor et al. 2013, 96). Related to the Latin *ingenium*, "innate ability," genius is both our inclination or natural gift, our inborn intellectual or imaginative power brought vibrantly alive in the creative process and also a transcendent state that allows us to "soar about the wakeful constraints of time and space."[29] As such, it connects us to a higher level of perception, to the "implicate order" (Burkhart 2011, 37), so that, for example, "Mozart's compositions could come to him from an outside source as complete wholes" (Panati 1974, 136).

It requires good generic intelligence, unique inherent talents, and an assortment of other gifts or attributes, as well as an excessive degree of mental energy, deeply focused concentration, and an openness to new and unexpected ideas (Lykken 1998, 18; Eysenck 1995, 18). With few constraints on the range and freedom of thought, "the creative genius must be willing to work hard and long on ambitious projects that verge on the unrealistic—a scientific magnum opus, an epic novel, a grandiose opera" (Simonton 1999, 102).

[29] Panati 1974, 137; see also Eysenck 1994, 200; 1995, 11-13; Simonton 1999, 2. More studies appear in Maslow 1966b; Penrose 1989, 444; Steptoe 1998.

Like creativity, genius emerges best when the mind is at rest, in a hypo-egoic state of ease and low self-consciousness (Goleman 2011, 27). "While most people work with a dual-process system, deliberately and systematically using conscious thought to weigh important considerations, search for relevant information, and override unwanted impulses and emotions, geniuses process information non-consciously and automatically without intentional effort or self-awareness yet controlled by evolved dispositions, cognitive scripts, and trained circuitry" (Leary and Guadagno 2011, 137). They do so best in stress-free situations such as the bath, the bed, and the bus (Simonton 1999, 69). The combination of low level ego-involvement and minimal desire for a particular outcome echoes the Daoist ideal of nonaction. Characterized by positive attitudes such as joy, flow, awe, amusement, interest, and love, it allows the mind to work a great deal faster and process many more pieces of information in a much wider range of neural circuitry (Leary and Guadagno 2011, 138-39).

Socially, there is no predicting the emergence of genius. While some are born into gifted families, many come from disadvantaged circumstances, as for example, the French thinker Jean-Jacques Rousseau and the Indian mathematician Srinivasa Ramanujan (Lykken 1998, 30; Eysenck 1995, 14; see also Albert 1998). Its recognition, on the other hand, is subject to certain rules. A genius is a person "credited with creative ideas or products that have left a large impression on a particular domain of intellectual or aesthetic activity," someone of "eminence" in society and even humanity as a whole (Simonton 1999, 6). In other words, from a social science perspective, "the location of genius is not in the mind, but in a virtual space, a system or social field" as determined by "a consensus of peers" (Csikszentmihalyi 1998, 39).

Emerging through the successful cooperation between supraliminal and subliminal modes of cognition (Kelly and Gasso 2007, 475; Simonton 1999, 44), genius often works through divine inspiration in the form of serendipity or chance, leading to intuitive leaps, sudden insights, accidental discoveries, or unexpected understanding (1999, 35-39; 2004, 84). "Indeed, so involuntary are these events that creators sometimes insist illuminations took place largely in opposition to voluntary control," to the point even where Nietzsche speaks of being "the mouthpiece or medium of some almighty power" (1999, 69). David R. Hawkins echoes this,

> Genius is by definition a style of consciousness characterized by the ability to access high-energy attractor patterns. The process of animating genius most commonly involves first formulating a question, then waiting an indefinite interval for consciousness to work with the problem—until suddenly, the answer appears in a flash, in a form that is characteristically nonverbal. . . . Attractor energy patterns have harmonics, as do musical tones. The higher the harmonic's frequency, the higher the power. What the genius arrives at is a new harmonic. (2002, 195-96)

Divinity

In other words, we are each connected to everything around us and to the greater universe in our bones, our history, our atoms, and our minds. Since we live in a cosmos of a multitude of holographically interlocking fields, the higher level of energy gauge symmetry or attractor harmony we attain, the more we can access patterns and information that seem far out, elusive, and beyond ordinary limitations. The result is divinity, a new perception of self and completely different kind of awareness:

> Instead of thinkingness, there is a self-revealing knowingness that imparts complete understanding and is self-explanatory by its self-effulgent essence. It is as though everything speaks silently and presents itself in its entirety in the absolute beauty of its perfection. In so doing, it manifests its glory and its intrinsic Divinity. (Hawkins 2001, 5)

In terms of neurophysiology, knowingness or attractor harmony matches a reduced activity in the orientation association area on the fringes of the neocortex, the part that orients the individual in space and provides boundaries of self and identity. With a calm, focused mind—as in nuns at prayer, Buddhist meditators, or practicing mystics—fewer sensory data enter, blinding the orientation area (Newberg and Waldman 2009, 51). Via the thalamus, this state causes the hippocampus to dampen the flow of neural input, leading to a subjective sense of opening and widening. With a fully established calming neural ciruit and a further reduction in data, moreover, "the brain would have no choice but to perceive that the self is endless and intimately interwoven with everyone and everything" (Newberg et al. 2001, 6).

> In this state of total deafferentiation of the orientation area, the mind would perceive a neurological reality consistent with many mystical descriptions of the ultimate spiritual union. There would be no discrete objects or beings, no sense of space or the passage of time, no line between the self and the rest of the universe. In fact, there would be no subjective self at all; there would only be an absolute sense of unity. (2001, 119)

This unity, moreover, is real, reflecting what we now know to be true about the universe and the nonlocal, holographic nature of mind and world. Experiences of mystical oneness, creative illumination, genius insight, and immortality—"states that involve the perception of a unitary reality" (Newberg 2012, 168), part of what traditional religions have called God, Brahman, or Dao—represent in fact "a reality that cannot be undone by ideas," a transcendent presence or "absolute unitary being" that encompasses and contains the material world.[30]

It is therefore entirely plausible that a scientist struck by lightning would become obsessed with piano music (Sacks 2007, 5): his neurocircuitry was opened to a different frequency and he plugged into a new attractor harmony. It is also entirely reasonable that some people experience death due to shock, trauma, or disease. Free from pain and suffering, they leave the body, float off, move through a tunnel toward a white light, where they see loved ones or divine figures, then return to physical existence, often with great reluctance. After coming back, they *know* that God is real. As a result, they no longer fear death, instead feeling connected to all existence luminous serenity. Centering their lives on love and compassion, they are eager to be of service.[31]

A powerful example is Eben Alexander (b. 1953), a professor of neurosurgery who, in November 2008, suffered from bacterial meningitis and was kept alive solely by machines for an entire week. First reborn into a primitive mucky Jell-o-like substance, the Realm of the Earthworm's-Eye View, he encountered "a beautiful girl with high cheekbones and deep blue eyes" who assured him that he was loved forever and had nothing to fear (2012, 30, 40-41). She took him into the Core, an immense void that was both pitch black and brimming with light, where he "sensed and the infinite vastness of the Creator," an all-loving God he called Om (2012, 47).

Returning again to the lower realm, he received the ultimate truth that "unconditional love is the basis of everything," changing his overall outlook and purpose in life (2012, 71). As he says, "This other, vastly grander universe isn't far away at all. In fact, it is right here—right here where I am, typing this sentence, and right there where you are, reading it. It is not far away physically, but simply exists on a different frequency" (2012, 156).

Daoists speak of this vastly grander power in terms of Dao and spirit—closely matching Ken Wilber's understanding. He notes,

> Spirit is the Condition of all conditions, the Being of all beings, the Nature of all natures. As such, it neither evolves nor involves, grows or develops, ascends or descends. It is the simply suchness or isness—the perfect isness—of all that is, of each and every thing in manifestation.

---

[30] Newberg et al. 2001, 139, 142, 147; Hardy 1979, 141; Beauregard and O'Leary 2007, 202.

[31] For studies and discussions of the so-called near-death experience, see Alvarado 2000, 183; Beauregard 2012, ch. 7; and O'Leary 2007, 157-58; Irwin 1999, 199-218; Targ and Katra 163-65; see also Bailey and Yates 1996; Blackmore 1993; Moody 1975; 1988; Van Lommel 2010. Traditional medical explanations include hallucination, fantasy, hypoxic unconsciousness, heavy right hemisphere intrusion, and temporal lobe dysfunction (Greyson 2000, 332-35).

> There is no contacting immanent Spirit, no way to reach it, no way to commune with it, for there is nothing it is not.
>
> Being completely and totally present at every single point of space and time, it is fully and completely present here and now, and thus we can no more attain immanent spirit than we could, say, attain our feet. (2004, 67-68; 1993, 43-44)

The same holds true also for the mystic understanding of God in a description that could just as easily apply to Dao:

> God is beyond perception, duality, positionality, or having parts. God is beyond all opposites, such as good and bad, right and wrong, win and lose. Like the sun, God shines equally on all. God's love is not reserved for the favored few, but it shines thorugh the clouds via the love we experience with others, including even pets and nature. (Hawkins 2001, 150)

Rather than an ultimate reality far beyond our lives, this is real reality, the place and time and life where we are right now, the original Self we had before the Big Bang and also the practical self we have right now in lived perfection. We are spirit, we are the universe, we are infinite, we are eternal. We are amazing, cosmic, light, and powerful beyond measure.

Bibliography

Abelson, R. P. 1986. "Beliefs Are Like Possessions." Journal for the Theory of Social Behavior 16:223-50.

Abrams, Nancy Ellen, and Joel R. Primack. 2011. *The New Universe and the Human Future: How a Shared Cosmology Could Transform the World.* New Haven, Conn.: Yale University Press.

Abuhamdeh, Sami, and Mihaly Csikszentmihalyi. 2004. "The Artistic Personality: A Systems Perspective." In *Creativity: From Potential to Realization*, edited by Robert J. Sternberg, Elena L. Grigorenko, and Jerome L. Singer, 31-42. Washington, DC: American Psychological Association.

Adorno, Theodor. 1950. *The Authoritarian Personality.* New York: Harper.

Albert, Robert S. 1998. "Mathematical Giftedness and Mathematical Genius: A Comparison of G. H. Hardy and Srinivas Ramanujan." In *Genius and the Mind: Studies of Creativity and Temperament*, edited by Andrew Steptoe, 111-40. New York: Oxford University Press.

Alcock, James E. 1990. *Science and Supernature: A Critical Appraisal of Parapsychology.* Buffalo, NY: Prometheus Books.

Alexander, Eben. 2012. *Proof of Heaven: A Neurosurgeon's Journey into the Afterlife.* New York: Simon & Schuster.

_____. 2014. *Map of Heaven.* New York: Simon & Schuster.

Alexander, F. Matthias. 1989 [1932]. *The Use of the Self: Its Conscious Direction in Relation to Diagnosis, Functioning and the Control of Reaction.* New York: E. P. Dutton.s

Alexander, Stephon H. S. 2009. "Just What Is Dark Energy?" In *What's Next? Dis-patches on the Future of Science*, edited by Max Brockman, 52-67. New York: Vintage Books.

Allinson, Robert Elliott. 2015. "How Metaphor Functions in the *Zhuangzi*: The Case of the Unlikely Messenger." In *New Visions of the Zhuangzi*, edited by Livia Kohn, 95-118. St. Petersburg, Fla.: Three Pines Press.

Allport, Gordon. 1954. *The Nature of Prejudice.* Cambridge, Mass.: Addison-Wesley.

_____. 1961 [1937]. *Personality: A Psychological Interpretation.* New York: Holt.

Alvarado, Carlos S. 2000. "Out-of-Body Experiences." In *Varieties of Anomalous Experience: Examining the Scientific Evidence*, edited by Etzel Cardeña, Steven Jay Lynn, and Stanley Krippner, 183-218. Washington, DC: American Psychological Association.

Amabile, Teresa. 1983. *The Social Psychology of Creativity.* New York: Springer.

_____. 1996. *Creativity in Context.* Boulder, Col.: Westview Press.

Ambrose, Kala. 2011. *The Awakened Aura.* Woodbury, Minn.: Llewellyn Publishers.

Ames, Roger T. 1994. "The Meaning of Body in Classical Chinese Philosophy." In *Self as Person in Asian Theory and Practice*, edited by Roger T. Ames, Wimal Dissanayake, and Thomas P. Kasulis, 157-77. Albany: State University of New York Press.

______. 1998. "Knowing in the *Zhuangzi*: From Here, on the Bridge, over the River Hao." In *Wandering at Ease in the Zhuangzi*, edited by Roger Ames, 219-30. Albany: State University of New York Press.

Amodie, David M, and Matthew D. Lieberman. 2009. "Pictures in Our Heads: Contributions of fMRI to the Study of Prejudice and Stereotyping." In *Handbook of Prejudice, Stereotyping, and Discrimination*, edited by Todd D. Nelson, 347-65. New York: Taylor & Francis.

Andersen, Poul. 1980. *The Method of Holding the Three Ones*. London: Curzon Press.

______. 1990. "The Practice of *Bugang*." *Cahiers d'Extrême-Asie* 5: 15-53.

Andrews, Cecile. 2009a. "Introduction." In *Less Is More: Embracing Simplicity for a Healthy Planet, a Caring Economy, and Lasting Happiness*, edited by Cecile Andrews and Wanda Urbanska, 1-7. Gabriola Island: New Society Publishers.

______. 2009b. "The Circle of Simplicity." In *Less Is More: Embracing Simplicity for a Healthy Planet, a Caring Economy, and Lasting Happiness*, edited by Cecile Andrews and Wanda Urbanska, 53-63. Gabriola Island: New Society Publishers.

______, and Wanda Urbanska, eds. 2009. *Less Is More: Embracing Simplicity for a Healthy Planet, a Caring Economy, and Lasting Happiness*. Gabriola Island: New Society Publishers.

Ardila, Alfredo. 2009. "Origins of the Language: Correlation between Brain Evolution and Language Development." In *Foundations in Evolutionary Cognitive Neuroscience*, edited by Steven M. Platek and Todd K. Shackelford, 153-74. Cambridge: Cambridge University Press.

Ariely, Dan. 2008. *Predictably Irrational: The Hidden Forces That Shape Our Decisions*. New York: HarperCollins.

Arthur, Shawn. 2013. *Early Daoist Dietary Practices: Examining Ways to Health and Longevity*. New York: Lexington Books.

AtKisson, Alan. 2009. "The *Lagom* Solution." In *Less Is More: Embracing Simplicity for a Healthy Planet, a Caring Economy, and Lasting Happiness*, edited by Cecile Andrews and Wanda Urbanska, 101-06. Gabriola Island: New Society Publishers.

Attenborough, David. 1995. *The Private Life of Plants: A Natural History of Plant Behavior*. Princeton: Princeton University Press.

Aziz, Robert. 1990. *C. G. Jung's Psychology of Religion and Synchronicity*. Albany: State University of New York Press.

Bachorowski, Jo-Anne, and Michael J. Owren. 2002. "Vocal Acoustics in Emotional Intelligence." In *The Wisdom in Feeling: Psychological Processes in Emotional Intelligence*, edited by Lisa Feldman Barrett and Peter Salovey, 11-36. New York: Guilford Press.

Baggini, Julian. 2011. *The Ego Trick*. London: Granta.

Bagley, Robert W. 2004. "Anyang Writing and the Origin of the Chinese Writing System." In *The First Writing: Script Invention as History and Process*, edited by Stephen D. Houston, 190-429. Cambridge: Cambridge University Press.

Bailey, Lee W., and Jenny Yates, eds. 1996. *The Near-Death Experience" A Reader*. New York: Routledge.

Baines, John. 2004. "The Earliest Egyptian Writing: Development, Context, Purpose." In *The First Writing: Script Invention as History and Process*, edited by Stephen D. Houston, 150-89. Cambridge: Cambridge University Press.

Barad, Karen Michelle. 2007. *Meeting the Universe Halfway: Quantum Physics and the Entanglement of Matter and Meaning*. Durham: Duke University Press.

Barbot, Baptiste, Mei Tan, and Elena L. Grigorenko. 2013. "The Genetics of Creativity: The Generative and Receptive Sides of the Creativity Equation." In *Neuroscience of Creativity*, edited by Oshin Vartanian, Adam S. Bristol, and James C. Kaufman, 71-94. Cambridge, Mass.: MIT Press.

Barlow, Horace. 1990. "What Does the Brain See? How Does It Understand?" In *Images and Understanding: Thoughts about Images, Ideas about Understanding*, edited by Horace Barlow, Colin Blakemore, and Miranda Weston-Smith, 5-25. Cambridge: Cambridge University Press.

_____, Colin Blakemore, and Miranda Weston-Smith eds. 1990. *Images and Understanding: Thoughts about Images, Ideas about Understanding*. Cambridge: Cambridge University Press.

Barron, Frank. 1969. *Creative Person and Creative Process*. New York: Holt, Rinehart and Winston.

_____. 1976. "The Psychology of Creativity." In *The Creativity Question*, edited by Albert Rothenberg and Carl A. Hausman, 189-99. Durham, NC: Duke University Press.

_____. 1980. "The Creative Personality: Akin to Madness." In *Understanding Mysticism*, edited by Richard Woods, 312-320. New York: Image Books.

Barrow, John D., and Frank Tipler. 1986. *The Anthropic Cosmological Principle*. New York: Oxford University Press.

Bates, John E., Jackson A. Goodnight, and Jennifer E. Fife. 2008. "Temperament and Emotions." In *Handbook of Emotions*, edited by Michael Lewis, Jeannette M. Haviland-Jones, and Lisa Feldman Barrett, 485-96. New York: Guilford Press.

Baumeister, Ray F. 1999. *The Self in Social Psychology*. Philadelphia: Psychology Press.

Beauregard, Mario. 2004. *Consciousness, Emotional Self-Regulation, and the Brain*. Philadelphia: John Benjamins Publications.

_____. 2012. *Brain Wars: The Scientific Battle Over the Existence of the Mind and the Proof that Will Change the Way We Live Our Lives*. New York: HarperOne.

_____, and Denise O'Leary. 2007. *The Spiritual Brain: A Neuroscientist's Case for the Existence of the Soul.* New York: HarperOne.

Beck, Aaron T. 2004. *Cognitive Therapy of Personality Disorders*. New York: Guilford Press.

Becker, Robert O. 1982. *Electromagnetism and Life*. Albany: State University of New York Press.

______. 1990. *Cross Currents: The Perils of Electropollution—The Promise of Electromedicine*. New York: Putnam.

______, and Gary Sheldon. 1985. *The Body Electric: Electromagnitism and the Foundation of Life*. New York: William Morrow and Co.

Bedell, Leila G. 1885. *The Abdominal Brain*. Chicago: Grass and Delbridge.

Begley, Sharon, ed. 2007. *Train Your Mind to Change Your Brain*. New York: Ballentine.

Bellah, Robert N. 2011. *Religion in Human Evolution: From the Paleolithic to the Axial Age*. Cambridge, Mass.: Harvard University Press.

Bellwood, Peter S. 2005. *First Farmers: The Origins of Agricultural Societies*. Malden, Mass.: Blackwell.

Beloff, John. 2008. "Psi Phenomena: Causal Versus Acausal Interpretation." In *Synchronicity: Multiple Perspectives on Meaningful Coincidence*, edited by Lance Storm, 99-108. Pari: Pari Publishing.

Benaji, Makzarin R., and R. Bhashar. 2000. "Implicit Stereotypes and Memory: The Bounded Rationality of Social Beliefs." In *Memory, Brain, and Belief*, edited by Daniel L. Schacter and Elaine Sacrry, 139-75. Cambridge, Mass.: Harvard University Press.

Benedetti, F. 2014. *Placebo Effects*. New York: Oxford University Press.

Benor, D. 2001. *Spiritual Healing: Scientific Validation of a Healing Revolution*. Southfield, Mich.: Vision Publications.

Benson, Herbert. 1976. *The Relaxation Response*. New York: Avon.

______. 1996. *Timeless Healing: The Power and Biology of Belief*. New York: Simon & Schuster.

______, and William Proctor. 1985. *Beyond the Relaxation Response*. New York: Times Books.

Bentov, Itchak. 1977. *Stalking the Wild Pendulum: On the Mechanics of Consciousness*. New York: E. P. Dutton.

Bergounioux, F. M. 1961. "Notes on the Mentality of Primitive Man." In *Social Life of Early Man*, edited by Sherwood L. Washburn, 106-19. Chicago: Aldine.

Berman, Morris. 1989. *Coming to Our Senses: Body and Spirit in the Hidden History of the West*. New York: Simon & Schuster.

Beversdorf, David Q. 2013. "Pharmacological Effects on Creativity." In *Neuroscience of Creativity*, edited by Oshin Vartanian, Adam S. Bristol, and James C. Kaufman, 151-74. Cambridge, Mass.: MIT Press.

Bianco, Carla. 1974. *The Two Rosetos*. Bloomington: Indiana University Press.

Bickerton, Derek. 1990. *Language and Species*. Chicago: University of C Press.

______. 2010. "On Two Incompatible Theories of Language Evolution." In *The Evolution of Human Language: Biolinguistic Perspectives*, edited by Richard K. Larson, Viviane Déprez, and Hiroko Yamakido, 199-210. Cambridge: Cambridge University Press.

Bidlack, Bede Benjamin. 2015. *In Good Company: The Body and Divinization in Pierre Teilhard de Chardin, SJ and Daoist Xiao Yingsou*. Leiden: Brill.

Billeter, Jean François. 2010. *Leçons sur le Tchouang Tseu*. Paris: Éditions Allia.

Bingham, Paul M. 2010. "On the Evolution of Language: Implications of a New and General Theory of Human Origins, Properties, and History." In *The Evolution of Human Language: Biolinguistic Perspectives*, edited by Richard K. Larson, Viviane Déprez, and Hiroko Yamakido, 211-24. Cambridge: Cambridge University Press.

Biswas-Diener, Robert M. 2008. "Material Wealth and Subjective Well-Being." In *The Science of Subjective Well-Being*, edited by Michael Eid and Randy J. Larsen, 307-22. New York: Guilford Press.

Blackmore, Susan. 1993. *Dying to Live: Near-Death Experiences*. Buffalo, NY: Prometheus Books.

_____. 1999. *The Meme Machine*. New York: Oxford University Press.

_____. 2007. "Imitation Makes Us Human." In *What Makes Us Human?* edited by Charles Pasternak, 1-16. New York: Oxford University Press.

Blair, Forbes Robbins. 2004. *Instant Self-Hypnosis*. Naperville, Ill.: Sourcebooks Inc.

Blass, Thomas. 2004. *The Man Who Shocked the World: The Life and Legacy of Stanley Migram*. New York: Basic Books.

Bloom, Harold. 2002. *Genius: A Mosaic of One Hundred Exemplary Creative Minds*. New York: Warner Books.

Bock-Möbius, Imke. 2012. *Qigong Meets Quantum Physics*. Dunedin, Fla: Three Pines Press.

Bodde, Derk. 1959. "The Chinese Cosmic Magic Known as Watching for the Ethers." In *Studia Serica Bernard Karlgren Dedicata*, edited by Søren Egerod, 14-35. Kopenhagen: E. Munksgaard.

Boden, Margaret A. 1994. "What Is Creativity? " In *Dimensions of Creativity*, edited by Margaret A. Boden, 75-118. Cambridge, Mass.: MIT Press.

_____. 1998. "What Is Creativity?" In *Creativity in Human Evolution and Prehistory*, edited by Steven Mithen, 22-60. London: Routledge.

_____. 2004. *The Creative Mind: Myths and Mechanisms*. London: Routledge.

_____. 2013. "Creativity as a Neuroscientific Mystery." In *Neuroscience of Creativity*, edited by Oshin Vartanian, Adam S. Bristol, and James C. Kaufman, 3-18. Cambridge, Mass.: MIT Press.

Bodenhausen, Galen V., Andrew R. Todd, and Jennifer A. Richeson. 2009. "Controlling Prejudice and Stereotyping: Antecedents, Mechanisms, and Contexts." In *Handbook of Prejudice, Stereotyping, and Discrimination*, edited by Todd D. Nelson, 111-36. New York: Taylor & Francis.

Bohm, David. 1951. *Quantum Theory*. New York: Prentice Hall.

_____. 1980. *Wholeness and the Implicate Order*. London: Routledge & Kegan Paul.

_____. 1987. "Hidden Variables and the Implicate Order." In *Quantum Implications*, edited by Basil J. Hiley and F. David Peat. London: Routledge & Kegan Paul.

_____, and B. J. Hiley. 1993. *The Undivided Universe: An Ontological Interpretation of Quantum Theory*. London: Routledge.

Bok, Sesela. 2010. *Exploring Happiness: From Aristotle to Science*. New Haven, Conn.: Yale University Press.

Bokenkamp, Stephen R. 1997. *Early Daoist Scriptures*. With a contribution by Peter Nickerson. Berkeley: University of California Press.

Boltz, William G. 1994. *The Origin and Early Development of the Chinese Writing System*. New Haven, Conn.: Yale University Press.

Bonnanno, George A., Laura Goovin, and Karin G. Coifman. 2008. "Sadness and Grief." In *Handbook of Emotions*, edited by Michael Lewis, Jeannette M. Haviland-Jones, and Lisa Feldman Barrett, 797-810. New York: Guilford Press.

Boroditsky, Lera. 2000. "Metaphoric Structuring: Understanding Time through Spatial Metaphors." *Cognition* 75:1-28.

_____. 2009. "How Does Our Language Shape the Way We Think?" In *What's Next? Dispatches on the Future of Science*, edited by Max Brockman, 116-29. New York: Vintage Books.

Borysenko, Joan, with Larry Rothstein. 1987. *Minding the Body, Mending the Mind*. Reading, Mass.: Addison-Wesley.

Bottéro, Françoise. 2004. "Writing on Shell and Bone in China." In *The First Writing: Script Invention as History and Process*, edited by Stephen D. Houston, 250-61. Cambridge: Cambridge University Press.

Bradberry, Travis and Greaves, Jean. 2009. *Emotional Intelligence 2.0*. San Francisco: Publishers Group West.

Braud, William G. 2003. *Disting Mental Influence: Its Contributions to Science and Healing*. Charlottesville, VA; Hampton Roads Publishing.

Breaux, Charles. 1989. *Journey into Consciousness: The Chakras, Tantra, and Jungian Psychology*. York Beach, ME: Nicolas-Hays.

Brennan, Barbara Ann. 1987. *Hands of Light: A Guide to Healing Through the Human Energy Field*. New York: Bantam Books.

_____. 1993. *Light Emerging: The Journey of Personal Healing*. New York: Bantam Books.

Brickman, P., D. Coates, and R. Janoff-Bulman. 1978. "Lotter Winners and Accident Victims: Is Happiness Relative?" *Journal of Personality and Social Psychology* 36:919-27.

Brindley, Erica F. 2016. "Spontaneous Arising: Creative Change in the *Hengxian*." *Journal of Daoist Studies* 9:1-17.

_____, Paul R. Goldin, and Esther S. Klein. 2013. "A Philosophical Translation of the *Heng Xian*." *Dao: A Journal of Comparative Philosophy* 12.2:145-51.

Bronowski, Jacob. 1965. *Science and Human Values*. New York: Harper & Row.

Brown, Kirk Warren, and Melissa Holt. 2011. "Experiential Processing and the Integration of Bright and Dark Sides in the Human Psyche." In *Designing Positive Psychology: Taking Stock and Moving Forward*, edited by Kennon M. Sheldon, Todd B. Kashdan, and Michael F. Steger, 147-59. New York: Oxford University Press.

Buchanan, Mark. 2002. *Nexus: Small Worlds and the Groundbreaking Science of Networks*. New York: W. W. Norton.

Bucke, R. M. 1961. *Cosmic Consciousness: A Study of the Evolution of the Human Mind.* Hyde Park: University Books.

Burkhart, Brian Yazzie. 2011. "The Physics of Spirit: The Indigenous Continuity of Science and Religion" In *The Routledge Companion to Religion and Science*, edited by James W. Haag, Gregory R. Peterson, and Michael L. Spezio, 34-42. London: Routledge.

Burrow, Trigant. 1964. *Preconscious Foundations of Human Experience*. New York: Basic Books.

Buzsáki, G. 2006. *Rhythms of the Brain*. New York: Oxford University Press.

Byrne, Richard. 1998. "The Early Evolution of Creative Thinking: Evidence from Monkeys and Apes." In *Creativity in Human Evolution and Prehistory*, edited by Steven Mithen, 110-24. London: Routledge.

Callahan, Roger J., with Richard Trubo. 2001. *Tapping the Healer Within*. Chicago: Contemporary Books.

Cameron, Oliver G. 2002. *Visceral Sensory Neuroscience: Interoception*. New York: Oxford University Press.

Campany, Robert Ford. 2002. *To Live As Long As Heaven and Earth: A Translation and Study of Ge Hong's Traditions of Divine Transcendents*. Berkeley: University of California Press.

_____. 2014. "The Sword Scripture: Recovering and Interpreting a Lost 4th-Century Daoist Method for Cheating Death." *Daoism: Religion, History and Society* 6:33-84.

Cannon, Charles. 2007. *The Synchronicity Experience: Holistic Lifestyle and Contemporary High-Tech Meditation*. Nellysford, VA: Synchronicity Foundation for Modern Spirituality.

Capra, Fritjof. 1975. *The Tao of Physics: An Exploration of the Parallels Between Modern Physics and Eastern Mysticism*. Boulder: Shambhala.

_____. 1996. *The Web of Life: A New Scientific Understanding of Living Systems*. New York: Anchor Books.

Carlson, Ed, and Livia Kohn. 2012. *Core Health: The Quantum Way to Inner Power*. St. Petersburg, Fla.: Energy Essentials.

Carr, Bernard, ed. 2007. *Universe or Multiverse?* Cambridge: Cambridge University Press.

Carr, Michael. 2006. "The *Shi* 'Corpse/Personator' Ceremony in Ancient China." In *Reflections on the Dawn of Consciousness: Julian Jaynes's Bicameral Mind Theory Revisited*, edited by Marcel Kuijsten, 343-416. Henderson, Nev.: Julian Jaynes Society.

Carson, Shelley. 2013. "Creativity and Psychopathology: Shared Neurocognitive Vulnerabilities." In *Neuroscience of Creativity*, edited by Oshin Vartanian, Adam S. Bristol, and James C. Kaufman, 175-203. Cambridge, Mass.: MIT Press.

Cavalli-Sforza, Luigi Luca. 2000. *Genes, Peoples, and Languages.* New York: North Point Press.

Cedzich, Ursula-Angelika. 2001. "Corpse Deliverance, Substitute Bodies, Name Change, and Feigned Death: Aspects of Metamorphosis and Immortality in Early Medieval China." *Journal of Chinese Religions* 29:1-68.

Chambers, David John. 1996. *The Conscious Mind: In Search of a Fundamental Theory.* New York: Oxford University Press.

Champoux, François, et al. 2009. "The Neurophysiology of Early Motor Resonance." In *Mirror Neuron Systems: The Role of Mirroring Processes in Social Cognition*, edited by Jaime A. Pineda, 63-76. New York: Humana.

Chan, Alan K. L. 1991. *Two Visions of the Way: A Study of the Wang Pi and the Ho-shang-kung Commentaries on the Laozi.* Albany: State University of New York Press.

Chan, Shirley. 2014. "Oneness: Reading the 'All Things Flow in Form' (*Fanwu liu-xing*) of the Shanghai Museum Bamboo Texts." *Journal of Chinese Philosophy* 41. www.academia.edu.

Chan, Wing-tsit. 1963. *A Source Book in Chinese Philosophy.* Princeton: Princeton University Press.

Chang, Leo S., and Yu Feng. 1998. *The Four Political Treatises of the Yellow Emperor: Original Mawangdui Texts with Complete English Translation and an Introduction.* Honolulu: University of Hawaii Press.

Chess, S., and A. Thomas. 1986. *Temperament in Clinical Practice.* New York: Guilford Press.

Chia, Mantak, and Maneewan Chia. 1986. *Iron Shirt Chi Kung.* New York: Healing Dao Center.

_____. 1993. *Awaken Healing Light of the Tao.* Huntington, NY: Healing Dao Books.

Childre, Doc Lew, Howard Martin, and Donna Beach.1999. *The Heart-Math Solution.* San Francisco: HarperSanFrancisco.

Chomsky, Noam. 2002. *New Horizons in the Study of Language and Mind.* New York: Oxford University Press.

_____. 2010. "Some Simple Evo Devo Theses: How True Might They Be for Language." In *The Evolution of Human Language: Biolinguistic Perspectives*, edited by Richard K. Larson, Viviane Déprez, and Hiroko Yamakido, 45-62. Cambridge: Cambridge University Press.

Chong, Kim-chong. 2010. "Zhuangzi and Hui Shi on *Qing*." *Qinghua Journal of Chinese Studies* 40.1:21-45.

_____. 2011. "Zhuangzi's *Cheng Xin* and Its Implications for Virtue and Perspective." *Dao: A Journal of Comparative Philosophy* 10.4:427-43.

Chopra, Deepak, and Rudolph E. Tanzi. 2015. *Supergenes: Unlock the Astonishing Power of your DNA for Optimum Health and Well-Being.* New York: Harmony Books.:

Christian, David. 2008. *Big History: The Big Bang, Life on Earth, and the Rise of Humanity.* Chantilly, VA: The Teaching Company.

Claridge, Gordon. 1998. "Creativity and Madness: Clues from Modern Psychiatric Diagnosi." In *Genius and the Mind: Studies of Creativity and Temperament*, edited by Andrew Steptoe, 227-52. New York: Oxford University Press.

Clark, Margaret S., and Ian Brissette. 2000. "Relationship Beliefs and Emotions: Reciprocal Effects." In *Emotions and Beliefs: How Feelings Influence Thoughts*, edited by Nico H.Frijda, A. S. R. Manstead, and Sacha Bem, 212-40. Cambridge: Cambridge University Press.

Clay, Zanna, and Klaus Zuberbühler. 2014. "Vocal Communication and Social Awareness in Chimpanzees and Bonobos." In *The Social Origins of Language*, edited by Daniel Dor, Chris Knight, and Jerome Lewis, 141-56. New York: Oxford University Press.

Cleary, Thomas. 1984. *The Flower Ornament Scripture*. Boston: Shambhala.

Clore, Gerald L., and Karen Gasper. 2000. "Feeling Is Believing: Some Affective Influences on Belief." In *Emotions and Beliefs: How Feelings Influence Thoughts*, edited by Nico H. Frijda, A. S. R. Manstead, and Sacha Bem, 10-44. Cambridge: Cambridge University Press.

Close, Frank. 2011. *The Infinity Puzzle: Quantum Field Theory and the Hunt for an Orderly Universe*. New York: Basic Books.

Cochran, Gregory, and Henry Harpending. 2009. *The 10,000 Year Explosion: How Civilization Accelerated Human Evolution*. New York: Basic Books.

Coghill, Roger. 2000. *The Book of Magnet Healing: A Holistic Approach to Pain Relief*. New York: Simon & Schuster.

Cohen, Kenneth S. 1997. *The Way of Qigong: The Art and Science of Chinese Energy Healing*. New York: Ballantine Books.

Cohen, Mark Nathan. 1977. *The Food Crisis in Pre-History: Overpopulation and Origins of Agricultures*. New Haven: Yale University Press.

Cohn, Michael A., and Barbara L. Fredrickson. 2009. "Positive Emotions." In *Oxford Handbook of Positive Psychology*, edited by C. R. Snyder and Shane J. Lopez, 13-24. New York: Oxford University Press.

Colavito, Maria M. 1992. *The New Theogony: Mythology for the Real World*. Albany: State University of New York Press.

Cook, Constance. 1997. "Wealth and the Western Zhou." *Bulletin of the School of Oriental and African Studies* 60.2:253-94.

Cook, Francis H. 1977. *Hua-yen Buddhism: The Jewel Net of Indra*. University Park and London: Pennsylvania State University Press.

Cooke, Sam. 2009. "Memory Enhancement, Memory Erasure: The Future of Our Past." In *What's Next? Dispatches on the Future of Science*, edited by Max Brockman, 130-43. New York: Vintage Books.

Cooper, Jerrold S. 2004. "Babylonian Beginnings: The Origin of the Cuneiform Writing System in Comparative Perspective." In *The First Writing: Script Invention as History and Process*, edited by Stephen D. Houston, 71-99. Cambridge: Cambridge University Press.

Corballis, Michael C. 2002. *From Hand to Mouth: The Origins of Language*. Princeton: Princeton University Press.

_____. 2010. "Did Language Evolve Before Speech?" In *The Evolution of Human Language: Biolinguistic Perspectives*, edited by Richard K. Larson, Viviane Déprez, and Hiroko Yamakido, 115-23. Cambridge: Cambridge University Press.

_____. 2011. *The Recursive Mind: The Origins of Human Language, Thought, and Civilization*. Princeton: Princeton University Press.

_____, and Thomas Suddendorf. 2007. "Memory, Time, and Language." In *What Makes Us Human?* edited by Charles Pasternak, 17-36. New York: Oxford University Press.

Coutinho, Steve. 2004. *Zhuangzi and Early Chinese Philosophy: Vagueness, Transformation, and Paradox*. Burlington: Ashgate Press.

Cowan, C. Wesley, and Patty Jo Watson, eds. 1992. *The Origins of Agriculture: An International Perspective*. Washington, D.C.: Smithsonian Institution Press.

Cox, Brian, and Jeff Forshaw. 2011. *The Quantum Universe: And Why Anything That Can Happen, Does*. Boston: DaCapo Press.

Craig, A. D. 2008. "Interoception and Emotion: A Neuroanatomical Perspective." In *Handbook of Emotions*, edited by Michael Lewis, Jeannette M. Haviland-Jones, and Lisa Feldman Barrett, 272-88. New York: Guilford Press.

Craig, Gary. 2011. *The EFT Manual.* Santa Rosa, Calif.: Energy Psychology Press.

Craig, William L. 2001. *God, Time, and Eternity*. Dordrecht: Kluwer Academic.

Crandall, Michael M. 2010 [1983]. "On Walking Without Touching the Ground: 'Play' in the Inner Chapters of the *Zhuangzi*." In *Experimental Essays on Zhuangzi*, edited by Victor H. Mair, 99-121. Dunedin, Fla.: Three Pines Press.

Crocker, Jennifer, and Julie A. Garcia. 2009. "Downward and Upward Spirals in Intergroup Interaction: The Role of Ecosystems and Ecosystem Goals." In *Handbook of Prejudice, Stereotyping, and Discrimination*, edited by Todd D. Nelson, 229-45. New York: Taylor & Francis.

Csikszentmihalyi, Mihaly. 1975. *Beyond Boredom and Anxiety*. San Francisco: Jossey Bass.

_____. 1990. *Flow: The Psychology of Optimal Experience*. New York: Harper & Row.

_____. 1996. *Creativity: Flow and the Psychology of Discovery and Invention*. New York: HarperCollins.

_____. 1998. "Creativity and Genius: A Systems Perspective." In *Genius and the Mind: Studies of Creativity and Temperament*, edited by Andrew Steptoe, 39-66. New York: Oxford University Press.

Dacey, John S., and Kathleen Lennon. 1998. *Understanding Creativity: The Interplay of Biological, Psychological, and Social Factors*. San Francisco: Jossey-Bass.

Dalai Lama. 1999. *Ethics for the New Millennium*. New York: Riverhead Books.

_____. 2002. *How to Practice: The Way to a Meaningful Life*. New York: Pocket Books.

_____. 2005. *The Universe in a Single Atom: The Convergence of Science and Spirituality*. New York: Morgan Road Books.

Damasio, Antonio. 1999. *The Feeling of What Happens*. New York: Harcourt.

_____. 2003. *Looking for Spinoza: Joy, Sorrow, and the Feeling Brain*. New York: Harcourt.

Dames, Major Ed, and Joel Harry Newman. 2011. *Tell Me What You See: Remote Viewing Cases from the World's Premier Psychic Spy*. Hoboken: John Wiley & Sons.

Darwin, Charles. 2009 [1890]. *The Expression of the Emotions in Man and Animals*. New York: New York University Press.

Davidson, Julian M. 1984. "The Physiology of Meditation and Mystical States of Consciousness." In *Meditation: Classic and Contemporary Perspectives*, edited by Deane H. Shapiro, Jr. and Roger Walsh, 376-95. New York: Aldine.

Davidson, Richard J. 2003. "Alterations in Brain and Immune Function Produced by Mindfulness Meditation." *Psychosomatic Medicine* 65:564-70.

_____, Andrew Fox, and Ned H. Kalin. 2007. "Neural Bases of Emotion Regulation in Nonhuman Primates and Humans." In *Handbook of Emotion Regulation*, edited by James J. Gross, 47-68. New York: Guilford Press.

_____, and Anne Harrington, eds. 2002. *Visions of Compassion: Western Scientists and Tibetan Buddhists Examine Human Nature*. New York: Oxford University Press.

_____, and Sharon Begley. 2012. *The Emotional Life of Your Brain*. New York: Hudson Street Press.

Davies, Paul C. W. 2006. *The Goldilocks Enigma: Why Is the Universe Just Right for Life?* London: Allen Lane.

_____. 2007. *Cosmic Jackpot: Why Our Universe Is Just Right for Life*. Boston: Houghton Mifflin.

Dawkins, Richard. 1976. *The Selfish Gene*. New York: Oxford University Press.

_____. 1986. *The Blind Watchmaker*. New York: W. W. Norton.

De Becker, Gavin. 1997. *The Gift of Fear*. Boston: Little, Brown & Co.

De Moor, Marleen H. M., Mark Patrick Roeling, and Dorret I. Boomsma. 2013. "Creativity and Talent: Etiology of Family Clustering." In *Neuroscience of Creativity*, edited by Oshin Vartanian, Adam S. Bristol, and James C. Kaufman, 95-111. Cambridge, Mass.: MIT Press.

Deacon, Terrence W. 1998. *The Symbolic Species: The Co-Evolution of Language and the Brain*. New York: W. W. Norton.

Dediu, Dan, and Stephen C. Levinson. 2014. "The Time Frame of the Emergence of Modern Language and Its Implications." In *The Social Origins of Language*, edited by Daniel Dor, Chris Knight, and Jerome Lewis, 184-95. New York: Oxford University Press.

Dehaene, Stanislas. 2014. *Consciousness and the Brain: Deciphering How the Brain Codes Our Thoughts*. New York: Viking.

Deikman, Arthur J. 1980a [1966]. "Deautomatization and the Mystic Experience." In *Understanding Mysticism*, edited by Richard Woods, 240-60. New York: Image Books.

_____. 1980b. "Bimodal Consciousness and the the Mystic Experience." In *Understanding Mysticism*, edited by Richard Woods, 261-69. New York: Image Books.

_____. 1982. *The Observing Self: Mysticism and Psychotherapy*. Boston: Beacon Press.

DeMeyer, Jan. 2006. *Wu Yun's Way: Life and Works of an Eighth-Century Daoist Master*. Leiden: Brill.

Dennett, Daniel D. 1991. *Consciousness Explained*. Boston: Little, Brown.

Denney, Mike. 2002. "Walking the Quantum Talk." *IONS Noetic Sciences Review* 7.

Derrida, Jacques. 1981. *Positions*. Translated by Alan Bass. Chicago: University of Chicago Press.

DeSalle, Rob, and Ian Tattersall. 2012. *The Brain: Big Bangs, Behaviors, and Beliefs*. New Haven, Conn.: Yale University Press.

Despeux, Catherine. 2006. "The Six Healing Breaths." In *Daoist Body Cultivation*, edited by Livia Kohn, 37-67. Magdalena, NM: Three Pines Press.

Deutsch, David. 2004. "It from Qubit." In *Science and Ultimate Reality: Quantum Theory, Cosmology, and Complexity*, edited by John D. Barrow, P. C. W. Davies, and Charles L. Harper, 90-102. Cambridge: Cambridge University Press.

Deutsch, Eliot. 1969. *Advaita Vedanta: A Philosophical Reconstruction*. Honolulu: East-West Center Press.

Devine, Patricia G., and Lindsay B. Sharp. 2009. "Automaticity and Control in Stereotyping and Prejudice." In *Handbook of Prejudice, Stereotyping, and Discrimination*, edited by Todd D. Nelson, 61-87. New York: Taylor & Francis.

Dewey, John. 1933. *How We Think*. Boston: Heath.

DeWoskin, Kenneth J. 1982. *A Song for One or Two: Music and the Concept of Art in Ancient China*. Ann Arbor: University of Michigan, Center for Chinese Studies.

Diamond, Jared. 1998. *Guns, Germs, and Steel: The Fates of Human Societies*. New York: W. W. Norton.

Diamond, John. 1979. *Behavioral Kinesiology: How to Activate Your Thymus and Increase Your Life Energy*. New York: Harper & Row.

_____. 1985. *Life Energy: Using the Meridians to Unlock the Hidden Power of Your Emotions*. St. Paul, Minn.: Paragon House.

_____. 1986. *The Life Energy in Music*. 3 vols. Valley Cottage, NY: Archaeus Press.

Dick Steven J. 2001. *Life on Other Worlds: The 20th Century Extraterrestrial Life Debate*. Cambridge: Cambridge University Press.

Dickerson, Sally S., and Peggy M. Zoccola. 2011. "Toward a Biology of Social Support." In *Oxford Handbook of Positive Psychology*, edited by C. R. Snyder and Shane J. Lopez, 519-26. New York: Oxford University Press.

Diener, Ed, Shigehiro Oishi, and Richard E. Lucas. 2009. "Subjective Well-Being: The Science of Happiness and Life Satisfaction." In *Oxford Handbook of Positive Psychology*, edited by C. R. Snyder and Shane J. Lopez, 187-94. New York: Oxford University Press.

Dienstbier, Richard A., and Lisa M. Pytlik Zillig. 2011. "Toughness." In *Oxford Handbook of Positive Psychology*, edited by C. R. Snyder and Shane J. Lopez, 537-48. New York: Oxford University Press.

Dill, Karen E. 2009. *How Fantasy Becomes Reality: Seeing Through Media Influence*. New York: Oxford University Press.

Donald, Merlin. 1991. *Origins of the Modern Mind: Three Stages in the Evolution of Culture and Cognition*. Cambridge, Mass.: Harvard University Press.

_____. 2001. *A Mind So Rare: The Evolution of Human Consciousness*. New York: W. W. Norton.

Donaldson, O. Fred. 1993. *Playing by Heart: The Vision and Practice of Belonging*. Deerfield Beach, Fla.: Health Communications.

Donati, Marialuisa. 2008. "Beyond Synchronicity: The Worldview of Carl Gustav Jung and Wolfgang Pauli." In *Synchronicity: Multiple Perspectives on Meaningful Coincidence*, edited by Lance Storm, 42-63. Pari: Pari Publishing.

Dor, Daniel. 2014. "The Instruction of Imagination: Language and Its Evolution as a Communication Technology." In *The Social Origins of Language*, edited by Daniel Dor, Chris Knight, and Jerome Lewis, 105-25. New York: Oxford University Press.

_____, and Eva Jablonka. 2010. "Plasticity and Canalization in the Evolution of Linguistic Communication: An Evolutionary Developmental Approach." In *The Evolution of Human Language: Biolinguistic Perspectives*, edited by Richard K. Larson, Viviane Déprez, and Hiroko Yamakido, 135-47. Cambridge: Cambridge University Press.

_____, and Eva Jablonka. 2014. "Why We Need to Move from Gene-Culture Co-Evolution to Culturally Driven Co-Evolution." In *The Social Origins of Language*, edited by Daniel Dor, Chris Knight, and Jerome Lewis, 15-30. New York: Oxford University Press.

_____, et al. 2014. "Introduction: A Social Perspective on How Language Began." In *The Social Origins of Language*, edited by Daniel Dor, Chris Knight, and Jerome Lewis, 1-12. New York: Oxford University Press.

Dossey, Larry. 1993. *Healing Words: The Power of Prayer and the Practice of Medicine*. San Francisco: Harper.

_____. 1994. *Reinventing Medicine: Beyond Mind-Body to a New Era of Healing*. San Francisco: Harper.

_____. 2001. *Healing Beyond the Body: Medicine and the Infinite Reach of the Mind*. Boston: Shambhala.

_____. 2009. *The Power of Premonitions: How Knowing the Future Can Shape Our Lives*. New York: Dutton.

Dunbar, Robin. 1996. *Grooming, Gossip, and the Evolution of Language*. Cambridge, Mass.: Harvard University Press.

_____. 2007. "Why are Humans Not Just Great Apes?" In *What Makes Us Human?* edited by Charles Pasternak, 37-48. New York: Oxford University Press.

Duncan, Steven M. 1995. *A Primer of Modern Virtue Ethics*. New York: University Press of America.

Durlacher, James V. 1995. *Freedom from Fear Forever*. Mesa, Ariz.: Van Ness Publishing.

Dychtwald, Ken. 1986. *Bodymind*. New York: Penguin Putnam.

Dyer, Wayne W. 2004. *The Power of Intention: Learning to Co-create Your World Your Way*. Carlsbad, Calif.: Hay House.

Eagleman, David M. 2009. "Brain Time." In *What's Next? Dispatches on the Future of Science*, edited by Max Brockman, 155-69. New York: Vintage Books.

Eakin, Paul John. 2000. "Autobiography, Identity, and the Fictions of Memory." In *Memory, Brain, and Belief*, edited by Daniel L. Schacter and Elaine Sacrry, 290-306. Cambridge, Mass.: Harvard University Press.

Eden, Donna. 2008. *Energy Medicine for Women*. New York: Jeremy P. Tarcher.

_____, with David Feinstein. 1998. *Energy Medicine: Balancing Your Body's Energies for Optimal Health, Joy, and Vitality*. London: Penguin.

Egizii, Rita. 2011. "Daoist Principles as a Solution for Sustainable Business." *Journal of Daoist Studies* 4:190-201.

Eichenbaum, Howard, and J. Alexander Bodkin. 2000. "Belief and Knowledge as Distinct Forms of Memory." In *Memory, Brain, and Belief*, edited by Daniel L. Schacter and Elaine Sacrry, 176-207. Cambridge, Mass.: Harvard University Press.

Eichhorn, Werner. 1957. "T'ai-p'ing und T'ai-p'ing Religion." *Mitteilungen des Instituts für Orientforschung* 5: 113-40.

Ekman, Paul, Wallace V. Friesen, and Phoebe Ellsworth. 1972. *Emotion in the Human Face: Guidelines for Research and an Integration of Findings*. New York: Pergamon Press.

Elfenbein, Hillary Anger, Abigail A. Marsh, and Nalini Ambady. 2002. "Emotional Intelligence and the Recognition of Emotion from Facial Expressions." In *The Wisdom in Feeling: Psychological Processes in Emotional Intelligence*, edited by Lisa Feldman Barrett and Peter Salovey, 37-59. New York: Guilford Press.

Eliade, Mircea. 1957. "Time and Eternity in Indian Thought." *Eranos Jahrbuch* 1957:173–201.

Elias, Jason, and Katherine Ketcham. 1998. *The Five Elements of Self-Healing: Using Chinese Medicine for Maximum Immunity, Wellness, and Health*. New York: Harmony Books.

Ellis, George F. R. 2004. "True Complexity and Its Associated Ontology. " In *Science and Ultimate Reality: Quantum Theory, Cosmology, and Complexity*, edited by John D. Barrow, P. C. W. Davies, and Charles L. Harper, 607-36. Cambridge: Cambridge University Press.

Emmons, Robert A. 2006. "Spirituality." In *A Life Worth Living: Contributions to Positive Psychology*, edited by Mihaly Csikszentmihalyi and Isabella Selega Csikszentmihalyi, 62-81. New York: Oxford University Press.

_____. 2008. "Gratitude, Subjective Well-Being, and the Brain." In *The Science of Subjective Well-Being*, edited by Michael Eid and Randy J. Larsen, 469-89. New York: Guilford Press.

_____, and Anjali Mishra. 2011. "Why Gratitude Enhances Well-Being: What We Know, What We Need to Know." In *Designing Positive Psychology: Taking Stock and Moving Forward*, edited by Kennon M. Sheldon, Todd B. Kashdan, and Michael F. Steger, 248-62. New York: Oxford University Press.

Engelhardt, Ute. 1987. *Die klassische Tradition der Qi-Übungen. Eine Darstellung anhand des Tang-zeitlichen Textes Fuqi jingyi lun von Sima Chengzhen.* Wiesbaden: Franz Steiner.

_____. 2001. "*Daoyin tu* und *Yinshu*: Neue Erkenntnisse über die Übungen zur Lebenspflege in der frühen Han-Zeit." *Monumenta Serica* 49: 213-26.

Eno, Robert. 1996. "Cook Ding's Dao and the Limits of Philosophy." In *Essays on Skepticism, Relativism, and Ethics in the Zhuangzi*, edited by Paul Kjellberg and Philip J. Ivanhoe, 127-51. Albany: State University of New York Press.

Enzinger, Irmgard. 2002. "Bedeutungen des Begriffes "Herz": Das Körper-Denken in *Mengzi* und *Zhuangzi*." *Monumenta Serica* 50:95-170.

Erickson, Milton H, and Ronald A. Havens. 1985. *The Wisdom of Milton H. Erickson.* New York: Irvington Publisherss.

Eysenck, H. J. 1994. "The Measurement of Creativity." In *Dimensions of Creativity*, edited by Margaret A. Boden, 199-242. Cambridge, Mass.: MIT Press.

_____. 1995. *Genius: The Natural History of Creativity.* Cambridge: Cambridge University Press.

Eysenck, Michael W. 1997. *Anxiety and Cognition: A Unified Theory.* Hove, UK: Psychology Press.

_____. 2000. "Anxiety, Cognitive Biases, and Beliefs." In *Emotions and Beliefs: How Feelings Influence Thoughts*, edited by Nico H.Frijda, A. S. R. Manstead, and Sacha Bem, 171-84. Cambridge: Cambridge University Press.

Farthing, G. William. 1992. *The Psychology of Consciousness.* Englewood Cliffs, NJ: Prentice Hall.

Fayer, Michael D. 2010. *Absolutely Small: How Quantum Theory Explains Our Everyday World.* New York: American Management Association.

Feinstein, David. 2003. "Energy: The Missing Link." *IONS Noetic Sciences Review* 8:19-23, 36.

_____, Donna Eden, and Gary Craig. 2005. *The Promise of Energy Psychology.* New York: Penguin.

Feist, Gregory J. 2004. "The Evolved Fluid Specificity of Human Creative Talent." In *Creativity: From Potential to Realization*, edited by Robert J. Sternberg, Elena L. Grigorenko, and Jerome L. Singer, 57-82. Washington, DC: American Psychological Association.

Feldenkrais, M. 1970 [1949]. *Body and Mature Behavior.* New York: International Universities Press.

Ferreira, Pedro G. 2006. *The State of the Universe: A Primer in Modern Cosmology.* London: Phoenix.

Festinger, Leon. 1957. *A Theory of Cognitive Dissonance*. Stanford: Stanford University Press.

Feuerstein, Georg. 1998. *Tantra: The Path of Ecstasy*. Boston: Shambhala.

Fiedler, Klaus, and Herbert Bless. 2000. "The Formation of Beliefs at the Interface of Affective and Cognitive Processes." In *Emotions and Beliefs: How Feelings Influence Thoughts*, edited by Nico H.Frijda, A. S. R. Manstead, and Sacha Bem, 144-70. Cambridge: Cambridge University Press.

Filshie, Jacqueline, and Adrian White, eds. 1998. *Medical Acupuncture: A Western Scientific Approach*. New York: Churchill Livingstone.

Fink, Andreas, and Mathias Benedek. 2013. "The Creative Brain: Brain Correlates Underlying the Generation of Original Ideas." In *Neuroscience of Creativity*, edited by Oshin Vartanian, Adam S. Bristol, and James C. Kaufman, 207-32. Cambridge, Mass.: MIT Press.

Fitch, W. Tecumseh. 2010a. *The Evolution of Language*. Cambridge: Cambridge University Press.

_____. 2010b. "Three Meanings of 'Recursion': Key Distinctions for Biolinguists." In *The Evolution of Human Language: Biolinguistic Perspectives*, edited by Richard K. Larson, Viviane Déprez, and Hiroko Yamakido, 73-90. Cambridge: Cambridge University Press.

Fivush, Robyn, and Elaine Reese. 1992. "The Social Construction of Autobiographical Memory." In *Remembering Reconsidered: Ecological and Traditional Approaches to the Study of Memory*, edited by Ulric Neisser and E. Vinograd, 272-82. Cambridge: Cambridge University Press.

Ford, Julian, and Jon Wortman. 2013. *Hijacked by Your Brain: How to Free Yourself When Stress Takes Over*. Naperville, Ill.: Sourcebooks.

Ford, Kenneth W. 2004. *The Quantum World: Quantum Physics for Everyone*. Cambridge, Mass.: Harvard University Press.

Forgas, Joseph P. 2000. "Feeling Is Believing? The Role of Processing Strategies in Mediating Affective Influences on Beliefs." In *Emotions and Beliefs: How Feelings Influence Thoughts*, edited by Nico H.Frijda, A. S. R. Manstead, and Sacha Bem, 108-43. Cambridge: Cambridge University Press.

Foss, L., and K. Rothenberg. 1987. *The Second Medical Revolution: From Biomedicine to Infomedicine*. Boston: Shambhala.

Fouts, Roger, with Stephen Turkel Mills. 1998. *Next of Kin: My Conversations with Chimpanzees*. New York: Bard.

Francis, Richard C. 2011. *Epigenetics: The Ultimate Mystery of Inheritance*. New York: W. W. Norton.

Franks, David D. 2010. *Neurosociology: The Nexus between Neuroscience and Social Psychology*. New York: Springer.

Franz, Marie-Louise. 1980. *On Divination and Synchronicity: The Psychology of Meaningful Chance*. Toronto: Inner City Books.

Fraser, Chris. 2011. "Emotion and Agency in *Zhuangzi*." *Asian Philosophy* 21.1:97-121.

Fredrickson, Barbara L. 2006. "The Broaden-and-Build Theory of Positive Emotions." In *A Life Worth Living: Contributions to Positive Psychology*, edited by Mihaly Csikszentmihalyi and Isabella Selega Csikszentmihalyi, 85-103. New York: Oxford University Press.

_____. 2008. "Promoting Positive Affect." In *The Science of Subjective Well-Being*, edited by Michael Eid and Randy J. Larsen, 449-68. New York: Guilford Press.

_____. 2009. *Positivity*. New York: Crown Publishers.

_____, and Michael A. Cohn. 2008. "Positive Emotions." In *Handbook of Emotions*, edited by Michael Lewis, Jeannette M. Haviland-Jones, and Lisa Feldman Barrett, 777-96. New York: Guilford Press.

Freeman, Mark Philip. 1993. *Rewriting the Self: History, Memory, Narrative*. London: Routledge.

Freud, Sigmund. 1961 [1920]. *Beyond the Pleasure Principle*. New York: W. W. Norton.

Fried, Robert. 1993. *The Psychology and Physiology of Breathing: In Behavioral Medicine, Clinical Psychology, and Psychiatry*. With Joseph Grimaldi. New York: Plenum Press.

Frijda, Nico H. 1986. *The Emotions*. Cambridge: Cambridge University Press.

_____, and Batja Mesquita. 2000. "Beliefs through Emotions." In *Emotions and Beliefs: How Feelings Influence Thoughts*, edited by Nico H.Frijda, A. S. R. Manstead, and Sacha Bem, 45-77. Cambridge: Cambridge University Press.

Frith, Chris. 2007. *Making Up the Mind: How the Brain Creates Our Mental World*. Malden: Blackwell Publishing.

Fuller, R. Buckminster. 1992. *Cosmography: A Posthumous Scenario for the Future of Humanity*. New York: Macmillan

Fuster, Joaquin M. 2003. *Cortex and Mind: Unifying Cognition*. New York: Oxford University Press.

Gabora, Liane, and Apara Ranjan. 2013. "How Insight Emerges in a Distributed, Content-Addressalbe Memory." In *Neuroscience of Creativity*, edited by Oshin Vartanian, Adam S. Bristol, and James C. Kaufman, 19-44. Cambridge, Mass.: MIT Press.

Gach, Michael Reed, and Beth Ann Henning. 2004. *Acupressure for Emotional Healing*. New York: Bantam.

Gallese, Vittorio. 2009. "Mirror Neurons and the Neural Exploitation Hypothesis: From Embodied Simulation to Social Cognition." In *Mirror Neuron Systems: The Role of Mirroring Processes in Social Cognition*, edited by Jaime A. Pineda, 163-90. New York: Humana.

Gallistel, C. R., and Adam Philip King. 2009. *Memory and the Computational Brain: Why Cognitive Science Will Transform Neuroscience*. Malden, Mass.: Wiley-Blackwell.

Gallo, Fred P., ed. 2004. *Energy Psychology in Psychotherapy*. New York: W. W. Norton.

_____. 2000. *Energy Diagnostics and Treatment Methods*. New York: W. W. Norton.

_____, and Harry Vincenzi. 2000. *Energy Tapping*. Oakland, Calif.: New Harbinger Publications.

Gardner, Earnest. 1968. *Fundamentals of Neurology*. Philadelphia: W. B. Saunders Co.

Gardner, Howard. 1983. *Frames of Mind: The Theory of Multiple Intelligences.* New York: Basic Books.

______. 1993. *Creating Minds: An Anatomy of Creativity.* New York: Basic Books.

______. 1994. "The Creators' Patterns. " In *Dimensions of Creativity*, edited by Margaret A. Boden, 143-58. Cambridge, Mass.: MIT Press.

______. 1999. *Intelligence Reframed: Multiple Intelligences for the 21st Century.* New York: Basic Books.

Gardner, Martin. 1985. "Parapsychology and Quantum Mechanics." In *A Skeptic's Handbook of Parapsychology*, edited by Paul Kurtz, 585-98. Buffalo, NY: Prometheus Books.

Garvey, Catherine. 1990. *Play.* Cambridge, Mass.: Harvard University Press.

Gass, Robert. 1999. *Chanting: Discovering Spirit in Sound.* New York: Broadway Books.

Gauld, Alan. 2007. "Memory." In *Irreducible Mind: Toward a Psychology for the 21st Century*, edited by Edward F. Kelly and Emily Williams Kelly, 241-300. Lanham, MD: Rowan & Littlefield.

Gazzaniga, Michael S. 2008. *Human: The Science Behind What Makes Us Unique.* New York: HarperCollins.

______. 2011. *Who's in Charge? Free Will and the Science of the Brain.* New York: HarperCollins.

Gedgaugas, Nora T. 2009. *Primal Body, Primal Mind: Beyond the Paleo Diet for Total Health and a Longer Life.* Rochester, VT: Healing Arts Press.

Gentilucci, Maurizio, and Michael Corballis. 2007. "The Hominid That Talked." In *What Makes Us Human?* edited by Charles Pasternak, 49-70. New York: Oxford University Press.

Gerber, Richard. 1988. *Vibrational Medicine: New Choices for Healing Ourselves.* Santa Fe: Bear and Company.

Gilbert, Daniel. 2005. *Stumbling on Happiness.* New York: Vintage Books.

Gimello, Robert M. and Peter N. Gregory. 1983. *Studies in Ch'an and Hua-yen.* Honolulu: University of Hawaii Press, Kuroda Institute Studies in East Asian Buddhism 1.

Girardot, Norman J. 1985. "Behaving Cosmogonically in Early Taoism." In *Cosmogony and Ethical Order: New Studies in Comparative Ethics*, edited by Robin W. Lovin and Frank E. Reynolds, 67-97. Chicago: University of Chicago Press.

______. 2002. *The Victorian Translation of China: James Legge's Oriental Pilgrimage.* Berkeley: University of California Press.

______. 2008 [1983]. *Myth and Meaning in Early Taoism: The Theme of Chaos (Hundun).* Dunedin, Fla.: Three Pines Press.

Girden, Edward, and Ellen Girden. 1985. "Psychokinesis: Fifty Years Afterward." In *A Skeptic's Handbook of Parapsychology*, edited by Paul Kurtz, 129-46. Buffalo, NY: Prometheus Books.

Gladwell, Malcolm. 2008. *Outliers: The Story of Success.* New York: Little, Brown, and Co.

Gleiser, Marcelo. 2004. "The Three Origins: Cosmos, Life, and Mind." In *Science and Ultimate Reality: Quantum Theory, Cosmology, and Complexity*, edited by John D. Barrow, P. C. W. Davies, and Charles L. Harper, 637-53. Cambridge: Cambridge University Press.

_____. 2010. *A Tear at the Edge of Creation.* New York: Free Press.

Glover, John A., Royce A. Ronning, and Cecil R. Reynolds, eds. 1989. *Handbook of Creativity.* New York: Plenum Press.

Godwin, Gail. 2001. *Heart: A Personal Journey through Its Myths and Meanings.* New York: William Morrow.

Gohm, Carol L., and Gerald L. Clore. 2002. "Affect as Information: An Individual-Differences Approach." In *The Wisdom in Feeling: Psychological Processes in Emotional Intelligence*, edited by Lisa Feldman Barrett and Peter Salovey, 89-113. New York: Guilford Press.

Goleman, Daniel. 1988. *The Meditative Mind: The Variety of Meditative Experiences.* New York: Putnam.

_____. 1995. *Emotional Intelligence.* New York: Bantam Books.

_____, ed. 1997. *Healing Emotions: Conversations with the Dalai Lama on Mindfulness, Emotions, and Health.* Boston: Shambhala.

_____. 1998. *Working with Emotional Intelligence.* New York: Bantam Books.

_____. 2011. *The Brain and Emotional Intelligence: New Insights.* Northampton, Mass: More Than Sound.

_____. 2013. *Focus: The Hidden Driver of Excellence.* New York: HarperCollins.

_____, Paul Kaufman, and Michael Ray. 1992. *The Creative Spirit.* New York: Dutton.

Goodheart, George J. 1989. *You'll Be Better: The Story of Applied Kinesiology.* Geneva, OH: AK Printing.

Graham, A. C. 1960. *The Book of Lieh-tzu.* London: A. Murray.

_____. 1969. "Chuang-tzu's 'Essay on Seeing Things as Equal'." *History of Religions* 9:137-159.

_____. 1981. *Chuang-tzu: The Seven Inner Chapters and Other Writings from the Book of Chuang-tzu.* London: George Allen & Unwin.

_____. 1986. *Yin-Yang and the Nature of Correlative Thinking.* Singapore: The Institute for East Asian Philosophies.

_____. 1989. *Disputers of the Tao: Philosophical Argument in Ancient China.* La Salle, Ill.: Open Court Publishing Company.

Green, Barry, with W. Timothy Gallwey. 1986. *The Inner Game of Music.* Garden City, NY: Anchor Press/Doubleday.

Greene, Brian. 2003. *The Elegant Universe: Superstrings, Hidden Dimensions, and the Quest for the Ultimate Theory.* New York: W. W. Norton.

_____. 2004. *The Fabric of the Cosmos: Space, Time, and the Texture of Reality.* New York: Alfred A. Knopf.

_____. 2011. *The Hidden Reality: Parallel Universes and the Deep Laws of the Cosmos*. New York: Alfred A. Knopf.

Greenspan, Stanley I., and Stuart G. Shanker. 2004. *The First Idea: How Symbols, Language, and Intelligence Evolved from Our Primate Ancestors to Modern Humans*. Cambridge, Mass.: Da Capo Press.

Greer, Scott. 2006. "A Knowing Noos and a Slippery Psyche: Jaynes's Recipe for an Unnatural Theory of Consciousness." In *Reflections on the Dawn of Consciousness: Julian Jaynes's Bicameral Mind Theory Revisited*, edited by Marcel Kuijsten, 233-63. Henderson, Nev.: Julian Jaynes Society.

Greyson, Bruce. 2000. "Near-Death Experiences." In *Varieties of Anomalous Experience: Examining the Scientific Evidence*, edited by Etzel Cardeña, Steven Jay Lynn, and Stanley Krippner, 315-52. Washington, DC: American Psychological Association.

Griffin, Donald R. 1976. *The Question of Animal Awareness: Evolutionary Continuity of Mental Experience*. New York: Rockefeller University Press.

Griffin, Donald R. 1984. *Animal Thinking*. Cambridge, Mass.: Harvard University Press.

Grof, Stanislav. 1985. *Beyond the Brain*. Albany: State University of New York Press.

_____, with Hal Zina Bennett. 1992. *The Holotropic Mind*. San Francisco: Harper.

Gross, James J. 2008. "Emotion Regulation." In *Handbook of Emotions*, edited by Michael Lewis, Jeannette M. Haviland-Jones, and Lisa Feldman Barrett, 497-512. New York: Guilford Press.

_____, and Oliver P. John. 2002. "Wise Emotion Regulation." In *The Wisdom in Feeling: Psychological Processes in Emotional Intelligence*, edited by Lisa Feldman Barrett and Peter Salovey, 297-318. New York: Guilford Press.

Groves, J. Randall. 2006. "Daoism, Freedom, and Jazz Improvisation: A Rational Reconstruction of Chuang Tzu's Cook Ting Passage." *Interdisciplinary Humanities* 2006:99-108.

Gruen, Sara. 2010. *Ape House*. New York: Spiegel and Grau.

Gu, Ming Dong. 2009. "A Theory of the Dao and Taiji: A Chinese Model of the Mind." *Journal of Chinese Philosophy* 36.2:157-75.

Hamilton, John. 2006. "Auditory Hallucinations in Nonverbal Quadriplegics." In *Reflections on the Dawn of Consciousness: Julian Jaynes's Bicameral Mind Theory Revisited*, edited by Marcel Kuijsten, 141-66. Henderson, Nev.: Julian Jaynes Society.

Hammond, Richard. 2008. *The Unknown Universe: The Origin of the Universe, Quantum Gravity, Wormholes, and Other Things Science Still Can't Explain*. Franklin Lakes: New Page Books.

Hanna, Thomas. 1988. *Somatics: Reawakening the Mind's Control of Movement, Flexibility, and Health*. Cambridge, Mass.: Perseus Books.

Hansel, C. E. M. 1985. "The Search for a Demonstration of ESP." In *A Skeptic's Handbook of Parapsychology*, edited by Paul Kurtz, 97-128. Buffalo, NY: Prometheus Books.

Hansen, Chad. 1992. *A Daoist Theory of Chinese Thought: A Philosophical Interpretation*. New York: Oxford University Press.

Happold, F. C. 1970. *Mysticism: A Study and an Anthology*. Baltimore: Penguin.

Harbsmeier, Christoph. 2004. "The Semantics of *Qing* in Pre-Buddhist Chinese." In *Love and Emotions in Traditional Chinese Literature*, edited by Halvor Eifring, 69-149 Leiden: E. Brill.

Hardy, Alister Clavering. 1979. *The Spiritual Nature of Man: A Study of Contemporary Religious Experience*. New York: Oxford University Press.

Hariri, Ahmad R, and Erika E. Forbes. 2007. "Genetics of Emotion Regulation." In *Handbook of Emotion Regulation*, edited by James J. Gross, 110-32. New York: Guilford Press.

Harman, Willis, and Howard Rheingold. 1984. *Higher Creativity: Liberating the Unconscious for Breakthrough Insights*. Los Angeles: Jeremy P. Tarcher.

Harmon-Jones, Eddie. 2000. "A Cognitive Dissonance Theory Perspective on the Role of Emotion in the Maintenance and Change of Beliefs and Attitudes." In *Emotions and Beliefs: How Feelings Influence Thoughts*, edited by Nico H.Frijda, A. S. R. Manstead, and Sacha Bem, 185-211. Cambridge: Cambridge University Press.

Haroche, Serge. 2004. "Breeding Non-local Schrödinger's Cats: A Thought-Experiment to Explore the Quantum-Classical Boundary." In *Science and Ultimate Reality: Quantum Theory, Cosmology, and Complexity*, edited by John D. Barrow, P. C. W. Davies, and Charles L. Harper, 280-305. Cambridge: Cambridge University Press.

Harper, Donald. 1998. *Early Chinese Medical Manuscripts: The Mawangdui Medical Manuscripts*. London: Wellcome Asian Medical Monographs.

Harris, Eugene E. 2015. *Ancestors in Our Genome: The New Science of Human Evolution*. New York: Oxford University Press.

Harrison, Edward R. 1985. *Masks of the Universe*. New York: Macmillan.

Harth, Erich. 1993. *The Creative Loop: How the Brain Makes a Mind*. Reading, Mass.: Addison-Wesley.

Hatfield, Elaine, John T. Cacioppo, and Richard L. Rapson. 1994. *Emotional Contagion*. Cambridge: Cambridge University Press.

Hawking, Stephen W. 2001. *The Universe in a Nutshell*. New York: Bantam Books.

_____, and Leonard Mlodinow. 2010. *The Grand Design*. New York: Bantam Books.

_____, and Roger Penrose. 2000. *The Nature of Space and Time*. Princeton: Princeton University Press.

Hawkes, David. 1959. *Ch'u Tz'u: The Songs of the South*. Oxford: Clarendon Press.

Hawkins, David R. 2001. *The Eye of the I*. Sedona: Veritas.

_____. 2002. *Power vs. Force: The Hidden Determinants of Human Behavior*. Carlsbad, Calif: Hay House.

_____. 2006. *Transcending the Levels of Consciousness: The Stairway to Enlightenment*. Sedona: Veritas.

_____. 2008. *Reality, Spirituality, and Modern Man*. Toronto: Axial Publications.

Hebb, Donald O. 1949. *The Organization of Behavior: A Neurophysiological Theory*. Hoboken: John Wiley & Sons.

Henderson, Sheila J. 2004. "Inventors: The Ordinary Genius Next Door." In *Creativity: From Potential to Realization*, edited by Robert J. Sternberg, Elena L. Grigorenko, and Jerome L. Singer, 103-26. Washington, DC: American Psychological Association.

Hendrischke, Barbara. 2000. "Early Daoist Movements." In *Daoism Handbook*, edited by Livia Kohn, 134-64. Leiden: Brill.

_____. 2006. *The Scripture on Great Peace: The Taipingjing and the Beginnings of Daoism*. Berkeley: University of California Press.

Henricks, Robert. 2000. *Lao Tzu's Tao Te Ching: A Translation of the Startling New Documents Found at Guodian*. New York: Columbia University Press.

Henshaw, John M. 2012. *A Tour of the Senses: How Your Brain Interprets the World*. Baltimore: Johns Hopkins University Press.

Hickok, Gregory. 2014. *The Myth of Mirror Neurons: The Real Neuroscience of Communication and Cognition*. New York: W. W. Norton.

Hodder, Ian. 1998. "Creative Thought: A Long-term Perspective." In *Creativity in Human Evolution and Prehistory*, edited by Steven Mithen, 61-77. London: Routledge.

Homann, Rolf. 1971. *Die wichtigsten Körpergottheiten im Huang-t'ing-ching*. Göppingen: Alfred Kümmerle.

Hood, Bruce M. 2012. *The Self Illusion: How the Social Brain Creates Identity*. New York: Oxford University Press.

Hotz, Robert Lee. 2008. "How Alphabets Shape the Brain." *Wall Street Journal*, May 2, A10.

Huang, Yong. 2005. "A Copper Rule versus the Golden Rule: A Daoist-Confucian Proposal for Global Ethics." *Philosophy East & West* 55.3:394-425

_____. 2010. "The Ethics of Difference in the *Zhuangzi*." *Journal of the American Academy of Religion* 78.1:65-99.

Huizinga, Johan. 1955. *Homo Ludens: A Study of the Play Element in Culture*. Boston: Beacon Press.

Hutschnecker, Arnold A. 1978 [1951]. *The Will to Live*. New York: Cornerstone Library.

Huxley, Aldous. 1963. *The Doors of Perception and Heaven and Hell*. New York: Vintage Books.

Hyman, Ray. 1985. "A Critical Historical Overview of Psychical Research." In *A Skeptic's Handbook of Parapsychology*, edited by Paul Kurtz, 3-96. Buffalo, NY: Prometheus Books.

Iacoboni, Marco. 2008. *Mirroring People*. New York: Farrar, Straus, and Giroux.

_____. 2009a. *Mirroring People: The Science of Empathy and How We Connect with Others*. New York: Farrar, Straus, and Giroux.

_____. 2009b. "The Problem of Other Minds Is Not a Problem: Mirror Neurons and Intersubjectivity." In *Mirror Neuron Systems: The Role of Mirroring Processes in Social Cognition*, edited by Jaime A. Pineda, 121-34. New York: Humana.

Irwin, H. J. 1994. *An Introduction to Parapsychology*. Jefferson, N.C.: McFarland & Co.

Isen, Alice M. 2011. "A Role for Neuropsychology in Understanding the Facilitating Influence of Positive Affect on Social Behavior and Cognitive Processes." In *Oxford Handbook of Positive Psychology*, edited by C. R. Snyder and Shane J. Lopez, 503-18. New York: Oxford University Press.

Ishida, Hidemi. 1989. "Body and Mind: The Chinese Perspective." In *Daoist Meditation and Longevity Techniques*, edited by Livia Kohn, 41-70. Ann Arbor: University of Michigan, Center for Chinese Studies Publications.

Ivanhoe, Philip J. 1993. "Zhuangzi on Skepticism, Skill, and the Ineffable Dao." *Journal of the American Academy of Religion* 61.4:639-54.

_____. 1996. "Was Zhuangzi a Relativist?" In *Essays on Skepticism, Relativism, and Ethics in the Zhuangzi*, edited by Paul Kjellberg and Philip J. Ivanhoe, 196-214. Albany: State University of New York Press.

Iyengar, B. K. S. 1976. *Light on Yoga*. New York: Schocken Books.

Jablonka, Eva, and Geva Rechav. 1996. "The Evolution of Language in Light of the Evolution of Literacy." In *Origins of Language*, edited by Jürgen Trabant, 70-88. Budapest: Collegium Budapest.

Jackowicz, Stephen. 2006. "Ingestion, Digestion, and Regestation: The Complexities of the Absorption of *Qi*." In *Daoist Body Cultivation*, edited by Livia Kohn, 68-90. Magdalena, NM: Three Pines Press.

_____. 2011. "Daoist Incantations for Acupuncture." *Journal of Daoist Studies* 4:63-79.

Jahnke, Roger. 2002. *The Healing Promise of Qi: Creating Extraordinary Wellness Through Qigong and Tai Chi*. New York: Contemporary Books.

James, William. 1936 [1902]. *The Varieties of Religious Experience*. New York: The Modern Library.

Jarrett, Lonny S. 2000. *Nourishing Destiny: The Inner Tradition of Chinese Medicine*. Stockbridge, Mass.: Spirit Path Press.

_____. 2003. *The Clinical Practice of Chinese Medicine*. Stockbridge, Mass.: Spirit Path Press.

_____. 2006. "Acupuncture and Spiritual Realization." In *Daoist Body Cultivation*, edited by Livia Kohn, 19-36. Magdalena, NM: Three Pines Press.

Jaspers, Karl. 1953. *The Origin and Goal of History*. New Haven, Conn.: Yale University Press.

Jaynes, Julian. 1990 [1976]. *The Origins of Consciousness in the Breakdown of the Bicameral Mind*. Boston: Houghton Mifflin.

_____. 2006a. "Verbal Hallucinations and Preconscious Mentality." In *Reflections on the Dawn of Consciousness: Julian Jaynes's Bicameral Mind Theory Revisited*, edited by Marcel Kuijsten, 75-94. Henderson, Nev.: Julian Jaynes Society.

_____. 2006b. "The Ghost of a Flea: Visions of William Blake." In *Reflections on the Dawn of Consciousness: Julian Jaynes's Bicameral Mind Theory Revisited*, edited by Marcel Kuijsten, 71-74. Henderson, Nev.: Julian Jaynes Society.

______. 2006c. "Dragons of the Shang Dynasty: The Hidden Faces." In *Reflections on the Dawn of Consciousness: Julian Jaynes's Bicameral Mind Theory Revisited*, edited by Marcel Kuijsten, 337-42. Henderson, Nev.: Julian Jaynes Society.

Jensen, Clayne R., and Gordon W. Schultz. 1977. *Applied Kinesiology: The Scientific Study of Human Performance*. New York: McGraw-Hill.

Jochim, Chris. 1998. "Just Say No to "No Self" in *Zhuangzi*." In *Wandering at Ease in the Zhuangzi*, edited by Roger Ames, 34-74. Albany: State University of New York Press.

Johansson, Sverker. 2014. "How Can a Social Theory of Language Evolution Be Grounded in Evidence?" In *The Social Origins of Language*, edited by Daniel Dor, Chris Knight, and Jerome Lewis, 56-64. New York: Oxford University Press.

Johnson, Jerry Alan. 2000. *Chinese Medical Qigong Therapy: A Comprehensive Clinical Text*. Pacific Grove: International Institute of Medical Qigong.

______. 2014a. *The Secret Teachings of Chinese Energetic Medicine: Volume 1: Energetic Anatomy and Physiology*. Pacific Grove: International Institute of Medical Qigong.

______. 2014b. *The Secret Teachings of Chinese Energetic Medicine: Volume 2: Energetic Alchemy, Dao Yin Therapy, Healing Qi Deviations, Spirit Pathology*. Pacific Grove: International Institute of Medical Qigong.

______. 2014c. *The Secret Teachings of Chinese Energetic Medicine: Volume 3: Developing Intuitive and Perceptual Awareness, Energetic Foundations, Treatment Principles, and Clinical Applications*. Pacific Grove: International Institute of Medical Qigong.

Johnson, Kendall.1975. *The Living Aura: Radiation Field Photography and the Kirlian Effect*. New York: Hawthorn Books.

Johnson, Marcia K., and Carol L. Raye. 2000. "Cognitive and Brain Mechanisms of False Memories and Beliefs." In *Memory, Brain, and Belief*, edited by Daniel L. Schac-ter and Elaine Sacrry, 35-86. Cambridge, Mass.: Harvard University Press.

Johnstone, Keith. 1985. *Improvisation and the Theater*. New York: Theater Arts Books.

Jolly, Alison. 1999. *Lucy's Legacy: Sex and Intelligence in Human Evolution*. Cambridge, Mass.: Harvard University Press.

Jones, David, and John Culliney. 1999. "The Fractal Self and the Organization of Nature: The Daoist Sage and Chaos Theory." *Zygon: Journal of Science and Religion* 4:643-54.

Joordens, Steve. 2011. *Memory and the Human Lifespan*. Chantilly, VA: The Great Courses.

Joseph, R. 1993. *The Naked Neuron: Evolution and the Languages of the Body and Brain*. New York: Plenum Press.

Jullien, François. 1995. *The Propensity of Things: Toward a History of Efficacy in China*. New York: Zone Books.

______. 2007. *Vital Nourishment: Departing from Happiness*. Translated by Arthur Goldhammer. New York: Zone Books.

Jung, Carl G. 1955. *The Interpretation of Nature and the Psyche: Synchronicity*. London: Routledge & Kegan Paul.

_____. 1973 [1952]. *Synchronicity: An Acausal Connecting Principle.* Princeton: Princeton University Press.

_____, and Wolfgang Pauli. 1955. *The Interpretation of Nature and the Psyche.* New York: Pantheon Books.

Jung, Rex E., and Richard J. Haier. 2013. "Creativity and Intelligence: Brain Networks That Link and Differentiate the Expression of Genius." In *Neuroscience of Creativity*, edited by Oshin Vartanian, Adam S. Bristol, and James C. Kaufman, 233-54. Cambridge, Mass.: MIT Press.

Kabat-Zinn, Jon. 2005. *Coming to Our Senses: Healing Ourselves and the World through Mindfulness.* New York: Hyperion.

Kafatos, Menas, and Robert Nadeau. 2000. *The Conscious Universe: Parts and Whole in Modern Physical Theory.* Berlin: Springer Verlag.

Kaku, Michio. 2006. *Parallel Worlds: A Journey through Creation, Higher Dimensions, and the Future of the Cosmos.* New York: Anchor Books.

_____. 2008. *Physics of the Impossible: A Scientific Exploration into the World of Phrasers, Force Fields, Teleportation, and Time Travel.* New York: Doubleday.

Kalinowski, Marc. 1985. "La transmission du dispositif des Neuf Palais sous les Six-dynasties." In *Tantric and Taoist Studies*, edited by Michel Strickmann, 3:773-811. Brussels: Institut Belge des Hautes Etudes Chinoises.

Kaptchuk, Ted J. 2000 [1983]. *The Web that Has No Weaver: Understanding Chinese Medicine.* New York: Congdon & Weed.

Karagulla, Shafica, and Dora van Gelder Kunz. 1989. *The Chakras and Human Energy Fields.* Wheaton, Ill.: Theosophical Publishing House.

Karp, Gerald. 2014. *Cell Biology.* Hoboken: John Wiley & Sons.

Katz, Debra Lynne. 2008. *Extraordinary Psychic.* Woodbury, Minn.; Llewellyn Publications.

Kaufman, James C., and John Baer. 2004. "Hawking's Haiku, Madonna's Math: Why It Is Hard to Be Creative in Every Room of the House." In *Creativity: From Potential to Realization*, edited by Robert J. Sternberg, Elena L. Grigorenko, and Jerome L. Singer, 3-20. Washington, DC: American Psychological Association.

_____, and Robert J. Sternberg, eds. 2006. *Handbook of Creativity.* Cambridge: Cambridge University Press.

Keightley, David N. 1989. "The Origins of Writing in China: Scripts and Cultural Contexts." In *The Origins of Writing*, edited by Wayne M. Senner, 171-202. Lincoln: University of Nebraska Press.

_____. 1996. "Art, Ancestors, and the Origins of Writing." *Representations* 56:68-95.

Keinänen, Mia, and Howard Gardner. 2004. "Vertical and Horizontal Mentoring for Creativity." In *Creativity: From Potential to Realization*, edited by Robert J. Sternberg, Elena L. Grigorenko, and Jerome L. Singer, 169-94. Washington, DC: American Psychological Association.

Kelly, Edward F. and Michael Grosso. 2007. "Genius." In *Irreducible Mind: Toward a Psychology for the 21st Century*, edited by Edward F. Kelly and Emily Williams Kelly, 423-93. Lanham, MD: Rowan & Littlefield.

Kendall, Donald E. 2002. *Dao of Chinese Medicine: Understanding an Ancient Healing Art.* New York: Oxford University Press.

Keysers, Christian. 2006. "Towards a Unifying Neural Theory of Social Cognition." *Progress in Brain Research* 156:379-401.

_____. 2009. "Mirror Neurons: Are We Ethical by Nature?" In *What's Next? Dispatches on the Future of Science*, edited by Max Brockman, 16-24. New York: Vintage Books.

_____. 2011. *The Empathic Brain: How the Discovery of Mirror Neurons Changes Our Understanding of Human Nature.* Lexington, KY: Social Brain Press.

_____, and Valeria Gazzola. 2009. "Unifying Social Cognition." In *Mirror Neuron Systems: The Role of Mirroring Processes in Social Cognition*, edited by Jaime A. Pineda, 3-37. New York: Humana.

Khalsa, Dharma Singh, and Cameron Stauth. 2001. *Meditation as Medicine.* New York: Pocket Books.

Kilner, Walter J. 1965 [1911]. *The Human Aura.* New Hyde Park, NJ: University Books.

King, Deborah. 2011. *Be Your Own Shaman: Heal Yourself and Others with 21st-Century Energy Medicine.* Carlsbad, Calif.: Hay House.

King, Laura A. 2008. "Interventions for Enhancing Subjective Well-Being: Can We Make People Happier and Should We?" In *The Science of Subjective Well-Being*, edited by Michael Eid and Randy J. Larsen, 431-48. New York: Guilford Press.

King, Winston L. 1980. *Theravada Meditation: The Buddhist Transformation of Yoga.*University Park: Pennsylvania State University Press.

Kingston, Karen. 1997. *Creating Sacred Space with Feng Shui.* New York: Broadway Books.

Kirby, Simon. 1999. *Function, Selection, and Innateness: The Emergence of Language Universals.* New York: Oxford University Press.

Klein, Melanie. 1957. *Envy and Gratitude.* New York: Basic Books.

Klein, Richard. 2005. "Hominin Dispersal in the Old World." In *The Human Past: World Prehistory and the Development of Human Societies*, edited by Chris Scarre, 84-123. London: Thames & Hudson.

Knoblock, John, and Jeffrey Riegel. 2000. *The Annals of Lü Buwei.* Stanford: Stanford University Press.

Koestler, Arthur. 1972. *The Roots of Coincidence.* London: Hutchinson.

Kohn, Livia. 1989a. "Taoist Insight Meditation: The Tang Practice of *Neiguan*." In *Taoist Meditation and Longevity Techniques*, edited by Livia Kohn, 193-224. Ann Arbor: University of Michigan, Center for Chinese Studies.

_____. 1989b. "Guarding the One: Concentrative Meditation in Taoism." In *Taoist Meditation and Longevity Techniques*, edited by Livia Kohn, 123-56. Ann Arbor: University of Michigan, Center for Chinese Studies.

_____. 1990a. "Transcending Personality: From Ordinary to Immortal Life." *Taoist Resources* 2.2:1-22.

_____. 1990b. "Eternal Life in Taoist Mysticism." *Journal of the American Oriental Society* 110:622-40.

_____. 1991. "Taoist Visions of the Body." *Journal of Chinese Philosophy* 18: 227-52.

_____. 1992. "Selfhood and Spontaneity in Ancient Chinese Thought." In *Selves, People, and Persons,* edited by Leroy Rouner, 123-38. South Bend: University of Notre Dame Press.

_____. 1993. *The Taoist Experience: An Anthology*. Albany: State University of New York Press.

_____. 1995. *Laughing at the Tao: Debates among Buddhists and Taoists in Medieval China*. Princeton: Princeton University Press.

_____. 1998a. *God of the Dao: Lord Lao in History and Myth*. University of Michigan, Center for Chinese Studies.

_____. 1998b. "Mind and Eyes: Sensory and Spiritual Experience in Taoist Mysticism." *Monumenta Serica* 46: 129-56.

_____. 2000a. "Doumu: The Mother of the Dipper." *Ming Qing Yanjiu* 8: 149-95.

_____. 2000b. "The Northern Celestial Masters." In *Daoism Handbook*, edited by Livia Kohn, 283-308. Leiden: Brill.

_____. 2002. *Living with the Dao: Conceptual Issues in Daoist Practice*. Cambridge, Mass.: Three Pines Press, E-Dao series.

_____. 2003. *Monastic Life in Medieval Daoism: A Cross-Cultural Perspective*. Honolulu: University of Hawaii Press.

_____. 2004a. *Cosmos and Community: The Ethical Dimension of Daoism*. Cambridge, Mass.: Three Pines Press.

_____. 2004b. *Supplement to Cosmos and Community*. Cambridge, Mass.: Three Pines Press, E-Dao Series.

_____. 2005. *Health and Long Life: The Chinese Way*. Cambridge, Mass.: Three Pines Press.

_____, ed. 2006. *Daoist Body Cultivation: Traditional Models and Contemporary Practices*. Magdalena, NM: Three Pines Press.

_____. 2007. *Daoist Mystical Philosophy: The Scripture of Western Ascension*. Magdalena, NM: Three Pines Press.

_____. 2008a. *Chinese Healing Exercises: The Tradition of Daoyin*. Honolulu: University of Hawai'i Press.

_____. 2008b. *Meditation Works: In the Daoist, Buddhist, and Hindu Traditions*. Magdalena, NM: Three Pines Press.

_____. 2009. *Readings in Chinese Mysticism*. Dunedin, Fla: Three Pines Press.

______. 2010a. *Sitting in Oblivion: The Heart of Daoist Meditation.* Dunedin, Fla.: Three Pines Press.

______. 2010b. *Daoist Dietetics: Food for Immortality.* Dunedin, Fla.: Three Pines Press.

______. 2011. *Chuang-tzu: The Tao of Perfect Happiness. Selections Annotated and Explained.* Woodstock, VT: Skylight Paths Press.

______. 2012. *A Source Book in Chinese Longevity.* St. Petersburg, FL: Three Pines Press.

______. 2014. *Zhuangzi: Text and Context.* St. Petersburg, Fla.: Three Pines Press.

______. 2015. "Forget or Not Forget? The Neurophysiology of *Zuowang.*" In *New Visions of the Zhuangzi*, edited by Livia Kohn, 161-79. St. Petersburg, Fla.: Three Pines Press.

Kondo, Marie. 2014. *The Life-changing Magic of Tidying Up: The Japanese Art of Decluttering and Organizing.* Berkeley: Ten Speed Press.

Krippner, Stanley, and Daniel Rubin, eds. 1974. *Galaxies of Life: A Conference on Kirlian Photography, Acupuncture, and the Human Aura.* Garden City, NJ: Anchor Books.

______, and Jeanne Achterberg. 2000. "Anomalous Healing Experiences." In *Varieties of Anomalous Experience: Examining the Scientific Evidence*, edited by Etzel Cardeña, Steven Jay Lynn, and Stanley Krippner, 353-96. Washington, DC: American Psychological Association.

Kroll, Paul W. 1996. "Body Gods and Inner Vision: *The Scripture of the Yellow Court.* In *Religions of China in Practice*, edited by Donald S. Lopez Jr., 149-55. Princeton: Princeton University Press.

Kubie, Lawrence S. 1976. "Creation and Neurosis." In *The Creativity Question*, edited by Albert Rothenberg and Carl A. Hausman, 143-48. Durham, NC: Duke University Press.

Kuhn, Thomas S. 1970. *The Structure of Scientific Revolutions.* Chicago: University of Chicago Press.

Kuijsten, Marcel. 2006. "Consciousness, Hallucinations, and the Bicameral Mind: Three Decades of New Research." In *Reflections on the Dawn of Consciousness: Julian Jaynes's Bicameral Mind Theory Revisited*, edited by Marcel Kuijsten, 95-140. Henderson, Nev.: Julian Jaynes Society.

Kunz, Dora. 1991. *The Personal Aura.* Wheaton, Ill.: Theosophical Publishing House.

Kupperman, Joel. 1996. "Spontaneity and Education of the Emotions in the *Zhuangzi.*" In *Essays on Skepticism, Relativism, and Ethics in the Zhuangzi*, edited by Paul Kjellberg and Philip J. Ivanhoe, 183-95. Albany: State University of New York Press.

Kuriyama, Shigehisa. 1999. *The Expressiveness of the Body and the Divergence of Greek and Chinese Medicine.* New York: Zone Books.

Kwok, Sun. 2013. *Stardust: The Cosmic Seeds of Life.* New York: Springer.

Lai, Karyn Lynne. 2006. "Philosophy and Philosophical Reasoning in the *Zhuangzi*: Dealing with Plurality." *Journal of Chinese Philosophy* 33.3:365-74.

Lakoff, George, and Mark Johnson. 1980. *Metaphors We Live By.* Chicago: University of Chicago Press.

Lambrou, Peter, and George Pratt. 2000. *Instant Emotional Healing.* New York: Broadway Books.

Lane, Richard D., and Lynn Nadel. 2000. *Cognitive Neuroscience of Emotion.* New York: Oxford University Press.

Larre, Claude, and Elisabeth Rochat de la Vallee. 1996. *Eight Extraordinary Vessels.* Cambridge: Monkey Press.

Larsen, Jeff T., et al. 2008. "The Psychophysiology of Emotions." In *Handbook of Emotions,* edited by Michael Lewis, Jeannette M. Haviland-Jones, and Lisa Feldman Barrett, 180-210. New York: Guilford Press.

Larsen, Randy J., and Zvjezdana Prizmic. 2008. "Regulation of Emotional Well-Being: Overcoming the Hedonic Treadmill." In *The Science of Subjective Well-Being,* edited by Michael Eid and Randy J. Larsen, 458-89. New York: Guilford Press.

Larson, Cynthia Sue. 2003. *Aura Advantage: How the Colors in Your Aura Can Help You Attain Your Desires and Attract Success.* Las Vegas: Lightworker Publications.

Lash, John. 1993. *The Tai Chi Journey.* Shaftesbury, Dorset: Element.

Lazarus, R. S. 1966. *Psychological Stress and the Coping Process.* New York: McGraw-Hill

_____. 1991. *Emotion and Adaptation.* New York: Oxford University Press.

Le Blanc, Charles. 1986. "A Re-examination of the Myth of Huang-ti." *Journal of Chinese Religions* 13-14:45-64.

Leadbeater, C. W. 1972 [1927]. *The Chakras: A Monograph.* Wheaton, Ill.: Theosophical Publishing House.

Leakey, Richard. 1994. *The Origin of Humankind.* New York: Basic Books.

_____, and Roger Lewin. 1977. *Origins: The Emergence and Evolution of Our Species and Its Possible Future.* New York: E. P. Dutton.

Leary, Mark R., and Jennifer Guadagno. 2011. "The Role of Hypo-egoic Self-Processes in Optimal Functioning and Subjective Well-Being." In *Designing Positive Psychology: Taking Stock and Moving Forward,* edited by Kennon M. Sheldon, Todd B. Kashdan, and Michael F. Steger, 135-46. New York: Oxford University Press.

Leary, Timothy. 1970. *The Politics of Ecstasy.* New York: Paladin.

Leboyer, Frederick. 1975. *Birth Without Violence.* New York: Alfred A. Knopf.

LeDoux, Joseph E., and Elizabeth A. Phelps. 2008. "Emotional Networks in the Brain." In *Handbook of Emotions,* edited by Michael Lewis, Jeannette M. Haviland-Jones, and Lisa Feldman Barrett, 159-79. New York: Guilford Press.

Lee, Jung H. 2000. "Finely Aware and Richly Responsible: The Daoist Imperative." *Journal of the American Academy of Religion* 68.3:511-36.

Lemerise, Elizabeth A. and Kenneth A. Dodge. 2008. "The Development of Anger and Hostile Interactions." In *Handbook of Emotions,* edited by Michael Lewis, Jeannette M. Haviland-Jones, and Lisa Feldman Barrett, 630-41. New York: Guilford Press.

Leontiev, Dmitry. 2006. "Positive Personality Development: Approaching Personal Autonomy." In *A Life Worth Living: Contributions to Positive Psychology*, edited by Mihaly Csikszentmihalyi and Isabella Selega Csikszentmihalyi, 49-61. New York: Oxford University Press.

Levinovitz, Alan. 2012. "The *Zhuangzi* and *You* 遊: Defining an Ideal without Contradiction." *Dao: A Journal of Comparative Philosophy* 11.4:479-96.

Levy, Susan L., and Carol Lehr, C. 1996. *Your Body Can Talk: The Art and Application of Clinical Kinesiology*. Prescott: Hohm Press.

Lewis, Jerome. 2014. "BaYaka Pygmy Multi-Modal and Mimetic Communication Traditions." In *The Social Origins of Language*, edited by Daniel Dor, Chris Knight, and Jerome Lewis, 77-91. New York: Oxford University Press.

Lewis, Mark Edward. 2006. *The Construction of Space in Early China*. Albany: State University of New York Press.

Libet, Benjamin. 1985. "Unconscious Cerebral Initiative and the Role of Conscious Will in Voluntary Action." *Behavioral and Brain Sciences* 8:529-66.

______. 2004. *Mind Time: The Temporal Factor in Consciousness*. Cambridge, Mass.: Harvard University Press.

Lieberman, J. Nina. 1977. *Playfulness: Its Relationship to Imagination and Creativity*. New York: Academic Press.

Lieberman, Philip. 1984. *The Biology and Evolution of Language*. Cambridge, Mass.: Harvard University Press.

______. 2010. "The Creative Capacity of Language, In What Manner It Is Unique, and Who Had It?" In *The Evolution of Human Language: Biolinguistic Perspectives*, edited by Richard K. Larson, Viviane Déprez, and Hiroko Yamakido, 163-75. Cambridge: Cambridge University Press.

Liedloff, Jean. 1986. *The Continuum Concept*. Harmondsworth: Penguin.

Lilly, John C. 1973. *The Center of the Cyclone: An Autobiography of Inner Space*. New York: Bantam Books.

Limber, John. 2006. "Language and Consciousness: Jaynes's 'Preposterous Idea' Reconsidered." In *Reflections on the Dawn of Consciousness: Julian Jaynes's Bicameral Mind Theory Revisited*, edited by Marcel Kuijsten, 169-202. Henderson, Nev.: Julian Jaynes Society.

Lincoln, Bruce. 1975. "The Indo-European Myth of Creation." *History of Religions* 15: 121-45.

Linde, Andrei. 2004. "Inflation, Quantum Cosmology, and the Anthropic Principle." In *Science and Ultimate Reality: Quantum Theory, Cosmology, and Complexity*, edited by John D. Barrow, P. C. W. Davies, and Charles L. Harper, 426-58. Cambridge: Cambridge University Press.

Lip, Evelyn. 1995. *Feng Shui: Environments of Power. A Study of Chinese Architecture*. London: Academy Editions.

Lipton, Bruce H. 2008. *The Biology of Belief: Unleashing the Power of Consciousness, Matter, and Miracles*. Carlsbad, Calif.: Hay House.

______, and Steve Bhaerman. 2009. *Spontaneous Evolution: Our Positive Future (and a Way to Get There)*. Carlsbad, Calif.: Hay House.

Liu, Xiaogan. 1991. "*Wuwei* (Non-Action): From *Laozi* to *Huainanzi*." *Taoist Resources* 3.1: 41-56.

Loehr, James E., and Jeffrey A. Migdow. 1986. *Breathe In, Breathe Out: Inhale Energy and Exhale Stress by Guiding and Controlling Your Breathing*. Alexandria, VA: Time Life Books.

Loewe, Michael. 1988. "The Oracles of the Clouds and the Winds." *Bulletin of the School of Oriental and African Studies* 51: 500-20.

Lovelock, James. 1979. *Gaia: A New Look at Life on Earth*. New York: Oxford University Press.

Lu, Gwei-djen. 1980. *Celestial Lancets: A History and Rationale of Acupuncture and Moxa*. Cambridge: Cambridge University Press.

Lubart, Todd, and Jacques-Henri Guignard. 2004. "The Generality-Specifity of Creativity: A Multivariate Approach." In *Creativity: From Potential to Realization*, edited by Robert J. Sternberg, Elena L. Grigorenko, and Jerome L. Singer, 43-56. Washington, DC: American Psychological Association.

Lucas, Richard E. 2008. "Personality and Subjective Well-Being." In *The Science of Subjective Well-Being*, edited by Michael Eid and Randy J. Larsen, 171-94. New York: Guilford Press.

Ludwig, Arnold M. 1995. *The Price of Greatness: Resolving the Creativity and Madness Contoversy*. New York: Guilford Press.

Luria, Alexander R. 1976a. *Cognitive Development: Its Cultural and Social Foundations*. Cambridge, Mass.: Harvard University Press.

______. 1976b. *The Neuropsychology of Memory*. New York: Halsted Press.

______. 1986. *The Mind of a Mnemonist*. New York: Basic Books.

Luttgens, Kathryn, and Katherine F. Wells. 1989. *Kinesiology: Scientific Basis of Human Motion*. Dubuque, IA: Wm. C. Brown Publishers.

Lykken, David T. 1998. "The Genetics of Genius." In *Genius and the Mind: Studies of Creativity and Temperament*, edited by Andrew Steptoe, 15-38. New York: Oxford University Press.

Lyons, Derek E. 2009. "The Rational Continuum of Human Imitation." In *Mirror Neuron Systems: The Role of Mirroring Processes in Social Cognition*, edited by Jaime A. Pineda, 77-103. New York: Humana.

Maciocia, Giovanni. 1989. *The Foundations of Chinese Medicine: A Comprehensive Text for Acupuncturists and Herbalists*. New York: Churchill Livingstone.

Main, Roderick. 2008. "Religion, Science, and Synchronicity." In *Synchronicity: Multiple Perspectives on Meaningful Coincidence*, edited by Lance Storm, 25-41. Pari: Pari Publishing.

Mair, Victor H. 1994.*Wandering on the Way: Early Taoist Tales and Parables of Chuang Tzu*. New York: Bantam.

Major, John S. 1978. "Myth, Cosmology, and the Origins of Chinese Science." *Journal of Chinese Philosophy* 5: 1-20.

Major, John S. 1984. "The Five Phases, Magic Squares, and Schematic Cosmography." In *Explorations in Early Chinese Cosmology*, edited by Henry Rosemont, 133-66 Chico: Scholars Press, American Academy of Religion.

_____. 1986. "New Light on the Dark Warrior." *Journal of Chinese Religions* 13/14: 65-87.

_____. 1993. *Heaven and Earth in Early Han Thought: Chapters Three, Four, and Five of the Huainanzi*. Albany: State University of New York Press.

_____, Sarah A. Queen, Andrew S. Meyer, and Harold D. Roth. 2010. *The Huainanzi: A Guide to the Theory and Practice of Government in Early Han China*. New York: Columbia University Press.

Mansfield, Victor, Sally Rhine-Feather, and James Hall. 2008. "The Rhine-Jung Letters: Distinguishing Parapsychological from Synchronistic Events." In *Synchronicity: Multiple Perspectives on Meaningful Coincidence*, edited by Lance Storm, 129-51. Pari: Pari Publishing.

Margulis, Lynn, and Michael F. Dolan. 2002. *Early Life: Evolution on the Precambrian Earth*. Boston: Jones and Bartlett.

Marks, Lawrence E. 2000. "Synesthesia." In *Varieties of Anomalous Experience: Examining the Scientific Evidence*, edited by Etzel Cardeña, Steven Jay Lynn, and Stanley Krippner, 121-50. Washington, DC: American Psychological Association.

Masicampo, E. J., and Roy F. Baumeister. 2011. "Finding Positive Value in Human Consciousness." In *Designing Positive Psychology: Taking Stock and Moving Forward*, edited by Kennon M. Sheldon, Todd B. Kashdan, and Michael F. Steger, 175-89. New York: Oxford University Press.

Maslow, Abraham H. 1954. *Motivation and Personality*. New York: Harper & Row.

_____. 1964. *Toward a Psychology of Being*. New York: Van Nostrand Reinhold.

_____. 1966a. *The Psychology of Science: A Reconnaissance*. New York: Harper & Row.

_____. 1966b. *The Creative Attitude*. New York: Ethical Culture Publications.

_____. 1970. *Religions, Values, and Peak Experiences*. New York: Viking.

_____. 1971. *The Further Reaches of Human Nature*. New York: Viking.

Mather, Richard B. 1976. *A New Account of Tales of the World*. Minneapolis: University of Minnesota Press.

Matsumoto, Kiiko, and Stephen Birch. 1985. *Five Elements and Ten Stems*. Brookline, Mass.: Paradigm Publications.

_____. 1986. *Extraordinary Vessels*. Brookline, Mass.: Paradigm Books.

Matthews, Gerald, Moshe Zeidner, and Richard D. Roberts. 2002. *Emotional Intelligence: Science and Myth*. Cambridge, Mass.: MIT Press.

_____. 2007. *The Science of Emotional Intelligence: Knowns and Unknowns*. New York: Oxford University Press.

McBrearty, Sally, and Alison Brooks. 2000. "The Revolution That Wasn't." *Journal of Human Evolution* 39:453-563.

McCraty, Rollin. 2004. "The Energetic Heart: Bioelectric Communication Within and Between People." In *Bioelectricomagnetic Medicine*, edited by Paul J. Rosch and M. S. Markov, 541-62. New York: Marcel Dekker.

_____, and Robert A. Rees. 2011. "The Central Role of the Heart in Generating and Sustaining Positive Emotions." In *Oxford Handbook of Positive Psychology*, edited by C. R. Snyder and Shane J. Lopez, 527-36. New York: Oxford University Press.

McEvenue, Kelly.2001. *The Actor and the Alexander Technique.* New York: Palgrave Macmillan.

McGill, Ormond. 1979. *Hypnotism and Mysticism of India.* Los Angeles: Westwood Publishing Company.

McLean, Lyn. 2002. *What's the Buzz? Understanding and Avoiding the Risks of Electromagnetic Radiation.* Melbourne: Scribe Publications.

McMillin, David L., Douglas G. Richards, Eric A. Mein, and Carl D. Nelson. 1999. "The Abdominal Brain and the Enteric Nervous System." *Journal of Alternative and Complementary Medicine* 5.6. www.meridianinstitute. com.

McTaggart, Lynne. 2003. *The Field: The Quest for the Secret Force of the Universe.* New York: Harper.

_____. 2007. *The Intention Experiment: Using Your Thoughts to Change Your Life and the World.* New York: Free Press.

_____. 2011. *The Bond: Connecting through the Space between Us*New York: Free Press.

McVeigh, Brian J. 2006. "The Self as Interiorized Social Relations: Applying a Jaynesian Approach to Agency and Volition. In *Reflections on the Dawn of Consciousness: Julian Jaynes's Bicameral Mind Theory Revisited*, edited by Marcel Kuijsten, 203-32. Henderson, Nev.: Julian Jaynes Society.

Meier, C. A. 2001. *Atom and Archetype: The Pauli/Jung Letters, 1932-1958.* Translated by David Roscoe. Princeton: Princeton University Press.

Mershin, Andreas, Hugo Sanabria, John H. Miller, et al. 2006. "Towards Experimental Tests of Quantum Effects in Cytoskeletal Proteins." In *The Emerging Physics of Consciousness*, edited by Jack A. Tuszynski, 95-170. New York: Springer.

Mersini-Houghton, Laura, and Rudi Vaas, eds. 2012. *The Arrows of Time: A Debate in Cosmology.* New York: Springer.

Merton, Thomas. 1969. *The Way of Chuang Tzu.* New York: New Directions.

Millar, Susanna. 1968. *The Psychology of Play.* Harmondsworth: Penguin Books.

Miller, Arthur G. 1986. *The Obedience Experiments: A Case Study of Controversy in Social Science.* New York: Praeger.

Miller, George A. 1960. *Plans and the Structure of Behavior.* New York: Holt. Miller, Jonathan. 1990. "Moving Pictures." In *Images and Understanding*, edited by Horace Barlow, Colin Blakemore, and Miranda Weston-Smith, 180-94. Cambridge: Cambridge University Press.

Min Zhiting 閔智亭. 1990. *Daojiao yifan* 道教儀範. Beijing: Zhongguo daojiao xueyuan.

Mitchell, Edgar D., and John White, eds. 1974. *Psychic Explorations: A Challenge for Science, Understanding the Nature and Power of Consciousness*. New York: Putnam.

Mitchell, Jason P. 2009. "Watching Minds Interact." In *What's Next? Dispatches on the Future of Science*, edited by Max Brockman, 77-88. New York: Vintage Books.

Mithen, Steven. 1998. "A Creative Explosion? Theory of Mind, Language, and the Disembodied Mind of the Upper Paleolithic." In *Creativity in Human Evolution and Prehistory*, edited by Steven Mithen, 165-91. London: Routledge.

______. 2004. *After the Ice: A Global Human History, 20,000-5,000 BC*. Cambridge, Mass.: Harvard University Press.

______. 2006. *The Singing Neanderthals: The Origins of Music, Language, Mind and Body*. Cambridge, Mass.: Harvard University Press.

Mitroff, Ian I., and Elizabeth A. Denton. 1999. *A Spiritual Audit of Corporate America: A Hard Look at Spirituality, Religion, and Values in the Workplace*. San Francisco: Jossey-Bass Publishers.

Miura, Kunio. 1989. "The Revival of *Qi*: Qigong in Contemporary China." In *Taoist Meditation and Longevity Techniques*, edited by L. Kohn, 329-58. Ann Arbor: University of Michigan, Center for Chinese Studies Publications.

Moeller, Hans-Georg. 2003. "Idiotic Irony in the *Zhuangzi*." CLEAR 30:117-23.

______. 2004. *Daoism Explained: From the Dream of the Butterfly to the Fishnet Allegory*. La Salle, IL: Open Court Publishing.

Møllgaard, Eske. 2007. *An Introduction to Daoist Thought: Action, Language, and Ethics in the Zhuangzi*. London: Routledge.

Mollier, Christine. 2000. "Les cuisines de Laozi et du Buddha." *Cahiers d'Extrême-Asie* 11:45-90.

Momigliano, Arnaldo. 1975. *Alien Wisdom: The Limits of Hellenization*. Cambridge: Cambridge University Press.

Monroe, Robert A. 1971. *Journeys Out of the Body*. Garden City, NY: Doubleday.

Montagu, Ashley. 1986. *Touching: The Human Significance of the Skin*. New York: Perennial Library.

Monteith, Margo J. and Aimee Y. Mark. 2009. "The Self-Regulation of Prejudice." In *Handbook of Prejudice, Stereotyping, and Discrimination*, edited by Todd D. Nelson, 507-23. New York: Taylor & Francis.

Moody, Raymond A. 1975. *Life After Life*. New York: Bantam Books.

______. 1988. *The Light Beyond*. New York: Bantam Books.

Morehouse, David. 2008. *Remote Viewing: The Complete User's Manual for Coordinate Remote Viewing*. Boulder: Sounds True.

Moss, Cynthia F., and S. Shettleworth, eds. 1996. *Neuroethological Studies of Cognitive and Perceptual Processes*. Boulder, Col.: Westview Press.

Moss, Thelma. 1974. *The Probability of the Impossible: Scientific Discoveries and Explorations in the Psychic World.* Los Angeles: Jeremy P. Tarcher.

Munroe, Kristen Renwick. 1996. *The Heart of Altruism: Perceptions of a Common Humanity.* Princeton: Princeton University Press.

Murdin, Paul. 2009. *Secrets of the Universe: How We Discovered the Cosmos.* Chicago: University of Chicago Press.

Murphy, Joseph. 1963. *The Power of Your Subconscious Mind.* Englewood Cliffs, NJ: Prentice Hall.

Murphy, M., et al. 1997. *The Physiological and Psychological Effects of Meditation: A Review of Contemporary Research with a Comprehensive Bibliography, 1931-1996.* Petaluma, Calif.: Institute of Noetic Sciences.

Myers, David G. 1992. *The Pursuit of Happiness: Who Is Happy and Why.* New York: William Morrow.

_____. 2008. "Religion and Human Flourishing." In *The Science of Subjective Well-Being,* edited by Michael Eid and Randy J. Larsen, 323-43. New York: Guilford Press.

Nadeau, Robert, and Menas Kafatos. 1999. *The Non-Local Universe: New Physics and Matters of the Mind.* New York: Oxford University Press.

Nagel, Thomas. 1970. *The Possibility of Altruism.* Oxford: Clarendon Press.

Nakamura, Jeanne, and Mihaly Csikszentmihalyi. 2009. "Flow Theory and Research." In *Oxford Handbook of Positive Psychology*, edited by C. R. Snyder and Shane J. Lopez, 195-206. New York: Oxford University Press.

Nash, Carroll B. 1986. *Parapsychology: The Science of Psilology.* Springfield, Ill.: Charles C. Thomas.

Neisser, Ulric. 1994. "Self-Narratives: True and False." In *The Remembering Self: Construction and Accuracy in the Self-Narrative*, edited by Ulric Neisser and Robyn Fivush, 1-18. Cambridge: Cambridge University Press.

Nelson, James B., and Mark E. Bouton. 2002. "Extinction, Inhibition, and Emotional Intelligence." In *The Wisdom in Feeling: Psychological Processes in Emotional Intelligence*, edited by Lisa Feldman Barrett and Peter Salovey, 60-85. New York: Guilford Press.

Nelson, Katherine. 2000. "Memory and Belief in Development." In *Memory, Brain, and Belief*, edited by Daniel L. Schacter and Elaine Sacrry, 259-89. Cambridge, Mass.: Harvard University Press.

Neswald, Sara Elaine. 2009. "Internal Landscapes." In *Internal Alchemy: Self, Society, and the Quest for Immortality*, edited by Livia Kohn and Robin R. Wang, 27-53. Magdalena, NM: Three Pines Press.

Neville, Robert. 1978. *Soldier, Sage, Saint.* New York: Fordham University Press.

Newberg, Andrew. 2012. *The Spiritual Brain: Science and Religious Experience.* Chantilly, VA: Teaching Company.

______, Eugene G. D'Aquili, and Vince Rause. 2001. *Why God Won't Go Away: Brain Science and the Biology of Belief.* New York: Ballentine.

______, and Mark Robert Waldman. 2009. *How God Changes Your Brain: Breakthrough Findings from a Leading Neuroscientist.* New York: Ballantine Books.

Nichols. T. L. 1853. *Esoteric Anthropology*. New York: Stringer & Townsend.

Nicholson, Philip T. 2004. "Restoring the One: Meditation and Light Visions in Early Daoist Texts." Paper presented at the 6th Conference of the International Society for Shamanic Research, Changchun, China.

Nishida, Kitaro. 1990. *An Inquiry into the Good.* New Haven, Conn.: Yale University Press.

Noble, William, and Iain Davidson. 1996. *Human Evolution, Language, and Mind: A Psychological and Archaeological Inquiry*. Cambridge: Cambridge University Press.

Nordenstrøm, B. E. W. 1983. *Biologically Closed Electric Circuits: Clinical, Experimental, and Theoretical Evidence for an Additional Circuitory System*. Stockholm: Nordic Medical Publications.

Nørretranders, Tor. 1998. *The User Illusion: Cutting Consciousness Down to Size*. Translated by Jonathan Sydenham. New York: Viking.

North, Claire. 2014. *The First Fifteen Lives of Harry August*. London: Orbit Books.

Nylan, Michael. 1992. *The Shifting Center: The Original "Great Plan" and Later Readings*. St. Augustin/ Nettetal: Steyler Verlag.

Oatley, Keith. 2000. "The Sentiments and Beliefs of Distributed Cognition." In *Emotions and Beliefs: How Feelings Influence Thoughts*, edited by Nico H.Frijda, A. S. R. Manstead, and Sacha Bem, 78-107. Cambridge: Cambridge University Press.

Ober, Clinton, Stephen T. Sinatra, and Martin Zucker. 2010. *Earthing: The Most Important Health Discovery Ever?* Laguna Beach, Calif.: Basic Health Publications.

Oberman, Lindsay M., and V. S. Ramachandran. 2009. "Reflection on the Mirror Neuron System: Their Evolutionary Function beyond Motor Representation." In *Mirror Neuron Systems: The Role of Mirroring Processes in Social Cognition*, edited by Jaime A. Pineda, 39-59. New York: Humana.

Ochsner, Kevin N. and James J. Gross. 2007. "The Neural Architecture of Emotion Regulation." In *Handbook of Emotion Regulation*, edited by James J. Gross, 87-109. New York: Guilford Press.

Olberding, Amy. 2007. "Sorrow and the Sage: Grief in the *Zhuangzi*." *Dao: A Journal of Comparative Philosophy* 6.4:339-59.

Olson, Carl. 2013. "The Ludic Quality of Life: A Comparison of the *Caitanaya-caritamrta* and the *Zhuangzi*." In *Brahman and Dao: Comparative Studies in Indian and Chinese Philosophy and Religion*, edited by Ithamar Theodor and Zhihua Yao, 247-62. New York: Lexington Books.

Ong, Walter J. 2002 [1982]. *Orality and Literacy: The Technologizing of the Word.* New York: Routledge.

Oppenheimer, Stephen. 2007. "What Makes Us Human?—Our Ancestors and the Weather." In *What Makes Us Human?* edited by Charles Pasternak, 93-113. New York: Oxford University Press.

Ornstein, Robert E. 1980. "Two Sides of the Brain." In *Understanding Mysticism*, edited by Richard Woods, 270-85. New York: Image Books.

Oschman, James. 2000. *Energy Medicine: The Scientific Basis*. New York: Churchill Livingstone.

_____. 2003. *Energy Medicine in Therapeutics and Human Performance*. Boston: Butterworth Heinemann.

_____. 2004. "Recent Developments in Bioelectricomagnetic Medicine." In *Bioelectricomagnetic Medicine*, edited by Paul J. Rosch and M. S. Markov, 77-92. New York: Marcel Dekker.

Ospina, Maria B., et al. 2007. *Meditation Practice for Health: State of the Research*. AHRQ Publication No. 07-E010. Rockville, Md: Agency for Healthcare Research and Quality. www.ahrq.gov.

Ostrander, Sheila, and Lynn Schroeder. 1970. *Psychic Discoveries Behind the Iron Curtain*. Englewood Cliffs: Prentice-Hall.

Ostriker, Jeremiah P., and Simon Mitton. 2013. *Heart of Darkness: Unraveling the Mysteries of the Invisible Universe*. Princeton: Princeton University Press.

Ott, John N. 1976. *Health and Light*. New York: Pocket Books.

Pagel, Mark. 2012. *Wired for Culture: Origins of the Human Social Mind*. New York: W. W. Norton.

Pagels, Heinz. 1982. *The Cosmic Code: Quantum Physics as the Language of Nature*. New York: Simon & Schuster.

Palmer, David. 2007. *Qigong Fever: Body, Science and Utopia in China*. New York: Columbia University Press.

Palmer, John. 2008. "Synchronicity and Psi: How Are They Related?" In *Synchronicity: Multiple Perspectives on Meaningful Coincidence*, edited by Lance Storm, 175-92. Pari: Pari Publishing.

Panati, Charles. 1974. *Supersenses: Our Potential for Parasensory Experience*. New York: Quadrangle.

Pankenier, David W. 2013. *Astrology and Cosmology in Early China: Conforming Earth to Heaven*. Cambridge: Cambridge University Press.

Panksepp, Jaak. 1998. *Affective Neuroscience: The Foundation of Human and Animal Emotions*. New York: Oxford University Press.

_____. 2008. "The Affective Brain and Core Consciousness: How Does Neural Activity Generate Emotional Feelings?" In *Handbook of Emotions*, edited by Michael Lewis, Jeannette M. Haviland-Jones, and Lisa Feldman Barrett, 47-66. New York: Guilford Press.

_____. 2011. "The Primary Process Affect in Human Development, Happiness, and Thriving." In *Designing Positive Psychology: Taking Stock and Moving Forward*, edited by Kennon M. Sheldon, Todd B. Kashdan, and Michael F. Steger, 51-85. New York: Oxford University Press.

Parrott, W. Gerrod. 2002. "The Functional Utility of Negative Emotions." In *The Wisdom in Feeling: Psychological Processes in Emotional Intelligence*, edited by Lisa Feldman Barrett and Peter Salovey, 341-59. New York: Guilford Press.

Pasternak, Charles. 2007. "Curiosity and Quest." In *What Makes Us Human?* edited by Charles Pasternak, 114-32. New York: Oxford University Press.

Pearsall, Paul. 1998. *The Heart's Code: Tapping the Wisdom and Power of Our Heart Energy*. New York: Broadway Books.

Peat, F. David. 1987. *Synchronicity: The Bridge between Matter and Mind.* New York: Bantam Books.

______. 1997. *Infinite Potential: The Life and Times of David Bohm*. New York: Helix Books.

______. 2008. "Divine Contenders: Wolfgang Pauli and the Symmetry of the World." In *Synchronicity: Multiple Perspectives on Meaningful Coincidence*, edited by Lance Storm, 15-24. Pari: Pari Publishing.

Pekala, Ronald J., and Etzel Cardeña. 2000. "Methodological Issues in the Study of Altered States of Consciousness and Anomalous Experiences." In *Varieties of Anomalous Experience: Examining the Scientific Evidence*, edited by Etzel Cardeña, Steven Jay Lynn, and Stanley Krippner, 47-82. Washington, DC: American Psychological Association.

Penfield, Wilder. 1975. *The Mystery of the Mind: A Critical Study of Consciousness and the Human Brain.* Princeton: Princeton University Press.

Penrose, Roger. 1989. *The Emperor's New Mind: Concerning Computers, Minds, and the Laws of Physics.* New York: Oxford University Press.

______. 1994. *Shadows of the Mind: A Search for the Missing Science of Consciousness.* New York: Oxford University Press.

______. 1997. *The Large, the Small, and the Human Mind.* Cambridge: Cambridge University Press.

______. 2005. *The Road to Reality: A Complete Guide to the Laws of the Universe*. New York: Alfred A. Knopf.

Perkins, David N. 1994. "Creativity: Beyond the Darwinian Paradigm. " In *Dimensions of Creativity*, edited by Margaret A. Boden, 119-42. Cambridge, Mass.: MIT Press.

Pert, Candace. 1997. *Molecules of Emotion: Why You Feel the Way You Feel.* New York: Scribner.

Peterson, Christopher, and Martin E. P. Seligman. 2004. *Character Strengths and Virtues: A Handbook and Classification.* Oxford: Oxford University Press.

Pettitt, Paul. 2005. "The Rise of Modern Humans." In *The Human Past: World Prehistory and the Development of Human Societies*, edited by Chris Scarre, 124-73. London: Thames & Hudson.

Phillips, Scott Park 2008. "Portrait of an American Daoist: Charles Belyea/Liu Ming." *Journal of Daoist Studies* 1:161-76.

______, and Daniel Mroz. 2016. "Daoyin Reimagined: A Comparison of Three Embodied Traditions." *Journal of Daoist Studies* 9:139-57.

Philpott, William H., Dwight K. Kalita, and B. Goldberg. 2000. *Magnet Therapy*. Tiburon: Alternative Medicine.

Piaget, Jean. 1976. *To Understand Is to Invent.* New York: Penguin.

Piattelli-Palmarino, Massimo. 2010. "What Is Language, That It May Have Evolved, and What Is Evolution, That It May Apply to Language." In *The Evolution of Human Language: Biolinguistic Perspectives*, edited by Richard K. Larson, Viviane Déprez, and Hiroko Yamakido, 148-62. Cambridge: Cambridge University Press.

Pika, Simone. 2014. "Chimpanzee Grooming Gestures and Sounds: What Might They Tell Us about How Language Evolved?" In *The Social Origins of Language*, edited by Daniel Dor, Chris Knight, and Jerome Lewis, 129-40. New York: Oxford University Press.

Pineda, Jaime A., A. Roxanne Moore, Hanie Elfenbein, and Roy Cox. 2009. "Hierarchically Organized Mirroring Processes in Social Cognition." In *Mirror Neuron Systems: The Role of Mirroring Processes in Social Cognition*, edited by Jaime A. Pineda, 135-60. New York: Humana.

Pinker, Steven. 1994. *The Language Instinct: How the Mind Creates Language*. New York: W. Morrow & Co.

_____. 1997. *How the Mind Works*. New York: W. W. Norton.

_____. 2007. *The Stuff of Thought: Language as a Window into Human Nature*. New York: Viking.

Platek, Steven M., and Todd K. Shackeford, eds. 2009. *Foundations in Evolutionary Cognitive Neuroscience*. Cambridge: Cambridge University Press.

Plucker, Jonathan A., and Ronald A. Beghetto. 2004. "Why Creativity is Domain General, Why It Looks Domain Specific,and Why the Distinction Does Not Matter." In *Creativity: From Potential to Realization*, edited by Robert J. Sternberg, Elena L. Grigorenko, and Jerome L. Singer, 153-68. Washington, DC: American Psychological Association.

Poizner, Howard, Edward S. Klima, and Ursula Bellugi. 1987. *What the Hands Reveal about the Brain.* Cambridge, Mass.: MIT Press.

Polich, Laura. 2005. *The Emergence of the Deaf Community in Nicaragua: With Sign Language You Can Learn So Much.* Washington, D.C.: Gallaudet University Press.

Popp, Fritz-Albert. 2002. "Biophotonics: A Powerful Tool for Investigating and Understanding Life." In *What Is Life? Scientific Approaches and Philosophical Positions*, edited by H.-P. Dürr, Fritz-Albert Popp, and Wolfram Schommers. Singapore: World Scientific.

Porkert, Manfred. 1974. *The Theoretical Foundations of Chinese Medicine*. Cambridge, Mass.: MIT Press.

Potter, Christopher.2009. *You Are Here: A Portable History of the Universe*. New York: HarperCollins.

Power, Camilla. 2014a. "Signal Evolution and the Social Brain." In *The Social Origins of Language*, edited by Daniel Dor, Chris Knight, and Jerome Lewis, 47-55. New York: Oxford University Press.

_____. 2014b. "The Evolution of Ritual as a Process of Sexual Selection." In *The Social Origins of Language*, edited by Daniel Dor, Chris Knight, and Jerome Lewis, 47-55. New York: Oxford University Press.

Pregadio, Fabrizio, ed. 2008. *The Encyclopedia of Taoism.* 2 vols. London: Routledge.

_____. 2004. "The Notion of 'Form' and the Ways of Liberation in Daoism." *Cahiers d'Extrême-Asie* 14:95-130.

Pribram, Karl H. 1971. *Languages of the Brain: Experimental Paradoxes and Principles in Neuropsychology*. Englewood Cliffs: Prentice-Hall.

_____. 1977. *Languages of the Brain: Experimental Paradoxes and Principles in Neuropsychology*. Monterey: Wadsworth Publishing.

_____. 1991. *Brain and Perception: Holonomy and Structure in Figural Processing.* Hillsdale, NJ: Lawrence Erlbaum Associates.

Price Douglas B., and Anna B. Gebauer, eds. 1995. *Last Hunters—First Farmers.* Santa Fe: School of American Research Press.

Priel, Avner, Jack A. Tuszynski, and Horacion F. Cantiello. 2006. "The Dendritic Cytoskeleton as a Computational Device: An Hypothesis." In *The Emerging Physics of Consciousness*, edited by Jack A. Tuszynski, 293-326. New York: Springer.

Primack, Joel R., and Nancy Ellen Abrams. 2006. *The View from the Center of the Universe: Discovering Our Extraordinary Place in the Cosmos.* New York: Riverhead Books.

_____. 2011. "Cosmology." In *The Routledge Companion to Religion and Science*, edited by James W. Haag, Gregory R. Peterson, and Michael L. Spezio, 103-12. London: Routledge.

Prince, Raymond H. 1980. "Cocoon Work: An Interpretation of the Concern of Contemporary Youth with the Mystical." In *Understanding Mysticism*, edited by Richard Woods, 338-54. New York: Image Books.

Proudfoot, Wayne. 1985. *Religious Experience.* Berkeley and Los Angeles: University of California Press.

Provine, Robert R. 2001. *Laughter: A Scientific Investigation.* New York: Penguin.

Puett, Michael J. 2002. *To Become a God: Cosmology, Sacrifice, and Self-Divinization in Early China.* Cambridge, Mass.: Harvard University Press.

_____. 2003. "Can Nothing Overcome Heaven? The Notion of Spirit in the *Zhuangzi*." In *Hiding the World in the World: Uneven Discourses on the Zhuangzi*, edited by Scott Cook, 248-62. Albany: State University of New York Press.

_____. 2004. "The Ethics of Responding Properly: The Notion of *Qing* in Early Chinese Thought." In *Love and Emotions in Traditional Chinese Literature*, edited by Halvor Eifring, 37-68. Leiden: E. Brill.

Quirk, Gregory J. 2007. "Prefrontal-Amygdala Interactions in the Regulation of Fear." In *Handbook of Emotion Regulation*, edited by James J. Gross, 27-46. New York: Guilford Press.

Radin, Dean. 1997. *The Conscious Universe: The Scientific Truth of Psychic Phenomena.* New York: HarperEdge.

_____. 2006. *Entangled Minds: Extrasensory Experiences in Quantum Reality*. New York: Paraview Pocket Books.

_____. 2013. *Supernormal: Science, Yoga, and the Evidence for Extraordinary Psychic Abilities*. New York: Random House.

Ramachandran, V. S. 2000. "Memory and the Brain: New Lessons fromOld Syndromes." In *Memory, Brain, and Belief*, edited by Daniel L. Schacter and Elaine Sacrry, 87-114. Cambridge, Mass.: Harvard University Press.

_____. 2011. *The Tell-Tale Brain: A Neuroscientist's Quest for What Makes Us Human*. New York: W. W. Norton & Co.

Raphals, Lisa. 1992. *Knowing Words: Wisdom and Cunning in the Classical Traditions of China and Greece*. Ithaca: Cornell University Press.

_____. 2003. "Fate, Fortune, Chance, and Luck in Chinese and Greek: A Comparative Semantic History." *Philosophy East & West* 53.4:537-74.

_____. 2005. "Languages of Fate: Semantic Fields in Chinese and Greek." In *The Magnitude of Ming: Command, Allotment, and Fate in Chinese Culture*, edited by Christopher Lupke, 70-106. Honolulu: University of Hawai'i Press.

Ratey, John J. 2002. *A User's Guide to the Brain: Perception, Attention, and the Four Theaters of the Brain*. New York: Vintage Books.

Redford, William. 1993. *Anger Kills: Seventeen Strategies for Controlling the Hostility That Can Harm Your Health*. New York: Times Books.

Rees, Martin. 2000. *Just Six Numbers: The Deep Forces That Shape the Universe*. New York: Basic Books.

_____. 2001. *Our Cosmic Habitat*. Princeton: Princeton University Press.

Remen, Naomi. 1980. *The Human Patient*. Garden City, NY: Anchor Press.

Réquéna, Yves. 1989. *Character and Health: The Relation of Acupuncture and Psychology*. Brookline, Mass.: Paradigm Publications.

_____. 2012. "The Biochemistry of Internal Alchemy: Decapitating the Red Dragon." *Journal of Daoist Studies* 5:141-52.

Restak, Richard. 2009. "The New Brain." In *The Brain*, edited by Kenneth Partridge, 19-21. New York: H. S. Wilson.

Richards, Ruth. 1999. "Everyday Creativity." In *Encyclopedia of Creativity*, edited by Marc A. Runco and Steven R. Pritzker, 1:683-87. San Diego: Academic Press.

_____. 2007. *Everyday Creativity and New Views of Human Nature: Psychological, Social, and Spiritual Perspectives*. Washington, DC: American Psychological Association.

Rickett, W. Allyn. 1998. *Guanzi: Political, Economic, and Philosophical Essays from Early China*. Vol. 2. Princeton: Princeton University Press.

Rinaldini, Michael. 2008. "How I Became a Daoist Priest." *Journal of Daoist Studies* 1:181-87.

_____. 2013. *A Daoist Practice Journal: Come Laugh with Me.* Sebastopol, Calif.: StoriesToTell-Books.

Robertson, John S. 2004. "The Possibility and Actuality of Writing." In *The First Writing: Script Invention as History and Process*, edited by Stephen D. Houston, 16-38. Cambridge: Cambridge University Press.

Robinet, Isabelle. 1977. *Les commentaires du Tao to king jusqu'au VIIe siècle.* Paris: Mémoirs de l'Institute des Hautes Etudes Chinoises 5.

_____. 1979. "Metamorphosis and Deliverance of the Corpse in Taoism." *History of Religions* 19:37-70.

_____. 1989. "Visualization and Ecstatic Flight in Shangqing Taoism." In *Taoist Meditation and Longevity Techniques*, edited by Livia Kohn, 159-91. Ann Arbor: University of Michigan, Center for Chinese Studies.

_____. 1993. *Taoist Meditation: The Mao-shan Tradition of Great Purity.* Translated by Norman Girardot and Julian Pas. Albany: State University of New York Press.

_____. 2000. "Shangqing—Highest Clarity." In *Daoism Handbook*, edited by Livia Kohn, 196-224. Leiden: Brill.

Robinson, Michael D., and Maya Tamir. 2011. "A Task-Focused Mind Is a Happy Mind: A Processing Perspective." In *Designing Positive Psychology: Taking Stock and Moving Forward*, edited by Kennon M. Sheldon, Todd B. Kashdan, and Michael F. Steger, 160-74. New York: Oxford University Press.

_____, and Rebecca J. Compton. 2008. "The Happy Mind in Action: The Cognitive Basis of Subjective Well-Being." In *The Science of Subjective Well-Being*, edited by Michael Eid and Randy J. Larsen, 220-38. New York: Guilford Press.

Rosch, Paul J. 2009. "Bioelectromagnetic and Subtle Energy Medicine: The Interface between Mind and Matter." *Annals of the New York Academy of Sciences* 1172:297-311.

Rosenberg, Larry. 1999. *Breath by Breath: The Liberating Practice of Insight Meditation.* Boston: Shambhala.

Rosenblum, Bruce, and Fred Kuttner. 2011. *Quantum Enigma: Physics Encounters Consciousness.* New York: Oxford University Press.

Rosenthal, Robert, and Lenore Jacobson. 1968. *Pygmalion in the Classroom.* New York: Holt, Rinehart, & Winston.

Ross, Michael, and Anne E. Wilson. 2000. "Constructing and Appraising Past Selves." In *Memory, Brain, and Belief*, edited by Daniel L. Schacter and Elaine Sacrry, 231-58. Cambridge, Mass.: Harvard University Press.

Rossbach, Sarah. 1983. *Feng Shui: The Chinese Art of Placement.* New York: Dutton.

Roth, Harold D. 1990. "The Early Taoist Concept of *Shen*: A Ghost in the Machinery?" In *Sagehood and Systematizing Thought in the Late Warring States and Early Han*, edited by Kidder Smith, 11-32. Brunswick, Maine: Bowdoin College.

_____. 1997a. "Evidence for Stages of Meditation in Early Taoism." *Bulletin of the School of Oriental and African Studies* 60: 295-314.

_____. 1997b. "The Yellow Emperor's Guru: A Narrative Analysis from *Chuang-tzu* 11." *Taoist Resources* 7.1:43-60.

_____. 1999. *Original Tao: Inward Training and the Foundations of Taoist Mysticism*. New York: Columbia University Press.

_____. 2000. "Bimodal Mystical Experience in the "Qiwulun" Chapter of *Zhuangzi*." *Journal of Chinese Religions* 28:31-50.

_____. 2010. "Bimodal Mystical Experience in the "Qiwulun" Chapter of *Zhuangzi*." In *Experimental Essays on Zhuangzi*, edited by Victor H. Mair, 195-211. Dunedin, Fla.: Three Pines Press.

Roth, Robert. 1987. *TM: Transcendental Meditation*. New York: Primus.

Rothbart, Mary Klevjord. 2011. *Becoming Who We Are: Temperament and Personality in Development*. New York: Guilford Press.

Ruhlen, Merritt.1994. *The Origin of Language: Tracing the Evolution of the Mother Tongue*. Hoboken: John Wiley & Sons.

Runco, Mark A. 2004. "Everyone Has Creative Potential." In *Creativity: From Potential to Realization*, edited by Robert J. Sternberg, Elena L. Grigorenko, and Jerome L. Singer, 21-30. Washington, DC: American Psychological Association.

Sabbadini, Shantena Augusto. 2008. "Synchronicity, Science, and the *I Ching*." In *Synchronicity: Multiple Perspectives on Meaningful Coincidence*, edited by Lance Storm, 78-83. Pari: Pari Publishing.

Sacks, Oliver W. 1985. *The Man Who Mistook His Wife for a Hat, and Other Clinical Tales*. New York: Harper.

_____. 1995. *An Anthropologist on Mars*. New York: Alfred A. Knopf.

_____. 2007. *Musicophilia: Tales of Music and the Brain*. New York: Alfred A. Knopf.

_____. 2012. *Hallucinations*. New York: Alfred A. Knopf.

Sagan, Carl. 2006. *The Varieties of Scientific Experience: A Personal View of the Search for God*. Edited by Ann Druyan. New York: Penguin Press.

Samuels, Mike, and Nancy Samuels. 1975. *Seeing with the Mind's Eye: The History, Technique, and Uses of Visualization*. New York: Random House.

Santee, Robert. 2008. "Stress Management and the *Zhuangzi*." *Journal of Daoist Studies* 1:93-123.

_____. 2011. "The *Zhuangzi*: A Holistic Approach to Healthcare and Well-being." In *Living Authentically: Daoist Contributions to Modern Psychology*, edited by Livia Kohn, 39-58. Dunedin, FL: Three Pines Press.

Saso, Michael. 1995. *The Gold Pavilion: Taoist Ways to Peace, Healing, and Long Life*. Boston: Charles E. Tuttle.

Savage-Rumbaugh, Sue, and Roger Levine. 1994. *Kanzi: The Ape at the Brink of the Human Mind*. Hoboken: John Wiley & Sons.

Sawyer, Ralph D. 1993. *The Seven Military Classics of Ancient China.* Boulder: Westview Press.

Scarre, Chris. 2005. "The World Transformed: From Foragers and Farmers to States and Empires." In *The Human Past: World Prehistory and the Development of Human Societies*, edited by Chris Scarre, 176-99. London: Thames & Hudson.

Schaberg, David. 2005. "Command and the Content of Tradition." In *The Magnitude of Ming: Command, Allotment, and Fate in Chinese Culture*, edited by Christopher Lupke, 23-48. Honolulu: University of Hawai'i Press.

Schafer, Edward H. 1977. *Pacing the Void.* Berkeley: University of California Press.

______. 1987. "The Dance of the Purple Culmen." *T'ang Studies* 5: 45-68.

______. 1997. "The Scripture of the Opening of Heaven by the Most High Lord Lao." *Taoist Resources* 7.2: 1-20.

Schipper, Kristofer. 1994. *The Taoist Body.* Translated by Karen C. Duval. Berkeley: University of California Press.

______, and Franciscus Verellen, eds. 2004. *The Taoist Canon: A Historical Companion to the Daozang.* 3 vols. Chicago: University of Chicago Press.

Schrijver, Karel, and Iris Schrijver. 2015. *Living with the Stars: How the Human Body Is Connected to the Life Cycles of the Earth, the Planets, and the Stars.* New York: Oxford University Press.

Schrödinger, Erwin. 1964. *My View of the World.* Cambridge: Cambridge University Press.

______. 1969. *What Is Life? and Mind and Matter.* Cambridge: Cambridge University Press.

Schul, Bill D. 1990. *Animal Immortality: Pets and Their Afterlife.* New York: Carroll & Graf.

Schwartz, Benjamin. 1985. *The World of Thought in Ancient China.* Cambridge, Mass: Harvard University Press.

Schwartz, Berthold Eric. 2008. "Synchronicity and Telepathy." In *Synchronicity: Multiple Perspectives on Meaningful Coincidence*, edited by Lance Storm, 67-77. Pari: Pari Publishing.

Schwartz, Gary E., and Linda G. S. Russek. 1999. *The Living Energy Universe.* Charlottesville, VA: Hampton Roads.

Schwartz, Jeffrey, and Sharon Begley. 2002. *The Mind and the Brain: Neuroplasticity and the Power of Mental Force.* New York: HarperCollins.

Schwarz, Norbert. 2002. "Situated Cognition and the Wisdom in Feelings: Cognitive Tuning." In *The Wisdom in Feeling: Psychological Processes in Emotional Intelligence*, edited by Lisa Feldman Barrett and Peter Salovey, 144-66. New York: Guilford Press.

Scott, Alwyn. 2006. "Physicalism, Chaos, and Reductionism." In *The Emerging Physics of Consciousness*, edited by Jack A. Tuszynski, 171-92. New York: Springer.

Seaman, Gary. 1992. "Winds, Waters, Seeds, and Souls: Folk Concepts of Physiology and Etiology in Chinese Geomancy." In *Paths to Asian Medical Knowledge*, edited by Charles Leslie and Allan Young, 74-97. Berkeley: University of California Press.

Seem, Mark D. 1989. *BodyMind Energetics: Toward a Dynamic Model of Health.* Rochester, VT: Healing Arts Press.

_____. 1990. *Acupuncture Imaging: Perceiving the Energy Pathways of the Body*. New York: Inner Traditions.

Segal, Jerome. 2009. "Graceful Living." In *Less Is More: Embracing Simplicity for a Healthy Planet, a Caring Economy, and Lasting Happiness*, edited by Cecile Andrews and Wanda Urbanska, 27-34. Gabriola Island: New Society Publishers.

Segerstrom, Suzanne C., Timothy W. Smith, and Tory A. Eisenlohn-Moul. 2011. "Positive Psychophysiology: The Body and Self-Regulation." In *Designing Positive Psychology: Taking Stock and Moving Forward*, edited by Kennon M. Sheldon, Todd B. Kashdan, and Michael F. Steger, 25-40. New York: Oxford University Press.

Seidel, Anna. 1969. *La divinisation de Lao-tseu dans le taoïsme des Han*. Paris: Ecole Française d'Extrême-Orient.

Sekida, Katsuki. 1975. *Zen Training*. New York: Weatherhill.

Selby, John, and Zackary Zelig. 1992. *Kundalini Awakening: A Gentle Guide to Chakra Activation and Spiritual Growth*. New York: Bantam New Age.

Seligman, Martin E. P. 2002. *Authentic Happiness: Using the New Positive Psychology to Realize Your Potential for Lasting Fulfillment*. New York: Free Press.

_____. 2011. *Flourish: A Visionary New Understanding of Happiness and Well-Being*. New York: Free Press.

Sellmann, James D. 1998. "Transformational Humor in the *Zhuangzi*." In *Wandering at Ease in the Zhuangzi*, edited by Roger Ames, 163-74. Albany: State University of New York Press.

Selye, Hans. 1984. *The Stress of Life*. New York: McGraw-Hill

Shang, Geling. 2002. "Embracing Differences and Many: The Signification of One in Zhuangzi's Utterance of Dao." *Dao: A Journal of Comparative Philosophy* 1.2: 229-50.

Shapiro, Deane N. 1984. "Overview: Clinical and Physiological Comparison of Meditation with Other Self-Control Strategies." In *Meditation: Classic and Contemporary Perspectives*, edited by Deane N. Shapiro and Roger N. Walsh, 5-12. 1984 New York: Aldine.

_____. and Roger N. Walsh. 1984. *Meditation: Classic and Contemporary Perspectives*. New York: Aldine.

Shealy, C. Norman. 2011. *Energy Medicine: Practical Applications and Scientific Proof*. Virginia Beach: 4th Dimension Press.

Shear, Jonathan. 2000. *Explaining Consciousness: The 'Hard Problem'*. Cambridge, Mass.: MIT Press.

Sherrill, Martha. 2000. *The Buddha from Brooklyn*. New York: Random House.

Shettleworth, Sara J. 2010. *Cognition, Evolution, and Behavior*. New York: Oxford University Press.

Shi, Jing. 2005. "An Interview with Liu Xingdi." *The Dragon's Mouth* 2005.3:2-8.

_____. 2006. "Sitting and Forgetting: An Introduction to *Zuowang*." *The Dragon's Mouth* 2006.1:10-13.

_____. 2007. "An Interview with Eva Wong." *The Dragon's Mouth* 2007.1:4-8.

Siegel, Daniel. 2007. *The Mindful Brain.* New York: W. W. Norton.

Silburn, Lilian. 1988. *Kundalini: The Energy of the Depths.* Albany: State University of New York Press.

Simonton, Dean Keith. 1999. *Origins of Genius: Darwinian Perspectives on Creativity.* New York: Oxford University Press.

_____. 2004. "Creativity as Constrained Stochastic Process." In *Creativity: From Potential to Realization*, edited by Robert J. Sternberg, Elena L. Grigorenko, and Jerome L. Singer, 83-102. Washington, DC: American Psychological Association.

Simonton, Oscar Carl. 1978. *Getting Well Again: A Step-by-Step, Self-Help Guide to Overcoming Cancer.* Los Angeles: J. P. Tardner.

Sinha, Chris. 2014. "Niche Construction and Semiosis: Biocultural and Social Dynamics." In *The Social Origins of Language*, edited by Daniel Dor, Chris Knight, and Jerome Lewis, 31-46. New York: Oxford University Press.

Slingerland, Edward. 2003. *Effortless Action: Wu-wei as a Conceptual Metaphor and Spiritual Ideal in Ancient China.* New York: Oxford University Press.

Smith, Bruce D. 1998. *The Emergence of Agriculture.* New York: Scientific American Library.

Somers, Margaret. 1994. "The Narrative Construction of Identity: A Relational and Network Approach." *Theory and Society* 23.5:605-49.

Sommer, Deborah. 2002. "Destroying Confucius: Iconoclasm in the Confucian Temple." In *On Sacred Ground: Culture, Society, Politics, and the Formation of the Cult of Confucius*, edited by Thomas A. Wilson, 95-133. Cambridge, Mass.: Harvard Asia Center.

_____. 2008. "Boundaries of the *Ti* Body." *Asia Major* (3rd ser.) 21.3:293-324.

_____. 2010. "Concepts of the Body in the *Zhuangzi*." In *Experimental Essays on Zhuangzi*, edited by Victor H. Mair, 212-27. Dunedin, Fla.: Three Pines Press.

Sounds True, ed. 2009. *The Mystery of 2012: Predictions, Prophecies, and Possibilities.* Boulder: Sounds True.

Spence, Dale W. 1975. *Essentials of Kinesiology: A Laboratory Manual.* Philadelphia: Lea & Febinger.

Spencer, Colin. 1993. *Vegetarianism: A History.* New York: Four Walls Eight Windows.

Stace, W.T. 1960. *Mysticism and Philosophy.* London: Macmillan.

Stangor, Charles. 2009. "The Study of Stereotyping, Prejudice, and Discrimination within Social Psychology: A Quick History of Theory and Research." In *Handbook of Prejudice, Stereotyping, and Discrimination*, edited by Todd D. Nelson, 1-22. New York: Taylor & Francis.

Starkes, Janet L. and K. Anders Ericcson, eds. 2003. *Expert Performance in Sports: Advances in Research on Sport Expertise.* Champaign, Ill.: Human Kinetics.

Stein, Kathleen. 2007. *The Genius Engine: Where Memory, Passion, Reason, Violence and Creativity Intersect in the Human Brain.* Hoboken: John Wiley & Sons.

Steinkirch, Maria von. 2011. "Introduction to Group Theory for Physicists." State University of New York at Stony Brook. http://astro.sunysb.edu/steinkirch/books/group.pdf

Stenger, Victor J. 2011. *The Fallacy of Fine-Tuning: Why the Universe is Not Designed for Us.* Buffalo, NY: Prometheus Books.

Steptoe, Andrew. 1998. "Mozart: Resilience under Stress." In *Genius and the Mind: Studies of Creativity and Temperament*, edited by Andrew Steptoe, 141-66. New York: Oxford University Press.

Sternberg, Robert J. 1996. *Successful Intelligence: How Practical and Creative Intelligence Determines Success in Life.* New York: Simon & Schuster.

_____, and Todd Lubart. 1995. *Defying the Crowd: Cultivating Creativity in a Culture of Conformity.* New York: Free Press.

Stevenson, Frank W. 2006. "Zhuangzi's Dao as Background Noise." *Philosophy East & West* 56.2:301-31.

Storm, Lance. 2008. "Synchronicity, Causality, and Acausality." In *Synchronicity: Multiple Perspectives on Meaningful Coincidence*, edited by Lance Storm, 153-74. Pari: Pari Publishing.

Strickmann, Michel. 1978. "The Mao-shan Revelations: Taoism and the Aristocracy." *T'oung Pao* 63: 1-63.

_____. 1981. *Le taoïsme du Mao chan: chronique d'une révélation.* Paris: Collège du France, Institut des Hautes Etudes Chinoises.

Susskind, Leonard. 2006. *The Cosmic Landscape: String Theory and the Illusion of Intelligent Design.* New York: Little, Brown and Co.

Swimme, Brian Thomas, and Mary Evelyn Tucker. 2011. *Journey of the Universe: The Epic Story of Cosmic, Earth, and Human Transformation.* New Haven, Conn.: Yale University Press.

Sylvia, Claire, and William Novak. 1997. *A Change of Heart.* Boston: Little & Brown.

Takano, Kazuaki. 2014. *Genocide of One.* New York: Mulholland Books.

Talbot, Michael. 1991. *The Holographic Universe.* New York: HarperCollins.

Tallerman, Maggie. 2005. *Language Origins: Perspectives on Evolution.* New York: Oxford University Press.

Tang, Yijie. 2003. "Emotion in Pre-Qin Ruist Moral Theory: Dao Begins in *Qing*." Translated by Brian Bruya and Wen Haiming. *Philosophy East & West* 53.2:271-81.

Tangney, June Price. 2009. "Humility." In *Oxford Handbook of Positive Psychology*, edited by C. R. Snyder and Shane J. Lopez, 483-90. New York: Oxford University Press.

Targ, Elisabeth, Marilyn Schlitz, and Harvey J. Irwin. 2000. "Psi-Related Experiences." In *Varieties of Anomalous Experience: Examining the Scientific Evidence*, edited by Etzel Cardeña, Steven Jay Lynn, and Stanley Krippner, 219-52. Washington, DC: American Psychological Association.

Targ, Russell. 2004. *Limitless Mind: A Guide to Remote Viewing and Transformation of Consciousness.* Novato, Calif.: New World Library.

_____. 2008. *Do You See What I See? Memoirs of a Blind Biker.* Charlottesville, VA: Hampton Roads.

_____. 2012. *The Reality of ESP: A Physicist's Proof of Psychic Abilities.* Wheaton, Ill.: Theosophical Publishing House.

_____, and Jane Katra. 1999. *Miracles of Mind: Exploring Nonlocal Consciousness and Spiritual Healing.* Novato, Calif.: New World Library.

_____, and Keith Harary. 1984. *The Mind Race: Understanding and Using Psychic Abilities.* New York: Villard Books.

Tart, Charles T., ed. 1969. *Altered States of Consciousness.* Hoboken: John Wiley & Sons.

_____. 2008. "Causality and Synchronicity: Steps toward Clarification." In *Synchronicity: Multiple Perspectives on Meaningful Coincidence*, edited by Lance Storm, 109-26. Pari: Pari Publishing.

Tattersall, Ian. 2007. "Human Evolution and the Human Condition." In *What Makes Us Human?* edited by Charles Pasternak, 133-45. New York: Oxford University Press.

_____. 2010. "A Putative Role for Language in the Origin of Human Consciousness." In *The Evolution of Human Language: Biolinguistic Perspectives*, edited by Richard K. Larson, Viviane Déprez, and Hiroko Yamakido, 193-98. Cambridge: Cambridge University Press.

Taylor, Jill Bolte. 2009. *My Stroke of Insight.* New York: Penguin-Plume.

Taylor, Rodney L. 1988. *The Confucian Way of Contemplation: Okada Takehiko and the Tradition of Quiet-Sitting.* Columbia: University of South Carolina Press.

Tegmark, Max. 2004. "Parallel Universes." In *Science and Ultimate Reality: Quantum Theory, Cosmology, and Complexity*, edited by John D. Barrow, P. C. W. Davies, and Charles L. Harper, 459-91. Cambridge: Cambridge University Press.

Teilhard de Chardin, Pierre. 1959. *The Phenomenon of Man.* New York: Harper.

Tennesen, Michael. 2015. *The Next Species: The Future of Evolution in the Aftermath of Man.* New York: Simon & Schuster.

Thomas, Linnie, Carrie Obry, and James L. Oschman, eds. 2010. *The Encyclopedia of Energy Medicine.* Minneapolis: Fairview Press.

Tiller, William A. 1997. *Science and Human Transformation: Subtle Energies, Intentionality, and Consciousness.* Walnut Creek, Calif.: Pavior Publishing.

_____. 2004a. "Subtle Energies and Their Roles in Bioelectricomagnetic Phenomena." In *Bioelectricomagnetic Medicine*, edited by Paul J. Rosch and M. S. Markov, 159-92. New York: Marcel Dekker.

_____. 2004b. "Electromagneticism and Bioelectromagneticsm." In *Bioelectricomagnetic Medicine*, edited by Paul J. Rosch and M. S. Markov, 193-206. New York: Marcel Dekker.

_____, David G. Boyers, and H. S. Dakin. 1974. *Towards a Kirlian Device for Monitoring Physiological State.* Stanford: Stanford University Press.

_____, Walter E. Dibble, and J. Greory Fandel. 2005. *Some Science Adventures with Real Magic.* Walnut Creek, Calif.: Pavior Publishing.

_____, Walter E. Dibble, and Michael J. Kohane. 2001. *Conscious Acts of Creation: The Emergence of the New Physics.* Walnut Creek, Calif.: Pavior Publishing.

Tipler, Frank J. 1994. *The Physics of Immortality: Modern Cosmology, God, and the Resurrection of the Dead.* New York: Doubleday.

Todeschi, Kevin J., and Carol Ann Liaros. 2011. *Edgar Cayce on Auras and Colors.* Virgina Beach: A. R. E. Press.

Tomasello, Michael. 1999. *The Cultural Origins of Human Cognition.* Cambridge, Mass.: Harvard University Press.

_____, and Josep Call. 1997. *Primate Cognition.* New York: Oxford University Press.

Tompkins, Peter, and Christopher Bird. 1973. *The Secret Life of Plants.* New York: Harper & Row.

Toth, Nicholas, and Kathy Schick. 2005. "African Origins." In *The Human Past: World Prehistory and the Development of Human Societies*, edited by Chris Scarre, 46-83. London: Thames & Hudson.

Trigger, Bruce G. 2004. "Writing Systems: A Case Study in Cultural Evolution." In *The First Writing: Script Invention as History and Process*, edited by Stephen D. Houston, 39-68. Cambridge: Cambridge University Press.

Tucker, Mary Evelyn. 2011. *Journey of the Universe: Educational Series.* 4 DVDs. New Haven, Conn.: Yale University Press.

Tugade, Michael M., and Barbara L. Fredrickson. 2002. "Positive Emotions and Emotional Intelligence." In *The Wisdom in Feeling: Psychological Processes in Emotional Intelligence*, edited by Lisa Feldman Barrett and Peter Salovey, 319-40. New York: Guilford Press.

Tulving, Endel. 1983. *Elements of Episodic Memory.* New York: Oxford University Press.

_____, ed. 2000. *The Oxford Handbook of Memory.* New York: Oxford University Press.

_____, and Martin Lepage. 2000. "Where in the Brain Is the Awareness of One's Past?" In *Memory, Brain, and Belief*, edited by Daniel L. Schacter and Elaine Sacrry, 208-28. Cambridge, Mass.: Harvard University Press.

Tuszynski, Jack A., and Nancy Woolf. 2006. "The Path Ahead." In *The Emerging Physics of Consciousness*, edited by Jack A. Tuszynski, 1-26. New York: Springer.

Twist, Lynne. 2003. *The Soul of Money: Transforming Your Relationship with Money and Life.* New York: W. W. Norton.

Tylen, K., et al. 2010. "Language as a Tool for Interacting Minds." *Mind and Language* 25:3-29.

Tyson, Niel deGrasse, and Thomas Goldsmith. 2004. *Origins: Fourteen Billion Years of Cosmic Evolution.* New York: W. W. Norton.

Underhill, Evelyn. 1911. *Mysticism.* London: Methuen & Co.

Valentine, Tom, and Carol Valentine. 1989. *Applied Kinesiology: Muscle Response in Diagnosis, Therapy, and Preventive Medicine.* Rochester, VT: Inner Traditions.

Van Lommel, Pim. 2010. *Consciousness beyond Life: The Science of the Near-Death Experience.* New York: HarperOne.

Van Oosterzee, Penny. 2000. *Dragon Bones: The Story of Peking Man.* Cambridge, Mass.: Perseus Publishing.

Vandermeersch, Leon. 1980. *Wangdao ou La voie royale. Recherches sur l'esprit des institutions de la Chine archaïque.* 2 vols. Paris: Ecole Française d'Extrême-Orient.

Vartanian, Oshin. 2013. "Fostering Creativity: Insights from Neuroscience." In *Neuroscience of Creativity*, edited by Oshin Vartanian, Adam S. Bristol, and James C. Kaufman, 257-72. Cambridge, Mass.: MIT Press.

Vedral, Vlatko. 2010. *Decoding Reality: The Universe as Quantum Information.* New York: Oxford University Press.

Veith, Ilza. 1972. *The Yellow Emperor's Classic of Internal Medicine.* Berkeley: University of California Press.

Viskontas, Indre V., and Bruce L. Miller. 2013. "Art and Dementia: How Degeneration of Some Brain Regions Can Lead to New Creative Impulses." In *Neuroscience of Creativity*, edited by Oshin Vartanian, Adam S. Bristol, and James C. Kaufman, 115-32. Cambridge, Mass.: MIT Press.

Von Franz, Marie-Louise. 1992. *Psyche and Matter.* Boston: Shambhala.

Wager, Tor D., et al. 2008. "The Neuroimaging of Emotion." In *Handbook of Emotions*, edited by Michael Lewis, Jeannette M. Haviland-Jones, and Lisa Feldman Barrett, 249-71. New York: Guilford Press.

Wakefield, Dan. 2001. *Releasing the Creative Spirit.* Woodstock, VT: Skylight Paths Publishing.

Walter, Chip. 2006. *Thumbs, Toes, and Tears: And Other Traits That Make Us Human.* New York: Walker & Company.

Walther, David S. 1981. *Applied Kinesiology.* Pueblo, Cols.: Systems DC.

Wang, Bo. 2014. *Zhuangzi: Thinking through the Inner Chapters.* Translated by Livia Kohn. St. Petersburg, Fla.: Three Pines Press.

Wang, Robin R. 2012. *Yinyang: The Way of Heaven and Earth in Chinese Thought and Culture.* Cambridge: Cambridge University Press.

Wang, Shumin, and Penelope Barrett. 2006. "Profile of a *Daoyin* Tradition: The 'Five Animal Mimes'." *Asian Medicine: Tradition and Modernity* 2.2:225-53.

Wang, Zhongjiang. 2015. *Daoism Excavated: Cosmos and Humanity in Early* Manuscripts. St. Petersburg, Fla.: Three Pines Press.

Wann, Dave. 2009. "Finding Real Wealth: Twice the Value for Half the Resources." In *Less Is More: Embracing Simplicity for a Healthy Planet, a Caring Economy, and Lasting Happiness*, edited by Cecile Andrews and Wanda Urbanska, 41-46. Gabriola Island: New Society Publishers.

Ward, Peter D., and Donald Brownlee. 2000. *Rare Earth: Why Complex Life in Uncommon in the Universe.* New York: Copernicus.

Ward, Thomas B., Ronald A. Finke, and Steven M. Smith. 1995. *Creativity and the Mind: Discovering the Genius Within.* New York: Plenum Press.

Ware, James R. 1966. *Alchemy, Medicine and Religion in the China of AD 320.* Cambridge, Mass.: MIT Press.

Washburn, David A., and Duane M. Rumbaugh. 2007. *Primate Perspectives on Behavior and Cognition.* Washington, DC: American Psychological Association.

Washburn, Sherwood L., ed. 1961. *Social Life of Early Man.* Chicago: Aldine.

Watson, Burton. 1968. *The Complete Works of Chuang-tzu.* New York: Columbia University Press.

Watson, David, and Kristin Naragon. 2009 "Positive Affectivity: The Disposition to Experience Positive Emotional States." In *Oxford Handbook of Positive Psychology*, edited by C. R. Snyder and Shane J. Lopez, 207-16. New York: Oxford University Press.

Watts, Alan. 1957. *The Ways of Zen.* New York: Vintage Books.

Watts, Ian. 2014. "The Red Thread: Pigment Use and the Evolution of Collective Ritual." In *The Social Origins of Language*, edited by Daniel Dor, Chris Knight, and Jerome Lewis, 208-27. New York: Oxford University Press.

Wearing, Deborah. 2005. *Forever Today.* New York: Doubleday.

Webb, Stephen. 2002. *Where Is Everybody? Fifty Solutions to the Fermi Paradox and the Problem of Extraterrestrial Life.* New York: Copernicus Books.

Wegner, Daniel M. 2002. *The Illusion of Conscious Will.* Cambridge, Mass.: MIT Press.

Weil, Andrew. 1983. *Health and Healing: Understanding Conventional and Alternative Medicine.* Boston: Houghton Mifflin.

_____. 1995. *Spontaneous Healing: How to Discover and Enhance Your Body's Natural Ability to Heal Itself.* New York: Knopf.

Weinberg, Stephen. 1979. *The First Three Minutes: A Modern View of the Origin of the Universe.* New York: Basic Books.

_____. 1993. *Dreams of a Final Theory: The Search for the Fundamental Laws of Nature.* New York: Pantheon Books.

Weisberg, Deena Skolnick. 2009. "The Vital Importance of Imagination." In *What's Next? Dispatches on the Future of Science*, edited by Max Brockman, 144-54. New York: Vintage Books.

Weisberg, Robert. 2010. "The Study of Creativity: From Genius to Cognitive Science." *International Journal of Cultural Policy* 16.3:235-53.

Wellman, Henry M. 1990. *The Child's Theory of Mind.* Cambridge, Mass.: Harvard University Press.

Wells, Marnix. 2013. *The Pheasant Cap Master and the End of History: Linking Religion to Philosophy in Ancient China.* St. Petersburg, Fla.: Three Pines Press.

Wenzel, Christian Helmut. 2003. "Ethics and Zhuangzi: Awareness, Freedom, and Autonomy." *Journal of Chinese Philosophy* 30.1:115-26.

Wetering, Janwillem van de. 1975. *A Glimpse of Nothingness: Experiences in an American Zen Community.* Boston: Houghton Mufflin Company.

Whitehead, Charles. 2014. "Why Humans and Not Apes: The Social Preconditions for the Emergence of Language." In *The Social Origins of Language*, edited by Daniel Dor, Chris Knight, and Jerome Lewis, 157-70. New York: Oxford University Press.

Whiten, Andrew. 2007. "The Place of 'Deep Social Mind' in the Evolution of Human Nature." In *What Makes Us Human?* edited by Charles Pasternak, 146-63. New York: Oxford University Press.

Whitman, Walt. 1954. *The Complete Poetry and Prose of Walt Whitman.* Garden City, NY: Garden City Books.

Wilber, Ken. 1979. "Are the Chakras Real? " In *Kundalini: Evolution and Enlightenment*, edited by John White, 120-31. New York: Paragon House.

_____. 1993. *The Spectrum of Consciousness.* Wheaton, Ill.: Quest Books.

_____. 1998. *The Marriage of Sense and Soul: Integrating Science and Religion.* New York: Random House.

_____. 2004. *The Simple Feeling of Being: Embracing Your True Nature.* Boston: Shambhala.

Williams, Bryan. 2007. "On Studies of the Human Aura." www.mind-energy.net.

Williamson, Marianne. 2002. *Everyday Grace: Having Hope, Finding Forgiveness, and Making Miracles.* New York: Riverhead Books.

Wolf, Fred Alan. 1996. *The Spiritual Universe: How Quantum Physics Proves the Existence of the Soul.* New York: Simon & Schuster.

Wolpert, Lewis. 2007. "Causal Belief Makes Us Human." In *What Makes Us Human?* edited by Charles Pasternak, 164-81. New York: Oxford University Press.

Wong, Eva. 1992. *Cultivating Stillness: A Taoist Manual for Transforming Body and Mind.* Boston: Shambhala.

Woodward, William R., and June F. Tower. 2006. "Julian Jaynes: Introducing His Life and Thought." In *Reflections on the Dawn of Consciousness: Julian Jaynes's Bicameral Mind Theory Revisited*, edited by Marcel Kuijsten, 13-68. Henderson, Nev.: Julian Jaynes Society.

Woolf, Nancy J. 2006. "Microtubules in the Cerebral Cortex: Role in Memory and Consciousness." In *The Emerging Physics of Consciousness*, edited by Jack A. Tuszynski, 49-94. New York: Springer.

Worsley, J. R. 1973. *Acupuncture: Is It for You?* New York: Harper & Row.

_____. 1982. *Traditional Chinese Acupuncture*. Tisbury: Element Books.

Worthington, Vivian. 1982. *A History of Yoga*. Boston: Routlege & Kegan Paul.

Wrangham, Richard W. 2007. "The Cooking Enigma." In *What Makes Us Human?* edited by Charles Pasternak, 182-203. New York: Oxford University Press.

_____. 2009. *How Cooking Made Us Human*. New York: Basic Books.

Wright, Robert. 1994. *The Moral Animal: The New Science of Evolutionary Psychology*. New York: Pantheon Books.

_____. 2000. *NonZero*. New York: Pantheon Books.

Wright, Ronald. 2005. *A Short History of Progress*. New York: Carroll & Graf.

Wu, Kuang-ming. 1982. *Chuang-tzu: World Philosopher at Play*. Albany: State University of New York Press.

_____. 1990. *The Butterfly as Companion: Meditations on the First Three Chapters of the Chuang-tzu*. New York: Crossroads Publications.

_____. 1991. "Non-World Making in *Chuang Tzu*." *Journal of Chinese Philosophy* 18.1:37-50.

_____. 2002. "*Wu-wei* in *Zhuangzi* as Life-Systematic." *International Journal of Transpersonal Studies* 21:71-77.

_____. 2007. "Emperor Hun-tun: A Cultural Hermeneutic." *Dao: A Journal of Comparative Philosophy* 6:263-79.

Wulff, David M. 2000. "Mystical Experience." In *Varieties of Anomalous Experience: Examining the Scientific Evidence*, edited by Etzel Cardeña, Steven Jay Lynn, and Stanley Krippner, 397-440. Washington, DC: American Psychological Association.

Xu, Kejian. 2011. "A Different Type of Individualism in *Zhuangzi*." *Dao: A Journal of Comparative Philosophy* 10:445-62.

Yamada, Toshiaki. 1989. "Longevity Techniques and the Compilation of the *Lingbao wufuxu*." In *Taoist Meditation and Longevity Techniques*, edited by L. Kohn, 97-122. Ann Arbor: University of Michigan, Center for Chinese Studies.

_____. 2000. "The Lingbao School." In *Daoism Handbook*, edited by Livia Kohn, 225-55. Leiden: Brill.

Yan, Wenming. 2005. "The Beginning of Farming." In *The Formation of Chinese Civilization: An Archaeological Perspective*, edited by Sarah Allan, 27-42. New Haven, Conn.: Yale University Press.

Yasudian, Selvarajan, and Elizabeth Haich. 1965. *Yoga and Health*. New York: Harper & Row.

Yates, Robin D. S. 1997. *Five Lost Classics: Tao, Huang-Lao, and Yin-Yang in Han China*. New York: Ballentine Books.

Yearley, Lee. 1996. "Zhuangzi's Understanding of Skillfulness and the Ultimate Spiritual State." In *Essays on Skepticism, Relativism, and Ethics in the Zhuangzi*, edited by Paul Kjellberg and Philip J. Ivanhoe, 152-82. Albany: State University of New York Press.

______. 2010. "The Perfected Person in the Radical *Zhuangzi.*" In *Experimental Essays on Zhuangzi*, edited by Victor H. Mair, 122-36. Dunedin, Fla.: Three Pines Press

Yessis, Michael. 1992. *Kinesiology of Exercise: A Safe and Efficient Way to Improve Athletic Performance.* Indianapolis: Masters Press.

Zaidel, Dahlia W. 2013. "Biological and Neuronal Underpinnings of Creativity in the Arts." In *Neuroscience of Creativity*, edited by Oshin Vartanian, Adam S. Bristol, and James C. Kaufman, 133-48. Cambridge, Mass.: MIT Press.

Zeh, H. Dieter. 2004. "The Wave Function: It or Bit?" In *Science and Ultimate Reality: Quantum Theory, Cosmology, and Complexity*, edited by John D. Barrow, P. C. W. Davies, and Charles L. Harper, 103-20. Cambridge: Cambridge University Press.

Zeidner, Moshe, Gerald Matthews, and Richard D. Roberts. 2009. *What We Know About Emotional Intelligence: How It Affects Learning, Work, Relationships, and Our Mental Health.* Cambridge, Mass.: MIT Press.

Zeki, S. 1993. *A Vision of the Brain.* Boston: Blackwell.

Zhang, Dainian. 2002. *Key Concepts in Chinese Philosophy.* New Haven, Conn.: Yale University Press.

Zhang, Yuhuan, and Ken Rose. 2001. *A Brief History of Qi.* Brookline, Mass.: Paradigm Books.

Zhou, Fan, and Imios Archangelis. 2010. *Jade Writing: Yellow Court Classic.* Lake Mary, Fla.: Avatar Solutions.

Zimbardo, Phil. 2007. *The Lucifer Effect: How Good People Turn Evil.* New York: Random House.

Zohar, Dana. 1990. *The Quantum Self.* New York: William Morrow.

Zukav, Gary. 1979. *The Dancing Wuli Masters: An Overview of the New Physics.* New York: Bantam.

______. 2002. *Soul Stories.* New York: Simon & Schuster.

Index